W9-BMQ-675

In Conversation with God

Meditations for each day of the year

Volume Six

Feasts: January – June

Francis Fernandez

In Conversation with God

Meditations for each day of the year

Volume Six

Feasts: January – June

SCEPTER
London – New York

This edition of *In Conversation with God – Volume 6* is published:
in England by Scepter (U.K.) Ltd., 21 Hinton Avenue, Hounslow TW4 6AP; e-mail: scepter@pobox.com;
in the United States by Scepter Publishers Inc.; 800-322-8773; e-mail: info@scepterpublishers.org; www.scepterpublishers.org

This is a translation of *Hablar con Dios – Vol VI*, first published in 1989 by Ediciones Palabra, Madrid, and in 1991 by Scepter.

With ecclesiastical approval

British Library Cataloguing in Publication Data

Fernandez-Carvajal, Francis
In Conversation with God — Volume 6
Feasts: January – June
1. Christian life — Daily Readings
I Title II Hablar con Dios *English*
242'.2

ISBN Volume 7 978-0-906138-36-6
ISBN Volume 6 978-0-906138-25-0
ISBN Volume 5 978-0-906138-24-3
ISBN Volume 4 978-0-906138-23-6
ISBN Volume 3 978-0-906138-22-9
ISBN Volume 2 978-0-906138-21-2
ISBN Volume 1 978-0-906138-20-5
ISBN Complete set 978-0-906138-19-9

Cover design & typeset in England by KIP Intermedia, and printed in China.

Contents

1 JANUARY
1. Mary, Mother of God **17**
1.1 God chose his Mother and bestowed upon her all manner of gifts and graces.
1.2 Mary and the Blessed Trinity.
1.3 Our Mother.

6 JANUARY
2. The Epiphany of Our Lord **24**
2.1 Corresponding to grace.
2.2 The paths that lead to Christ.
2.3 Renewing our apostolic spirit.

FIRST SUNDAY AFTER THE EPIPHANY
3. The Baptism of Our Lord **30**
3.1 The manifestation of the Blessed Trinity.
3.2 Our divine filiation in Christ through Baptism.
3.3 Baptism and daily life.

CHRISTIAN UNITY OCTAVE: DAY 1 – 18 JANUARY
4. Christ founded One Church **36**
4.1 The Will of Christ was to found one Church.
4.2 Christ's priestly prayer for unity.
4.3 Unity, a gift from God.

CHRISTIAN UNITY OCTAVE: DAY 2 – 19 JANUARY
5. Unity within the Church **42**
5.1 Union with Christ is the foundation for unity among the faithful.
5.2 Making unity a high priority.
5.3 The order of charity.

CHRISTIAN UNITY OCTAVE: DAY 3 – 20 JANUARY
6. The Deposit of Faith **47**
6.1 Fidelity to Revelation. Ecumenical dialogue needs to be based on a sincere love for divine truth.
6.2 Explaining doctrine in a clear fashion.
6.3 *Veritatem facientes in caritate.*

CHRISTIAN UNITY OCTAVE: DAY 4 – 21 JANUARY
7. The Foundation of Unity **53**
7.1 The primacy of Peter is realized in the Church in the person of the Roman Pontiff.
7.2 The *Vicar of Christ.*
7.3 The papacy is the guarantee of Christian unity and the well-spring of true ecumenism.

CHRISTIAN UNITY OCTAVE: DAY 5 – 22 JANUARY
8. Christ and the Church **58**
8.1 Christ is to be found in the Church.
8.2 Images of the Church. *The Mystical Body of Christ.*
8.3 The Church is a communion of faith, sacraments and government. The *Communion of Saints.*

CHRISTIAN UNITY OCTAVE: DAY 6 – 23 JANUARY
9. The new people of God **63**
9.1 Christians are *a chosen race, a royal priesthood, a people set apart* for Jesus Christ.
9.2 Participation of the laity in the priestly, prophetic and royal mission of Christ.
9.3 The ministerial priesthood.

CHRISTIAN UNITY OCTAVE: DAY 7 – 24 JANUARY
10. Mary, Mother of Unity **68**
10.1 The Mother of unity at the Incarnation.
10.2 Mary at Calvary.
10.3 Mary with the new-born Church at Pentecost.

24 JANUARY
11. St Francis De Sales 74
11.1 The virtue of friendliness or cordiality.
11.2 The virtues of social life are essential for apostolate.
11.3 Respect for others and care for material things.

25 JANUARY
12. The Conversion of Saint Paul 79
12.1 On the road to Damascus.
12.2 The life of Saint Paul is a beacon of hope.
12.3 Zeal for souls.

26 JANUARY
13. Saints Timothy and Titus 85
13.1 Protecting the deposit of faith.
13.2 Having a deep knowledge of the faith.
13.3 Spreading the Good News entrusted to the Church.

28 JANUARY
14. St Thomas Aquinas 91
14.1 The way to God: piety and doctrine.
14.2 The authority of Saint Thomas's writings.
14.3 Doctrine as the food of piety.

2 FEBRUARY
15. The Presentation of Our Lord 96
15.1 Mary offers Jesus to the Father.
15.2 To illuminate reality by the light of the Cross.
15.3 Jesus Christ, *sign of contradiction.*

2 FEBRUARY
16. The Purification of Our Lady 102
16.1 The Fourth Mystery of the Holy Rosary.
16.2 The Virgin leads us to Jesus, *light of the nations*.
16.3 We should offer to the Lord everything we are.

11 FEBRUARY
17. Our Lady of Lourdes **108**
17.1 The apparitions in the grotto. Holy Mary, *Salus infirmorum.*
17.2 The Christian meaning of pain and suffering.
17.3 Sanctifying pain. Going to the intercession of Our Lady.

14 FEBRUARY
18. Saints Cyril and Methodius **113**
18.1 The evangelization of the Slavic peoples.
18.2 Responding with a new evangelization.
18.3 Promoting Christian customs in ordinary life.

22 FEBRUARY
19. The Chair of St Peter **119**
19.1 Meaning of the feast.
19.2 Saint Peter in Rome.
19.3 Love and veneration due to the Roman Pontiff.

17 MARCH
19–A. Saint Patrick **124**
19-A.1 Saint Patrick based his apostolate on prayer and mortification.
19-A.2 Aiming at all levels of society.
19-A.3 Faith and culture.

THE SEVEN SUNDAYS OF SAINT JOSEPH:
THE FIRST SUNDAY
20. Vocation and Sanctity of Saint Joseph **130**
20.1 The greatest of the saints.
20.2 *The Lord prepares those whom he calls to do his work.*
20.3 Living our vocation: *God gives us the grace to overcome all obstacles.*

THE SEVEN SUNDAYS OF SAINT JOSEPH:
THE SECOND SUNDAY
21. The Virtues of Saint Joseph **136**
21.1 The humility of the Holy Patriarch.
21.2 Faith, hope and love.
21.3 Saint Joseph's human virtues.

THE SEVEN SUNDAYS OF SAINT JOSEPH:
THE THIRD SUNDAY
22. Joseph, Husband of Mary **141**
22.1 The married life of Mary and Joseph.
22.2 The most pure love of Joseph.
22.3 Joseph's paternal relationship to Jesus.

THE SEVEN SUNDAYS OF SAINT JOSEPH:
THE FOURTH SUNDAY
23. Joys and Sorrows -- I **147**
23.1 The Lord will always enlighten those who seek him with a clean heart.
23.2 The Nativity in Bethlehem. The Circumcision.
23.3 Simeon's prophecy.

THE SEVEN SUNDAYS OF SAINT JOSEPH:
THE FIFTH SUNDAY
24. Joys and Sorrows -- II **153**
24.1 The flight into Egypt.
24.2 The return to Nazareth.
24.3 Jesus is lost and found in the Temple.

THE SEVEN SUNDAYS OF SAINT JOSEPH:
THE SIXTH SUNDAY
25. Death and glorification of Saint Joseph **159**
25.1 The death of Saint Joseph, patron of a good death.
25.2 The glorification of Saint Joseph.
25.3 Prayer to Saint Joseph for vocations.

THE SEVEN SUNDAYS OF SAINT JOSEPH:
THE SEVENTH SUNDAY
26. The fatherly intercession of Saint Joseph 165
26.1 The intercession of the saints.
26.2 Going to Saint Joseph for our every need.
26.3 Perseverance.

19 MARCH
27. Saint Joseph 171
27.1 The promises of the Old Testament were realized in Jesus by means of Saint Joseph.
27.2 The fidelity of the Holy Patriarch to his vocation.
27.3 Our perseverance.

25 MARCH
28. The Annunciation of the Lord 176
28.1 True God and true man.
28.2 The ultimate expression of divine love.
28.3 The impact of the Incarnation on our life.

25 MARCH
29. The Vocation of Our Lady 182
29.1 Our Lady's example.
29.2 *I delight to do thy Will, O my God.*
29.3 *Ne timeas...*

25 APRIL
30. Saint Mark the Evangelist 188
30.1 Saint Mark, Saint Peter's co-worker.
30.2 To be good instruments of God we always have to be ready to make a new beginning.
30.3 The apostolic mandate.

27 APRIL
31. Our Lady of Montserrat **194**
31.1 Marian shrines are 'divine signs'.
31.2 Our Lady is our hope in all our needs.
31.3 Hope and divine filiation.

29 APRIL
32. Saint Catherine of Siena **200**
32.1 Love for the Church and the Pope, the 'sweet Christ on earth'.
32.2 Saint Catherine offered her life for the Church.
32.3 Making the truth known. Helping to shape public opinion.

1 MAY
33. Saint Joseph the Worker **207**
33.1 Work is a gift from God.
33.2 The natural and the supernatural meaning of work.
33.3 Loving our work.

3 MAY
34. Saints Philip and James **213**
34.1 The calling of Philip and James.
34.2 Jesus was always close to his disciples, and is now close to us.
34.3 Spreading the Apostles' message. Apostolate is based on a supernatural foundation.

13 MAY
35. Our Lady of Fatima **219**
35.1 Our Lady's apparitions at Fatima.
35.2 The Blessed Virgin asks us to do penance for the sins of mankind.
35.3 Consecration of the world to the Immaculate Heart of Mary.

14 MAY
36. Saint Matthias 226
36.1 God is the one who chooses.
36.2 We are never denied the graces necessary to respond to vocation.
36.3 Happiness and the meaning of life for every person consists in following God's call.

31 MAY
37. The Visitation of the Blessed Virgin 232
37.1 Serving cheerfully.
37.2 Seeking Jesus through Mary.
37.3 The *Magnificat.*

THURSDAY AFTER PENTECOST
38. Our Lord Jesus Christ Eternal High Priest 238
38.1 Jesus is High Priest forever.
38.2 All Christians have a priestly soul. Dignity of the priesthood.
38.3 The priest, an instrument of unity.

SUNDAY AFTER PENTECOST
39. The Blessed Trinity 245
39.1 Revelation of the mystery of the Trinity.
39.2 The soul's relationship with each of the Three Divine Persons.
39.3 Praying to the Blessed Trinity.

SUNDAY AFTER PENTECOST
40. The indwelling of the Holy Trinity in the Soul 251
40.1 The Presence of God, One and Three, in the soul in grace.
40.2 Supernatural life leads a Christian to know and to converse intimately with the Blessed Trinity.
40.3 Temples of God.

CORPUS CHRISTI
41. The Most Holy Body and Blood of Christ **258**
41.1 Love and Veneration for Jesus in the Blessed Sacrament.
41.2 Food for eternal life.
41.3 The *Corpus Christi* Procession.

CORPUS CHRISTI OCTAVE: DAY 2
42. A Hidden God **265**
42.1 Jesus remains hidden so that He may be sought out by our faith and our love.
42.2 The Holy Eucharist transforms us.
42.3 Christ gives himself to each one of us personally.

CORPUS CHRISTI OCTAVE: DAY 3
43. The Eucharist: Substantial Presence of Christ **271**
43.1 Transubstantiation.
43.2 The real presence of Christ in the tabernacle.
43.3 Trust and respect for Jesus in the Blessed Sacrament.

CORPUS CHRISTI OCTAVE: DAY 4
44. Like the Repentant Thief **278**
44.1 The tabernacles we find along our way.
44.2 We should imitate the Good Thief.
44.3 The purification of our faults.

CORPUS CHRISTI OCTAVE: DAY 5
45. The Wounds that Thomas saw **285**
45.1 Faith with deeds.
45.2 Faith and the Holy Eucharist.
45.3 Our conversation with Jesus who is present in the Tabernacle.

CORPUS CHRISTI OCTAVE: DAY 6

46. Food for the Weak **292**

46.1 The Eucharist: a memorial of the Passion.

46.2 Living Bread.

46.3 Sustenance for the journey. Ardently desiring to receive Holy Communion.

CORPUS CHRISTI OCTAVE: DAY 7

47. *Cleanse Me, Lord Jesus ...* **299**

47.1 Christ's surrender on the Cross, renewed in the Blessed Eucharist, purifies us of our weakness.

47.2 Jesus comes in Person to heal and strengthen us.

47.3 The Sacred Humanity of Christ in the Eucharist.

CORPUS CHRISTI OCTAVE: DAY 8

48. A pledge of Eternal Life **305**

48.1 A foretaste of Heaven.

48.2 Our participation in the Life that never ends.

48.3 Mary and the Blessed Eucharist.

THE SACRED HEART OF JESUS: I

49. The Sacred Heart of Jesus **311**

49.1 The origin and significance of this feast.

49.2 Christ's love for each one of us.

49.3 Reparatory love.

THE SACRED HEART OF JESUS: II

50. Christ's Love for us **318**

50.1 A unique and personal love for each individual.

50.2 Atonement and reparation.

50.3 A *furnace burning with charity*.

THE IMMACULATE HEART OF MARY
51. The Immaculate Heart of the Virgin Mary **325**
51.1 The Heart of Mary.
51.2 A motherly heart.
51.3 *Cor Mariae dulcissimum, iter para tutum.*

1 JUNE
52. Saint Justin **332**
52.1 Defence of the Faith in times of misunderstanding.
52.2 The greater the adversity, the more opportunity for apostolate.
52.3 We must live charity always. Charity with those who have no regard for us.

11 JUNE
53. Saint Barnabas **339**
53.1 The need for having a big heart in the apostolate.
53.2 Learning to understand people so as to be able to help them.
53.3 Cheerfulness and a positive spirit in our apostolate.

22 JUNE
54. Saints John Fisher and Thomas More **346**
54.1 A testimony of faith, even to the extent of martyrdom.
54.2 Fortitude and the life of prayer.
54.3 Christian coherence and unity of life.

24 JUNE
55. Birth of John the Baptist **352**
55.1 The mission of Saint John the Baptist.
55.2 Our mission is to prepare men's hearts so that Christ may enter in.
55.3 *Oportet illum crescere* ... Christ must ever increase in our lives.

26 JUNE
55-A. Saint Josemaría Escriva 359
55-A.1 Being led by the Holy Spirit.
55-A.2 Yearnings of love.
55-A.3 Sacrifice for the sake of love.

29 JUNE
56. Saint Peter 365
56.1 The Vocation of Peter.
56.2 The first of Christ's disciples.
56.3 His fidelity to the point of martyrdom.

29 JUNE
57. Saint Paul 372
57.1 Our Lord chooses his disciples.
57.2 God's call and the apostolic vocation.
57.3 The apostolate. A joyful task that demands sacrifice.

30 JUNE
58. The First Martyrs of the Church of Rome 378
58.1 Their exemplary behaviour in the middle of the world.
58.2 Our attitude in the face of opposition.
58.3 Apostolate in all circumstances.

Index to quotations from the Fathers and Popes 385

Subject Index 399

1 January

1. MARY, MOTHER OF GOD

Solemnity

The Christmas Octave concludes with the occasion of this Solemnity. Even though Mary was venerated as the Mother of God from the earliest days of the Church, the feast was not established until the fourth century, when this truth of faith was promulgated by the Council of Ephesus. In 1931, Pius XI decreed that the feast was to be celebrated on October 11th. Saint Paul VI decided to move the feast to the Christmas season so as to have it coincide with the beginning of the New Year. The prayer used after Communion is taken from a liturgy of the seventh century. This prayer is notable for the fact that it invokes Mary as Mother of the Church. It is the first recorded instance when this Marian title appears in the liturgy.

Whenever we venerate the Blessed Virgin as the Mother of God we simultaneously claim her to be our own Mother. We know that she takes very good care of her children, especially those who are most in need.

1.1 God chose his Mother and bestowed upon her all manner of gifts and graces.

But when the time had fully come, God sent forth his Son, born of woman ...,[1] we are told in the *Second Reading* of today's Mass.

It was only a few days ago that we were praying about the humble birth of Christ in a cave in Bethlehem. We saw him as a little baby, a defenceless child in the arms of his Mother. She shows the child to us so that we might adore him as our Redeemer and Lord. God the Father had taken into account all the circumstances surrounding his birth: the edict from Caesar Augustus, the census, the poverty in

---

[1] Gal 4:4

Bethlehem ... Above all, he had foreseen the Mother who would bring him into the world. This *Woman* was spoken of on various occasions in Holy Scripture. She had been predestined from all eternity. God had prepared her creation with more loving attention than he had given to the making of any other creature. This was so because she was to make a free choice to be his Mother.

In Genesis, God announced that he would put enmity between the serpent and the woman.[2] As the Lord said to the Prophet Ahaz in the book of Isaiah, *Behold, a young woman shall conceive and bear a son, and shall call his name Emmanuel.*[3] Our Lady was prefigured in the *ark of the covenant,* in the *house of gold,* in the *tower of ivory.* God chose her from among all women before the dawn of time. He loved her more than He loved the sum of all his creation. He loved her with such a love that he bestowed upon her the plenitude of his gifts and graces, more than He granted to his angels and his saints. He preserved her from any stain of sin or imperfection. As a result, no creature more beautiful or holy could ever have been conceived.[4] It is with reason that theologians and saints have taught that God could have created a better world, but He could not have created a more perfect mother than his own Mother.[5] Saint Bernard comments, *Why should we be astonished if the God who could work marvels in the Scripture and through his saints should choose to reveal himself even more marvellous by means of his Mother?*[6]

Saint Thomas Aquinas teaches that the divine maternity of Mary surpasses all graces and charisms such as the gift of

---

[2] Gen 3:15
[3] Is 7:14
[4] cf Pius IX, Bull, *Ineffabilis Deus,* 8 December 1854
[5] cf St Bonaventure, *Speculum,* 8
[6] St Bernard, *Homilies on the Blessed Virgin Mary,* II, 9

prophecy, the gift of tongues, the power to work miracles ...[7] *Almighty God, Omnipotent and Infinitely Wise, had to choose his Mother. What would you have done, if you had had to choose yours? I think that you and I would have chosen the mother we have, filling her with all graces. That is what God did: and that is why, after the Blessed Trinity, comes Mary. Theologians have given a rational explanation for her fullness of grace and why she cannot be subject to the devil: it was fitting that it should be so, God could do it, therefore he did it. That is the great proof: the clearest proof that God endowed his Mother with every privilege, from the very first moment. That is how she is: beautiful, and pure, and spotless in soul and body!*[8]

Today, as we look upon Mary, the Mother of God, we see her with the child in her arms. She offers her Son to us. We have to give thanks to God because surely this was *one of God's greatest mercies apart from creating us and redeeming us, namely, to choose to have a Mother who became our mother as well.*[9]

1.2 Mary and the Blessed Trinity.

Saint Thomas Aquinas teaches that Mary *is the one person next to God the Father who could say to the divine Son: You are my Son.*[10] According to Saint Bernard, Our Lady *calls God Almighty, the Lord of the angels, her Son when she asks in all simplicity: 'Son, why have you treated us so?' What angel would dare to say such a thing? ... But Mary, fully aware of her motherhood, does not hesitate to call the Lord of heaven and earth 'her Son'. And God is*

---

[7] cf St Thomas, *Summa Theologiae,* 1-2, q 3, a 5

[8] St. J. Escrivá, *The Forge,* 482

[9] Blessed Alonso de Orozco, *Commentary on the Seven Words of the Blessed Virgin Mary,* Madrid, 1966

[10] St Thomas, *op cit,* 3, q 36, a 1

not offended for being called what He wanted to be.[11] He truly is the Son of Mary.

Whenever we study the nature of Christ we are careful to distinguish between his eternal generation (his divine nature, the pre-existence of the Word) and his temporal birth. Being God, the Son is begotten, not made, by the Father *ab aeterno,* from all eternity. Being man, the Son was born, *he became man,* of the Virgin Mary. In the fullness of time the Anointed One of God, the Second Person of the Blessed Trinity, assumed a human nature. That is to say, He assumed a rational soul and human body formed in the womb of his Immaculate Mother. The human nature (soul and body) and the divine nature came together in the one Person of the Word. From the very moment when Our Lady gave her free consent to the Will of God, she became the Mother of the Word Incarnate. *It is similar to the case of each and every mother, in whose womb a human body is born, but not the rational soul. We logically consider these women to be mothers. So too should we think of Mary as the Mother of God because of the unity of Persons in her Son.*[12]

From their place in Heaven the angels and the saints contemplate in awe the supreme glory of Mary. They know full well that this dignity derives from the fact that she was and continues to be for all eternity the Mother of God, *Mater Creatoris, Mater Salvatoris* (Mother of our Creator, Mother of our Saviour).[13] It is for this reason that in the litany of the Rosary the first title of glory given to Our Lady is *Sancta Dei Genitrix* (Mother of God). The titles that follow are those which correspond to her divine maternity: *Holy Virgin of Virgins, Mother of divine grace, Mother most pure, Mother most chaste ...*

---

[11] St Bernard, *op cit,* I, 7

[12] Pius XI, Encyclical, *Lux veritatis,* 25 December 1931

[13] cf R. Garrigou-Lagrange, *The Mother of the Saviour,* Madrid, 1976

By nature of her being Mother of the Son of God made man, Mary has a unique relationship to the Most Blessed Trinity. She is *Daughter of God the Father,* as she has been called by the Fathers of the Church and in the constant teaching of the Magisterium.[14] Through her Son, the Blessed Virgin has a bond of consanguinity, *which thereby confers upon her earthly power and dominion over Jesus ... Jesus himself is bound to Mary by the same duties of justice which all children have to their parents.*[15] With regard to the Holy Spirit, Mary is *Temple and Tabernacle,* according to the teachings of the Fathers and, more recently, of St John Paul II.[16] Mary is *the great masterpiece of the Trinity.*[17]

This *masterpiece* ought not to be something accidental in the life of a Christian. *God does not bestow upon a person so many gifts just to impress us. This masterpiece of the Trinity is the Mother of the Redeemer and, at the same time, my Mother – Mother of such a wretched thing as myself, who am in this respect no different from any other person.*[18] *Mother of mine!*

Today we turn to Mary with thoughts filled with joy and praise ... and with a holy pride. *How men like to be reminded of their relationship with distinguished figures in literature, in politics, in the armed forces, in the Church! Sing to Mary Immaculate, reminding her: Hail Mary, Daughter of God the Father! Hail Mary, Mother of God the Son! Hail Mary, Spouse of God the Holy Spirit! Greater than you no one but God!*[19]

---

[14] cf Second Vatican Council, *Lumen gentium,* 53
[15] B. Hugon, *Marie, pleine de gráce,* quoted by R. Garrigou-Lagrange, *op cit*
[16] St John Paul II, Encyclical, *Redemptoris Mater,* 25 March 1987, 9
[17] M. M. Philipon, *The Gifts of the Holy Spirit,* Madrid, 1989
[18] J. Polo Carrasco, *Mary and the Blessed Trinity,* Madrid, 1987
[19] St. J. Escrivá, *The Way,* 496

1.3 Our Mother.

Salve, Mater misericordiae, Mater spei et Mater veniae ... Hail, Mother of Mercy, Mother of hope and of pardon, Mother of God and of grace, Mother full of holy joy.[20] We speak to Our Mother with the words of a traditional hymn.

With her maternal care, Our Lady continues to present to her Son the offerings made by his people on earth. She deals with us in a motherly manner. She sees Jesus in each Christian, in each person. As Co-Redeemer, she urgently desires that we become fully united to the divine life. She will always be ready to lend us a hand in whatever difficulties and temptations may befall us. She is our great ally in the apostolate which we Christians must make a reality in the middle of the world. *Invoke the Blessed Virgin. Keep asking her to show herself a Mother to you – 'monstra te esse Matrem!' As well as drawing down her Son's grace, may she bring the clarity of sound doctrine to your mind, and love and purity to your heart, so that you may know the way to God and take many souls to him.*[21] This prayer from the liturgy – *monstra te esse Matrem!* – can help us to be united to Mary on this feast day.[22] Mother of mine! Show me that you are my Mother! Help me in this or that necessity ..., with this friend who needs to come close to your Son.

As we begin the New Year, let us take advantage of the occasion to make a firm resolution to grow daily in our recourse to the Blessed Virgin. We will never find a more reliable ally. Let us imitate Saint John, who on Calvary received Mary on behalf of all mankind: *And from that*

---

[20] *Divine Office,* Hymn from the *Office of readings,* Presentation of Our Lady
[21] St. J. Escrivá, *The Forge,* 986
[22] Hymn, *Ave Maria Stella*

hour the disciple took her to his own home.[23] With how much love, with how much refinement he must have treated her! This is how we should deal with Our Lady in this New Year and always.

---

23 John 19:27

6 JANUARY

2. THE EPIPHANY OF OUR LORD
Solemnity

Epiphany means manifestation. In today's Solemnity the Church commemorates the first manifestation of the Son of God made Man to the pagan world, which took place during the adoration of the Magi. This feast proclaims the universal dimension of the mission of Christ. Christ came into the world to fulfil the promises made to Israel and to bring to fruition the salvation of all people.

The Solemnity of the Epiphany was born in the first centuries of Christianity in the Orient at which time it was known as the *Theophany* or *the Feast of the Illumination.* It was made into a universal feast of the Church in the fourth century. The feast has traditionally been celebrated on January 6th.

2.1 Corresponding to grace.

We have seen his star in the East, and have come with gifts to adore the Lord.[1]

The star over Bethlehem shone down upon all mankind. Its brilliance could be perceived from every corner of the earth. From his first moments as a man, the new-born Jesus *began to spread forth his light and his riches to the world, making use of a star in the heavens to draw men from distant lands to himself.*[2] *Epiphany* means 'manifestation'. On this feast, one of the oldest feasts in Christianity, we celebrate the universality of the Redemption. The people of Jerusalem who witnessed the arrival of the wise men from the East may well have recalled the

---

[1] *Communion Antiphon*: cf Matt 2:2
[2] Fr. Luis de Granada, *Life of Jesus Christ,* Madrid 1975, VI, p 54

prophecy of Isaiah which we find in today's *First Reading* of the Mass: *Arise, shine; for your light has come, and the glory of the Lord has risen upon you. For behold, darkness shall cover the earth, and thick darkness the peoples; but the Lord will arise upon you, and his glory will be seen upon you. And nations shall come to your light, and kings to the brightness of your rising. Lift up your eyes round about, and see; they all gather together, they come to you; your sons shall come from afar ...*[3]

The three wise men, the Magi, represent all the races and nations on earth. They have arrived at the end of their long journey. They are men with a *thirst for God,* a longing which has led them to put aside comforts, earthly goods and satisfactions *so as to adore the Lord God.* They have allowed themselves to be guided by an external sign, a star which shone with a special light. The star was in some sense *clearer and more brilliant than the rest, so much so that it captured the attention of those who looked upon it. It seemed only logical that something so marvellous would have some special significance.*[4] These men were astronomers dedicated to the study of the heavens. They were accustomed to look for signs in the sky. *Where is he who has been born king of the Jews? For we have seen his star in the east ...* Perhaps they had become aware of the coming of the Messiah through the Jewish people of the Diaspora, but we may also speculate that they had been inspired by an interior grace from God to follow the star. As Saint Bernard has observed, He who was to show them the way to Bethlehem had already been their instructor for quite some time. He who led them by the help of a star, He it was who had been guiding them in the intimacy of their hearts.[5] The feast of

---

[3] Is 60:1-6
[4] St Leo the Great, *Sermons on the Epiphany,* I, 1
[5] cf St Bernard, *On the Epiphany of the Lord,* I, 5

these holy men is a good opportunity to examine whether our lives are headed directly towards Jesus. Are we living up to the graces we receive from the Holy Spirit, especially that most important gift – that of our Christian vocation?

We look upon the Child in the arms of Mary. We tell him: *My Lord Jesus, grant that I may feel your grace and second it in such a way that I empty my heart, so that you, my Friend, my Brother, my King, my God, my Love ... may fill it.*[6]

2.2 The paths that lead to Christ.

Upon their arrival in Jerusalem the wise men may have thought that they had come to the end of their travels. But they did not find the one *born king of the Jews* in this great religious capital. Since they were looking for a king, we might expect that they would have gone directly to the palace of King Herod. Yet the ways of men do not always correspond to the ways of God. The wise men were led to ask the people of Jerusalem: *Where is he?* When we really want to find him, God shows us the way. He may even use means which seem least appropriate.

'Where is he who has been born King of the Jews?' Moved by this question, I too now contemplate Jesus 'lying in a manger', in a place fit only for animals. Lord, where is your kingship, your crown, your sword, your sceptre? They are his by right, but he does not want them. He reigns wrapped in swaddling clothes. Our king is unadorned. He comes to us as a defenceless little child ... Where is the king? Could it be that Jesus wants to reign above all in men's hearts, in your heart? That is why he has become a child, for who can help loving a little baby? Where then is the king? Where is the Christ whom the Holy Spirit wants to fashion in our souls?[7]

Following the footsteps of the Wise Men in search of Christ, we ask ourselves where he could be. *He cannot be*

---

[6] St. J. Escrivá, *The Forge,* 913
[7] *idem, Christ is passing by,* 31

present in the pride that separates us from God, nor in the lack of charity which cuts us off from others. Christ cannot be there. In that loveless state man is left alone.[8]

We need to find the true signs which will lead us to the Child-God. The wise men are representatives of all humanity, past, present and future. As we come closer to Christ by dint of our daily struggle we can certainly find something of ourselves in these men and their noble effort. Saint Bonaventure has observed that the star which guides us is composed of three parts: *Holy Scripture, our Blessed Mother and the graces which we receive from the Holy Spirit.*[9] Accompanied by this assistance, we will never lose the trail which leads to Bethlehem and the child Jesus.

The Lord has put into our hearts the longing to find him: *You did not choose me, but I chose you.*[10] We will find our way to him by reading the Holy Gospel, by living as good sons of Our Blessed Lady, by being faithful to our life of prayer and devotion to the sacraments, especially the Holy Eucharist. Our Mother in Heaven beckons us to pick up the pace. Her Son is eagerly awaiting our arrival.

At some moment in the future, perhaps not very far off, the star will come to shine perpetually upon us. We will at last find Jesus seated upon his throne at the right hand of God the Father. Jesus will be clothed in all the fullness of power and glory. Close by we will surely find his Mother. This indeed will be the perfect *epiphany,* the radiant manifestation of the Son of God.

2.3 Renewing our apostolic spirit.

The Solemnity of the Epiphany should move us to renew the apostolic spirit which we have received from the

---

[8] *ibid*
[9] cf St Bonaventure, *On the Epiphany of the Lord*
[10] John 15:16

Lord. From the earliest days of Christianity this feast has been considered the first manifestation of Christ to all mankind. *With the birth of Jesus a star has been lit up in the sky. It is a most luminous vocation. It inspires caravans of people to take to the road (cf Is 60:1 ff). New paths have been opened up for mankind, paths which lead to Christ. Christ has become the heart for a new system of circulation which will last forever. By merit of being our Redeemer, Christ has become indispensable to us ... Christ wants to be announced to the world ...*[11] Today's feast is yet another reminder that we have to bring Christ into the mainstream of our society. We can do this by means of our example and our conversation in family life, in hospitals, in shops, in the university, in our workplace ...

Lift up your eyes round about, and see ... your sons shall come from afar ... From afar, from every conceivable place and nation where men and women can be found. Our hearts resound with the invitation made by Our Lord: *Go therefore and make disciples of all nations ...*[12] Our families, friends and colleagues may or may not be from *afar* in relation to the Lord. Yet the grace of God is all-powerful. With his help, they may come to join us one day in adoration of the child Jesus.

On this feast day we cannot go to Jesus empty-handed. He does not need our gifts since he is the Creator of all things. But he wants us to be generous so that we may receive more graces and gifts from him. Today we put at his disposal *the gold* of our charity. This is our desire to love him more, to treat others with more love. We will present him with *the frankincense* of our prayers and good works. We will give him *the myrrh* of our sacrifices united to the Sacrifice of the Cross as renewed in the Mass. In this

---

[11] St Paul VI, *Homily,* 6 January 1973
[12] Matt 28:19

way we become co-redeemers with him.

The *Three Kings* are in heaven. They can certainly intercede for us. What, then, shall we ask of them? Surely we will not ask for gold, frankincense and myrrh? We can ask them to guide us along the path to finding Jesus, to help us not to lose heart along the way.

When they had heard the king they went their way; and lo, the star which they had seen in the East went before them, till it came to rest over the place where the child was. When they saw the star, they rejoiced with exceedingly great joy.[13] Theirs was the incomparable joy of discovering God after a long and demanding search and effort.

And going into the house they saw the child with Mary his mother, and they fell down and worshipped him. Then, opening their treasures, they offered him gifts, gold and frankincense and myrrh.[14] These gifts were highly valued at that time in the Orient. *The same Christ who in Bethlehem, as a Child, accepted the gifts of the Magi Kings, is still the One to whom men and whole peoples 'open their treasures.' The gifts of the human spirit, in the act of this opening before God Incarnate, take on a special value.*[15] Everything takes on a new value when it is offered to God.

---

[13] Matt 2:9-10
[14] Matt 2:11
[15] St John Paul II, *General Audience,* 24 January 1979

FIRST SUNDAY AFTER THE EPIPHANY

3. THE BAPTISM OF OUR LORD
Feast

The feast of the Baptism of Our Lord falls on the Sunday following the Solemnity of the Epiphany. The feast brings to our mind the mystery of Christ's Person and mission. At the same time it is an opportunity for us to give thanks to God for the innumerable gifts which we have received since the day we were baptized. The Church exhorts the faithful to renew *with deep faith those baptismal commitments which we assumed through our parents and godparents, particularly our loyalty to Christ and our determination to struggle against temptation* (St John Paul II).

3.1 The manifestation of the Blessed Trinity in the Baptism of Christ.

After the Lord was baptized, the heavens were opened, and the Spirit descended upon him like a dove, and the voice of the Father thundered: This is my beloved Son, with whom I am well pleased.[1]

Only a few days ago we celebrated the feast of the *Epiphany,* the manifestation of the Lord to the Gentiles, as represented in the person of the wise men. An earlier manifestation had been made to the shepherds on Christmas night. The shepherds had come to the stable bearing simple gifts. Today's feast is also an *epiphany* since it commemorates the manifestation of Christ's divinity by the voice of the Father and the descent of the Holy Spirit in the form of a dove. The Fathers of the Church were wont to point out a third manifestation of the divinity of Jesus. It took place in Cana of Galilee on the

[1] *Entrance Antiphon*: cf Matt 3:16-17

occasion of Christ's first miracle. Jesus *manifested his glory; and his disciples believed in him.*[2]

In today's *First Reading,* Isaiah prophesied the figure of the Messiah: *Behold my servant, whom I uphold, my chosen, in whom my soul delights; I have put my Spirit upon him ... a bruised reed he will not break, and a dimly burning wick he will not quench ... I am the Lord, I have called you ... to open the eyes that are blind, to bring out the prisoners from the dungeon, from the prison those who sit in darkness.*[3] This prophecy is fulfilled during the Baptism of the Lord. At that time *the Holy Spirit descended upon him in bodily form, as a dove, and a voice came from heaven, 'Thou art my beloved Son; with thee I am well pleased'.*[4] In this great epiphany on the shores of the Jordan, the three divine Persons of the Blessed Trinity are made manifest: the Father allows his voice to be heard as He gives testimony to the Son while the Holy Spirit appears above him. The expression from Isaiah *my servant* has been replaced with the phrase *my beloved Son.* These new words tell us about the Person and divine nature of Christ.

Following upon his baptism Jesus formally begins his salvific mission. It is at this moment that the Holy Spirit begins his action on souls by means of the Messiah, an influence which will last until the end of time.

The liturgy for this Sunday's Mass provides a good opportunity for us to recall with joy our own baptism and how that sacrament has affected our lives. Saint Augustine remembers his baptism with a special joy: *In those days I could not take my fill of meditating with wondrous sweetness on the depths of your counsel concerning the*

---

[2] John 2:11
[3] Is 42:1-4; 6-7
[4] Luke 3:22

salvation of mankind.[5] We ought to cultivate the same kind of sentiments today when we pray about our baptism in the name of the Father and the Son and the Holy Spirit.

The Baptism of Jesus is a mystery. *And from his fullness have we all received, grace upon grace.*[6] We have been baptized not only with water, as in the baptism of John, but *with the Holy Spirit,* which joins us to the life of God. We give thanks to God for that day when we were incorporated into the life of Christ. Our destiny is to be with him forever in heaven. We thank God that we were baptized soon after being born, following the long-standing custom of the Church, or for having been received into the Church in our adult life.

3.2 Our divine filiation in Christ through the sacrament of Baptism.

We have been baptized in the name of the Father and of the Son and of the Holy Spirit. We have entered into communion with the Most Blessed Trinity. Heaven has been opened up unto us. We can enter into the *house of the Lord* and learn about our divine filiation. As Saint Cyril of Jerusalem has written: *If you endeavour to have true piety the Holy Spirit will also descend upon you from above. You too will hear the voice of the Father saying, 'This is not my Son, but now that he has been baptized, he has been made mine'.*[7] One of the most important gifts which we received at Baptism was that of our divine filiation. Saint Paul teaches us about this filiation in those moving words: *So through God you are no longer a slave but a son, and if a son then an heir.*[8]

In the rite of this sacrament the Church reminds us that

---

[5] St Augustine, *Confessions,* I, 9, 6
[6] John 1:16
[7] St Cyril of Jerusalem, *Catechesis III, About Baptism,* 14
[8] Gal 4:7

our unity with Christ takes place by means of a spiritual rebirth. As Jesus tells Nicodemus: *Truly, truly, I say to you, unless one is born of water and the Spirit, he cannot enter the kingdom of God.*[9] *Christian baptism is, in fact, a mystery of death and resurrection: the immersion in the baptismal water symbolizes and actualizes the burial of Jesus in the earth and the death of the 'old man', while the coming up out of the water signifies Christ's resurrection and the birth of the 'new man'.*[10] This new birth is the basic foundation of our divine filiation. *Thus by Baptism men are grafted into the paschal mystery of Christ; they die with him, are buried with him, and rise with him. They receive the spirit of adoption as sons 'in which we cry, Abba, Father' (Rom 8:15) and thus become true adorers such as the Father seeks.*[11] This filiation brings with it the cleansing of all sin from the soul and the infusion of grace.

By means of Baptism we are forgiven and cleansed from original sin, from our personal sins as well as from the eternal and temporal penalties which we have merited because of our sins. The soul receives the infused virtues and gifts of the Holy Spirit. The doors of heaven are opened to the new Christian and the angels and saints rejoice. After Baptism, our human nature still is marked by the consequences of original sin. The baptized person remains prone to error and eventual death. Nevertheless, the sacrament has sown a divine seed in the human body, a seed which will lead to a glorious resurrection. The Christian *comes forth from Baptism resplendent like the sun. What is even more important, he has been converted into a son of God and a co-redeemer with Christ.*[12]

---

[9] John 3:5

[10] St John Paul II, *Angelus,* 8 January 1989

[11] Second Vatican Council, *Sacrosanctum Concilium,* 6

[12] St Hippolytus, *Homily on the Theophany*

We thank the Lord a great deal for all these gifts which we are praying about today. *We humbly entreat your mercy, O Lord, that, faithfully listening to your Only Begotten Son, we may be your children in name and truth.*[13] This is our greatest desire and aspiration.

3.3 Baptism and daily life.

In today's *Second Reading,* Saint Peter presents a brief review of Christ's public life. *You know the word which he sent to Israel, preaching good news of peace by Jesus Christ (he is Lord of all), the word which was proclaimed throughout all Judaea beginning from Galilee after the baptism which John preached: how God anointed Jesus of Nazareth with the Holy Spirit and with power; how He went about doing good and healing all that were oppressed by the devil ...*[14]

Pertransivit benefaciendo ..., he went about doing good ... This is an appropriate summary of Christ's life on this earth. This should be the description of the life of every baptized person since our lives are subject to the influence of the Holy Spirit. This ought to be so in our daily work, in our times of rest, whenever we help other people in our family or community.

Today's feast gives us an opportunity to have a renewed awareness of those baptismal commitments which we took ourselves, or on that day when our parents or godparents spoke on our behalf. We should reaffirm our devotion to Christ and our intention to come closer to him every day. We should resolve to separate ourselves from all sin, including venial sins. Having received this sacrament, we have been called by God to participate in his divine life.

Baptism makes us 'fideles', faithful. This is a word that

---

[13] *Prayer after Communion*
[14] *Second Reading of the Mass*: Acts 10:34-38

was used – like 'sancti', the saints – by the first followers of Jesus to refer to one another. These words are still used today: we speak of 'the faithful' of the Church.[15] We shall be faithful to the extent that our life is built upon the sure foundation of true prayer. In his gospel Saint Luke makes note of the fact that Christ *was praying*[16] after his baptism by John. Saint Thomas Aquinas has commented on this passage that *after one's baptism, a Christian needs to live a life of persevering prayer in order to win Heaven. Baptism does act to cleanse us from sins, but the baptized person is still prone to the temptations of sin, the flesh and the Devil.*[17]

We thank God for all the benefits we have received from this sacrament. Today is a good moment to renew our commitment to Christ and his Church by means of daily prayer.

---

[15] St. J. Escrivá, *The Forge,* 622

[16] cf Luke 3:21

[17] St Thomas, *Summa Theologiae,* 3, q 39, a 5

CHRISTIAN UNITY OCTAVE

DAY 1 – 18 JANUARY

4. CHRIST FOUNDED ONE CHURCH

Each year the Church prays for Christian unity during the Octave which precedes the feast of the Conversion of Saint Paul on January 25th.

In 1897, Pope Leo XIII announced in the encyclical *Satis cognitum* that the Church would especially pray for Christian unity during the nine days between the Ascension and Pentecost. In 1910, Pope Saint Pius X changed the feast to the current date. At that time the feast of *the Chair of Saint Peter* was celebrated on January 18th, the first day of the octave.

In its decree on ecumenism, the Second Vatican Council urged the faithful to unite in prayer for this intention ... this Council declares that it realizes that this holy objective – the reconciliation of all Christians in the unity of the one and only Church of Christ – transcends human powers and gifts (Decree, *Unitatis redintegratio*, 24).

4.1 The Will of Christ was to found one Church.

I believe ... in one, holy, catholic and apostolic Church.[1] How many times have we made this profession of faith in the course of our lives, savouring those characteristic marks: *one, holy, catholic and apostolic!* During the Christian Unity Octave, the Church asks us to pray with renewed devotion in company with the Pope, the bishops, Catholics around the world and all of our separated brethren. Although our separated brethren do not live in the fullness of the Faith, they are oriented to it by Christ himself who desires *ut omnes unum sint.*[2] This is Christ's priestly prayer, that all may be one.

---

[1] *Nicene Creed,* Dz 86 (150)

[2] John 17:21

Unity is a characteristic mark of Christ's Church. It forms part of her mystery.[3] Christ founded one Church, not several. *This is the sole Church of Christ which in the Creed we profess to be one, holy, catholic and apostolic, which our Saviour, after his resurrection, entrusted to Peter's pastoral care (cf John 21:17), commissioning him and the other apostles to extend and rule it (cf Matt 28:18 ff), and which he raised up for all ages as 'the pillar and mainstay of the truth' (1 Tim 3:15). This Church, constituted and organized as a society in the present world, subsists in the Catholic Church, which is governed by the successor of Peter and by the bishops in communion with him. Nevertheless, many elements of sanctification and of truth are found outside its visible confines. Since these are gifts belonging to the Church of Christ, they are forces impelling towards Catholic unity.*[4] The Church has frequently been compared to Christ's tunic which *was without seam, woven from top to bottom.*[5] According to Saint Augustine, the Church should not be divided because it also is without seam.[6]

Our Lord expressed his desire to found one Church on a number of occasions. He preached about the one flock and the one true shepherd.[7] He stated that a kingdom divided against itself cannot stand – *omne regnum divisum contra se, desolabitur.*[8] He gave the keys of the kingdom to Peter.[9] He promised to build his Church upon Peter.[10]

By means of the Communion of the Saints, of which we form part, let us unite in prayer *ut omnes unum sint,*

---

[3] cf St Paul VI, *Address,* 19 January 1977

[4] Second Vatican Council, *Lumen gentium,* 8

[5] cf John 19:23

[6] cf St Augustine, *Treatise on St John's Gospel,* 118, 4

[7] John 10:16

[8] Matt 12:25

[9] Matt 16:19

[10] Matt 16:18

that all may be one, gathered together under one shepherd.

4.2 Christ's priestly prayer for unity.

Christ's deep concern for unity is especially evident in his priestly prayer at the Last Supper: *And now I am no more in the world, but they are in the world, and I am coming to thee. Holy Father keep them in thy name, which thou hast given me, that they may be one, even as we are one ... I do not pray for these only, but also for those who believe in me through their word, that they may all be one; even as thou, Father, art in me, and I in thee, that they also may be in us, so that the world may believe that thou hast sent me.*[11]

Ut omnes unum sint ... Union with Christ is the cause and the condition of the unity of Christians. This unity is a great help for humanity, since the one Church beckons all people to believe in Jesus Christ, the one true Saviour. The Church continues Christ's salvific work in the world. In its decree on ecumenism, the Second Vatican Council has taught that the unity of the Church affects her universality and her salvific mission.[12]

Unity of faith and customs was the theme of the first Council of Jerusalem at the dawn of Christianity.[13] The letters of Saint Paul are replete with his insistence on unity. Saint Paul instructed the elders of the Church of Ephesus that their chief responsibility was to preserve unity.[14] He made the same point to his closest collaborators and successors.[15] This concern for unity can be found in the teachings and actions of all the Apostles.[16]

The Fathers of the Church sought to defend this unity

---

[11] John 17:11; 20-21

[12] cf Second Vatican Council, *Unitatis redintegratio,* 1

[13] Acts 15:1-30

[14] Acts 20:28-35

[15] cf 1 Tim 4:1-16; 6:3-6; Tit 1:5-16; etc.

[16] cf 1 Pet 2:1-9; 2 Pet 1:12-15; John 2:1-25; Jas 4:11-12; etc.

desired by Christ. They looked upon division in the Church as the worst of all evils.[17] In our own times there are those who advocate a false ecumenism which holds that all Christian religions are equally valid. They reject the existence of one visible Church linked to the Apostles and fulfilling the Will of Christ. According to the Second Vatican Council, *Christ the Lord founded one Church and one Church only. However, many Christian communions present themselves to men as the true inheritors of Jesus Christ; all indeed profess to be followers of the Lord, but they differ in mind and go their different ways, as if Christ himself were divided. Certainly, such division openly contradicts the Will of Christ, scandalizes the world, and damages that most holy cause, the preaching of the Gospel to every creature.*

Because of our love for the Church this scandal should be a motive for prayer and sacrifice. We have to offer up little mortifications in our daily work so as to win God's mercy to build up the unity of his Church. We have to put aside any obstacle which separates us from Christ and from our vocation to follow him. We have to lead lives which will bring people closer to Christ, not drive them farther away. We ought to look for what we have in common with our separated brethren. Perhaps our differences have traditionally attracted more attention than our similarities. *The Church knows that she is joined in many ways to the baptized who are honoured by the name of Christian, but do not however profess the Catholic faith in its entirety or have not preserved unity or communion under the successor of Peter. For there are many who hold Sacred Scripture in honour as a rule of faith and of life, who have a sincere religious zeal, who lovingly believe in God the Father Almighty and in Christ, the Son of God and the Saviour, who are sealed in baptism which unites them to*

---

[17] cf St Augustine, *Against the Parmenians,* 2, 2

Christ and who indeed recognize and receive other sacraments in their own Churches or ecclesiastical communities. Many of them possess the episcopate, celebrate the holy Eucharist and cultivate devotion to the Virgin Mother of God.[18] These separated brethren participate in the *Communion of the Saints* and benefit from its influence, being inspired by the Holy Spirit to lead exemplary lives.[19]

This desire for unity should lead us to pray for everyone and to be models of charity. We should live in such a way that people will remark: *See how they love one another.*[20]

4.3 Unity, a gift from God.

Unity is a gift from God. We have to ask for it in our prayer and make this intention an integral part of our ascetic struggle. *We will be able to do only very little, in the work for the whole Church which is my daily worry and yours, if we have not reached this close intimacy with the Lord Jesus, if we do not keep his word in us, trying to discover its hidden riches every day, if God's own love for his Christ is not deeply rooted in us.*[21]

Our love for God should move us to pray in particular for those brothers and sisters of ours who still maintain many ties with the Church. Through our efforts to seek sanctity in ordinary work, we will contribute in a most efficacious manner to the cause of Christian unity. Each Catholic ought to have a big heart, big enough to sense how to be of service to other Catholics, to other Christians and to people with other beliefs. We have to pray for other people so that they may come to live in the fullness of Christ and find happiness therein. With the liturgy of the

---

[18] *idem*, *Lumen gentium*, 15
[19] cf *ibid*
[20] Tertullian, *Apology*, 39
[21] St John Paul II, *Address during the Hour of Prayer for Christian Unity*, 23 January 1981

Mass, we pray: *Pour out on us, O Lord, the Spirit of your love and, in your kindness, make those who believe in you one in mind and heart by the power of this sacrifice.*[22]

[22] *Roman Missal, Mass for the Unity of Christians,* Cycle B. Prayer after Communion

Christian Unity Octave

Day 2 – 19 January

5. UNITY WITHIN THE CHURCH

5.1 Union with Christ is the foundation for unity among the faithful.

The Lord desired that we be joined to his Person with bonds as strong as those which unite the different parts of the body to one another. Jesus likened this relationship to that of the vine and the branches: *I am the true vine.*[1] In the vestibule of the Temple of Jerusalem there was a sculpture of an immense golden vine. Jesus taught his disciples according to their religious understanding. *Abide in me, and I in you. As the branch cannot bear fruit by itself, unless it abides in the vine, neither can you, unless you abide in me. I am the vine, you are the branches. He who abides in me, and I in him, he it is that bears much fruit, for apart from me you can do nothing.*[2] *You see, the branches are full of fruit, because they share in the sap that comes from the stem. Otherwise, from the tiny buds we knew just a few months back, they could not have produced the sweet ripe fruit that gladdens the eye and makes the heart rejoice. Here and there on the ground we may find some dry twigs, lying half-buried in the soil. Once they too were branches of the vine; now they lie there withered and dead, a perfect image of barrenness: 'for apart from me, you can do nothing'.*[3]

Union with Christ is the foundation for unity among the faithful. We are all bound together and strengthened in

---

[1] John 15:1
[2] John 15:4-6
[3] St. J. Escrivá, *Friends of God,* 254

the Mystical Body of Christ. In the *Acts of the Apostles* we read how the first Christians *with one accord devoted themselves to prayer*[4] and how they *had all things in common; and they sold their possessions and goods and distributed them to all, as any had need.*[5] Faith in Christ involves practical consequences with respect to our behaviour towards others. Faith in Jesus Christ should move us to act with brotherly love like the first Christians who *were of one heart and soul.*[6]

Saint Paul writes: *And they devoted themselves to the apostles' teaching and fellowship, to the breaking of bread and the prayers.*[7] In the words of St John Paul II, *Our union with Christ in the Eucharist must be expressed in the truth of our lives today – in our actions, in our behaviour, in our life-style, and in our relationships with others. For each one of us the Eucharist is a call to ever greater effort, so that we may live as true followers of Jesus: truthful in our speech, generous in our deeds, concerned, respectful of the dignity and rights of all persons – whatever their rank or income – self-sacrificing, fair and just, kind, compassionate and self-controlled ... The truth of our union with Jesus Christ in the Eucharist is tested by whether or not we really love our fellow men and women; it is tested by how we treat others; especially our families ..., by whether or not we try to be reconciled with our enemies, on whether or not we forgive those who hurt us or offend us.*[8]

Friendship with Christ will teach us to have a big heart, big enough to include those many people we meet along our way. This is especially true with respect to our relatives and friends.

---

[4] Acts 1:14
[5] Acts 2:44-45
[6] Acts 4:32
[7] Acts 2:42
[8] St John Paul II, *Homily in Phoenix Park,* 29 September 1979

5.2 Making unity a high priority.

One guarantee of ecumenical spirit is through dedicated sacrifice for the internal unity of the Church. *How do we suppose that people who do not have our Faith can come to the Holy Church if they see the unhandsome way in which those who call themselves followers of Christ treat each other?*[9]

This spirit will be shown in our charity towards other Catholics, our willingness to stand by our principles, our refined obedience to the Roman Pontiff and the bishops. Saint Paul VI has taught, *It is not sufficient to call ourselves Catholics. It is necessary to be truly united. The loyal sons and daughters of the Church ought to be the builders of authentic unity ... In our times there is a great deal of discussion about our separated brethren. That is all well and good. Ecumenism is a most meritorious enterprise to which everyone should make a real contribution. But we cannot forget our duty to work even harder for the internal unity of the Church, something which is essential to her spiritual and apostolic vitality.*[10]

The Lord established an unmistakable sign by which the world can identify his followers: *By this all men will know that you are my disciples, if you have love for one another.*[11] Fraternal charity acts like a cement that holds the *living stones* of the Church together, to use an expression of Saint Augustine.[12] As Saint Paul exhorted the Christians of the Church in Galatia: *So then, as we have opportunity, let us do good to all men, and especially to those who are of the household of faith.*[13] Saint Peter wrote

---

[9] St. J. Escrivá, *Furrow,* 751
[10] St Paul VI, *Address,* 31 March 1965
[11] cf John 13:35
[12] cf St Augustine, *Commentary on Psalm 44*
[13] Gal 6:10

in similar terms: *Honour all men. Love the brotherhood.*[14]

At the onset of the Roman persecutions the term *brother* acquired a deep meaning. Thanks to the external difficulties, the union among the faithful grew stronger. Today also we feel the need to *strengthen that which characterizes Catholicism: our sense of solidarity, of friendship, of mutual comprehension, of respect for our heritage of doctrine and customs, of obedience and authority of faith. This is the essence of the Church's power and beauty, that which proves her authenticity.*[15] If we ought to love those who are not fully incorporated into the Church, how much more charity should we exercise towards our brothers and sisters in the Faith?

Love for Christ will lead us to avoid giving in to any form of critical spirit about our fellow Catholics, especially with respect to members of the clergy and hierarchy. If we should ever happen to come across a Church leader who gives bad example, we should make an effort to pray for that individual and, if appropriate, give fraternal correction in a delicate and respectful manner. We should ask Our Lady to help us in this struggle. *Acquire the habit of speaking about everyone and about everything they do in a friendly manner, especially when you are speaking of those who labour in God's service. Whenever that is not possible, keep quiet. Sharp or irritated comment may border on gossip or slander.*[16]

5.3 The order of charity.

In the face of danger, everyone instinctively seeks to protect the head first. As Christians we should feel the same way when the Church is assailed. We ought to defend the Roman Pontiff and the bishops in the environment

[14] 1 Pet 2:17
[15] St Paul VI, *loc cit*
[16] St. J. Escrivá, *Furrow,* 902

where we live and work. The Lord is always pleased by our fidelity to his pastors. On a more positive note, we should pray every day for the Pope and the bishops and their intentions: *Dominus conservet eum et vivificet eum, et beatum faciat eum in terra* ... Here we pray that the Lord conserve them and strengthen them and increase their authority in the world ...

Love for unity will help us to maintain fraternal harmony. We will choose that which unites over that which divides: prayer, cordiality, fraternal correction, the Communion of the Saints.

We need to keep in mind that there is an order in charity. God has to be at the top of our priorities. The bonds of faith, of blood, of common interests, of work, of locale are also very important. It would be a strange form of charity indeed that would have us caring for strangers more than for our neighbours. Saint Augustine teaches that without excluding anyone he gave himself more generously to his friends and members of his own family. *In this expression of charity I have no regret, since I know that God is present in those who have been placed at my side.*[17] Saint Bernard asked the Lord to help him take good care of the parcel of land which had been entrusted to him.[18]

The internal unity of the Church is an excellent way to win people back to the Faith. Our love for our brothers and sisters in the Faith should be so attractive that people will feel a longing to join our spiritual family. Our prayer and sacrifice for the Church needs to be made specific in daily life. This testimony will, it is to be hoped, awaken those Catholics who find themselves fallen away from the Church and perhaps alienated from Jesus Christ.

---

[17] St Augustine, *Letter 73*

[18] St Bernard, *Sermon 49 on the Canticle of Canticles*

CHRISTIAN UNITY OCTAVE

DAY 3 – 20 JANUARY

6. THE DEPOSIT OF FAITH

6.1 Fidelity to Revelation. Ecumenical dialogue needs to be based on a sincere love for divine truth.

The Holy Spirit works to inspire all Christians to build up the unity desired by Christ.[1] The Lord encourages desires for ecumenical dialogue so as to attain this union. To be faithful to its origins, this dialogue has to be oriented to the truth. It is not simply a matter of exchanging opinions, nor is it a question of reaching a mutual accord about particular problems. This dialogue should be about the truths of the Faith which Christ entrusted to the Magisterium of the Church. Dialogue ought to lead to a greater understanding of dogma while fostering in souls renewed desire for personal sanctity.

The truths of the Faith can guide us to salvation because they are the fruit of divine revelation. These truths come to us from Jesus Christ who, in turn, gave them to the Apostles and their successors – the Pope and the bishops – who receive the continual assistance of the Holy Spirit. Each generation *receives* the deposit of the Faith revealed by Christ. Each generation *transmits* this deposit to the generation that follows, and so on until the end of time.

Saint Paul wrote to Timothy, *Guard what has been entrusted to you.*[2] Saint Vincent of Lérins has commented: *What is this 'deposit'? It is what you have believed, not what you have discovered. It is what you have received, not*

---

[1] cf Second Vatican Council, Decree *Unitatis redintegratio,* 4

[2] 1 Tim 6:20

what you have thought up. It is something which emanates from doctrine as opposed to human imagination. It is the fruit of a public tradition, not private property. It is something which has found you. You have not found it. You are not the author but the guardian; not the creator, but the protector; not the conductor, but the conducted. 'Guard what has been entrusted to you'. Preserve and protect the Catholic Faith. What you have believed, that is what will remain with you, that is what you will hand on to others. Gold has been delivered unto you, gold you must return. Do not substitute one thing for another. Do not put iron in the place of gold. Do not mix things in a fraudulent manner. I do not want the appearance of gold, but only pure gold.[3]

Ecumenical dialogue does not consist in thinking up new truths or in coming up with commonly-agreed-upon doctrines. One cannot compromise when it comes to revealed truth since it has been given to us by Christ. To treat this divine treasure as a merely human inheritance would be a real disservice to others. *Love and practise charity without setting any limits or discriminating between people, for it is the virtue which marks us out as disciples of the Master. Nevertheless, this charity cannot lead you to dampen your faith – for it would then cease to be a virtue. Nor should it blur the clear outlines that define the faith, nor soften it to the point of changing it, as some people try to do, into something amorphous and lacking the strength and power of God.*[4] Our desire for dialogue with our separated brethren and 'fallen-away' Catholics should move us to renew our personal commitment to formation and understanding of revealed truth. Today, let us pray about how well we make use of the means of

---

[3] St Vincent de Lérins, *Commonitorio,* 22
[4] St. J. Escrivá, *The Forge,* 456

formation we have at our disposal – spiritual reading, spiritual direction, retreats ...

6.2 Explaining doctrine in a clear fashion.

The Gospel is the source of salvation because it is the Gospel of Christ. Paul, aware of this, desired to compare his own proclamation with that of the other Apostles to assure himself of the authenticity of his own preaching (cf Gal 2:1-10). During his whole life he never tired of urging fidelity to the teaching which had been received because 'no one can lay a foundation other than the one already laid, which is Jesus Christ' (1 Cor 3:11).[5]

The truth which we have received from the Lord is one and immutable, integrally preserved from the beginning and down through the centuries. It cannot be brought 'up-to-date' or improved. As St John Paul II reminded us, *Every attack against the unity of the Faith is an attack against Christ himself. Paul was so profoundly convinced of this that, in the face of factions emerging in the primitive community in the name of one or other of the apostles, he responds with that anguished question whose echo does not cease to resound in the Church today: Has Christ perhaps been divided? (1 Cor 1:13).*[6] *Now I would remind you, brethren, in what terms I preached to you the gospel, which you received, in which you stand, by which you are saved, if you hold it fast – unless you believed in vain. For I delivered to you as of first importance what I also received, that Christ died for our sins in accordance with the scriptures, that He was buried, that He was raised on the third day in accordance with the scriptures, and that He appeared to Cephas, then to the twelve. Then He appeared to more than five hundred brethren at one time, most of whom are still alive, though some have fallen*

---

[5] St John Paul II, *Homily,* 25 January 1987

[6] *ibid*

asleep.[7]

The Apostle taught the first Christians that the Faith was not a matter of personal theory but the doctrine of *the twelve.* The content of the Faith is to be found in the *Creed.* According to the Second Vatican Council, *The manner and order in which Catholic belief is expressed should in no way become an obstacle to dialogue with our brethren. It is, of course, essential that the doctrine be clearly presented in its entirety. Nothing is so foreign to the spirit of ecumenism as a false irenicism which harms the purity of Catholic doctrine and obscures its genuine and certain meaning.*[8]

The proper object of ecumenical dialogue is to find communion in the saving truth of Jesus Christ. Progress in understanding and accepting this truth requires the continual assistance of the Holy Spirit. During this octave for Christian unity, we pray with renewed fervour for the help of the Holy Spirit. As Saint Paul VI affirmed, *Yesterday and today, the Church gives so much importance to the conservation of authentic revelation. This is the Church's inviolable treasure. She is fully aware of her fundamental duty to defend and transmit the truths of the Faith in unequivocal terms. Orthodoxy is her first concern. Pastoral teaching is her primary and divinely-ordered duty. As the apostle Paul insisted: 'depositum custodi' (1 Tim 6:20; 2 Tim 1:14). This is the Church's mission. She cannot betray this trust. The Church teaches her doctrine. She does not invent it. She is the witness, custodian, interpreter and transmitter. In what refers to the truths of the Christian message, the Church can be said to be the steadfast guardian. Those who want her to make the Faith less demanding, more in accord with the spirit of our*

---

[7] 1 Cor 15:1-6

[8] Second Vatican Council, *loc cit,* 11

times, let them consider the words of the Apostles: non possumus, we cannot do it *(Acts 4:20).*[9] These words should help us in our personal apostolate when we deal with Catholics who may desire to make the Faith more 'up-to-date'.

6.3 *Veritatem facientes in caritate.* Giving the truth with charity.

Saint Paul reminded the first Christians in Ephesus to *speak the truth in love: veritatem facientes in caritate.*[10] This is how we ought to behave towards other people who are seeking the truth. *Veritatem facientes in caritate* with those whom we meet and work with every day. We ought to be understanding and cordial without compromising our beliefs. Even more, if for whatever reason we find ourselves in a more or less anti-Christian environment, we should follow the wise counsel of Saint John of the Cross: *Think of nothing else but that everything be ordered to God. Where there is no love, put love and you will draw out love ...*[11] We have many opportunities to put this advice into practice. Perhaps we already know of cases where we have changed a hostile or indifferent environment in this fashion.

We need to give people good doctrine in its full integrity. Yet we need to do so in an attractive manner – without negative polemics, without violence. Every person has a right to his or her good name, no matter how right or wrong that person may be. We cannot ever judge another person, much less condemn anyone. The spirit of charity which impels us to be loyal to Christ in the Faith is the same charity which leads us to love other people, to be

---

[9] St Paul VI, *General Audience,* 19 January 1972

[10] Eph 4:15

[11] St John of the Cross, *Letter to M. María de la Encarnación,* 6 July 1591

understanding, to be forgiving, to be patient, to trust in the action of grace, to respect freedom of conscience.

We should want to satisfy the greatest longing of the human heart – to know the truth and live in the truth with joy. God has impressed this desire on the heart of every person. It is our common experience that each person has a unique path to the truth. We might think of our role as serving as a bridge between our friends and God.

Let us ask Our Lady for her guidance to teach us how to deal with each person in the proper manner – with immense love and respect for the individual, with immense love and respect for the truth.

Christian Unity Octave

Day 4 – 21 January

7. THE FOUNDATION OF UNITY

7.1 The primacy of Peter is realized in the Church in the person of the Roman Pontiff.

Saint John begins his narration of the public life of Jesus by recounting the gathering of the first disciples. When Andrew introduced Jesus to his brother Peter, the Lord said: *So, you are Simon the son of John? You shall be called Cephas (which means Peter).*[1] *Cephas* is the Greek translation of the Aramaic word for *rock,* foundation. *Cephas* was not a proper name. The Lord called his apostle by this name to indicate his future mission. In Biblical history, the act of naming is equivalent to assuming control over the named. For example, when God gave man the power to name every creature, man exercised authority and dominion over the beasts.[2] The name of *Noah* was given to him to represent new hope after the flood.[3] God changed Abram's name to *Abraham* to signify that he would be *the father of a multitude of nations.*[4]

The first Christians were so taken up with the symbolism of the name *Cephas* that they became accustomed to use it without translation.[5] Some time later the translation from 'rock' to 'Petrus' became popular, which led to neglect of the original name of Simon. Christ himself was

---

[1] John 1:42

[2] Gen 2:20

[3] Gen 5:20

[4] Gen 17:5

[5] cf Gal 2:9; 11; 14

wont to call his apostle *Simon Peter,* thereby joining the proper name of the apostle with the mission entrusted to him. It is especially significant that this name of *Cephas* or *Peter* chosen by Jesus was not a proper name common to that time and place.

Right from the very start, Peter occupied a singular position among Christ's disciples. In each of the four listings of the Twelve Apostles which appear in the New Testament, Simon Peter is in the first place. Jesus gave special attention to Peter, even though John seems to have been his favourite. Jesus stayed in Peter's house.[6] Jesus asked Peter to pay the temple tax for both of them.[7] It may have been that Peter was the first to see the risen Jesus.[8] There are a number of instances when Peter simply sticks out from among the group of the apostles. For example, Saint Luke makes reference to *Peter and those who were with him,*[9] and *Peter and his companions ...*[10] The angel at the tomb of the Lord tells the women: *But go, tell his disciples and Peter ...*[11] On several occasions, Peter acts as the spokesman for the Twelve. Peter is the one who asks the Lord to explain his parables.[12]

Everyone seems to have known about the pre-eminent position of Simon. The tax-collectors say as much when they go to Peter to collect the temple tax from the Master.[13] Peter's superiority is not due to his personality but to his vocation from Christ. The Second Vatican Council has taught, *The Roman Pontiff, as the successor of Peter, is the perpetual and visible source and foundation of the unity both of the*

---

[6] Luke 4:38-41
[7] Matt 17:27
[8] Luke 24:34
[9] Luke 9:32
[10] Luke 8:45
[11] Mark 16:7
[12] Luke 12:41
[13] Matt 17:24

bishops and of the whole company of the faithful.[14]

During these days when we are praying especially for Christian unity we ought to keep in mind the Pope, who is the personification of unity. We should pray for his person and intentions: Dominus conservet eum et vivificet eum ... We pray that the Lord conserve him, strengthen him and make him happy here on earth. Surely this is a most pleasing prayer to Our Lord.

7.2 The Vicar of Christ.

While they were in Caesarea Philippi Jesus asked his disciples what people were saying about him. With poignant simplicity, the disciples proceeded to report what they had heard from the crowds. Then Jesus asked the disciples what they themselves thought about him: *But who do you say that I am?* Peter stands forth and speaks for the group: *You are the Christ, the Son of the living God.* The Lord responds to this profession of faith with some of the most pivotal words in the history of the Church and of the world: *Blessed are you, Simon Bar-Jona! For flesh and blood has not revealed this to you, but my Father who is in heaven. And I tell you, you are Peter, and on this rock I will build my church, and the powers of death shall not prevail against it. I will give you the keys of the kingdom of heaven, and whatever you bind on earth shall be bound in heaven, and whatever you loose on earth shall be loosed in heaven.*[15]

This text can be found in all of the ancient codices. It is cited by many of the early Christian authors.[16] The Lord builds his Church upon the very person of Simon: *You are Peter, and on this rock*[17]*...* Jesus speaks directly to Peter: *You ...* Here is an obvious allusion to their first encounter.

---

[14] Second Vatican Council, *Lumen gentium,* 23
[15] Matt 16:16-20
[16] cf J. Auer, J. Ratzinger, *Course in Dogmatic Theology,* Barcelona 1986
[17] John 1:42

The disciple is to be the sure foundation for the building up of Christ's church. The Biblical prerogative of Christ to be the one *cornerstone*[18]has been given over to Peter. This is the origin for the later title given to Peter's successors, *Vicar of Christ.* This is also the source of that loving title which Saint Catherine of Siena gave to the Pope: the *sweet Christ on earth.*[19] According to Saint Leo the Great, the Lord says to Peter, *Even though I am the foundation and without me there is no other, nevertheless I have chosen you, Peter, to be the rock. I desire that you shall serve as the foundation. I hand on my powers to you.*[20]

In those days of walled cities, *giving over the keys* was symbolic of handing over public authority. Christ entrusted Peter with the responsibility of guarding and caring for the Church. He gave Peter supreme authority over the Church and her affairs. *To bind and to loose* – in the Semitic language of the day these words signified 'prohibit and permit'. Peter and his successors are charged with guiding, mandating, prohibiting, directing. This power finds its ratification in Heaven. The *Vicar of Christ* is responsible for nourishing the other apostles and all Christians, regardless of his own personal inadequacies. During the Last Supper, Jesus told Peter: *Simon, Simon, behold, Satan demanded to have you, that he might sift you like wheat, but I have prayed for you that your faith may not fail; and when you have turned again, strengthen your brethren.*[21] In these moments following the institution of the Eucharist, when his death was so imminent, Christ renews his covenant with Peter. The faith of Peter will not fail, since it is rooted in the prayer of Christ.

Because of the prayer of Jesus, Peter did not fail in his

---

[18] cf 1 Pet 2:6-8

[19] St Catherine of Siena, *Letter 207*

[20] St Leo the Great, *Sermon 4*

[21] Luke 22:31-32

faith, despite his betrayals. He got up from his fall. He confirmed his brethren in the Faith. He became the *cornerstone* of the Church. Saint Ambrose has written: *Where there is Peter, there is the Church. Where there is the Church, there is no death, only life.*[22] This prayer of Jesus redounds through the course of history.[23]

7.3 The papacy is the guarantee of Christian unity and the well-spring of true ecumenism. Love and veneration for the Pope.

The promise made by Jesus to Peter in Caesarea Philippi was fulfilled after the Resurrection on the shore of the Sea of Tiberias. The occasion was a miraculous catch of fish reminiscent of Peter's first encounter with the Lord.[24]

Christ confirmed Peter in his leadership by using the pastoral symbolism of the shepherd and the sheep.

The charism of Saint Peter has been handed on to his successors.[25] Peter was destined to die a martyr's death, but it was Christ's desire that the office of supreme shepherd would endure until the end of time.[26]

The Papacy is the guarantee of Christian unity and is the well-spring of true ecumenism. The Pope takes the place of Christ on earth. We have to love him and listen to him. He is the voice of the truth. We should do our best to have that voice and that truth echo throughout every quarter of the globe. We should live the Communion of the Saints by praying every day for his person and intentions.

Love for the Pope is a distinguishing characteristic of Catholics, and is a bond of unity. The Pope represents for us the tangible presence of Jesus, *the sweet Christ on earth.*

---

[22] St Ambrose, *Commentary on Psalm 12*

[23] cf First Vatican Council, Constitution, *Pastor aeternus,* 3

[24] John 21:15-17

[25] St John Paul II, *Address,* 30 December 1980

[26] First Vatican Council, *loc cit,* 2

CHRISTIAN UNITY OCTAVE

DAY 5 – 22 JANUARY

8. CHRIST AND THE CHURCH

8.1 Christ is to be found in the Church.

Christ's mission did not come to an end with his Ascension into heaven. Jesus is not simply a figure in history who was born, lived and rose from the dead, and who is now seated at the *right hand of God the Father*. In a mysterious way, Christ continues to live among us.

There was a real danger in the early church that the first Christians would think of Christ solely in terms of nostalgia for the past or of expectation for the future. It is against this misconception that the author of the *Letter to the Hebrews* writes: *Jesus Christ is the same yesterday and today and for ever.*[1] Even though the apostles and the first believers would eventually die, their testimony would not die with them. Men pass away, but Christ remains eternally present among us. He existed *yesterday* in history. He lives *today* in heaven at the *right hand of the Father*. He exists *today* at our very side, giving us his Life through the sacraments. The Holy Humanity of Christ was assumed only for a period of time. The Incarnation was decided upon from all eternity. The Son of God was born into time and space in the days of Caesar Augustus. He remains man for all time. The marks of his Passion are to be found on his glorified body.[2]

Christ lives in heaven in a resurrected and glorified state. He also lives in his Church in a mysterious way. The Church is not merely a religious movement inspired by Christ's teachings. The Church is Jesus Christ. Christ is to

---

[1] Heb 13:8

[2] cf *The Navarre Bible*, note to Heb 13:8

be found in the Church.

The glory of the Church resides in her intimate relationship with Jesus. This is a mystery which no words can fully describe. The Church has her origin in the Person of Jesus. She has her finality in perpetuating Christ's salvific presence to all mankind. The Church has the responsibility to witness to the truth of Christ's final promise to the apostles: *I am with you always, to the close of the age.*[3] According to the Second Vatican Council, *All those who in faith look towards Jesus, the author of salvation and the principle of unity and peace, God has gathered together and established as the Church, that it may be for each and every one the visible sacrament of this saving unity.*[4]

8.2 Images of the Church. The Mystical Body of Christ.

Saint Paul VI taught that it is essential for Christians to understand the nature of the Church. *This knowledge is all the more important for Catholics in these days when erroneous ideas enjoy such a wide circulation. How many people have forgotten that the Church is a mystery! This is true not only in the profundity of her life, but in the deeper sense that she is divine and therefore beyond our natural capacity for knowledge.*[5]

The nature of the Church is explained in Scripture through the use of a variety of complementary images. These images are oriented towards Jesus Christ and to his emphasis on unity. There is, for example, the *sheepfold* that has Christ as the gate; similarly, the *flock* which is guided by Christ as the Good Shepherd; the *lands and vineyards* of the Lord; the *building* whose *cornerstone* is Christ, whose cement is the Apostles and whose *living stones* are the faithful. The Church which is termed *Jerus-*

[3] Matt 28:20
[4] Second Vatican Council, *Lumen gentium,* 9
[5] St Paul VI, *Address,* 27 April 1966

alem on high and *our Mother* is also described as an *immaculate spouse.*[6] Saint Paul taught the early Christians that the Church is *the Mystical Body of Christ.*[7] By means of this image he gave a clear sense that the Church belongs to Christ and is united to Him. The ties between the Church and Christ are unbreakable.[8] Because of their basic union, things can be said of the one which might be said of the other. When the Church is persecuted, then Jesus Christ is persecuted.[9] Christ is beloved when the members of his body are beloved. Christ is rejected when people refuse to help the needy.[10] We might join Pope Pius XI in saying that *Christ's passion renewed us. In some way, this passion renews and completes the Mystical Body which is the Church ... It is logical that Jesus Christ would want us to join him in this work of expiation. It is natural that, being united to the Head, the members of the Body would participate in Christ's suffering.*[11] This is a strong bond of unity.

This union should not get in the way of each person's individuality. The personality of each person will not be annulled by union with Christ or his Church. The faithful receive the life of sanctifying grace from the Lord, thereby participating in a divine union. This intimate communion of the faithful affects the internal as well as the external character of the Church. *But if the Church is a body, it must be an organism, one and indivisible, according to the words of Saint Paul, We, being many, are one body in Christ* (Rom 7:5). Nor is it sufficient to say one and indivisible; it must also be concrete and perceptible to the senses ... Therefore, they are straying from divine truth

---

[6] cf Second Vatican Council, *loc cit,* 6
[7] cf 1 Cor 12:12-17
[8] cf Second Vatican Council, *loc cit,* 7
[9] cf Acts 9:5
[10] cf Matt 25:35-45
[11] Pius XI, Encyclical, *Miserentissimus Redemptor,* 8 May 1928

who imagine the Church to be something which can neither be touched nor seen, that it is something merely 'spiritual', as they say, in which many Christian communities, although separated from one another by faith, could be joined by some kind of invisible link. But a body also requires many members, united among themselves in such a way that they can be of mutual assistance.[12]

8.3 The Church is a communion of faith, sacraments and government. The Communion of Saints.

The faithful are united by a communion of faith, sacraments and government. The governmental hierarchy is ruled by the Pope.

The Church is a *communion of faith.* It is composed of all those persons who have been baptized. As a consequence of their shared Christian identity, the faithful confess the same doctrine and are united by the same divine grace. Doctrine and life become one. In early Christianity, when one of the baptized separated himself from the faith, he was considered as *ex-communicated,* that is to say, he had broken the community of faith. This process of separation later grew into a juridical power of the Church for extreme cases.

There is a *communion of spiritual goods* in the Mystical Body of Christ. We partake of these goods through the sacraments. The sacraments give divine life to the faithful. The Holy Eucharist is the most perfect food since it allows for the greatest union possible between Christ and his disciples. In the words of the Second Vatican Council, the Holy Eucharist is *the source and the summit of all preaching of the Gospel.*[13]

The Church is also a *communion of mutual supernatural help.* There is a great variety of charisms and vocations in the Church, all of which are ordered in unity to the hierarchy. Without their link to Peter, these paths

---

[12] Pius XII, Encyclical, *Mystici Corporis,* 29 June 1943

[13] cf Second Vatican Council, *Lumen gentium,* 11

would lack their full and proper efficacy.

The unity of the Church is manifested in the *Communion of the Saints.* With this dogma the Church explains the union among Christians. *If one member suffers, all suffer together; if one member is honoured, all rejoice together.*[14] *The interdependence of Christians united in Christ by the sacraments has no limits. Give to everyone the treasures of all.*[15] We are each of us in need. Each of us can be of help. We are all benefiting from the spiritual goods of the Church. Our prayer, the offering up of our daily work and sacrifices – these spiritual goods are a real help to our brothers and sisters in the Faith. They are of benefit to those who are not in full communion with the Church. As St Thomas Aquinas taught, *Just as in the case of a natural body the activity of one member can redound to the benefit of the whole, so too with regard to the spiritual body of the Church. Since all of the faithful form one body, the good performed by one member benefits the whole.*[16] These considerations should move us to live our faith with renewed devotion. Then one day when we contemplate the face of God we will be pleased to see the good we have contributed to the Church from our ordinary activities. We should not lose an hour of work. Everything ought to be converted into grace, united with Christ and his Mystical Body.

Look with favour on your people, Lord, we pray, and pour out upon them the gifts of your Spirit, that they may grow constantly in love of the truth and devote themselves with zeal to perfect unity among all Christians.[17]

---

[14] 1 Cor 12:26

[15] C. Journet, *Theology of the Church,* Bilbao 1960, p 252

[16] St Thomas, *On the Creed,* Madrid, 1975

[17] *Roman Missal, Mass for the unity of Christians,* Cycle C. Collect.

Christian Unity Octave

Day 6 – 23 January

9. THE NEW PEOPLE OF GOD

9.1 Christians are a chosen race, a royal priesthood, a people set apart for Jesus Christ.

God calls each and every person by his or her name.[1] *God, however, does not make men holy and save them merely as individuals, without bond or link between one another. Rather has it pleased him to bring men together as one people, a people which acknowledges him in truth and serves him in holiness.*[2] He chose the race of Israel to be his witnesses, to reveal his plans for mankind. He made a covenant with this people, a covenant which He renewed time and time again. This relationship was forged by way of preparation and as a figure of a new and perfect covenant to be ratified by Christ, a covenant which would fulfil the Old Testament titles of a *chosen race,*[3] *the people whom I formed for myself that they might declare my praise.*[4]

According to the Second Vatican Council, *the state of this people is that of the dignity and freedom of the sons of God, in whose hearts the Holy Spirit dwells as in his temple. Its law is the new commandment to love one another as Christ loved us (cf John 13:34). Its end is the kingdom of God, which has been begun by God himself on earth ...*[5] As Saint Peter taught the early Christians: *But you are a chosen*

---

[1] Is 43:1

[2] Second Vatican Council, *Lumen gentium,* 9

[3] cf Ex 19:5-6

[4] Is 43:20-21

[5] Second Vatican Council, *loc cit*

race, a royal priesthood, a holy nation, God's own people, that you may declare the wonderful deeds of him who called you out of darkness into his marvellous light. Once you were no people, but now you are God's people; once you had not received mercy, but now you have received mercy.[6]

In this new People there is but one priest, Jesus Christ, and one sacrifice, the sacrifice of Calvary, which is renewed each day in the Holy Mass. Everyone who belongs to this people are of the *chosen race.* All participate in the priesthood of Christ. All act as mediators in their apostolate and life of piety. It is in this manner that temporal activities may be converted into *spiritual sacrifices acceptable to God.*[7] This is then a real priesthood, although it is essentially distinct from the ministerial priesthood in which the priest takes the place of Christ. Nevertheless, both priest and laity are ordained to participate in the unique priesthood of Christ, each in his own manner. Through this participation we become sanctified and find the graces necessary to help the others.

9.2 Participation of the laity in the priestly, prophetic and royal mission of Christ. The sanctification of temporal realities.

The faithful participate in the mission of Christ and thereby convert their lives and the world itself according to the spirit of the Lord. Through prayer, through family and social life, through apostolic initiatives, through work and rest, through trials and tribulations, the faithful raise up a holy offering to God, principally through the Holy Mass, the *centre and root* of the Christian life.[8]

The faithful participate in the *priestly mission of Christ* when they lead lives centred on the Holy Mass. Yet their

---

[6] 1 Pet 2:9-10

[7] 1 Pet 2:5

[8] cf St. J. Escrivá, *Christ is passing by,* 87

eucharistic participation is not limited to the duration of the liturgy or to liturgical celebrations alone. The principal field of activity for the laity lies in the realm of professional work, in the fulfilment of family and social duties.

The laity take part in the *prophetic mission of Christ.* They are called to proclaim the word of God not just in the confines of the Church, but out in the middle of the world: in the factory, the office, the club, the home.[9] By their example the laity are to proclaim the 'Good News' to colleagues, relatives and neighbours. The laity take the place of Christ when they act as good friends and virtuous citizens.

Christians also participate in the *royal mission of Christ.* They do so with regard to their professional work. They do not allow themselves to become enslaved by their work. They work with rectitude of intention for the glory of God.[10] The role of the laity should not be thought of as simply an extension of the clerical state. Perhaps some lay people will tend towards church-related activities, but this avenue is not the fulfilment of the secular vocation.[11] The laity will practise their unity with Christ in the real world of work and family. As Saint Paul VI pointed out, *Their principal and primary function is not to establish or promote ecclesial communities, which is the special function of pastors, but to develop and make effective all those latent Christian and evangelical possibilities which already exist and operate in the world.*[12] The laity are to influence the social order with those Christian principles which will act to humanize and elevate, principles such as the dignity and primacy of the human person, social solidarity, the sanctity of the family and marriage, liberty

[9] cf St John Paul II, Apostolic Exhortation, *Christifideles laici,* 30 December 1988, 14

[10] cf *idem, Laborem exercens,* 14 September 1981, 5

[11] cf C. Burke, *Authority and Freedom in the Church,* Ignatius, p 123

[12] St Paul VI, *Evangelii nuntiandi,* 8 December 1975, 70

with responsibility, love for the truth, the pursuit of justice, mutual understanding and fraternal charity. *The laity are not, and were never meant to be, the 'long arm' of the hierarchy. They are not a part or an extension of an official Catholic system. They are, or rather each one is, in his or her own right and on the basis of his or her piety and competence and doctrine, meant to be the presence of Christ in secular affairs.*[13] Today we might pause to consider whether our behaviour moves other people to draw closer to Christ, whether our work and our life of service is in fact bringing the world to God.

9.3 The ministerial priesthood.

This new People of God has Christ as the Eternal High Priest. The Lord assumed the ancient tradition and transformed it into an eternal priesthood. The priest is an instrument of the Lord and a tangible prolongation of his Holy Humanity. The priest does not act in his own name. He is not merely a representative of the people. He is Christ himself. *For every high priest chosen from among men is appointed to act on behalf of men in relation to God.*[14]

Christ truly acts through his priests. His priesthood is intimately and inseparably united to them. The priest is father, brother, friend ... His person belongs to the Church.[15] The Church loves the priest with a complete love. On the occasion of a large ordination ceremony in Brazil, St John Paul II observed: *To such an extent does Jesus identify us with himself in the exercise of the powers which He has conferred on us, that our personality disappears, in a way, before his, since it is He who acts through us. 'The sacrament of Orders, in effect, equips the priest to lend Our Lord his voice, his hands, his whole*

[13] C. Burke, *op cit,* p 131
[14] Heb 5:1-4
[15] cf Bl. A. del Portillo, *On Priesthood,* p 83

being', someone said appropriately. 'It is Jesus Christ who, in the Holy Mass, through the words of the consecration, changes the substance of the bread and wine into his Body, Blood, Soul and Divinity' (cf J. Escrivá, 'In Love with the Church', 39). And we can continue: It is Jesus himself who, in the sacrament of Penance, speaks the authoritative and fatherly word: 'Your sins are forgiven' (Matt 9:2; Luke 5:20; 7:48; cf John 20:23). It is He who speaks when the priest, exercising his ministry in the name and in the spirit of the Church, announces the word of God. It is again Jesus Christ himself who takes care of the sick, children and sinners, when the love and pastoral solicitude of the sacred ministers encompasses them.[16]

Through priestly ordination man receives the highest level of dignity which is possible. Through this sacrament the priest is constituted a minister of God and a dispenser of divine treasure.[17] These treasures consist principally in the celebration of the Holy Mass and the power to forgive sins. The priest is converted into a channel of divine grace. The priest is a mediator between God and man, between heaven and earth. On the one hand he obtains the treasures of divine mercy, while on the other he distributes them to his fellow Christians. Each priest is of tremendous value to the Church and mankind. We have to pray that we may never lack good and holy priests, priests who are ever mindful of their dignity and mission. We would do well to recall those memorable words of Saint J. H. Newman: *If ever there was a time when a priest was a spectacle before men and the angels, certainly this is the time.*[18] We cannot fail to pray for the intentions of our priests.

---

[16] St John Paul II, *Homily,* 2 July 1980
[17] cf 1 Cor 4:1
[18] St J. H. Newman, *Sermon on the inauguration of St Bernard's Seminary,* 3 October 1873

CHRISTIAN UNITY OCTAVE

DAY 7 – 24 JANUARY

10. MARY, MOTHER OF UNITY

10.1 The Mother of unity at the moment of the Incarnation.

The disciples devoted themselves with one accord to prayer with Mary, the Mother of Jesus.[1] Through the intercession of Our Lady, the Church prays to God for the unity of Christians and of all mankind, that they may be brought together into the one people of the new Covenant.[2] The Church believes that the cause of unity is intimately related to the spiritual maternity of the Blessed Virgin Mary over all men and women, especially those who have been baptized.[3] Saint Paul VI was wont to pray to Mary under the title of *Mother of unity.*[4] St John Paul II offered to Our Lady this prayer full of loving trust: *You, who are the first Handmaid of the unity of Christ's Body, help us, help all the faithful who feel so keenly the tragedy of the historical divisions of Christianity, to seek persistently the path to the perfect unity of the Body of Christ through unreserved fidelity to the Spirit of Truth and Love ...*[5]

The Church was born with Christ and she 'grew up' in the house of Nazareth with Christ. The Church today is in an invisible and mysterious fashion the same Christ living

---

[1] *Roman Missal, Entrance Antiphon, Votive Mass of the Blessed Virgin Mary, Mother of the Church*

[2] cf *Roman Missal, Opening Prayer*

[3] cf Leo XIII, Encyclical, *Auditricem populi,* 5 September 1895

[4] cf St Paul VI, *Insegnamenti,* vol II, p 69

[5] St John Paul II, *Radio message commemorating the Council of Ephesus,* 7 June 1981

among us. Mary is the Mother of the Church from the Church's very beginnings.[6] We Christians form one Body, and Mary is the Mother of the Mystical Body. What mother would willingly allow her children to be separated from the family and the home? Who will be more attentive to our prayers for unity than Mary, our Mother?

Saint Bernard has written a beautiful account of the whole creation praying that Mary pronounce her *fiat* at the moment of the Annunciation. Heaven and earth, the sinners and the just, the past, the present and the future come together in that epochal event in Nazareth.[7] Once she had given her free consent, that *fiat,* that *be it done unto me,* Our Lady became the Mother of Christ, the Mother of the Church and, in some sense, the Mother of all Creation. Sin had shattered the unity of the human race and ruptured the order of the Universe. Mary was the creature chosen by God to bring about the Incarnation of his Son. With her free decision she, too, was a cause of Christ's saving work.

The Church as the Mystical Body of Christ finds the primary reason for unity in the Incarnation, that is, in the womb of Mary. *Receiving your Word in her Immaculate Heart, she was found worthy to conceive him in her virgin's womb and, giving birth to the Creator, she nurtured the beginnings of the Church.*[8]

10.2 Mary at Calvary.

Christ consummated the Redemption on Calvary. The new Covenant was sealed with his Blood on the Cross. It brought man back into harmony with God, as well as with other men. Saint Paul taught that the Lord brought down all the walls of division so as to form his true Church, his one

---

[6] St Paul VI, *Discourse to the Council,* 21 September 1964

[7] cf St Bernard, *Homilies on the Blessed Virgin Mary,* 2

[8] *Roman Missal, Preface*

people.[9] The unity which Christ won for us cannot be rent asunder by differences of race, nationality, language or social condition. At the very moment when Christ consummated the Redemption, the new People of the sons and daughters of God was born, the first fruit of the God-Man's sacrifice on the Cross. *Raised to the glory of heaven, she accompanies your pilgrim Church with a mother's love and watches in kindness over the Church's homeward steps, until the Lord's Day shall come in glorious splendour.*[10]

During those painful moments of the Passion, the Blessed Virgin was pondering in her heart the ways of God and men. Perhaps she was meditating on those sublime words about fraternity and unity which were spoken by her son the night before. *'Ut omnes unum sint, sicut tu, Pater, in me et ego in te ...' That they may all be one; even as thou, Father, art in me, and I in thee.*[11] Jesus prays that his followers may experience an earthly unity reflecting the heavenly unity which exists between the Three Persons of the Blessed Trinity. Our Lady participates in this divine unity in a unique and absolutely extraordinary way.[12]

Our Lady at the foot of the Cross is intimately united to her Son. She is co-redeeming with him. *When Jesus saw his mother and the disciple whom He loved standing near He said to his mother, 'Woman, behold your son!' Then he said to the disciple, 'Behold your mother!' And from that hour the disciple took her to his own home.*[13] Our Blessed Mother was always united to her Son as no other creature had been or ever will be. Her union was especially strong during those moments on Calvary. In the words of the

[9] cf Eph 2:14
[10] *Roman Missal, Preface*
[11] John 17:21
[12] cf St John Paul II, *Homily,* 30 January 1979
[13] John 19:26-27

Second Vatican Council: ... *the Blessed Virgin advanced in her pilgrimage of faith, and faithfully persevered in her union with her Son unto the cross, where she stood, in keeping with the divine plan, grieving exceedingly with her only begotten Son, uniting herself with a maternal heart to his sacrifice, and lovingly consenting to the immolation of this Victim which she herself had brought forth. Finally, she was given by the same Christ Jesus dying on the cross as a mother to his disciple ...*[14] We know that that disciple, Saint John, represented all of mankind. Mary is the Mother of the entire human race and particularly of those, the baptized, who have been incorporated into Christ. How can our Mother fail to hear us during these days when we are praying so insistently for the unity of her children?

In the closing words of the Dogmatic Constitution on the Church the Second Vatican Council urges us to have recourse to our Mother in Heaven: *The entire body of the faithful pours forth instant supplications to the Mother of God and Mother of men that she, who aided the beginnings of the Church by her prayers, may now, exalted as she is above all the angels and saints, intercede before her Son in the fellowship of all the saints, until all families of people, whether they are honoured with the title of Christian or whether they still do not know the Saviour, may be happily gathered together in peace and harmony into one people of God, for the glory of the Most Holy and Undivided Trinity.*[15] We ask Our Lady to increase our love for unity, that this love might grow stronger with each passing day. *Invoke the Blessed Virgin. Keep asking her to show herself a Mother to you – 'monstra te esse Matrem!' As well as drawing down her Son's grace, may she bring the clarity of sound doctrine to your mind, and love and purity to your*

---

[14] Second Vatican Council, *Lumen gentium*, 58
[15] *ibid*, 69

heart, so that you may know the way to God and take many souls to him.[16]

10.3 Mary with the new-born Church at Pentecost.

As the Apostles awaited the Spirit you had promised, she joined her supplication to the prayers of the disciples and so became the pattern of the Church at prayer.[17]

Jesus Christ desired that his Church should manifest from its very beginning a visible unity in faith, hope, charity, prayer, sacraments and government. This visible and external unity is a sign of the divine nature of the Church, of the presence of God within her. This was Christ's prayer at the Last Supper.[18] This was how the first Christians lived their faith – united to each other and subject to the authority of the Apostles.

When the Apostles gathered together at the Cenacle to receive the Holy Spirit, it is no mere coincidence that Our Lady was with them. The Apostles were the *living stones* of the universal Church. *Mary is there in the midst of them, acting like a heart which gives life to all the members of the body.*[19] The Apostles *devoted themselves to prayer, together with the women and Mary the mother of Jesus ...*[20] In the *Acts of the Apostles,* Saint Luke tells us that Mary occupied a central place in the birth of the Church. *Here we see Mary as the spiritual centre round which Jesus' intimate friends gather: tradition has meditated on this 'tableau', and found it to depict Our Lady's motherhood over the whole Church, both at its beginning and over the centuries.*[21] *Mary created an atmosphere of charity,*

---

[16] St. J. Escrivá, *The Forge,* 986
[17] *Roman Missal, Preface*
[18] John 17:23
[19] R. M. Spiazzi, *Mary in the Christian Mystery,* Madrid, 1958
[20] Acts 1:14
[21] *The Navarre Bible,* Acts of the Apostles, *in loc*

solidarity and unity. She was the most helpful collaborator of Peter and the Apostles in the organization and government of the early Church.[22]

After Christ's Ascension into Heaven, Mary looked after the unity of the members of his Body on earth. The faithful have never ceased to pray to Mary for the cause of unity. *The experience of the Cenacle would not reflect the hour of grace of the outpouring of the Spirit, if it had not the grace and joy of Mary's presence. 'Together with Mary the mother of Jesus' (Acts 1:14), we read of the great hour of Pentecost ... May she, the mother of love and unity, bind us deeply, in order that, like the first community born from the Cenacle, we may be 'one heart and soul'. May she, 'mater unitatis', in whose womb the Son of God was united with humanity, inaugurating mystically the nuptial union of the Lord with all men, help us to be 'one' and to become instruments of unity among our faithful and among all men.*[23]

---

[22] R. M. Spiazzi, *op cit,* p 70
[23] St John Paul II, *Homily,* 24 March 1980

24 January

11. ST FRANCIS DE SALES

Bishop and Doctor of the Church

Memorial

Born in Thorens, Savoy (France), Saint Francis de Sales (1567-1622) fought Calvinism with apostolic zeal. He was Bishop of Geneva. With Saint Frances Fremyot de Chantal, he founded the Order of the Visitation. He wrote *Introduction to the Devout Life,* a classic of spiritual direction. He died in Lyons and was canonized in 1655. In 1877, Pius IX proclaimed him Doctor of the Church. Pius XI declared him as Patron Saint of journalists and other writers.

11.1 The virtue of friendliness or cordiality.

Saint Francis de Sales spent his entire priestly life in a tireless effort to keep his countrymen loyal to the Roman See. As a bishop he was an outstanding model of the Good Shepherd to his priests and faithful. Saint Francis gave good doctrine to souls by means of his indefatigable preaching and writing.

The liturgy of today's Mass moves us to ask the Lord to help us to *imitate on earth the charity and meekness of Saint Francis de Sales and so attain like him the glory of heaven.*[1] For this reason, let us meditate about the virtues of *cordiality* and *meekness of heart* which are so evident in the holy life of the Bishop of Geneva. He knew how to stand firm in the truth while at the same time maintaining friendships with people who had different beliefs.

It is these virtues which make life in society amenable. According to Saint Francis, *meekness, temperance, integrity and humility are virtues that must mark all our actions in*

[1] *Roman Missal, Prayer after Communion*

life... We must always have on hand a good supply of these general virtues since we must use them almost constantly.[2] These virtues are indispensable for the apostolate, family life and all our friendships.

Each and every day we meet all kinds of people in our work, on the street, through our friends and relatives. The fact that we struggle to be friends with everyone is very pleasing to Our Lord. Saint Thomas Aquinas points out that we need to exercise a special effort to *give proper attention to human relationships, in word as well as in deed.*[3] Our basic challenge is to make the sacrifices necessary so that life will be more pleasing for those around us. In this way we will help others to reach the final homeland of Heaven. Without a doubt these virtues go completely against self-centred lifestyles. Our conversation should be warm and respectful, especially towards those with whom we live and work on a daily basis. As Saint Francis takes care to warn us, *Those who appear in public as angels but are devils in their own homes greatly fail in this regard.*[4] Cordiality opens the doors to friendship and apostolate.

11.2 The virtues of social life are essential for apostolate.

There are a number of virtues which come together to make up the practice of cordiality. Saint Francis de Sales gave many examples of these virtues in his life and writings. These virtues may not attract that much attention, but they are fundamental to the practice of charity and apostolate. These virtues include *prudence* whereby we judge other people and their actions with respect and refinement, *forbearance* towards the defects and mistakes of other people, *good manners* in our speech and behaviour,

---

[2] cf St Francis de Sales, *Introduction to the Devout Life,* 3, I

[3] St Thomas, *Summa Theologiae,* 2-2, q 114, a 1

[4] St Francis de Sales, *op cit,* 3, 8

gratitude and *respect.* The Christian should convert all the many manifestations of these human virtues into acts of supernatural virtue. What is done for love of man should also be done for love of God. The Christian should see his or her neighbours as children of God, children who deserve every consideration possible.

Saint Francis taught that humility is indispensable if we are to get along with others. *Humility is not only charity. It is also sweetness. Charity is the humility which appears on the outside. Humility is the charity which is on the inside.*[5] Both of these virtues are closely intertwined. If we struggle to be humble, we will know how to venerate *the image of God which is in each and every man.*[6]

To *respect* is to appreciate, to realize the real worth of other people. The word *respect* comes from the Latin *respectus* which means due consideration.[7] If we are to live peacefully with other people, we have to respect them as people. We will also have to respect the goods which God has created for the service of mankind. To respect the order of creation is to give glory to God. Respect is also a prerequisite for personal and social progress. Without mutual respect, fraternal correction and guidance is next to impossible.

It is interesting to note how the Evangelists refer on several occasions to the loving glance of Our Lord, which must have been incredible to behold. They tell us that Jesus looked with love upon that rich young man who said he wanted to be better. He looked with love on the poor widow who gave all that she had to the Temple offering. He looked with affection at Zacchaeus who was sitting in a tree. Jesus looked at everyone with great respect, the healthy, the sick, the young, the old, beggars, sinners. This

---

[5] *idem, Spiritual considerations,* 11, 2
[6] St. J. Escrivá, *Friends of God,* 230
[7] cf J. Corominas, *Etymological Dictionary,* Madrid 1987

is the way of life which we must imitate. We should look upon people as the Lord would look upon them – with sympathy, warmth and welcome. *In those persons who we are not naturally attracted to we have to see souls that have been saved by the Blood of Christ, souls that belong to the Mystical Body of Christ, souls which might even be closer to his Sacred Heart than our own. It often happens that we spend many years alongside very beautiful souls without our ever noticing it.*[8] Let us take a look around us and think about those people we are in contact with every day in our homes, offices, communities, etc. Let us reflect upon whether we look on our neighbours with Christ's loving vision.

11.3 Respect for others and care for material things.

Saint Francis insisted that *we have to be indignant towards evil while at the same time being as polite as possible towards our neighbour.*[9] Saint Francis practised this counsel on a continual basis as he sought to win Calvinists back to the Faith. He was doing this apostolate at a time in history when the wounds of division were particularly sensitive to the touch. Take for example the visit he made to a famous Calvinist theologian, a visit he undertook at the request of the Pope. The saint began his conversation with the thinker in a very cordial manner. He asked the man, *Is it possible for a person to be saved in the Catholic Church?* After a period of reflection, the theologian answered in the affirmative. In this way a door was opened which had seemed to be definitively shut.[10]

The virtue of understanding leads us to be open to other people, to be sympathetic to their struggles, to be conscious of the virtues and defects that exist in every man

---

[8] R. Garrigou-Lagrange, *The Three Ages of the Interior Life,* II, p 734
[9] St Francis de Sales, *Epistolario,* fragm. 110 in *Complete Works*
[10] cf *idem, Meditations on the Church*

and woman. If we really seek to understand others, we will be able to penetrate to the depth of their souls. We will be able to find the good qualities that exist in every person. Without understanding, we will find ourselves operating on the basis of prejudice and poor judgments which will invariably lead to disharmony.

The Lord knows the most profound reasons for human conduct. He understands and he pardons. Once we are understanding towards others, then we can be of service to them. Think of the case of the Samaritan woman, the good thief, the woman caught in adultery, Saint Peter who betrayed Our Lord, Saint Thomas who would not believe in the Resurrection. There must have been many other cases like these during the three years of Christ's public ministry. Try to imagine all the works of forgiveness of the Lord in the centuries which have followed.

In the final years of his life, Saint Francis wrote to the Pope regarding a special mission he had been entrusted with. *When we first arrived in that region there were barely one hundred Catholics. Today there are barely one hundred heretics.*[11] We ask this Saint on this his feast to teach us to live these all important virtues of social life which can be of such great help to us in the apostolate. *O God, who for the salvation of souls willed that the Bishop Saint Francis de Sales become all things to all, graciously grant that, following his example, we may always display the gentleness of your charity in the service of our neighbour.*[12]

---

[11] cf *ibid,* quoted in the Introduction, p 10
[12] *Roman Missal, Collect*

25 January

12. THE CONVERSION OF SAINT PAUL

Apostle

Feast

This feast marks the end of the Octave for Christian Unity. The grace of God changed Saint Paul from a persecutor of Christians to a messenger of the Gospel. This fact teaches us that our faith has its basis in grace and the free correspondence of each person. The best way to bring about the unity of Christians is to encourage personal conversions among those around us.

12.1 On the road to Damascus.

I know the one in whom I have believed and I am sure that he, the just judge, the mighty, will keep safe what is my due until that day.[1]

As a zealous defender of the Mosaic Law, Saul looked upon the Christians as a mortal threat to Judaism. He dedicated his every waking hour to the extermination of the early Church. Saul first appears in the *Acts of the Apostles* as one of the witnesses to the execution of Saint Stephen, the first Christian martyr.[2] Saint Augustine has observed that the final prayer of the martyr bore fruit in the life of one of his persecutors.[3] Some time after that event, Saul set out with *letters to the synagogues at Damascus, so that if he found any belonging to the Way, men or women, he might bring them bound to Jerusalem.*[4] Thanks to the workings of the Holy Spirit and the lively apostolate of the

---

[1] *Entrance Antiphon*: 2 Tim 1:12; 4:8

[2] cf Acts 7:60

[3] cf St Augustine, *Sermon 315*

[4] Acts 9:2

early Christians, the Church had expanded quite rapidly despite the most adverse of conditions: *Now those who were scattered went about preaching the word.*[5]

Saul was travelling along the road to Damascus, *breathing threats and murder against the disciples of the Lord,* but God had other plans for this man of action. It was around mid-day as he was approaching the city when *suddenly a light from heaven flashed about him. And he fell to the ground and heard a voice saying to him, 'Saul, Saul, why do you persecute me?' And he said, 'Who are you, Lord?' And he said, 'I am Jesus, whom you are persecuting.*[6] At this very moment Saul poses the most important question of his life to Jesus, *What shall I do, Lord?*[7] Saul was now another man. He had become Paul. In the act of conversion he understood everything at once. His new faith led him to an attitude of complete self-giving in the hands of God. What do you want me to do, my Lord? What do you expect of me?

There have been many occasions when the Lord has wanted to attract our attention, to get into our lives. He wants to reveal his wonderful plans for us. *'Blessed be God' you said after having finished your sacramental Confession. And you thought: it is as if I had just been born again. You then continued calmly: 'Domine, quid me vis facere? – Lord, what would you have me do?' And you yourself came up with the reply: 'By the help of your grace I will let nothing and no one come between me and the fulfilment of your most Holy Will: Serviam – I will serve you unconditionally'.*[8]

---

[5] Acts 8:4
[6] Acts 9:3-5
[7] Acts 22:10
[8] St. J. Escrivá, *The Forge,* 238

12.2 The life of Saint Paul is a beacon of hope. Corresponding to God's grace.

I live by faith in the Son of God, who has loved me and given himself up for me.[9]

Surely we will never forget those times when Jesus has stepped into our lives perhaps without prior warning. Saint Paul certainly never forgot his memorable encounter with the risen Lord. *On the road to Damascus...* Saint Paul uses this phrase to mark when his life began anew. On other occasions he states that this was the turning point of his entire life. *Last of all, as to one untimely born, he appeared also to me.*[10]

The life of Saint Paul is a beacon of hope because *who can say that they cannot overcome their faults when one of the most zealous persecutors of the believers could be transformed into the Apostle to the Gentiles?*[11] God's grace can still work miracles in human hearts in our day. But the power of God depends upon our correspondence to grace. God's grace is sufficient. What is necessary is our free, whole-hearted assent to grace. With regard to Saint Paul's adage *not because of me but because of the grace of God in me,* Saint Augustine comments, *This is to say, not because of me alone but because of God working with me. And for this reason, not because of the grace of God alone nor myself alone, but the grace of God and Him.*[12]

If we live our lives counting upon the help of God's grace, we will find ourselves able to overcome any defect or disappointment. The Lord is constantly calling to us to begin again, to convert our hearts, to walk in peace and joy along the divine ways of the earth. Like Saint Paul, we

---

[9] *Communion Antiphon*: Gal 2:20
[10] 1 Cor 15:8-10
[11] St Bernard, *Sermon on the Conversion of Saint Paul,* 1
[12] St Augustine, *On grace and free will,* 5, 12

have to respond to the Lord's invitation. *What shall I do, Lord?* In what areas do you want me to struggle harder? In what ways do you want me to change my behaviour? Since Jesus is always seeking us out, Saint Teresa advises us, *It is paramount that we draw forth new energy to be useful as well as being very grateful for that gift. These are the conditions which the Lord sets down. If we do not manage his treasures well, he will give them to another and we end up paupers. The Lord will give his jewels to someone who will make them shine more radiantly.*[13]

What shall I do, Lord? Let us ask this question from the depths of our hearts many times during the course of the day. Jesus will show us where our love has fallen short or has not deepened as God has wanted it.

12.3 Zeal for souls.

I know whom I have believed...

These few words explain the rest of Paul's adult life. He had met the Christ. Everything else faded into shadow compared to this luminous reality. Nothing had any value unless it was in Christ and for Christ. *The one thing which he now feared was to offend God. From now on, that was all that mattered. The only thing he lived for was to be faithful to the Lord and to make him known to all people.*[14] This is the attitude which we should aspire to.

From the time of his encounter with Jesus, Paul gave over his entire being to God with all his heart. He took the same enthusiasm and drive which he used to persecute the Christians and put it to the service of the Church. He received the apostolic mission which Christ gave to his disciples and made it his own. *Go out to the whole world; proclaim the Good News to all creation.*[15] *Paul accepted*

---

[13] St Teresa, *Life,* 10

[14] St John Chrysostom, *Homily 2 about the glories of Saint Paul*

[15] Mark 16:15

this task and made of it, from that moment, the very purpose of his life. His 'conversion' lies precisely in this, that he allowed the Christ he encountered on the road to Damascus to enter into his life and to orient it towards one single goal: the preaching of the Gospel. 'I owe a debt to the Greeks as well as to the barbarians, to the learned as well as to the ignorant... I am not ashamed of the Gospel because it is the power of God unto salvation for whoever believes' (Rom 1:14-16).[16]

I know whom I have believed... For the sake of Christ, Paul would take on himself risks and dangers without number. He would endure long hours of work, exhaustion, apparent failures, betrayals, whatever was necessary to win souls for God. *Five times I have received at the hands of the Jews the forty lashes less one. Three times I have been beaten with rods; once I was stoned. Three times I have been shipwrecked; a night and a day I have been adrift at sea; on frequent journeys, in danger from rivers, danger from robbers, danger from my own people, danger from Gentiles, danger in the city, danger in the wilderness, danger at sea, danger from false brethren; in toil and hardship, through many a sleepless night, in hunger and thirst, often without food, in cold and exposure. And, apart from other things, there is the daily pressure upon me of my anxiety for all the churches. Who is weak, and I am not weak? Who is made to fall, and I am not indignant?*[17]

Paul centred his life on the Lord. Even though he had suffered a great deal for Christ, at the end of his days he was able to write, *For as we share in Christ's sufferings, so through Christ we share abundantly in comfort too.* Paul found joy not in the absence of difficulties but in the presence of Christ.

---

[16] St John Paul II, *Homily,* 25 January 1987
[17] 2 Cor 11:24-29

Let us finish our meditation with this prayer from the liturgy: *O God, who taught the whole world through the preaching of the blessed Apostle Paul, draw us, we pray, nearer to you through the example of him whose conversion we celebrate today.*[18]

[18] *Roman Missal, Collect*

26 January

13. SAINTS TIMOTHY AND TITUS

Bishops
Memorial

Timothy was born in Lystra, Asia Minor, of a Jewish mother and a Gentile father. During Saint Paul's first trip to that city, Timothy was converted to the Faith. He was totally devoted to the Apostle. It seems that Timothy was quite young at the time since Saint Paul pleads with the believers in Corinth to treat the disciple with respect. Timothy was fairly young when he was appointed bishop of Ephesus. Tradition tells us that he died a martyr's death in that city.

Titus was one of Saint Paul's most valued disciples. The son of pagan parents, he seems surely to have been converted by the Apostle himself. Titus attended the Council of Jerusalem with Saint Paul and Saint Barnabas. In the pastoral letters Saint Paul describes Titus as a strong defender of the truth against the false teachers and erroneous doctrines of the day. Titus was nearly a centenarian when he died in the year 105.

13.1 Protecting the deposit of faith.

Titus and Timothy were very close disciples of Saint Paul. Timothy accompanied Saint Paul on many of his missionary journeys *as a son with a father.*[1] Saint Paul had great affection for him. During Saint Paul's final trip through Asia Minor he put Timothy in charge of the Church in Ephesus while he gave Titus responsibility for the Church on Crete. While under house arrest in Rome Saint Paul wrote letters to both of these bishops in which he reminded them to protect the deposit of faith which they had received. Saint Paul urged his two followers to keep alive the piety of the faithful despite the fact of their pagan

[1] Phil 2:22

surroundings and the occasional appearance of false teachers. Their primary responsibility, however, was to preserve intact the deposit of faith.[2] Timothy and Titus were to be totally dedicated to the giving of good doctrine.[3] They were to share their unshakeable conviction that the Church is the pillar and bulwark of the truth.[4] It is for this reason that the bishops were expected to be so vigilant concerning bad doctrine.[5]

From her earliest days the Church has taught the truths of the faith to her children in a clear and simple style so as to avoid possible confusion. We see this practice at work in these words of the Apostle to Saint Timothy: *As I urged you when I was going to Macedonia, remain at Ephesus that you may charge certain persons not to teach any different doctrine, nor to occupy themselves with myths and endless genealogies which promote speculations rather than the divine training that is in faith.*[6] With reference to this passage, St John Paul II taught: *Catechists for their part must have the wisdom to pick from the field of theological research those points that can provide light for their own reflection and their teaching, drawing, like the theologians, from the true sources, in the light of the Magisterium. They must refuse to trouble the minds of the children and young people, at this stage of their catechesis, with outlandish theories, useless questions and unproductive discussions, things that Saint Paul often condemned in his pastoral letters.*[7]

Teachers of the faith ought to teach the truths of the faith, not personal theories or doubts. It sometimes happens

---

[2] 1 Tim 6:20
[3] 1 Tim 6:16
[4] 1 Tim 3:15
[5] 1 Tim 1:13
[6] 1 Tim 1:3-4
[7] St John Paul II, *Catechesis tradendae,* 16 October 1979, 61

that people who seek to make the truths of the faith comprehensible to the *modern world* end up changing not only catechetical teaching methods but change the revealed truth itself.

In today's world we find that a great many weeds have been sown among the good wheat. Radio, television, literature, intellectual discourse... all of these powerful means of communication can be used to spread truths or falsehoods. Mixed in with good and laudable messages we can oftentimes find subtle and not so subtle attacks on Catholic doctrine regarding faith and morals. We Christians cannot consider ourselves immune from this widespread epidemic afflicting our society. The teachers of error seem to have increased in number and cultural influence since the days of the Apostle, making Saint Paul's warning all the more timely. Saint Paul VI called this phenomenon a *brutal and universal earthquake*:[8] *earthquake* because it has a subversive impact; *brutal* because it is aimed directly at fundamental truths; and *universal* because the phenomenon can be found throughout the world.[9]

We know in our hearts that the faith is a great treasure. We have to use the means necessary to conserve the faith in ourselves and in those around us. We need to be humble. We have to be on guard that we do not catch the contagion. We have to be prudent with regard to what we read, what we watch, where we go. We should get guidance about films, television shows, books, magazines, etc. The faith is worth more than anything else we can imagine.

13.2 Having a deep knowledge of the truths of the faith.

Guard the truth that has been entrusted to you by the Holy Spirit who dwells within us.[10]

---

[8] cf Paul VI, Apostolic Exhortation, *Petrum et Paulum,* 22 February 1967
[9] cf P. Rodriguez, *Faith and Life of Faith,* Pamplona 1974
[10] 2 Tim 1:14

In the vocabulary of Roman law the word *depositum* means those goods which are entrusted by one person to another with the understanding that they will be returned intact on request.[11] Saint Paul applied this legal term to truths of Revelation and this is how it entered into Catholic teaching. The truths of the faith are entrusted by one generation to another. These truths are not the product of human reasoning. They proceed directly from God. Those people who are not faithful to these truths ought to contemplate the divinely inspired words of the Prophet Jeremiah: *For my people have committed two evils: they have forsaken me, the fountain of living waters, and hewed out cisterns for themselves, broken cisterns, that can hold no water.*[12] Whosoever ignores the teachings of the Magisterium can only provide the teachings of men, teachings which can undermine the faith and put at risk one's salvation. *The preacher of the Gospel will therefore be a person who, even at the price of personal renunciation and suffering, always seeks the truth that he must transmit to others. He never betrays or hides truth out of a desire to please men, in order to astonish or shock, nor for the sake of originality or a desire to make an impression.*[13]

Through the course of the centuries the Church has carefully defined the dogmas of the faith. In many cases these definitions came about due to major religious crises of doctrinal controversy and confusion. Monsignor Ronald Knox has likened these dogmas to buoys which one finds at the mouth of a river. The buoys mark off the limits of safe navigation. Beyond these limits one runs the risk of running aground. Insofar as a person keeps to the sure way

---

[11] cf *The Navarre Bible,* Thessalonians Pastoral Letters, note to 1 Tim 6:20

[12] Jer 2:13

[13] St Paul VI, Apostolic Exhortation, *Evangelii nuntiandi,* 8 December 1975, 78

in what refers to faith and morals, that person will advance without any problems. To neglect these guidelines would be to put one's boat, one's voyage, in danger. So it should be clear that the issue is not about sacrificing one's freedom. Quite the contrary, the question is about preserving everything that makes freedom worth having and sharing.[14]

From her earliest days the Church has produced short *Catechisms* to provide a summary of the faith within the understanding of most people. Catechesis is one of the principal missions of the Church. In as much as possible, we should participate in this vital apostolate. That simple Catechism which was so helpful to us in our youth may still prove instructive to us in our maturity. Yet we ought to do more than merely review the basic ideas of our faith. As St John Paul II reminded a group of young pilgrims, *It is not enough to be Christians because of the Baptism received or because of the historico-social conditions in which you are born and live. As you grow in years and culture, new problems and new requirements of clarity and certainty come into consciousness. It is then necessary to set out in a responsible way in search of the motivations of your own Christian faith. If you do not become personally aware and do not have an adequate understanding of what must be believed and of the reasons for this faith, at a certain moment everything may inevitably collapse and be swept away, in spite of the good will of parents and educators.*[15] The better we know our faith, the better we will be able to know and love Our Lord.

13.3 Spreading the Good News entrusted to the Church.

This was Saint Paul's advice to Saint Timothy: *Take heed to yourself and to your teaching: hold to that, for by*

[14] cf R. A. Knox, *The Hidden Stream*

[15] St John Paul II, *Address,* 24 March 1979

so doing you will save both yourself and your hearers.[16] We should take advantage of the means of formation which are at our disposal. This would include studying Sacred Theology, making good retreats, being attentive in the spiritual reading. This all comes down to acquiring a good doctrinal formation in accord with our personal circumstances. We need to know God very well so that we can better make him known to others. With this formation in hand we will find ourselves well prepared to handle the contagion of false doctrine which is running rampant in the world.

Doctrine gives us light for our life. Our Christian life enables the human heart to know God. The Lord asks us to respond to his call and to his Revelation with our full, informed consent. God wants us to know and love him on more than a theoretical plane. We have to live according to our beliefs: confident in the fact that we are children of God, that we enjoy the constant protection of our Guardian Angel, that we can rely on the supernatural support of our fellow Christians. With this kind of life of faith we will introduce many people to the Lord, almost without our realizing it.

[16] 1 Tim 4:16

28 January

14. SAINT THOMAS AQUINAS

Doctor of the Church

Memorial

(1224-1274). He was educated at the Abbey of Monte Cassino and at the University of Naples. In 1244, he joined the Dominican Order. Considered one of the greatest philosophers and theologians of all times, Saint Thomas gained the title of 'Angelic Doctor'. He had an undisputed mastery of scholastic theology and a profound holiness of life. Pope Leo XIII declared him Patron of Catholic Schools. His monumental work, the *Summa Theologiae,* was still unfinished when he died.

14.1 The way to God: piety and doctrine.

In the midst of the Church he opened his mouth, and the Lord filled him with the spirit of wisdom and understanding and clothed him in a robe of glory.[1]

As a young student at the Abbey of Monte Cassino, Saint Thomas kept asking his professor the same query: *Who is God? Please explain to me what is God?* Eventually Saint Thomas came to the conclusion that knowing God required more than teachers and books could provide. Knowing God is more than anything else a spiritual endeavour. The prayerful soul has to seek the truth with a clean and humble heart. We find, then, in the life of Saint Thomas a wonderful example of the fruitful harmony of faith and reason. Saint Thomas always sought the guidance of the Holy Spirit before he would begin to teach or to write. While engaged in his study of the sacrament of the Eucharist he spent many hours in prayer before the Tabernacle.

---

[1] *Entrance Antiphon*: Eccles 15:5

Blessed with an incredible intelligence, Saint Thomas brought about one of the most remarkable works of theology of all time. His fairly brief life was an impassioned pursuit of a profound understanding of God, man and Creation. Thanks to his deep knowledge of classical philosophy and the Fathers of the Church, Saint Thomas was able to devise a harmonious synthesis between faith and reason. In later centuries the Church has repeatedly pointed to Saint Thomas as a role model of fidelity to the Magisterium and the highest aspirations of the human mind and spirit.

Saint Thomas is an example of humility and rectitude of intention in professional work. One day while he was praying, Saint Thomas heard these words from the crucified Jesus: *Thomas, you have written well of me. What reward do you wish for your work?* Saint Thomas responded: *Lord, I want nothing else but You.*[2] Here we also see the wisdom and holiness of the saint.

Even though he had incredible talent and wisdom, Saint Thomas always kept in mind the smallness of his efforts in comparison to the immensity of God. It was after saying Holy Mass one day that Saint Thomas decided to leave unfinished his life's work, the *Summa Theologiae.* When asked why he had come to that decision he explained: *After what God saw fit to show me on the feast of Saint Nicholas, it seems to me that everything which I have written is worthless. And so, I am unable to write anything more.*[3] God is always *more* than anything which the human mind and heart can possibly conceive.

The Angelic Doctor teaches us how we should seek the Lord: with our intelligence, with the help of profound

---

[2] cf *Fontes vitae Sancti Tomae,* p. 108

[3] Bartolome de Capua, in the *Neapolitan Process of Canonization,* 79: *Fontes vitae Sancti Tomae,* p. 3777

spiritual formation, with a life of love and prayer.[4]

14.2 The authority of Saint Thomas's writings. Our need for formation.

The Magisterium of the Church has on many occasions recommended that the faithful treat Saint Thomas as a guide in philosophical and theological study. The Church has taken the teachings of Saint Thomas as her own inasmuch as they are the best synthesis available of revealed truth, the writings of the Fathers and the demands of human reason.[5] The Second Vatican Council urged the faithful to obtain a deeper understanding of the mysteries of the Faith *with Saint Thomas as teacher.*[6] The works of Saint Thomas act as streetlights which shed their light on the most important questions in philosophy. They make it possible for us to better understand our faith in today's world.[7]

The feast of this great saint should lead us to pray about our need for a solid doctrinal and religious formation. This formation is an indispensable support for our life of faith. By studying and meditating upon the chief points of Catholic teaching we will be able to challenge the wave of religious ignorance which is afflicting our society. With the help of good doctrine that is well understood, we will not be at the mercy of our feelings or moods. We can give this formation a good start by studying a reliable catechism of Christian doctrine.

In these days when error and confusion abound, it might be said that this kind of intellectual formation has become indispensable. Our cry ought to be: *I believe all*

---

[4] cf St John Paul II, *Discourse at the Pontifical University of Saint Thomas Aquinas,* 17 November 1979
[5] cf John XXIII, *Address,* 28 September 1960
[6] Second Vatican Council, *Optatam totius,* 16
[7] cf Paul VI, Apostolic Letter, *Lumen Ecclesiae,* 20 November 1974

that God has revealed to me. We need to grow in our understanding of the truths of the Faith. Saint Teresa of Avila would often say that *the person who knows God is better able to do his works.*[8] A modern lay theologian makes the argument in this fashion: *I cannot say how often I have been told that some old Irishman saying his rosary is holier than I am, with all my study. I daresay he is. For his own sake, I hope he is. But if the only evidence is that he knows less theology than I, then it is evidence that would convince neither him nor me. It would not convince him, because all those rosary-loving, tabernacle-loving old Irishmen I have ever known (and my own ancestry is rich with them) were avid for more knowledge of the Faith. It does not convince me because while it is obvious that an ignorant man can be virtuous, it is equally obvious that ignorance is not a virtue; men have been martyred who could not have stated a doctrine of the Church correctly, and martyrdom is the supreme proof of love: yet with more knowledge of God they would have loved Him more still.*[9]

14.3 Doctrine as the food of piety.

Reflecting upon the life and work of Saint Thomas, we may notice how a life of true piety requires doctrine. It is for this reason that doctrinal formation should lead us to a deep and childlike piety. Saint Thomas, for example, while writing his *Summa contra Gentiles* wrote the prayer *Ave Maria* along the margins of the text as a way to maintain presence of God. Whenever he tested his pen he would write this along with many other prayers.[10] All of his writings and sermons serve to bring the soul closer to God. He demonstrated that in the same manner as if all human science was contained in a single book, we would want that

---

[8] St Teresa, *Foundations,* 3, 5

[9] F. J. Sheed, *Theology for Beginners,* Sheed and Ward, London, p. 5

[10] cf St Thomas, *Summa contra Gentiles,* vol. 13, Pref. p. VIII b.

book, so too ought we to seek only Christ who holds all the treasures of wisdom and science.[11] The doctrine which we learn should lead us to love Christ more, to want to serve him with joy.

The piety of children and the doctrine of theologians – that was the goal set by St Josemaria Escrivá. A sound faith is built on sound doctrinal formation. It is shown forth in a childlike life of piety. Saint Thomas taught that love leads to the knowledge of the truth.[12] In addition, all knowledge is ordered to charity as its end.[13] As we come to know God better, we should find ourselves making many acts of love to Him. While the mind is focused on the little details of the moment, the heart has its focus set on God the Father, God the Son and God the Holy Spirit.

Due to this kind of doctrinal formation we should have a wonderful grasp of the Holy Humanity of Our Lord, the Motherhood of Mary, the holiness of Saint Joseph, *our Father and Lord,* the helpful presence of the Guardian Angels, the intentions of the holy souls in Purgatory... Today let us examine our determination to acquire the formation we need to love God more and to help others in the apostolate.

---

[11] cf *idem, Commentary on the Epistle to the Thessalonians,* 2, 3, 1
[12] cf *idem, Commentary on St John,* 5, 6
[13] cf *ibid,* 15, 2

2 FEBRUARY

15. THE PRESENTATION OF OUR LORD

Feast

The feast was first observed in the Eastern Church as "The Encounter". In the sixth century, it began to be observed in the West: in Rome, with a more penitential character, and in Gaul (France) with solemn blessings and processions of candles, popularly known as "Candlemas". The presentation of the Lord concludes the celebration of the Nativity and, with the offerings of the Virgin Mother and the prophecy of Simeon, the events now point towards Easter.

15.1 Mary offers Jesus to the Father.

And the Lord you are seeking will suddenly enter his Temple; and the angel of the covenant whom you are longing for, yes, he is coming, says the Lord of hosts.[1]

Jesus arrives at the Temple in the arms of his mother Mary. According to the Jewish law, the first-born male had to be presented to the Lord forty days after his birth. Due to the action of the Holy Spirit in their souls, Simeon and Anna are the only people who recognize the Messiah in this ordinary infant. In today's *Responsorial psalm* the Church recalls how the Jewish people celebrated the entrance of the Ark of the Covenant. *O gates, lift up your heads; grow higher, ancient doors. Let him enter, the king of glory!*[2]

There were two precepts of the ancient law concerning the birth of first-born sons. According to Leviticus, a woman who bore a child was unclean. The period of legal impurity ended, in the case of a mother of a male child,

---

[1] *First Reading,* Mal 3:1

[2] *Responsorial Psalm,* Ps 23:7

after forty days, with a rite of purification. With regard to first-born sons, it is written in the Book of Exodus: *The Lord said to Moses, 'Consecrate to me all the first-born; whatever is the first to open the womb among the people of Israel, both of man and of beast, is mine'.*[3] This offering was a living memorial to how the Lord had delivered the people of Israel from their captivity in Egypt. Every first-born male, then, belonged to God and had to be set apart for the Lord, that is, dedicated to the service of God. However, once divine worship was reserved to the tribe of Levi, first-born who did not belong to that tribe were not dedicated to God's service, and to show that they continued to be God's special property, a rite of redemption was performed. The Law laid down that the Israelites should offer in sacrifice some lesser victim as a symbolic form of ransom.

Our Lady prepared her soul to present the Son of God to the Father and to offer herself to Him. In doing this she renewed her *fiat,* her *be it done unto me,* and once again put her whole life at the disposition of the Lord. Jesus was presented to the Father in the hands of Mary. This was a very special offering at the Temple which would never be repeated. More than thirty years later, Jesus would make the supreme offering of himself outside the city on Calvary.[4]

Today's feast is an open invitation for us to renew our dedication to the Lord. We should offer him our entire being, our thoughts, our works, everything we are, everything we do.

We can make this offering in many different ways. Today we might make our own this moving prayer of Saint Alphonsus Liguori: *Today, Oh my queen, I also, in*

---

[3] cf Ex 13:2,12-13; Lev 12:2-8
[4] cf F. Fernandez Carvajal, *The Gospel of Saint Luke,* Madrid 1988

imitation of thee wish to offer my poor heart to God... Offer me as thine to the eternal Father and to Jesus, and pray him that through the merits of his Son, and by thy favour, he may accept me, and take me for his own.[5]

15.2 To illuminate reality by the light of the Cross.

Mary and Joseph arrived at the Temple ready to fulfil the precepts of the Law. Because they had no money, they were obliged to offer up the ransom of the poor, that being a pair of turtle-doves.[6] It is at this juncture that they meet Simeon, a righteous and devout man, *who was looking for the consolation of Israel.* The Holy Spirit had revealed to him what remained hidden to almost everyone else. Simeon took the Child into his arms and blessed God, saying: *Lord, now lettest thou thy servant depart in peace, according to thy word; for mine eyes have seen thy salvation which thou hast prepared in the presence of all peoples, a light for revelation to the Gentiles, and for glory to thy people Israel.*

Saint Bernard wrote a sermon for this feast in which he refers to the long-standing tradition of mounting a procession of candles in church.[7] *Today the Virgin Mary brought to the Temple the Lord of the Temple. Joseph presents to God his adopted son, the Beloved One. Anna the widow joins in with words of thanksgiving. These four people performed the first procession, a joyful procession which will be continued throughout time in every corner of the earth.*[8]

The procession of candles in today's liturgy symbolizes how the life of each Christian should give light

---

[5] St Alphonsus Liguori, *Glories of Mary,* II, 6

[6] cf Luke 2:24

[7] cf *Journey of the Virgin of Egeria,* Madrid 1980; A. G. Martimort, *The Church at Prayer,* Barcelona 1986

[8] St Bernard, *Homily on the Purification of the Blessed Virgin Mary,* I, 1

to others. Christ is the Light of the world. *'Light'* as a word is frequently used to signify *life* and *truth.* The absence of light suggests solitude, doubt and error. Christ is the *Life* of the world and every person, the *Light* that shows the way, the *Truth* that saves, the *Love* that fulfils... When we carry a burning candle in today's procession, we are taking part in the light of Christ.

And his father and his mother marvelled at what was said about him. Mary listened to the prophecy of Simeon with the same recollection that she listened to the words of Saint Gabriel and the shepherds. The Child which she held in her arms was the *Light* sent by God the Father, *a light for revelation to the Gentiles, and for glory to thy people Israel.* From the moment of our baptism, our participation in the mission of Christ depends a great deal upon our personal generosity. *We have to learn how to give ourselves, to burn before God like the light placed on a lampstand to give light to those who walk in darkness; like the sanctuary lamps that burn by the altar, giving off light till their last drop is consumed.*[9] Is this our disposition towards the Lord? Are we giving ourselves without conditions, without limitations? Lord, my life is for You. I do not want it if it does not bring me closer to You.

Saint Bernard reminds us that *it is prohibited to come before the Lord with empty hands.*[10] Since we normally have only little things to offer him, let us pray about the poor value of Mary's offering to the Lord, those two turtle-doves. Learn to join your poor offerings to those of Christ. Join your prayers with his prayers, your tears with his tears, your fasts with his fasts. In this way you will take something of little value and give it an infinite worth. One drop of water by itself is nothing more than one drop of

---

[9] St. J. Escrivá, *The Forge,* 44
[10] St Bernard, *Homilies,* II, 2

water. One drop of water poured into a cask of wine becomes something of greater value. This is the way it is with our human labours. By themselves they are of small value. Yet when they are joined with the labours of Christ they acquire an inestimable worth.[11]

15.3 Jesus Christ, *sign of contradiction.*

Simeon blessed the parents and then *said to Mary his mother, 'Behold, this child is set for the fall and rising of many in Israel, and for a sign that is spoken against – and a sword will pierce through your own soul also, that thoughts out of many hearts may be revealed'.*[12]

Jesus brings salvation to all people. Nevertheless, for some he is a *sign that is spoken against* or *a sign of contradiction. The times in which we are living provide particularly strong confirmation of the truth of what Simeon said: Jesus is both the light that shines for mankind and at the same time a sign of contradiction... Jesus Christ is once again revealing himself to men as the light of the world. Has he not also become at one and the same time that sign which, more than ever, men are resolved to oppose?*[13] No one can treat Christ with indifference. We ask him to be our Light and our Hope.

The Evangelist takes care to note that Simeon addressed to Mary a message of warning. This warning establishes a link between the future of both the mother and the Son. *And a sword will pierce through your own soul.*[14] *With the old man's words in mind we too turn our gaze from the Son to the Mother, from Jesus to Mary. The mystery of this bond which unites her with Christ, the*

---

[11] Fr. Luis de Granada, *Life of Jesus Christ,* ch. 7
[12] Luke 2:34-35
[13] K. Wojtyla, *Sign of Contradiction,* p. 198
[14] Luke 2:35

Christ who is a 'sign of contradiction' is truly amazing.[15]

At the Presentation, Mary learns that her destiny is intimately united to that of her Son. The sword which Simeon speaks of is Mary's painful participation in the sufferings of her Son. The Lord suffered on the Cross for our sins. It is our sins which cause the sufferings of Mary. *Therefore, we have a duty to atone not only to God but also to his Mother, who is our Mother too.*[16]

---

[15] K. Wojtyla, *op cit,* p. 201

[16] cf *The Navarre Bible,* note to Luke 2:34-35

2 February

16. THE PURIFICATION OF OUR LADY

16.1 The Fourth Mystery of the Holy Rosary.

The Mosaic Law prescribed not only the offering up of the first-born male, but also the purification of the mother. Mary was not obliged by this law since she was most pure, having conceived of the Son in a miraculous manner. Yet Our Lady never sought to get out of social obligations. As Saint Bernard has written: *Don't you think that Our Lady could have complained and said, 'What need have I of purification? Why should the authorities block my entrance into the temple when my womb has been turned into the temple of the Holy Spirit? Why can't I go into the temple when I have brought to life the Lord of the temple? There has been nothing impure, nothing illicit, nothing to purify in this conception and this birth. This Child is the source of all purity. He has come to purify us from our sins. What then is there to purify in me when he has made me most pure in this immaculate birth?'*[1]

Nevertheless, as in so many other instances, Mary chose to act like any other Jewish woman of the time. She wanted to be an example of obedience and humility. Mary had the humility to avoid drawing any attention to herself for the wonderful graces God bestowed on her. Even though she was the Mother of God, or perhaps because of that fact, she went to the temple just like any other woman. She guarded within her heart the treasures she had received from God. Mary could have asked for special treatment. She would have definitely been more than entitled to it.

---

[1] St Bernard, *Homily on the Purification of the Blessed Virgin Mary,* III, 2

She prefers to teach us how to pass unnoticed among our contemporaries with our hearts on fire with love for God. Mary encourages us to live our lives as ordinary citizens, exercising the same rights and duties shared by our contemporaries.

Today we contemplate Mary on this her feast, the Fourth Joyful Mystery of the Holy Rosary. We see Mary most pure as she submits to an obligation which she could have avoided. We look at our own behaviour. How many times we have sought special treatment! How many times we have shown ingratitude to the love of God! *You and I surely do need purification! Atonement, and more than atonement, Love. Love as a searing iron to cauterize our souls' uncleanness, and as a fire to kindle with divine flames the wretched tinder of our hearts.*[2] This is the presentation we have to make to God through Holy Mary.

16.2 The Virgin leads us to Jesus, *light of the nations*, our light. Our need of purification.

And presently the Lord whom you seek, and the angel of the testament whom you desire, shall come to his temple... For he is like a refining fire, and like the fuller's herb: and he shall sit refining and cleansing the silver. And he shall purify the sons of Levi, and shall refine them as gold, and as silver, and they shall offer sacrifices to the Lord in justice.[3] This passage comes from the *First Reading* of today's Mass.

Today's Liturgy represents and makes present again a 'mystery' of Christ's life: in the Temple, the religious centre of the Jewish nation, in which animals were continually being sacrificed to be offered to God, there makes his first entry, humble and modest, he who, according to the prophecy of Malachi, will sit 'as a refiner and purifier' (Mal

---

[2] St. J. Escrivá, *Holy Rosary,* Fourth Joyful Mystery
[3] Mal 3:1-4

3:3), in particular of persons consecrated to worship and to service of God. There makes his first entry in the Temple he who 'had to be made like his brethren in every respect, so that he might become a merciful and faithful high priest in the service of God, to make expiation for the sins of the people'[4] in the words of the *Second Reading.*[5] Jesus comes to purify us from our sins by means of pardon and mercy.

This prophecy refers directly to the priests of the tribe of Levi. These priests prefigure all Christians who through Baptism become members of the royal priesthood of Christ. If we allow ourselves to be cleansed and purified, we too can offer up our work and our lives *in justice.*

Today is a feast day of the Lord who, despite his infancy, is *a light of revelation to the Gentiles.*[6] *It is also her feast: Mary's. She carries the child in her arms. He, even, in her hands, is the light of our souls, the light that illumines the darkness of knowledge and of human existence, of the intellect and the heart. The thoughts of so many hearts are revealed when her mother's hands carry this great divine Light, when they bring it closer to man.*[7]

Our Lady wants to encourage us that we purify our hearts, that we make the offering of ourselves pleasing to God, that we find Christ in all the circumstances of our everyday existence. She wanted to go through with the required rite of purification, even though she didn't have to do it, because she wanted us to give a high regard for the purification of our souls.

From the earliest days of Christianity, the Fathers of the Church have written of Mary's purity in glowing terms. They have called Her an *'iris among spines, immaculate*

---

[4] St John Paul II, *Homily,* 2 February 1981
[5] Heb 2:14-18
[6] Luke 2:32
[7] St John Paul II, *Homily,* 2 February 1979

virgin, forever blessed, free of all contagion of sin, tree of everlasting life, fountain most pure', free from all sin, more beautiful than beauty itself, holier than all sanctity, more exalted than all the angels and saints...[8] Mary's immaculate life is a call to each one of us to throw off whatever separates us from the Lord.

Ask the Father, the Son and the Holy Spirit, and your Mother, to make you know yourself and weep for all those foul things that have passed through you, and which, alas, have left such dregs behind... And at the same time, without wishing to stop considering all that, say to him: Jesus, give me a Love that will act like a purifying fire in which my miserable flesh, my miserable heart, my miserable soul, my miserable body may be consumed and cleansed of all earthly wretchedness. And when I have been emptied of myself, fill me with yourself. May I never become attached to anything here below. May Love always sustain me.[9]

16.3 We should offer to the Lord everything we are through the hands of Our Lady. We should turn to Our Lady in times of trial.

Saint Paul teaches us: *But we carry this treasure in vessels of clay, to show that the abundance of the power is God's and not ours.*[10] A vessel of clay can be broken rather easily. It can also be put together again without too much trouble. Within the merciful plans of the Lord, there is a remedy for every kind of damage. The Lord only asks that we be humble, that we go to him in sacramental Confession when necessary, that we have a firm resolve to sin no more. Our small and not so small weaknesses can be an excellent opportunity for us to increase our desires for reparation. Whenever we hurt someone we love, we do our

---

[8] cf Pius XII, Encyclical, *Fulgens corona,* 8 September 1953
[9] St. J. Escrivá, *The Forge,* 41
[10] cf 2 Cor 4:7

best to make up for the harm done. This is the way we should feel about hurting Jesus. *If children are ill, they have additional claim to be loved by their mother. And we, too, if by chance we are sick with badness, on the wrong track, have yet another claim to be loved by the Lord.*[11]

We should have a great sense of peace when we contemplate all the abundant supernatural means which God has placed at our disposal for penance and purification. He has given himself to us in the Holy Eucharist to serve as a most powerful spiritual food. He has given us the sacrament of Confession so that when we fall, we might find forgiveness and return to the struggle. He has given us our Guardian Angel to guard us along the way. We can also find support in our brothers in the Faith through the Communion of Saints. We can learn from the good example of so many practising Christians in our own communities. In a very special way we are able to count on the help of Holy Mary, Mother of God and our Mother. We should go to Mary on a regular basis but especially whenever we feel worn out or a bit overwhelmed.

Meditating upon today's feast, Saint Alphonsus Liguori explained Mary's power with the use of a legend from antiquity: *Plutarch relates that Antipater wrote to Alexander the Great a long letter of accusations against Olympias, the mother of Alexander. Having read the letter, he answered: 'Does not Antipater know that one tear of my mother is enough to cancel an endless number of letters of accusation?'* Saint Alphonsus takes these noble words and puts them on the lips of Jesus: *Does not Lucifer know that one prayer of my mother, in favour of a sinner, is enough to make me forget all the accusations of offences committed against me?* The saint makes this added commentary: *Saint Simeon received a promise from God*

---

[11] John Paul I, *Angelus,* 10 September 1978

that he should not die until he had seen the Messiah born... But he did not receive this grace except by means of Mary, for he did not see the Saviour until he saw him in the arms of Mary. Hence, whoever wishes to find Jesus, will not find him except through Mary. Let us, then, go to this divine Mother if we wish to find Jesus; and let us go with great confidence.[12] We ask Mary to cleanse and purify our hearts. We put ourselves in her motherly hands so that she might offer us to Jesus. *Holy Father, through the Immaculate Heart of Mary I offer Jesus, your Beloved Son, to you. I offer myself to you through Him and with Him in the name of all of your creatures.*[13]

---

[12] St Alphonsus Liguori, *Glories of Mary,* II, 6
[13] P. M. Sulamitis, *Prayer of Offering to the Merciful Love*

11 February

17. OUR LADY OF LOURDES

Memorial

This day marks the first apparition of the Blessed Virgin Mary in 1858 to fourteen-year-old Marie Bernade (Saint Bernadette) Soubirous. There were eighteen apparitions in all, the last of which was on 16 July 1858. The message of Lourdes is a call to personal conversion, prayer, and charity. Pope Leo XIII approved this feast day and Pope Saint Pius X extended it to the universal Church. Bernadette was beatified and canonized by Pope Pius XI in 1925.

17.1 The apparitions in the grotto. Holy Mary, *Salus infirmorum.*

In 1854 the Church defined as infallible the dogma of the Immaculate Conception of Mary. Four years later in the little town of Lourdes in southern France, Our Lady made a number of appearances to a fourteen-year-old peasant girl named Bernadette Soubirous. Saint Bernadette later recounted that the Blessed Virgin was so beautiful that it was impossible to describe her.[1] Many years after the apparitions a well-known sculptor was asked to create a statue of Our Lady for the shrine. He asked Saint Bernadette whether his work, which turned out quite beautiful, bore any resemblance to Mary of the apparitions. With great simplicity Saint Bernadette replied: *Oh, no, sir, not at all. It does not look like her in the least.*

There were a total of eighteen apparitions of Our Lady over the course of several months. When the young girl asked the woman what was her name, at first she only *smiled sweetly.* Finally, Our Lady revealed herself to Saint

---

[1] *Divine Office, Second Reading, Letter of Saint Bernadette to Father Godrand,* 1861

Bernadette as the Immaculate Conception. In the years following this wonderful event there have been many miracles at Lourdes of both a physical and spiritual nature. Truly, the cures have been without number. Many people have regained their faith and have left the shrine with a loving acceptance of the divine will.

In the *First Reading* of today's Mass we are asked to consider the words of the Prophet Isaiah as he consoles the chosen people in their exile. *For thus says the Lord: Now towards her I send flowing peace, like a river, and like a stream in spate the glory of the nations. At her breast will her nurslings be carried and fondled in her lap. Like a son comforted by his mother will I comfort you.*[2]

As we pray about today's feast, we can see how the Lord has wanted to entrust Mary with all the genuine riches which men and women require. Those eighteen apparitions to little Bernadette are yet one more reminder of the infinite mercy of God as made manifest in Holy Mary.

The Blessed Virgin is always *Health of the Sick* and *Comfort of the Afflicted.* As we pray today, let us bring to Mary our every need. She knows us very well. She hears our petitions, no matter where we may be. This motherly assistance should fill us with peace and joy. Like small children who do not stray from their mother, so too we should not become separated from our mother in heaven. *Mother, Mother of mine...* In the intimacy of our personal prayer we can ask her for so many things: help in the apostolate, lights for our interior life, favours for our friends.

17.2 The Christian meaning of pain and suffering.

Our Lady had a clear message in mind when she appeared in the grotto. She wanted to remind humanity of the need for conversion and penance. Our Mother wanted

---

[2] Is 66:10-14

to emphasize that all souls had been redeemed by Christ's sacrifice on the Cross. She also spoke of how we can be co-redeemers with Christ through our pain, suffering and voluntary mortifications.

What humanly speaking might be considered a great tragedy might in fact be a great good when considered with eyes of faith. Sickness, poverty, pain, failure, scandal, unemployment – each of these problems can lead us to God. With the help of grace, we can find in each of these problems *true humility* since they make us so dependent on God. Sickness can help us to be *much less tied to the things of the earth.* We recognize our need to depend on God's loving providence, to *fortify our supernatural hope.*

Sickness helps us to *trust more in God,* to put God's power above our meagre efforts.[3] Because of our divine filiation, we should develop a sense of confidence that God will never let us down. He is fully aware of our strengths and weaknesses. He will never ask us to do more than we can handle together. Sickness is a good opportunity to put into practice that wise maxim of Saint Augustine: do everything possible and ask for what is impossible.[4]

The true test of love is for us to accept sickness and death itself according to the will of God. We ought to give up our life as an oblation and sacrifice for Christ for the good of his Mystical Body, the Church. Our pains and sufferings lose their bitterness when they are elevated to Heaven. *Poenae sunt pennae – hardships are the wings,* so goes the old Latin saying. Sickness can serve as the wings which will permit us to rise up to God. How great is the contrast between a person who accepts their illness with faith and humility and someone who reacts to infirmity with resentment and grief!

---

[3] cf 1 Cor 10:13

[4] cf St Augustine, *Treatise on nature and grace,* 43, 5

17.3 Sanctifying pain. Going to the intercession of Our Lady.

And the mother of Jesus was there.[5] How marvellous it is to see the many different kinds of people who go to shrines of Our Lady and seek her intercession. Perhaps a good number of them would not have asked her help if they had not become ill or burdened with difficulties.

In this regard Blessed John Paul II asked: *Why is it precisely the sick who go on pilgrimage to Lourdes? Why – we wonder – has that place become for them almost a 'Cana of Galilee', to which they feel invited particularly? What draws them to Lourdes with such power?... Because they know that as at Cana, 'the mother of Jesus is there': and where she is, her Son cannot fail to be. This is the certainty that moves the multitudes who pour into Lourdes every year in search of relief, comfort and hope...*

The miraculous cure remains, however, in spite of everything, an exceptional event. Christ's salvific power, propitiated by the intercession of his Mother, is revealed at Lourdes particularly in the spiritual sphere. It is in the hearts of the sick that Mary makes the thaumaturgic voice of her Son heard: a voice that dissolves miraculously the stiffening of bitterness and rebellion, and restores eyes to the soul to see in a new light the world, others and one's own destiny.[6]

Mary always leads us to her Son who has a special love for the sick. Saint Peter summarized the life of Christ with these few words: *Jesus of Nazareth ... went about doing good and healing all...*[7] The Evangelists never seem to tire of describing the Master's solicitude for the sick and the suffering. Christ dedicated a large portion of his ministry on earth to sick people. *He was sensitive to every*

---

[5] cf John 2:1
[6] St John Paul II, *Homily,* 11 February 1980
[7] Acts 10:38

human suffering, whether of the body or of the soul.[8] The Lord is compassionate yet he wants us to use the means at our disposal. He will never test us beyond our strength. He will always give us sufficient graces so that difficult circumstances will only serve to draw us and our friends closer to him. We can certainly ask the Lord to cure our infirmities or resolve our problems. Above all, we need to ask him to make us more docile to his grace, to increase our faith, hope and charity.

We should put our pains and sufferings into the hands of God. *Therefore do not be anxious about tomorrow; for tomorrow will have anxieties of its own. Sufficient for the day is its own trouble.*[9] We cannot forget that *all of us are called to suffer in this life, though not all in the same manner or to the same degree. Each one has to correspond generously to the will of God for him or her. Suffering, which in the eyes of men is so disagreeable, can indeed be a fountain of sanctification and apostolate when it is united to Jesus.*[10] We have here an opportunity to co-redeem with Jesus, to feel ourselves to be sons of God in a very special way.

Let us go wholeheartedly to Mary. She will always be there at our side. She will get us what we want or what we need, so that *good might be drawn from evil. Great good can be drawn from great evil.* No matter what our situation may be, she will never fail to give us consolation. *Consolatrix afflictorum, Salus infirmorum, Auxilium christianorum ... ora pro eis ... ora pro me. Come to our aid in our time of trial, God of mercy. On this feast of the Immaculate Mother of your Son, grant that through her intercession we might be freed from our sins.*[11]

---

[8] St John Paul II, Apostolic Letter, *Salvifici doloris,* 11 February 1984
[9] Matt 6:34
[10] A. Tanquerey, *The divinization of suffering,* Madrid 1955
[11] *Divine Office,* Closing prayer of Morning Prayer

14 FEBRUARY

18. SAINTS CYRIL, MONK AND METHODIUS, BISHOP

Co-Patrons and Evangelizers of Europe
Memorial

Cyril and Methodius were the youngest and oldest brothers, respectively, of a family of seven children. Born in Thessalonica (Greece), they were sons of a high official in the Byzantine Empire. Cyril had an excellent education in Constantinople and eventually became a professor at the imperial university. Methodius followed a political career and rose to become a governor before entering a monastery in Bithynia. Both men dedicated their lives to the evangelization of the Slavic peoples. Cyril put to use his expertise in languages so as to compose an alphabet for the Slavic language. He translated Holy Scripture as well as the liturgy into Slav. Years later, Methodius completed this work of translation begun by his brother.

Cyril died in Rome on 14 February 869, and was buried next to the remains of Saint Clementine. Methodius died on 6 April 885. His body was buried next to his brother. St John Paul II named these two saints along with Saint Benedict as the Co-Patrons of Europe.

18.1 The evangelization of the Slavic peoples.

Wholly dedicated to the conversion of the Slavic peoples, *Cyril and Methodius carried out their missionary service in union both with the Church of Constantinople, by which they had been sent, and with Peter's Roman See, by which they were confirmed. In this way they manifested the unity of the Church...*[1]

---

[1] St John Paul II, Apostolic Constitution, *Egregiae virtutis,* 31 December 1980

St John Paul II spoke out on many occasions about the Christian roots of Europe: *It can be said that the European identity is not understandable without Christianity, and that it is precisely in Christianity that are found those common roots by which the continent has seen its civilization mature: its culture, its dynamism, its activity, its capacity for constructive expansion in other continents as well; in a word, all that makes up its glory.*[2] The very name of *Europe* is of fairly recent origin. For many centuries the more commonly used name for the region was *Christendom.*[3]

Whenever a building is erected with unstable foundations it is prone to collapse at the slightest tremor. It is for this reason that the Pope has been so insistent about the deterioration of the Faith in Europe. He has been issuing the call far and wide for a new evangelization of the continent. As he told a large group of young pilgrims at Santiago de Compostela: *Today, the Church is preparing for a new Christianization, which is a challenge she must face, as in times past.*[4] These words are directed at all the faithful.

In certain areas this new evangelization will be taken up with the most fundamental aspects of culture, as was the case for Saints Cyril and Methodius. It appears that certain areas have completely regressed to paganism, perhaps a more absolute paganism than was ever known in antiquity. In earlier times primitive peoples appeared to have some religious sensibility. This is a job which involves every one of us. We have to re-christianize our environment, our social customs. We will have to focus on those people and circumstances which are within our immediate influence.

---

[2] *idem, Address,* Santiago de Compostela, 9 November 1982, 2

[3] cf L. Suarez, *The Christian roots of Europe,* Madrid 1986

[4] St John Paul II, *Address,* Santiago de Compostela, 19 August 1989

We need to speak to people about God with clarity and without fear of rejection. We need to teach our neighbours that all human endeavour which ignores God's presence in Creation is doomed to failure. We should invite our friends to the means of formation with a sense of daring. We should distribute good reading material. We have to do an active work of apostolate for the sacrament of Confession.

18.2 Responding with a new evangelization.

Christianity gave Europe its unity. A multitude of races and cultures came together through the Church and based their co-existence on Christian principles. The conversion of Europe did not happen overnight. It ended up by taking over one thousand years. *This was an endeavour full of triumphs and apparent failures, an enterprise to which each people contributed their particular genius. As always, the Providence of God was predicated on the cooperation of men. Above all else, the conversion of Europe was a religious phenomenon which at the same time figured as an essential factor in the development of Western culture.*[5]

Even to this day Europe remains somewhat united according to certain essential principles in law and custom which derive from her Christian roots. These contemporary values include the dignity of the human person, the desire for social justice and human freedom, industriousness, the spirit of enterprise and initiative, love for the family, respect for life, respect for other peoples, the longing for social harmony and international peace.[6]

Side by side with these noble values we also find in modern Europe the steady growth of atheism and scepticism. We see widespread moral uncertainty, the disintegrat-

[5] J. Orlandis, *The Conversion of Europe to Christianity,* Madrid 1988
[6] cf St John Paul II, *Address,* Santiago de Compostela, 9 November 1982, 4

ion of the family and the deterioration of Christian customs.[7] Many countries have adopted anti-human legislation such as legalized abortion, a social tragedy which gives the notion of modern progress an ominously barbaric character. The only way to respond to this *new paganism* is with a *new evangelization.* It is the Christian's vocation to overcome evil with an abundance of good. This is what the Lord is asking of all of us whether we are many or few, young or old. We need to reach out to the people who are around us.

We would do well to recall that moving call of the Holy Father at Santiago de Compostela during his first visit to Spain: *I, Bishop of Rome and Shepherd of the Universal Church, from Santiago, utter to you, Europe of the ages, a cry full of love: Find yourself again. Be yourself. Discover your origins, revive your roots. Return to those authentic values which made your history a glorious one and your presence so beneficent in the other continents.*[8]

God is counting on us to re-christianize society in the same way that the first Christians did. How much work there is to do! Without abandoning our professional and family duties, we need to put our best efforts into this momentous task. We have to lead lives of faith. We have to become men and women of prayer, people who *know how to deal personally with the one who loves us above everything.*[9] It is essential that all our activity be anchored in the Holy Mass, the *centre and root* of the interior life. In addition, we need to draw strength and receive pardon in the sacrament of Penance.

18.3 Promoting Christian customs in ordinary life.

Saint Luke describes the first steps in the evangeliz-

---

[7] *idem, Address,* 6 November 1981

[8] *idem, Address,* Santiago de Compostela, 9 November 1982

[9] St Teresa, *Life,* 8, 2

ation of Europe with this account of the travels of Saint Paul and his company: *Passing through Phrygia and the Galatian country, they were forbidden by the Holy Spirit to speak the word in the province of Asia. And when they came to Mysia, they tried to get into Bithynia, but the Spirit of Jesus did not permit them; so passing by Mysia, they went down to Troas. And Paul had a vision one night; a Macedonian was standing, appealing to him and saying, 'Come over into Macedonia and help us'. As soon as he had the vision, straightway we made efforts to set out for Macedonia, being sure that God had called us to preach the gospel to them.*[10] Two thousand years later, we should still be attuned to the Macedonian's call: *Come... and help us.*

It is unlikely that the Lord wants us to imitate Saint Paul in the sense that he travelled throughout the known world of his time. We have to christianize the world that we know in our ordinary lives. We have to bring faith and optimism to this world without becoming overwhelmed by the difficulties involved. *If there are many obstacles, there will be abundant grace available. God himself will move the obstacles by using each one of us as his instruments.*[11]

Let us take advantage of all the circumstances of life that come our way: the birth or death of a relative or friend, sickness, family celebrations... There are always opportunities to suggest to someone a good book that will bring them closer to God. We can also give a word of encouragement or counsel to someone who is going through a rough time. We can suggest that new homeowners have their house blessed. We can teach people to go to their Guardian Angels for help throughout the day. We can suggest that people hang images of Our Lady in the home to give

[10] Acts 16:9
[11] Bl. A. del Portillo, *Letter,* 25 December 1985, 10

honour to the Mother of God. These are some of the simple customs which Christians have practised for many centuries. They are like the plasma which animates the life of faith. We need to make God a participant in the thousand little moments of ordinary life. This can be done by the way in which we offer up our work, the manner in which we take our vacations, how we choose to rest. The Faith should penetrate all of our actions so as to enrich them and make them pleasing to God. We will find that this supernatural effort will help to make our activities more human.

St John Paul II urged all Catholics to become fully aware of their baptismal responsibilities. This awareness will move us to make Christ known to others. If each and every Christian were to be wholly committed to the practice of the Faith, it would not take long to change the world. We would make the world a more human place to live in. This is because we would recognise God's rightful place in our affairs. Let us begin with our own lives and the lives of those closest to us. Apostolate then becomes like the proverbial pebble dropped into the lake which has a wider and wider ripple effect.[12] Through the intercession of Saints Cyril and Methodius, let us ask the Lord: *Grant that our hearts may grasp the words of your teaching, and perfect us as a people of one accord in true faith and right confession.*[13]

We turn with hope to Holy Mary, *Regina mundi.* Let us ask her that *the Church be rejuvenated, that she be firmly united, that her faithful be renewed in desires for holiness and apostolate.*[14] We pray that Christ might reign in all hearts and in all human activities.

---

[12] cf St. J. Escrivá, *The Way,* 831
[13] *Roman Missal, Collect*
[14] Bl. A. del Portillo, *op cit,* 12

22 February

19. THE CHAIR OF ST PETER

Apostle

Feast

This feast celebrates the fact that Peter established his See in Rome. Christians were known to have celebrated this feast before the Fourth Century. The original name found on the ancient calendars was *Natale Petri de Cathedra* and the original date was 22 February.

19.1 Meaning of the feast.

The Lord says to Simon Peter: I have prayed for you that your faith may not fail, and, once you have turned back, strengthen your brothers.[1]

The *Chair* of Saint Peter refers to his seat of authority. The Fathers of the Church used this term as a symbol of a bishop's authority, paying special regard to the Bishop of Rome. In the Third Century, Saint Cyprian wrote: *Peter holds primacy so as to show that Christ's Church is one, that his Chair is one.* He goes on to emphasize the matter of unity with these words: *God is one. The Lord is one. The Church is one. The Chair founded by Christ is one.*[2]

For many years, the people of Rome had on display a wooden chair which Saint Peter reputedly sat upon. Saint Damasus moved this relic to the baptistry of the newly built Vatican in the fourth century. The chair was seen and honoured by thousands of pilgrims from all over Christendom. At the time when the present Basilica of Saint Peter was erected, it was thought advisable to preserve the chair in bronze and gold.

---

[1] *Entrance Antiphon*: Luke 22:32

[2] St Cyprian, *Epistle 43,* 5

Before the fourth century, in the earliest liturgical calendars of the Church one finds this feast, *Natale Petri de Cathedra,* the celebration of the institution of the papacy. This feast highlights the fact that the Bishop of Rome has jurisdiction throughout the entire world. It has been a long-standing custom to commemorate the consecration of bishops in their respective dioceses. Yet these commemorations pertained solely to the limits of each diocese. The *Chair* of Peter, however, is unique in that it extends to all Christianity and has done so from the first centuries. As Saint Augustine has pointed out on a sermon for this feast: *Our forefathers gave the name 'Chair' to this feast so that we might remember that the Prince of the Apostles was entrusted with the 'Chair' of the episcopate.*[3] We should be sure to review the quality of our love and obedience to the Pope.

19.2 Saint Peter in Rome.

We know from the tradition of the Church[4]that Saint Peter lived for a period of time in the city of Antioch where *the disciples were first called 'Christians'.*[5] There he preached the Good News and then returned to Jerusalem where a bloody persecution had broken out. *Now at this time Herod the king set hands on certain members of the Church to persecute them. He killed James the brother of John with the sword, and seeing that it pleased the Jews, he proceeded to arrest Peter also, during the days of the Unleavened Bread.*[6] Freed from prison by the intercession of an angel, Peter left Palestine and *went to another place.*[7]

---

[3] St Augustine, *Sermon 15 on the Saints*

[4] cf St Leo the Great, *Homily 82 on the feast of the Apostles Peter and Paul,* 5

[5] Acts 11:26

[6] Acts 12:3

[7] Acts 12:17

The *Acts of the Apostles* does not state where Saint Peter went, but tradition tells us that he began to make his way to the Eternal City. Saint Jerome claims that Peter arrived in Rome during the second year of the reign of Claudius (43 A.D.) and remained there for twenty-five years until his death.[8] Other authors believe that Peter made two trips to Rome: one immediately following his captivity in Jersusalem, and having gone to Palestine on the occasion of the Council of Jerusalem in 49 A.D., he returned to Rome. Later he carried out other missionary journeys.

Saint Peter arrived at this the capital of the world *to better spread the light of the truth from the head to the rest of the body,* reasoned Saint Leo the Great. *What race was not represented in this city? What peoples would ignore what Rome said? This was the proper place to refute false philosophies, to challenge the foolishness of purely human reasoning, to destroy the empty sacrifices of the cults. For it was in Rome that all the different errors had come together, as it were.*[9]

This fisherman from Galilee became the rock and foundation of the Church. He chose to establish this foundation in the Eternal City. Here he preached the Good News as he had done in Judaea, in Samaria, in Galilee and in Antioch. From his *Chair* in Rome, Peter governed the whole Church. It was there in Rome that Peter gave up his own life for the Faith in imitation of the Master.

The tomb of the Prince of the Apostles lies directly beneath the main altar of Saint Peter's Basilica. This has been the constant tradition and it has recently been confirmed by archaeological investigation. The tomb serves as an enduring symbol that Simon Peter is by divine election the Church's firm foundation. The voice of Our

---

[8] St Jerome, *De viris illustribus,* 1
[9] St Leo the Great, *loc cit,* 3-4

Saviour can be heard down through the centuries in the teachings of the Roman Pontiffs.

19.3 Love and veneration due to the Roman Pontiff.

Today's Gospel passage records that immortal promise made by Jesus to Peter and all of this successors as Pope: *And I say to thee, thou art Peter, and upon this rock I will build my Church, and the gates of hell shall not prevail against it. And I will give thee the keys of the kingdom of heaven; and whatever thou shalt bind on earth shall be bound in heaven, and whatever thou shalt loose on earth shall be loosed in heaven.*[10] Saint Augustine comments about this passage: *Blessed be God, who deigned to exalt the Apostle Peter over the whole Church. It is most fitting that this foundation be honoured since it is the means by which we may ascend to Heaven.*[11]

Acting from Rome, Peter consoled, instructed and strengthened the many Christian churches which were developing throughout the Roman Empire. In the *First Reading* of today's Mass, Peter exhorts church leaders in Asia Minor to shepherd their flocks with charity: *Tend the flock of God which is among you, governing not under constraint, but willingly, according to God; nor yet for the sake of base gain, but eagerly.*[12] These words of Peter harken back to the teachings of the Master about the Good Shepherd.[13] We may specifically recall that moving scene after the Resurrection when Jesus said to Simon Peter: *Feed my lambs... Feed my sheep.*[14]

This is the mission which the Lord has entrusted to Peter and each of his successors: to take good care of the

---

[10] Matt 16:13-16
[11] St Augustine, *loc cit*
[12] 1 Pet 5:2
[13] John 10:1 ff
[14] John 21:15-17

Lord's flock, to confirm the faith of the People of God, to safeguard doctrine and customs, to interpret the truths contained in divine Revelation with the help of the Holy Spirit. As Saint Peter writes in his Second Epistle: *Therefore I shall begin to remind you always of these things; although indeed you know them and are well established in the present truth. As long as I am in this tabernacle, I think it right to arouse you by a reminder, knowing as I do that the putting off of my tabernacle is at hand, just as our Lord Jesus Christ signified to me. Moreover I will endeavour that even after my death you may often have occasion to call these things to mind.*[15]

Today's feast gives us a good opportunity to deepen our filial devotion to the Holy Father and to his teachings. We should examine the quality of our personal commitment to know his teachings and to put them into practice.

Love for the Pope is a good indicator of our love for Christ. This love and veneration needs to be specified in daily prayer and sacrifice for his intentions: *Dominus conservet eum et vivificet eum et beatum faciat eum in terra... May the Lord preserve him and give him life and make him blessed on earth, and not deliver him up to the will of his enemies.* We should show this love in real life: whenever we make a trip for apostolic purposes, when we are sick, whenever people are attacking the Church, when we are introducing our friends to the Faith. *Catholic, apostolic, Roman! I want you to be very Roman, ever anxious to make your 'pilgrimage' to Rome, videre Petrum – 'to see Peter'.*[16]

---

[15] 2 Pet 1:12-15
[16] St. J. Escrivá, *The Way,* 520

17 MARCH

19-A. SAINT PATRICK

Optional Memorial

19-A.1 Saint Patrick based his apostolate on prayer and mortification.

The story of Saint Patrick's life is from start to finish a divine adventure. Born of a Christian family in Roman Britain towards the close of the fourth century A.D., while still a teenager he was carried off by Irish pirates in one of those periodic raids which became progressively more pronounced as the once great civilization slowly sank into decay. In Ireland he was sold to a petty chieftain who put him to work as a swineherd; according to tradition the place of his captivity was Slemish in modern-day Antrim.

Patrick always regarded this calamity as a divine punishment for his sins. As he himself describes it, *I was then about sixteen years of age. I knew not the true God; and I went into captivity to Ireland with many thousands of persons, according to our deserts, because we departed away from God, and kept not his commandments, and were not obedient to our priests, who used to admonish us for our salvation.*[1]

However, in his misfortune he remembered the lessons of his youth and turned to God. *Now, after I came to Ireland, tending flocks was my daily occupation; and constantly I used to pray in the day time. Love of God and the fear of him increased more and more, and faith grew, and the spirit was moved, so that in one day I would say as many as a hundred prayers, and at night nearly as many, so that I used to stay even in the woods and on the*

[1] St Patrick, *Confession,* 1

mountain to this end. And before daybreak I used to be roused to prayer, in snow, in frost, in rain. And I felt no hurt, nor was there any sluggishness in me – as I now see, because the spirit was then fervent within me.[2]

After six years in these conditions Patrick contrived to escape, first to Gaul with the help of some friendly traders, and eventually back to his kindred, where he was received with great rejoicing. At that time he had no intention of ever returning to the place of his captivity, but God, as we shall see, had other plans. *And there verily I saw in the night visions, a man whose name was Victoricus coming as it were from Ireland with countless letters. And he gave me one of them, and I read the beginning of the letter, which was entitled 'The Voice of the Irish'; and while I was reading aloud the beginning of the letter, I thought that at that very moment I heard the voice of those who lived beside the Wood of Foclut, which is nigh unto the Western Sea. And thus they cried, as with one mouth: 'We beseech thee, O holy youth, to come and walk once more among us.' And I was exceedingly broken in heart, and would read no further. And so I awoke. Thanks be to God, that after very many years the Lord granted to them according to their cry.*[3]

Patrick thereafter spent some years in Gaul, where he prepared for his mission by studying under Saint Germanus of Auxerre, who had been empowered by Pope Celestine I to prepare the mission to Ireland. However, to Patrick's bitter disappointment, when the time came he was not chosen for the expedition; instead the task was given to a man named Palladius.[4] But Palladius died shortly after arriving in Ireland, whereupon his companions returned to

---

[2] *idem,* 16
[3] *idem,* 23
[4] cf E. MacNeill, *St Patrick,* Sheed & Ward, London 1934

Auxerre. In the circumstances Patrick was chosen to go in his place and was consecrated bishop by Germanus.

19-A.2 Aiming at all levels of society.

When Patrick landed in Ireland – in the year 432 A.D. – charged with the mission of evangelizing that pagan and warlike people, he brought with him a serene faith that stood to him in all the trials that lay ahead, allied to a shrewdly practical mind and a knowledge of the country, its language and customs.

In his work Patrick followed a fairly stereotyped pattern. Whenever he entered a district he would first present himself to the local chieftain and preach the Gospel to him and, following the custom of the time, make him an offering of presents. Although some of the chiefs did embrace the faith, the ancient annals make no secret of the fact that by and large those worldly-wise men were content to retain the less demanding customs of their ancestors. However, Patrick always asked for two further favours, which were invariably granted: a title to a plot of land where he could build a church; and the chief's permission to preach to the people.

Patrick next directed his efforts to the chiefs' sons and daughters; and here, by contrast, he was spectacularly successful. *Wherefore then in Ireland they who never had the knowledge of God, but until now only worshipped idols and abominations – now there has lately been prepared a people of the Lord, and they are called children of God. The sons and daughters of the Irish chieftains are seen to become monks and virgins of Christ.*

In especial there was one blessed lady of Irish birth, of noble rank, most beautiful, grown up, whom I baptized; and after a few days she came to us for a certain cause. She disclosed to us that she had been warned by an angel of God, and that he counselled her to become a virgin of

Christ, and live closer to God. Thanks be to God, six days after, most admirably and eagerly she seized on that which all virgins of God do in like manner; not with the consent of their fathers; but they endure persecutions and lying reproaches from their kindred; and nevertheless their number increases more and more. And as for those of our race who are born there, we know not the number of them, besides widows and continent persons.[5]

That this laid the basis for a subsequent massive conversion of ordinary folk is clear from Patrick's reference to having personally baptized 'many thousands': *wherefore it was exceedingly necessary that we should spread our nets so that a great multitude and a throng should be taken for God, and that everywhere there should be (ordained) clergy to baptize and to exhort a poor and needy people.*[6]

It should not be thought, however, that from then on everything was plain sailing. Time and time again Patrick's life was in danger from various quarters, principally from his mortal enemies the Druids; that he managed to survive them all was due to his own shrewdness and, on more than one occasion, to the special intervention of divine Providence. However, Patrick always regarded his greatest trial to be the opposition to his mission which originated within the circle of his fellow Christians in Britain and Gaul, who circulated so many scurrilous stories about him that he felt called upon to defend himself in writing; thanks to this we are fortunate enough to have his *Confession,* which is the main source of the details about his life.

19-A.3 Faith and culture.

The church that Patrick founded was from the first endowed with a number of very well defined

---

[5] *Confession,* 41-42
[6] *idem,* 40

characteristics. The Gospel message took root in the native Celtic culture, transforming it from within without replacing it, so that with the perspective of centuries behind us we now find it difficult to conceive of the people and their culture as anything but profoundly Christian. And so it always is with the faith. *We can say of catechesis, as well as of evangelization in general, that it is called to bring the power of the Gospel into the very heart of culture and cultures. For this very purpose, catechesis will seek to know these cultures and their essential components; it will learn their most significant expressions; it will respect their particular values and riches ... Two things must however be kept in mind.*

On the one hand, the Gospel message cannot be purely and simply isolated from the culture in which is was first inserted (the Biblical world, or, more accurately, the cultural milieu in which Jesus of Nazareth lived), nor, without serious loss, from the cultures in which it has already been expressed down the centuries ...

On the other hand, the power of the Gospel everywhere transforms and regenerates. When that power enters into a culture, it is no surprise that it rectifies many of its elements. There would be no catechesis if it were the Gospel that had to change when it came into contact with cultures. To forget this would simply amount to what Saint Paul very forcefully calls 'emptying the Cross of Christ of its power' (1 Cor 1:17).[7]

The second characteristic of the new church was its profoundly apostolic nature. The first to feel the benefit of this impulse were the pagan Picts of Scotland, and later still the barbarian tribes then settling in the ruins of the Roman provinces of Northern Europe: Gaul, Germany, and as far afield as Lombardy. It is from this period that the

---

[7] St John Paul II, *Catechesi tradendae,* 53

missionaries' homeland acquired the fame for holiness and learning that caused it to be known throughout Christendom as 'the island of saints and scholars.' And although this Golden Age was brought to an abrupt end in the ninth century when it was Ireland's turn to fall victim to foreign invaders, this time the Vikings, Patrick's legacy continued unabated and has survived the vicissitudes of history.

The third characteristic of the faith enkindled by Patrick was the link with the See of Peter, ever since Pope Celestine's initial mandate. Thus Patrick could describe his dearly loved people as the *Church of the Irish, nay of the Romans.*[8] In the century following Saint Patrick's death, Saint Columbanus could address Pope Boniface IV in these words: *We Irish ... are disciples of Saints Peter and Paul ... We hold unbroken that Catholic faith which we first received from you,*[9] a statement reiterated by St John Paul II: *Ireland 'semper fidelis', always faithful.*[10]

Today, as we thank Our Lord for the gift of faith that Saint Patrick handed on, and resolve to follow his example in our own generation, we do so in words attributed to the saint himself:

Christ beside me, Christ before me
Christ behind me, Christ within me
Christ under me, Christ over me
Christ to right of me, Christ to left of me
Christ in lying down, Christ in sitting, Christ in rising up
Christ in the heart of every person who may think of me
Christ in the mouth of every person who may speak of me
Christ in every eye that may look on me
Christ in every ear that may hear me.[11]

---

[8] From the '*Dicta Patricii*' in the medieval *Book of Armagh*
[9] Quoted by St John Paul II, *Address at Clonmacnois,* 30 September 1979
[10] St John Paul II, *Address at Shannon,* 1 October 1979
[11] Hymn, *St Patrick's breastplate*

THE SEVEN SUNDAYS OF SAINT JOSEPH
THE FIRST SUNDAY

20. VOCATION AND SANCTITY OF SAINT JOSEPH

Devotion to Saint Joseph has developed spontaneously from the heart of Christian people. For many people the Holy Patriarch is an excellent model of humility, industriousness and fidelity to one's vocation.

One of the most popular devotions to this saint is *the Seven Sundays of Saint Joseph.* This is an extended opportunity to meditate about the Holy Patriarch and to pray for his intercession.

20.1 The greatest of the saints.

Today we will renew a long-standing custom of preparing for the Feast of Saint Joseph during the seven Sundays prior to that feast day. On each of these Sundays of preparation, we will meditate on the life of the Holy Patriarch, a life which is full of lessons for us.

Following Our Lady, Saint Joseph is the greatest of all the saints in Heaven. Such is the common teaching of Catholic doctrine.[1] This humble carpenter from Nazareth exceeds in grace and blessing all the patriarchs, prophets, Saint John the Baptist, Saint Peter, Saint Paul, the Apostles, the holy martyrs and doctors of the Church.[2] The Church recognizes Saint Joseph's excellence in the First Eucharistic Prayer (the Roman Canon) where his name follows immediately upon that of Our Lady.

Christians from every period are under the care of the Holy Patriarch. The Church pays homage to this protection

---

[1] cf Leo XIII, Encyclical, *Quamquam pluries,* 15 August 1889

[2] cf St Bernardine of Siena, *Homily 1 on St Joseph*

in the *Litany of Saint Joseph* which names Saint Joseph *illustrious descendant of David, light of the patriarchs, spouse of the Mother of God..., model of the working man, tribute to the domestic life, guardian of virgins, consoler of the afflicted, hope of the sick, patron of the dying, scourge of demons, protector of the Holy Church...* No other creature aside from Our Lady has ever merited such praises. The Church sees in Saint Joseph her protector and patron. St John Paul II taught: *This patronage must be invoked as ever necessary for the Church, not only as a defence against all dangers, but also, and indeed primarily, as an impetus for her renewed commitment to evangelization in those lands and nations where – as I wrote in the Apostolic Exhortation 'Christifideles Laici' – 'religion and the Christian life were formerly flourishing and... are now put to a hard test'. In order to bring the first proclamation of Christ, or to bring it anew wherever it has been neglected or forgotten, the Church has need of special 'power from on high' (cf Luke 24:49; Acts 1:8): a gift of the Spirit of the Lord, a gift which is not unrelated to the intercession and example of his saints.*[3]

Through the course of these seven weeks, we should renew and deepen our devotion to the Holy Patriarch. These are moments to draw especially close to him. *Love Saint Joseph a lot. Love him with all your soul, because he, together with Jesus, is the person who has most loved our Blessed Lady and has been closest to God. He is the person who has most loved God, after our Mother. He deserves your affection, and it will do you good to get to know him, because he is the Master of the interior life, and has great power before the Lord and before the Mother of God.*[4] We

---

[3] St John Paul II, Apostolic Exhortation, *Redemptoris custos,* 15 August 1989, 19

[4] St. J. Escrivá, *The Forge,* 554

should take advantage of this opportunity to go to his powerful intercession regarding that matter which worries us the most.

20.2 The Lord prepares those whom he calls to do his work.

We may apply to Saint Joseph that principle formulated by Saint Thomas with reference to the sanctity of Our Lady: *The Lord prepares those whom he calls to do his work.*[5]

It is for this reason that the Blessed Virgin Mother was not only conceived without original sin but from her very conception she was filled with grace. She was given more grace than that possessed by all the saints in heaven combined. As the creature closest to the fountain of all grace, Mary has benefited more than any other creature. Right after Mary, no one was ever closer to Jesus than Saint Joseph, his foster father on earth. Next to Mary, no one has received such a unique mission as did Joseph. No one has loved Jesus more. No one has given Jesus more attention. No other person has been so intimate with the Son of God. *This is precisely the mystery in which Joseph of Nazareth 'shared' like no other human being except Mary, the Mother of the Incarnate Word. He shared in it with her; he was involved in the same salvific event; he was the guardian of the same love, through the power of which the eternal Father 'destined us to be his sons through Jesus Christ' (Eph 1:5).*[6]

It was certainly most fitting that God prepared Joseph's soul to carry out his extraordinary vocation. God was entrusting Joseph with the care of his beloved Son. Joseph's mission was so important that it cannot be equated with the services performed by all the hosts of

---

[5] St Thomas, *Summa Theologiae,* 3, q. 27, a. 4, c.

[6] St John Paul II, *ibid,* 2

angels.[7]

Saint Joseph participated in the fullness of Christ even more than the Apostles did. *He loved Christ. He lived with Christ. He listened to him. He touched him. He was continually at the supernatural fountain of grace, enriching his interior life. He also participated in the spiritual fullness of the Blessed Virgin Mary in their married life. Surely Mary did not deprive her spouse of the benefits deriving from her perfection. Mary led a most grace-filled life in the presence of Christ and the angels. The only person she would have been able to communicate these blessings to would have been Saint Joseph. It was in this fashion that Mary fulfilled the precept of the Lord that the two partners in marriage should become one flesh.*[8]

O blessed Joseph, happy man whose privilege it was, not only to see and hear that God whom many a king has longed to see, yet saw not, longed to hear, yet heard not; but also to carry him in your arms and kiss him, to clothe him and watch over him! Pray for us, blessed Joseph.[9] Favour us with your powerful intercession. For how can Jesus deny you anything?

20.3 Living our vocation: God gives us the grace to overcome all obstacles.

Saint Bernardine of Siena has taught, following the writings of Saint Thomas, that *whenever God chooses someone to do some important work for him, God grants that person the necessary graces. The perfect example of this truth can be seen in the life of Saint Joseph, foster father of Our Lord Jesus Christ and spouse of Mary.*[10] Sanctity consists in fulfilling one's vocation. For Saint

---

[7] cf B. Llamera, *Theology of St Joseph,* Madrid 1953

[8] Isidoro de Isolano, *The Gifts of St Joseph,* III, 17

[9] *Roman Missal, Prayers before Mass,* p. 2007

[10] St Bernardine of Siena, *loc cit*

Joseph, that vocation entailed preserving Mary's commitment to virginity while living in authentic matrimony. *An angel of the Lord appeared to him in a dream, saying, 'Do not be afraid, Joseph, son of David, to take to thee Mary thy wife, for that which is begotten in her is of the Holy Spirit.*[11] Joseph loved Mary with a love so pure and refined that it is beyond our imagination.

With respect to Jesus, Joseph watched over him, protected him, taught him a trade, helped in his education. *Joseph is called 'foster father' but words cannot express the intimate and mysterious relationship which he actually enjoyed with the Son of God. In normal circumstances a man becomes a foster father by accident. In the case of Joseph, however, this is no accidental relationship. Joseph was created so as to live out this transcendent responsibility. This was his predestination, the purpose of all the graces which he received.*[12]

Saint Joseph is a great saint because he corresponded in a heroic way to the graces given to him. We should contemplate about how well we are corresponding to the grace in our own vocation in the middle of the world.

We can never forget the maxim that *whenever God chooses someone to do some important work for him, God grants that person the necessary graces.* How do we react to difficulties in our life of faith? Do we ever doubt God's support in our struggle to raise a family, to give ourselves generously to God's requests, to live a commitment of apostolic celibacy? Do we firmly believe that *because I have a vocation, because I have the grace of God, I can overcome any obstacle?* Do I put my trust in God so that difficulties only make me more faithful?

You saw it quite clearly: while so many people do not

---

[11] Matt 1:20; Luke 2:5

[12] R. Garrigou-Lagrange, *The Mother of the Saviour,* p. 389

know God, he has looked to you. He wants you to form a part of the foundations, a firm stone upon which the life of the Church can rest. Meditate upon this reality and you will draw many practical consequences for your ordinary behaviour: the foundations, made of blocks of stone – hidden and possibly rather dull – have to be solid, not fragile. They have to serve as a support for the building. If not, they are useless.[13]

Saint Joseph was the firm foundation upon which Jesus and Mary were able to rest. He teaches us how to be faithful to our vocation. He will help us always to be faithful. We need only go to his intercession. *Sancte Joseph..., ora pro nobis..., ora pro me.* This is a simple prayer which we can recite many times today.

---

[13] St. J. Escrivá, *The Forge,* 472

THE SEVEN SUNDAYS OF SAINT JOSEPH
THE SECOND SUNDAY

21. THE VIRTUES OF SAINT JOSEPH

21.1 The humility of the Holy Patriarch.

For this second Sunday dedicated to Saint Joseph let us contemplate the virtues which he practised in his ordinary life of work. While describing the virginal birth, Saint Matthew chose to describe the Holy Patriarch as *Joseph her husband, ... a just man ...*[1] This is how the Evangelists portray the foster father of Our Saviour. He is *a just man.* In the case of Saint Joseph justice refers not only to the virtue of giving to each person his due. Justice also has to do with sanctity, with the habitual fulfilment of one's duty and the Will of God. In the Old Testament we find that the idea of *a just man* is the same as that of a saint. The just man has a clean heart and a right intention. He observes all that God has commanded in his social and personal behaviour.[2] Joseph was a just man in every sense of the word.

When considering the virtues of Saint Joseph we need to keep in mind that God's perspective on human actions is frequently quite different from the world's perspective. We men and women have a habit of *giving all our attention to exterior things while neglecting the interior realities. We tend to work against the clock. We accept appearances and give little importance to what is most important. We worry so much about how things will look to others instead of being concerned for the way they ought to be. It is for this*

---

[1] cf Matt 1:18
[2] cf J. Dheilly, *Biblical Dictionary,* Barcelona 1970

reason that the most esteemed virtues are those that are associated with 'getting on in life' and lead to success in business. As a consequence, the interior and hidden virtues are rarely practised or, for that matter, rarely understood. Yet these are the virtues that pertain to man's relationship with God. This dilemma (or paradox) is the key to the mystery of true virtue ... Joseph, the honest man, seeks God. Joseph, the selfless man, finds God. Joseph, the hidden man, delights in God's presence.[3] We need to follow the Holy Patriarch's example by seeking God's presence in the course of our ordinary work.

One of the most important virtues we observe in Saint Joseph's life is *humility.* This virtue is shown by Saint Joseph's reaction to his vocation. We can imagine that Saint Joseph would sometimes glance at the child Jesus and wonder to himself: why did God choose me and not another? What do I have to offer that has earned me this holy charge? He did not receive an answer to these ponderings, since the ways of the Lord are beyond the calculations of men. God calls whom he wants and He grants the graces necessary for every vocation. It is useful to remember in this connection that *the name Joseph, in Hebrew, means 'God will add.' God adds unsuspected dimensions to the holy lives of those who do his Will. He adds the one important dimension which gives meaning to everything, the divine dimension. To the humble and holy life of Joseph He added – if I may put it this way – the lives of the Virgin Mary and of Jesus, our Lord. God does not allow himself to be outdone in generosity. Joseph could make his own the words of Mary, his wife: 'He has looked graciously upon the lowliness of his handmaid ... because he who is mighty, he whose name is holy, has wrought for me his wonders' (Luke 1:48-49). Saint Joseph was an ordinary sort*

---

[3] Bossuet, *Second panegyric on St Joseph*

of man on whom God relied to do great things.[4]

The humility of Saint Joseph is also shown by his strong sense of gratitude to God. Our Lord wants us to imitate the Holy Patriarch in this disposition. We need to see all the events of our lives with eyes of faith, with a real determination to live out our vocation in the middle of the world.[5]

21.2 Faith, hope and love.

He did not give in to the temptation of disbelief before the promise of the Lord. Instead he became stronger in his faith and gave glory to God.[6]

Because Saint Joseph was a truly humble man he was able to remain steadfast in his faith through every trial. When the angel explained to him the manner of the Saviour's conception, Joseph believed without any hesitation. It is reasonable for us to assume that Joseph found it hard to understand why God wanted his Son to grow up in such a poor family. How was Joseph supposed to react to the wicked threat posed by Herod? He must have found it strange that the Son of God would have to run away from a minor despot. How often have we found ourselves in tough situations where the logic of God stands opposed to the logic of men? Saint Joseph knew how to see God in everything that happened. This is because he lived a very holy life.

Saint Joseph's hope grew as he awaited the arrival of the Redeemer. Later on, this virtue came into play as he watched the child Jesus develop into manhood. Perhaps he asked Jesus when He would manifest himself to the world. His sincere love for Jesus and Mary became deeper every

---

[4] St. J. Escrivá, *Christ is passing by,* 40

[5] cf St John Paul II, Apostolic Exhortation, *Christifideles laici,* 30 December 1988

[6] *Divine Office, Solemnity of St Joseph,* Responsorial Psalm to the First Reading

day. No one will ever love them as he loved them. This affection was demonstrated in the ordinary events of his working day, of his family life and social relations.

21.3 Saint Joseph's human virtues.

... being a just man ... Supernatural grace helps each person to reach the fullness of his or her potentiality according to the providential plan of God. Grace does not just heal the wounds of our human nature. Saint Joseph received countless supernatural gifts from God. By his heroic correspondence with these graces Joseph acquired the human and supernatural virtues to a superlative degree. St Josemaria Escrivá has written: *The Gospels give us a picture of Joseph as a remarkably sound man who was in no way frightened or shy of life ... I see him as a strong young man, perhaps a few years older than our Lady, but in the prime of his life and work.*[7]

Through his just behaviour and holiness before God Saint Joseph served his neighbours unstintingly. He was a man of his word in business dealings and personal friendships. This was the man whom God had entrusted with his Mother and Son. And God was not disappointed.

The life of the Holy Patriarch was full of work from his time in Nazareth and Bethlehem, in Egypt and then once again in Nazareth. Everyone knew of Joseph because he was such a hard worker. He probably gave great importance to the development of a manly character, the type of character that shines through the episodes of the Gospels. Saint Matthew repeatedly shows us how promptly Joseph responded to whatever God was asking of him.

During those times in Palestine the job of a 'carpenter' required dexterity and wide-ranging talents.[8] This trades-

---

[7] St. J. Escrivá, *op cit,* 40

[8] cf H. Daniel-Rops, *Daily Life in the Time of Jesus,* New York 1964, p. 239

man was therefore well-respected in the community. He was responsible for the most varied manufacturing projects, from constructing farming implements to making home furniture. He needed to be adept with any number of tools and implements. He also had to be familiar with the properties of the various materials, their strengths, their endurance, their proper uses.

The human and supernatural virtues of Saint Joseph are summarized by the Gospel writers in those few words: *he was a just man.* Saint Joseph was just towards God and just towards other people. His is the kind of behaviour we should all aspire to. This is what God expects from each one of us.

The justice of Saint Joseph is most evident in the testimony of his cleanness of heart, of his readiness to learn the will of God and bring it to fruition. He would have been a cheerful and friendly member of his community. Although the Gospels have not recorded anything Saint Joseph ever said, they do nevertheless give us a clear picture of his life and works. This record should serve as a point of reference for us in our efforts to achieve sanctity in ordinary life. *What is crucially important here is the sanctification of daily life, a sanctification which each person must acquire according to his or her own state, and one which can be promoted according to a model accessible to all people: 'Saint Joseph is the model of those humble ones that Christianity raises up to great destinies; ... he is the proof that in order to be a good and genuine follower of Christ, there is no need of great things – it is enough to have the common, simple and human virtues, but they need to be true and authentic' (Saint Paul VI, Address, 19 March 1969).*[9]

[9] St John Paul II, Apostolic Exhortation, *Redemptoris custos,* 15 August 1989, 24

THE SEVEN SUNDAYS OF SAINT JOSEPH
THE THIRD SUNDAY

22. JOSEPH, HUSBAND OF MARY

22.1 The married life of Mary and Joseph. Joseph the *guardian of her virginity*.

It is customary for saints to be outstanding and become well-known for some particular virtue or aspect of their struggle which makes them conspicuous exemplars for the faithful. For example, Saint Francis of Assisi is revered for his heroic life of poverty. The Holy Curé of Ars is a model of extraordinary priestly service to souls. Saint Thomas More is remembered for his devotion to both God and country, but to God first, even at the price of martyrdom. In the case of Saint Joseph, we have only to dwell upon the words of Saint Matthew: *Joseph, the husband of Mary.*[1] Here we have the summary of Joseph's vocation and the setting for his sanctity. With the exception of Jesus, no one ever cared for Our Lady more than Saint Joseph did. No one protected her with more vigilance. No one has given his life to the Lord with such total generosity as the Holy Patriarch did.

God's loving providence ordained that Jesus would be born into a human family. Joseph was not only the guardian of Mary; he was also her husband. According to Jewish custom of the time, matrimony involved two distinct ceremonies separated by a period of time: betrothal and the formal wedding. In the ceremony of betrothal, the spouses made a firm promise as regards their future wedding and matrimonial union. The bridegroom would

---

[1] Matt 1:16

place the rings in the hands of the future bride and both would receive a blessing. From that moment on, the woman would be known as *the wife of ...* The normal interval between betrothal and wedding ceremony was about the space of a year. It was within this period that the Virgin received the news of her vocation from the Angel Gabriel, and that the Incarnation took place. At the same time Saint Joseph learned about God's plans through a dream. *'So Joseph, arising from sleep, did as the angel of the Lord had commanded him, and took unto him his wife' (Matt 1:24). He took Mary as his wife in humble acceptance of the mystery of her maternity. He accepted her along with her Son who would come to the world by the action of the Holy Spirit. Saint Joseph can therefore be compared to Our Lady in his great docility to the will of God as revealed to him by an angel.*[2]

The wedding ceremony was the fulfilment of the marital contract entered into at the betrothal. It was customary for the bride to be brought to the home of the bridegroom amid great rejoicing.[3] In this manner the union was validated before the entire community and, therefore, her offspring would be recognised as legitimate.

It is of the essence of the marital union that the spouses give their bodies to one another. Because the marriage of Mary and Joseph was an authentic marriage, these reciprocal rights existed in their union. Because of what they had learned from God, by mutual agreement Mary and Joseph had renounced the exercise of these rights. The denial of them would have been cause for annulment. In the case of Joseph and Mary, however, we have something different because here we have a case of

---

[2] St John Paul II, Apostolic Exhortation, *Redemptoris custos,* 15 August 1989, 3

[3] F. M. Willam, *Life of Mary*

mutual voluntary renunciation. This understanding was the fruit of a most refined, prayerful environment. We can get some understanding of this union if we look upon it and try to comprehend it with a clean heart. Joseph became a virgin for the sake of the Virgin. He protected her with great delicacy and affection.[4]

Saint Thomas gives various reasons for the appropriateness of the Virgin's being united to Joseph in true matrimony.[5] It was appropriate and necessary so that Mary's pregnancy would not be a cause of scandal among relatives and neighbours. It was useful that Jesus would be born into a human family as an apparently legitimate son, since no one would thus know of the mystery of his supernatural conception. It was helpful that Jesus and Mary would find support for mother and child in their life with Saint Joseph. In this way the arrival of the Messiah would also be hidden from the Devil. With this union Mary gives due honour both to the state of matrimony and virginity. Our Lady loved Joseph with a deep and pure love. She knew and understood him well, and she wants us to go to him for assistance. Joseph and Mary are the model husband and wife. They are the perfect image of total self-giving to God, *indiviso corde,* in either apostolic celibacy or virginity lived in the middle of the world. *Virginity or celibacy for the sake of the Kingdom of God not only does not contradict the dignity of marriage, but presupposes it and confirms it. Marriage and virginity or celibacy are two ways of expressing and living the one mystery of the covenant of God with his people.*[6]

---

[4] cf St Augustine, *On Holy Virginity,* 1, 4

[5] St Thomas, *Summa Theologiae,* 3, q 29, a 1

[6] St John Paul II, Apostolic Exhortation, *Familiaris consortio,* 22 December 1981, 16

22.2 The most pure love of Joseph.

Joseph and Mary were married in Nazareth. Here in this little village the Word became flesh. In the wedding ceremony Mary would receive a small dowry as was customary. It would consist of a jewel of modest value, clothing and furniture.[7] Perhaps she would have received a patrimony of some land. In any event, all of this did not add up to very much. But when someone is poor, gifts of little worth take on an enhanced value. Since Joseph was a carpenter he would have built the best furniture possible for their home. The news of the wedding must have passed from one town to another: 'Mary has married Joseph the carpenter'. The Virgin wanted these ceremonies to take place even though she had given herself completely to God. *Marriage to a man like Joseph gave her security and tranquillity.*[8] Joseph and Mary allowed themselves to be led by divine inspiration. We might apply to this holy couple the following truth taught by Saint Thomas: *It is natural and typical that the just find in all of their works inspiration from the Holy Spirit.*[9] God was attentive to the human love between Joseph and Mary. He supplied abundant graces to strengthen that devotion.

Joseph eventually came to understand that Mary's child was from the Holy Spirit, and that Mary was to be the Mother of the Redeemer. As a consequence, he loved Mary more than ever. *Joseph loved Our Lady, not with a brotherly love but with a conjugal love. It was so deep that any carnal relation was made totally superfluous. So refined was it that he became not only a witness of Mary's virginal purity – virgin before birth, in birth and after birth*

---

[7] cf F. M. Willam, *op cit,* p. 66
[8] J. Maria Lagrange, *St Luke's Gospel,* Paris 1923
[9] cf St Thomas, *op cit,* 3, q 36, a 5, c and ad 2

as the Church teaches – but became its custodian.[10] God the Father took the greatest care to prepare this virginal family for his only-begotten Son.

Painters have traditionally depicted Joseph as an elderly man in order to emphasize the perpetual virginity of Mary. Yet it is more likely that Joseph was not much older than his wife. *You don't have to wait to be old or lifeless to practise the virtue of chastity. Purity comes from love; and the strength and joy of youth are no obstacle to a noble love. Joseph had a young heart and a young body when he married Mary, when he learned of the mystery of her divine motherhood, when he lived in her company, respecting the integrity God wished to give the world as one more sign that he had come to share the life of his creatures.*[11]

Let us ask the Holy Patriarch to teach us how to live this kind of love in the circumstances to which God has called us. We want this love *that lights up the heart*[12] so that we may perform our ordinary work with joy.

22.3 Joseph's paternal relationship to Jesus.

In the Gospels, Saint Joseph is repeatedly referred to as *father.*[13] Without a doubt, this is how Jesus called the Holy Patriarch in the intimacy of their home in Nazareth. Jesus was known in the community as the *son of Joseph.*[14] Joseph certainly fulfilled the duties corresponding to those of a father in the Holy Family. He gave Jesus his name. He led the Holy Family into Egypt. He decided where they would live on their return to Palestine. Jesus obeyed Joseph as if he were his natural father: *And he went down with*

---

[10] F. Suarez, *Joseph of Nazareth,* p. 40
[11] St. J. Escrivá, *Christ is passing by,* 40
[12] St Thomas, *On Charity*
[13] Luke 2:27, 33, 41, 48
[14] cf Luke 3:23

them and came to Nazareth, and was subject to them.[15]

Jesus was conceived in a miraculous way by the action of the Holy Spirit. He was born from the virginal womb of Mary according to the divine Will. God wanted Jesus to be born within a family, to be raised by a father and mother. Just as God chose Mary to be his Mother, God chose Joseph from among all men to be his father.[16]

Saint Joseph behaved and felt like a father towards Jesus. He had an ardent love for the Son of God and for the Mother of God. This love was even greater than the natural love a natural father may have for his natural son. This is because Joseph cared for Jesus as a son and at the same time worshipped him as his God. He was greatly moved at the sight of a God who would give himself so generously for the good of mankind. This amazing spectacle caused Joseph to love Jesus in an ever-increasing way.

Joseph loved Jesus almost as if he had really begotten him. He looked upon Jesus as a wondrous gift God had bestowed on him in his ordinary human life. Joseph consecrated his energies, his time, his greatest concern, his care to this gift. He sought no compensation other than the opportunity to give more of himself. His love was strong and sweet, tranquil and fervent, emotional and tender. We can think of Joseph with Jesus in his arms, teaching the child songs, watching over his sleep, making him little toys, treating the child with the affection shown by any parent.[17] How often must Joseph have been humbled at the awesome thought that the Son of God also wanted to be *his* son! Let us ask the Holy Patriarch to teach us how to love and cherish Jesus as he himself did.

---

[15] Luke 2:51

[16] cf Jose Antonio of the Child Jesus, *St Joseph, his mission, his life, his times, his life*

[17] cf M. Gasnier, *Joseph the Silent,* Madrid 1988

THE SEVEN SUNDAYS OF SAINT JOSEPH
THE FOURTH SUNDAY

23. JOYS AND SORROWS – I

23.1 The Lord always enlightens those who seek him with a clean heart. The mystery of the Immaculate Conception.

To think about the life of Saint Joseph is to discover a life full of joys and sorrows. The Lord teaches us through the life of the Holy Patriarch that true happiness is never far from the Cross. If we bear suffering and trial with supernatural spirit, we will soon be rewarded with clarity and peace. With Christ at our side, sorrows turn into joys.

The Gospel relates the first sorrow and first joy of the Holy Patriarch. *When Mary his mother had been betrothed to Joseph, before they came together, she was found to be with child by the Holy Spirit.*[1] Joseph was well aware of the holiness of his spouse, even though he could not understand the evident fact of her maternity. He was deeply perplexed. He loved Mary with a pure and deep human love. Yet he felt obliged by his upright conscience to follow the Mosaic Law in this regrettable situation. In order to protect Mary from public shame, Joseph decided to put her aside privately. This was a most painful test for both Joseph and Mary.

Just as his sorrow was great, so was Joseph's joy immeasurable when at last he was shown the ways of God's Providence. *But while he thought on these things ...* These were the things that he could not hope to fathom, that he was unable to share with anyone. In the midst of

---

[1] Matt 1:18

this trial Joseph was visited by an angel who said: *Do not be afraid, Joseph, son of David, to take to thee Mary thy wife, for that which is begotten in her is of the Holy Spirit.*[2] All of Joseph's doubts vanished at once. Everything had become clear. His soul had become filled with God's peace. He now understood that he was the recipient of two incredible treasures, Jesus and Mary. He had been given for his wife the Mother of God. He had been given for a son the Son of God. Joseph had become a different person: *he became a unique guardian of the mystery 'hidden for ages in God' (Eph 3:9).*[3]

We can learn from Joseph's first sorrow and joy that the Lord will always enlighten those who seek him with a clean heart. God's light can shine through the most perplexing situations imaginable.[4] How often does it happen that we fail to grasp the meaning of God's plans, the 'why' behind different circumstances and events. If we take care to trust in the Lord, we will come to appreciate his divine wisdom. With that realization we will discover a deep sense of peace and joy in our soul.

23.2 The Nativity in Bethlehem. The Circumcision.

A few months later, Joseph and Mary set off from Nazareth to Bethlehem to enroll in the census decreed by Caesar Augustus.[5] After this three or four-day journey they were tired and worn out. This must have been especially true of Mary, a mother with child. They had arrived at the town of their forefathers but they had no place to stay. There was no room for them at the inn. There was no home for them in anywhere. We can imagine Joseph going from

---

[2] Matt 1:20

[3] St John Paul II, Apostolic Exhortation, *Redemptoris custos,* 15 August 1989, 5

[4] cf *The Navarre Bible,* note to Matt 1:20

[5] cf Luke 2:1

door to door in search of shelter and hospitality for his pregnant wife. At each door he would have made the same simple request: 'We have just arrived in town. My wife is about to deliver a child.' Everywhere he must have received the same negative reply. Mary was probably close by on their donkey, a silent witness to this trying search. What must this terrible experience have been like for Saint Joseph? What were his feelings at the sight of his weary wife, her clothing travel-stained and every feature proclaiming her utter exhaustion?

Eventually they learned of some caves on the outskirts of the town. Joseph took the Blessed Virgin to one of these places which served as a stable. Our Lady could go no farther. *And it came to pass while they were there, that the days for her to be delivered were fulfilled. And she brought forth her firstborn son, and wrapped him in swaddling clothes, and laid him in a manger ...*[6]

All of this anxiety and suffering was quickly forgotten from the moment Mary held the Son of God in her arms. Saint Joseph realized that the Son of God was now his son as well. He kissed him and worshipped him. In the midst of this simplicity and poverty, a multitude of the heavenly host appeared and proclaimed: *Glory to God in the highest ...*[7] Our Lady experienced a great joy in these moments, and Saint Joseph participated in her happiness. He contemplated the way she looked upon her Son, the way she spoke to him, the way she watched over him with loving reverence.[8]

This alternating sorrow and joy should teach us that serving God is worth the effort, even though we will encounter difficulties, and perhaps poverty and pain. In the final analysis, a single look from Our Lady will more than

---

[6] Luke 2:6-7
[7] Luke 2:13-14
[8] cf F. Suarez, *Joseph of Nazareth,* p. 87-88

make up for the little and not-so-little sufferings which may come our way.

And when eight days were fulfilled for his circumcision, his name was called Jesus, the name given him by the angel before he was conceived in the womb.[9] By means of this rite each male was initiated into the community of the chosen people. The ceremony took place either in the paternal home or in the local synagogue. The boy's name was imposed at the time of the circumcision. The actual ceremony was sometimes performed by the father.

The giving of names had a special significance for the Jewish people. The name Jesus means *Saviour*; it had been chosen by God himself and communicated through the message of the angel: *thou shalt call his name Jesus; for he shall save his people from their sins.*[10] It was the desire of the Holy Trinity that the Son should commence his salvific mission on earth in suffering. It would seem fitting that Joseph was the one to inaugurate the mystery of the Redemption by shedding the first drops of his Son's holy blood. This blood would yield its full effect in the awful context of the Passion.[11] The Child who cried upon the receipt of his name had thereupon begun his work of salvation.

Saint Joseph was himself pained at the sight of these first drops of blood. He was well versed in the Scriptures and he knew, if only in an imperfect way, that there would come a day when his Son would have to shed his blood even to the last drop. Joseph was filled with joy to carry the child in his arms and call him Jesus, a name which countless people would later repeat with awe, with profound respect and devotion. Joseph was always aware of the mystery involved in that name.

---

[9] Luke 2:21
[10] Matt 1:21
[11] cf M. Gasnier, *Joseph the Silent*

23.3 Simeon's prophecy.

And when the days of her purification were fulfilled according to the Law of Moses, they took him up to Jerusalem to present him to the Lord.[12] The Temple was to be the setting for the *purification of Mary* and the *presentation of the Lord,* as prescribed by the Mosaic Law. Upon their arrival at the Temple, the Holy Family were met by an elderly man called Simeon who was inspired by the Holy Spirit. Simeon took the child into his arms and with immense joy he praised God.

Simeon prophesized that this young child would become a *sign of contradiction* which many would obstinately reject. He foretold that Mary would be intimately united with the redemptive work of her Son. A *sword* would pass through her heart. This *sword* signifies a deep and lasting wound. Mary then understood the immensity of her Son's sacrifice as well as the immensity of her own. The sorrow in this sacrifice was to be all the greater because some would reject as unwanted the graces won for them by her Son. The prophecy of Simeon, *the sword in the heart of Mary is also the sword in the heart of Joseph since they were of one heart, 'cor unum et anima una'. This sword represents the battle for or against Jesus. Mary is, therefore, directly tied ... to the many diverse acts which constitute the history of mankind. It should be evident to us, however, that Joseph is also heavily involved in this struggle inasmuch as he was a loyal and loving husband.*[13] When Joseph heard the prophecy of Simeon, surely a sword must have pierced his heart as well.

On that day in the Temple Joseph and Mary were given a more profound insight into the mystery of the Redemption which their Son would bring to completion.

---

[12] Luke 2:22

[13] L. Cristiani, *St Joseph, Patron of the universal Church,* Madrid 1978

Saint Joseph was now able to understand a little better the sorrow of his wife and Son. He made this suffering his own. He would never forget the words which he heard that morning in the Temple.

Alongside this pain there was, of course, the joy of the impending universal redemption. Jesus was the salvation *prepared before the face of all peoples: a light of revelation to the Gentiles, and a glory for thy people Israel.* No pain is greater than beholding a stubborn resistance to grace. No joy is comparable to understanding that the Redemption is being carried out in our time and that many souls are coming close to Christ. Haven't we all experienced this joy when a friend has returned to the Sacrament of Penance or when a friend has given his or her life to God without conditions?

O, most holy and lovable Virgin! Help us to share in the sufferings of Jesus as you yourself did. Help us to have a profound horror of sin, an ever greater desire for holiness and a generous love for Jesus and his cross. We would like to make reparation through our acts of love for your great sufferings and humiliations.[14] Saint Joseph, our Father and Lord, help us by your powerful intercession to bring Jesus to many people who live out their lives apart from him.

---

[14] A. Tanquerey, *The divinization of suffering*

The Seven Sundays of Saint Joseph
The Fifth Sunday

24. JOYS AND SORROWS – II

24.1 The flight into Egypt.

Having at last found a place for themselves in Bethlehem, the Holy Family received the unexpected homage of the Magi with their precious gifts for the divine Child. *But when they had departed, behold, an angel of the Lord appeared in a dream to Joseph, saying, 'Arise, and take the child and his mother, and flee into Egypt, and remain there until I tell thee. For Herod will seek the child to destroy him'.*[1]

Joseph's great joy at the visit of the Magi did not last long. He had to abandon his new-found home and business to flee to a foreign land. Herod wanted to kill the Child. Joseph's joy was changed to dread. Once again, God was testing him. Joy and sorrow are never far from one another in souls that love God.[2] Saint John Chrysostom comments on this passage: *The Lord loves his people. That is why he mixes suffering and delight in the lives of his saints. He takes care to intersperse dangers and consolations on the tapestry of the lives of his just ones. This is how He dealt with Joseph.*[3]

Heeding the message of the angel the Holy Family set out at once for Egypt. They could take with them only the bare essentials. *Because Joseph was a poor man, it was easy for him to leave at a moment's notice. His human fortune was certainly no obstacle! He had no impediments.*

---

[1] Matt 2:13

[2] cf *The Navarre Bible,* note to Matt 2:14

[3] St John Chrysostom, *Homilies on St Matthew's Gospel,* 8

Together with his walking-staff, his donkey and his few belongings, he escaped from Bethlehem with Mary and the Child. They passed without notice because of their evident lack of means. In addition to his life of poverty, Joseph practised the virtues of humility and obedience in an extraordinary way. He followed the will of God without delays or complaint.[4]

Meanwhile, many local infants who had not reached two years of age were giving their lives for Jesus in Bethlehem without even knowing it. Their martyrdom opened up for them the gates of Heaven. Today, together with their mothers – surely sanctified by their enormous grief's serving as an instrument for their salvation – they behold the Holy Family in eternal bliss.

Saint Joseph probably had little idea of how he was going to make ends meet for the Holy Family from one day to another. He had to rebuild a home and a clientele in a strange country. After a while he would have been able to give the family some financial stability. Being the kind of man he was, he would have used all the human means at his disposal. Even though he was in a foreign country, Joseph still had the joy of living with Jesus and Mary. We do not know for certain how long the Holy Family remained in exile. Once back in Nazareth, however, Joseph and Mary probably looked back upon that period as the 'years in Egypt.' They would recall their hurried escape along with the worries and problems of their first months on foreign soil. They would also remember their joy at watching Jesus grow up into boyhood.

From the very start of his life Jesus is rarely far from the Cross. Close to him and therefore to the Cross are those who loved him most, Mary and Joseph. The Holy Patriarch surely suffered in his life, but he humbly submitted to the

---

[4] L. Cristiani, *St Joseph, Patron of the Universal Church*

divine plan which he could not understand. *We ought never, then, to be alarmed by contradictions, by pain or by injustice; nor can we allow these humbling setbacks to make us lose our peace of mind. Everything has been foreseen.*[5]

24.2 The return to Nazareth.

The Holy Family remained in Egypt until Herod's death.[6] *But when Herod was dead, behold, an angel of the Lord appeared in a dream to Joseph in Egypt, saying, 'Arise, and take the child and his mother, and go into the land of Israel, for those who sought the child's life are dead'.*[7] This is what Joseph did. *In the different circumstances of his life, Saint Joseph never refuses to think, never neglects his responsibilities. On the contrary, he puts his human experience at the service of the faith. When he returns from Egypt, 'learning that Archelaus had succeeded his father Herod as ruler of Judaea, he was afraid to go there' (Matt 2:22). In other words, he had learned to work within the divine plan. And to confirm that he was doing the right thing, Joseph received an instruction to return to Galilee.*[8] The Holy Family went to live in Nazareth.[9]

Joseph prepared the Holy Family for their return to Palestine. At first, he thought they would be going to Judaea, most probably to Bethlehem. Once again on this occasion God did not spare his faithful servant anxiety and difficulty. On their way out of Egypt Joseph learned that Archelaus, Herod's wicked son, had assumed the throne in Judaea. Joseph guarded too great a treasure to expose it to

---

[5] F. Suarez, *Joseph of Nazareth,* p. 132
[6] Matt 2:14
[7] Matt 2:19
[8] St. J. Escrivá, *Christ is passing by,* 42
[9] Matt 2:23

this sort of danger. *He was afraid to go there.* While reflecting on what would be best for Jesus, Joseph was told in a dream to continue onward to Galilee. We take note that Jesus is always at the centre of Joseph's concerns. Upon their arrival in Nazareth, the Holy Family renewed their acquaintance with relatives and old friends. At long last, this family could settle into a home.

Let us ask Mary and Joseph to teach us how to take advantage of difficulties and contradictions so that we may love God more. We should not be troubled to find that as we follow our Lord ever more closely, we will feel ourselves closer to the Cross as well. *O, Blessed Virgin, who knew how to make the most of your time of exile, help us to serve you better in this valley of tears! Following your example, we offer to God our work, our worries and our sorrows so that Jesus Christ may reign in our hearts and the hearts of our friends.*[10] We ask Saint Joseph to help us to be strong in times of trial. We have to keep our eyes on Jesus, who is always at our side. He will be our strength.

24.3 Jesus is lost and found in the Temple.

In this final sorrow and joy we contemplate the time when Jesus was lost, and found in the Temple.

The Mosaic Law obliged all the Jews who could do so to go on pilgrimage to the Temple in Jerusalem during the three principal feasts of Passover, Pentecost and the Feast of Lights. This rule covered all Jews from their twelfth birthday. If a family lived more than a day's journey from the Temple they need only make one pilgrimage a year. The Law said nothing about the participation of women in this journey, but it seems to have been customary that women accompanied their husbands. Mary and Joseph

---

[10] A. Tanquerey, *The divinization of suffering*

went every year to Jerusalem during Passover. When Jesus reached the age of twelve he travelled with his parents to the Temple.[11] Families who came from distant villages typically travelled in groups. Jerusalem was about three or four days journey from Nazareth.

The Passover celebration lasted for a week. At its close the family caravans would regroup outside the city walls and then begin their return home. The men often travelled in one section of the caravan, while the women would be grouped in another. Children on the road would move about indiscriminately from one group to another. Husband and wife would normally meet together with their families for the evening meal.

When Joseph and Mary accordingly rejoined each other, they realized immediately that Jesus was missing. At first they looked for him among the other caravan groups, but he was not to be found. No one had seen him during the return trip! Joseph and Mary spent the following day searching anxiously among their relatives and acquaintances. No one had any news! Mary and Joseph would have been totally beside themselves with anxiety. What could have possibly happened? That night before they returned to Jerusalem must have been agony for them. Very early the next day they made haste back to Jerusalem. They looked for Jesus everywhere. Where was He? What had happened? They asked people. They described the Child. No one had any idea. *They made their earnest search in a most memorable fashion: he with furrowed brow, she seemingly doubled over with sorrow. Thus they taught all of us how to behave whenever we have the misfortune to lose Jesus.*[12]

Perhaps worst of all was the apparent silence of God. She, the Virgin, was the Father's favourite daughter. He,

---

[11] cf Luke 2:41-42

[12] M. Gasnier, *Joseph the Silent*

Joseph, had been chosen to care for the two of them, and he too had experienced God's intervention in human affairs. Through the angel he had been forewarned of the danger Jesus would run in Bethlehem. He had been urged to flee to Egypt. On moving to Judaea once more he was told to settle in Nazareth, to avoid possible evils. How is it that on this occasion there was no one to advise him? How, after two days of crying out to heaven, of incessant searching and with ever-mounting anxiety for the child, could God remain deaf to his supplication and his suffering?[13]

There are times during life when God seems silent. It may seem that we have lost him. In some instances, this happens through our own fault. In other cases, however, it is almost as if God has deliberately hidden himself so that we will try to find him. *Jesus, may I never lose you again ...*[14] We ought to repeat this simple prayer in the depths of our hearts.

On the third day, when every possibility had been exhausted, suddenly they found Jesus. We can only imagine the wave of joy which must have swept over Mary and Joseph when they discovered him. They would take the Child home between the two of them so as not to lose him again. If they did not actually fear losing him again, at least they wanted to make up for the three days they had lived without him.

Jesus, may I never lose you again ... We ask Saint Joseph to help us never to lose Jesus through sin. Nor do we want to lose sight of him through our human weakness. We ask St Joseph to teach us how to look for Jesus with our whole heart if we should ever suffer the misfortune of losing him.

---

[13] F. Suarez, *op cit,* p 148
[14] St. J. Escrivá, *Holy Rosary,* Fourth Joyful Mystery

THE SEVEN SUNDAYS OF SAINT JOSEPH
THE SIXTH SUNDAY

25. DEATH AND GLORIFICATION OF SAINT JOSEPH

25.1 The death of Saint Joseph, patron of a good death.

Most blessed among men was Joseph, in being attended at the hour of his death by the Lord himself and his Mother ... Having thus triumphed over death, bedecked in celestial light, Joseph travelled to the House of the Father.[1]

The time had come for Joseph to leave this world, and with it his precious treasures, Jesus and Mary. They had been entrusted to Joseph's care. With his daily work and God's help Joseph had supported and looked after the Holy Family. He had taught the Son of God to be a craftsman, besides the countless other lessons passed on in such circumstances from father to son. He fulfilled his paternal responsibilities up to the last moment with complete faithfulness.

We do not know when exactly the Holy Patriarch passed away. Joseph's final appearance in the Gospel narrative occurs when Jesus had turned twelve years old. It seems likely that he died before Jesus began his public life of preaching. When Jesus returned to Nazareth to preach, the people asked one another: *Is not this the carpenter, the son of Mary?*[2] It was customary in the East to refer to sons through their father. People spoke of the mother only in the case of the father's demise. In another social situation, we

---

[1] *Divine Office,* Hymn, *Iste quem laeti*
[2] cf Mark 6:3

recall that while Mary was invited to the wedding at Cana, no mention is made of Joseph. Based on what we know of contemporary Jewish culture, it would be hard to believe that Joseph had been overlooked. Nor is Joseph mentioned at all during the public life of his Son. The people of Nazareth do speak of Jesus as *the son of a carpenter.* This would suggest, perhaps, that not very much time had elapsed since Joseph's death. Joseph was still remembered as the carpenter who had taught his son Jesus his trade. If all of this speculation were not proof enough, we might think of the scene at Calvary with Mary standing at the foot of the Cross. Had Joseph been alive, without a doubt he would have been with her at his Son's side. Following the same line of reasoning, the fact that Jesus entrusted Mary to his beloved apostle Saint John presupposes that Joseph was dead. Most authors are of the opinion now that his death took place shortly before Jesus began his public ministry.

Saint Joseph could not have wished for a happier or more peaceful death, attended as he must have been by Jesus and Mary. Jesus would comfort his father with the promise of everlasting life. Mary would take care of her husband with tremendous devotion. *The filial piety of Jesus comforted Joseph in his agony. Jesus probably told his father that their separation would be very brief. They would be in one another's company again very shortly. Jesus would speak to him of his invitation to the celestial banquet given by his Heavenly Father: 'Well done, good and faithful servant, the work day has come to a close for you. Come into my mansion to receive your just wage. For I was hungry and you gave me to eat. I was homeless and you gave me shelter. I was naked and you gave me clothing' ...* [3]

Jesus and Mary would have closed the eyes of Joseph

[3] M. Gasnier, *Joseph the Silent*

and prepared his body for burial. The man who would later weep before the tomb of his friend Lazarus surely wept now. What tears he must have shed at the death of his earthly father! And those who may have seen him weep would have uttered the same words as were later to be spoken at Bethany: See how he loved him!

It is perfectly fitting that Saint Joseph has been proclaimed the *Patron of a Good Death.* Certainly no one can ever have experienced a more serene departure from this life than Joseph's in the physical presence of Jesus and Mary. Let us go to Saint Joseph whenever we are helping someone to prepare for death. Let us ask his help when our time arrives to go to the House of the Father. Joseph will lead us by the hand to Jesus and Mary.

25.2 The glorification of Saint Joseph.

After Our Lady, Saint Joseph enjoys the greatest glory accorded to a creature.[4] This is only fitting considering his holiness on earth. Joseph gave his entire life to the care of the Son of God and his Blessed Mother. *Since Jesus honoured Joseph as his father during his earthly life, sincerely calling him 'father,' He would certainly want to exalt Joseph in heaven after his death.*[5]

At the moment of his death the *soul* of Saint Joseph went directly to the *bosom of Abraham.* This is where the Patriarchs and the just from past ages awaited the hour of redemption. Joseph announced to the Patriarchs that the Redeemer was on earth and that soon he would open the gates of Heaven. *The just then became filled with thanksgiving and expectation. They surrounded Joseph and intoned a canticle of praise which goes on and will continue until the end of time.*[6]

---

[4] cf B. Llamera, *Theology of St Joseph*

[5] Isidoro de Isolano, *The Gifts of St Joseph*

[6] *ibid*

Since the sixteenth century many authors have contended that the *body* of Saint Joseph is now united in glory with his soul in heaven. They reason that the glorification of Joseph took place after the Resurrection of Jesus. This teaching is grounded in part on the words of Saint Matthew: ... *many bodies of the saints who had fallen asleep arose.*[7] Doctors of the Church and theologians have argued that it would have been fitting for Jesus to resurrect his adopted father from the dead to affirm the triumph of the Cross. What would this encounter of Joseph and Jesus have been like? Saint Francis de Sales writes: *The glorious patriarch had earned a tremendous reward in Heaven for all that he had done for the Son, preparing the way for his heavenly mission ... How could Jesus deny his gift of eternal bliss to the person whom he had obeyed so faithfully on earth? I believe that on seeing Jesus, Joseph would have told him: 'My Lord, remember that when you came down from Heaven I received you into my family and my home. When you appeared on the earth it was I who took you tenderly into my arms. Now take me into yours. Just as I once fed you and looked after you on earth, be so kind now as to lead me to eternal life'.*[8] Jesus would have been delighted to fulfil this wish.

A young fellow once asked the Founder of Opus Dei, St Josemaria Escrivá, about the exact location of the body of Saint Joseph. He responded: *His body is in Heaven, my son. It is in Heaven. Scripture tells us that many saints were resurrected when Our Lord overcame death. I truly believe that Saint Joseph was among that company.* To a similar question on another occasion, St Josemaria Escrivá answered: *Today is Saturday. Let us consider the Joyful Mysteries ... Let us contemplate the Fourth Mystery, the*

[7] Matt 27:52

[8] St Francis de Sales, *Sermon on St Joseph,* 7

Assumption of Our Lady. Tradition tells us that Saint Joseph died in the presence of the Blessed Virgin and Our Lord. Some years later, when Christ left his tomb alive in glory, Scripture relates that many saints were also resurrected to proceed with Christ to Heaven ... Doesn't it make sense that Jesus would have wanted Joseph at his side, the same man who had nurtured him as a father on earth?[9]

Today we might contemplate the Holy Patriarch with his glorious body in the company of Jesus and Mary. He is ready to intercede for us in our every need. *Fecit te Deus quasi patrem Regis et dominum universae domus eius.* God made you father of the King and lord of his home. Pray for us.[10]

25.3 Prayer to Saint Joseph for vocations.

Saint Bernardine of Siena has written: *Although it is not defined dogma, we are free to believe that Jesus honoured his adopted father in the same way as he has honoured his Blessed Mother. In the same way that Mary was to be assumed into Heaven, Jesus, it is thought, deigned to glorify Joseph on the day of the Resurrection. In this way all of the Holy Family – Jesus, Mary and Joseph – who lived together on earth would reign together in Heaven.*[11]

Theologians give several other reasons for the fittingness of this doctrine. The special dignity of Saint Joseph increased in accord with his singular fidelity to his vocation. The gift of glorification would be a further confirmation of this heroic loyalty. Jesus and Mary shared

---

[9] Quoted by L. M. Herran, *Devotion to St Joseph in the life and teachings of Monsignor Escrivá*

[10] cf *Divine Office, Solemnity of St Joseph,* Response to the Second Reading

[11] St Bernardine of Siena, *Homily 3 on St Joseph*

a great love for the Holy Patriarch. This love would have moved them to seek the glorification of Saint Joseph, rather than await the final judgment. The greatness of Joseph's holiness exceeds that of all the saints. It would be appropriate that God should reward him before the others. Due to his closeness to Jesus and Mary, his intimacy with the Redeemer and the Mother of Our Saviour, Joseph's relations in Heaven – these two – would surely have wanted to preserve him from corruption. As universal Patron of the Church, Joseph enjoys a special position among the faithful which could very well extend to the privilege of freedom from corruption.[12]

Saint Joseph fulfilled the mission which God had entrusted to him. His whole life was an unconditional gift to God for the good of the Holy Family and all people.[13] From his place in Heaven, he continues to have *a deep and lively interest in the concerns of mankind.*[14] Saint Joseph has a special concern for those who share his vocation to serve the Son of God in their professional work. Let us ask Saint Joseph that many people will discover their vocation to Christian holiness. We pray that our friends, colleagues and relations will respond generously to this great gift from God.

We pray to the Holy Patriarch that all Christians will be good instruments, well attuned to the Lord's call. The harvest is great, but the labourers are few in number.[15]

---

[12] cf B. Llamera, *op cit,* pp 305-306

[13] cf St John Paul II, Apostolic Exhortation, *Redemptoris custos,* 15 August 1989, 17

[14] St Paul VI, *Homily,* 19 March 1969

[15] cf Matt 9:37

THE SEVEN SUNDAYS OF SAINT JOSEPH
THE SEVENTH SUNDAY

26. THE FATHERLY INTERCESSION OF SAINT JOSEPH

26.1 The intercession of the saints.

The Church has taught on any number of occasions that the saints in Heaven offer to God for the benefit of the faithful the merits which they won while on earth. The Church has also recommended that people pray to the saints to make intercession before the Lord.[1] Saint Thomas has explained that the mediation of the saints is an appropriate way for God to share his mercy. In this way, God respects the natural order of things since his saints are, in fact, the people closest to him. This is why the intercession of the saints is by no means a sign of imperfection in God.[2] The saints partake in God's glory by helping those in need. They are collaborators with God, *above whom there is nothing more divine.*[3]

Even though the saints do not actually 'deserve' divine attention, they are able to win divine favour because of the merit gained by their holy lives. They ask for God's mercy by offering up their own past works and our good works also.[4] The saints are *able to help others because their prayers were heard by God during their lifetime.*[5] The

---

[1] cf Council of Trent, Session 25; Second Vatican Council, *Lumen gentium,* 49

[2] cf St Thomas, *Summa Theologiae,* q 72, a 2 c and ad 1

[3] cf *ibid,* a 1

[4] *ibid,* a 3

[5] *ibid,* a 4

degree to which a saint can be of help to us depends on the degree of his or her sanctity.[6] It also depends on how great a devotion we have to that saint, and whether *God wants to make manifest that person's sanctity.*[7] Certain saints are known to be powerful intercessors for particular intentions: to get someone who has gone astray to come back to God through the sacrament of Penance, to attend to family needs, to help in problems concerning work or in sickness.[8] According to Saint Thomas, the intercession of the saints *depends a great deal on the 'accidental' merit which they obtained in their lives. The saint who acquired extraordinary merit in sickness or in the execution of some particular task should have a special ability to help those who suffer from the same sickness or have to perform a similar task.*[9]

With regard to the intercession of Saint Joseph, Saint Teresa of Avila has written: *To other Saints our Lord seems to have given graces to succour men in some special necessity; but to this glorious Saint, as I know by experience, (He has given graces) to help us in all; and our Lord would have us understand that, as He was himself subject to him upon earth – for Saint Joseph, having the title of father, and being his guardian, could command him – so now in heaven He performs all his petitions.*[10] We should not fail to go to Saint Joseph for his help in everything that concerns us.

26.2 Going to Saint Joseph for our every need.

With the exception of the Blessed Virgin, Saint Joseph is the most powerful intercessor in Heaven by reason of his personal holiness in taking care of the Holy Family. Saint

---

[6] *ibid,* 1-2, q 114, a 4
[7] *ibid,* 2-2, q 83, a 11 ad 1 and 4
[8] *ibid,* q 72, a 2 ad 2
[9] B. Llamera, *Theology of St Joseph,* p 312
[10] St Teresa, *Life,* 6

Joseph's intercession has a universal character which applies to every problem, be it material or spiritual, and to every person without distinction. Saint Paul VI explained this intercession in these words: *A house lamp gives off a familiar and tranquil glow which is also intimate and confidential. It gives comfort in times of worry and separation ... So does the light of Saint Joseph diffuse its rays in the House of God which is the Church. He fills the House with the wonderful memories of the days when God became man for our sake. God lived under the protection of a simple craftsman from Nazareth. Saint Joseph is an incomparable example for us. He is the most blessed of saints because of his communion with Christ and Mary in service and in love.*[11]

By the example of their life in Nazareth Jesus and Mary invite us to seek Joseph's assistance. They frequently went to Joseph for his help in all kinds of needs. Their attitude and behaviour is a wonderful model for us to imitate. When *we go to Joseph for help we should have no fear at all. We ought to have a steadfast faith that what we are doing is most pleasing to God Almighty and the Queen of Angels.*[12] With the exception of God himself, Our Lady loved no one more than she loved Saint Joseph, her husband. Who can imagine the strength of Joseph's petition before Our Lady, Mediatrix of all graces? Spiritual authors have seen fit to make this comparison: *Christ is the one mediator before the Father, and the way to reach Christ is through Mary, his Mother. Similarly, the best way to reach Mary is through Saint Joseph. The ascending order is from Joseph to Mary, from Mary to Christ, from Christ to the Father.*[13]

---

[11] St Paul VI, *Homily,* 19 March 1966

[12] Isidoro de Isolano, *The Gifts of St Joseph*

[13] B. Llamera, *op cit,* p 315

The Church asks from Saint Joseph the same support and protection as he gave to the Holy Family in Nazareth.[14] The fatherly intercession of Saint Joseph extends to the universal Church, especially to those souls who seek sanctity in their ordinary work, to Christian families and to those who are near death.

I am sure Joseph knew how to lend a hand in many difficulties ... His skilled work was in the service of others, to brighten the lives of others in the town; and with a friendly word, a passing quip, he would restore confidence and happiness to those in danger of losing them.[15]

26.3 Perseverance.

The fatherly intercession of Saint Joseph in the Church is a prolongation of the authority he exercised over Jesus Christ, the head of the Church, and Mary, Mother of the Church. This is the reason why Saint Joseph has been declared *Patron of the Universal Church.*[16] That home in Nazareth contained all the elements of the nascent Church. It is fitting that *Joseph care for the Church in the same holy manner in which he watched over the Holy Family in Nazareth.*[17] Pope Leo XIII made this declaration during a period of great stress for the Church, the causes of which persist to the present day.[18] We seek Joseph's intercession whenever the Church is attacked or pushed to the sidelines in public life. The Popes have continuously encouraged devotion to Saint Joseph.[19]

---

[14] cf E. S. Gibert, *St Joseph, a Man of God,* Barcelona 1972

[15] St. J. Escrivá, *Christ is passing by,* 51

[16] cf Pius IX, Decree, *Quemadmodum Deus,* 8 December 1870; Apostolic Letter, *Inclytum Patriarcam,* 7 July 1871

[17] Leo XIII, Encyclical, *Quamquam pluries,* 15 August 1889

[18] cf St John Paul II, Apostolic Exhortation, *Redemptoris custos,* 15 August 1989, 31

[19] St Pius X, *Letter to Cardinal Lepicier,* 11 February 1908; Benedict XV, Brief, *Bonum sane,* 25 July 1920; Pius XI, *Address,* 21 April 1926

Saint Joseph's mission extends to the end of time. His fatherhood applies to each one of us. Saint Teresa of Avila has written: *Would that I could persuade all men to have devotion to this glorious Saint; for I know by long experience what blessings he can obtain for us from God. I have never known any one who was really devoted to him, and who honoured him by particular services, who did not visibly grow more and more in virtue; for he helps in a special way those souls who commend themselves to him. It is now some years since I have always on his feast asked him for something, and I have always received it. If the petition be in any way amiss, he directs it aright for my greater good.*

If I could write what I wanted, I should be delighted to go on and on almost interminably and down to every last tiny detail about the favours this great saint has granted to me and to others ... Listen. For the Love of God. Anyone who doesn't believe me has only to try out what I say for himself. He will find out from experience what enormous advantages come from commending himself to this glorious Patriarch and having devotion to him always. Those who practise prayer should have a tremendous devotion to him always. I simply don't know how anyone can think of the Queen of the Angels during the time she suffered so much with the Child Jesus without pouring out thanks to Saint Joseph for the way he helped them ...[20]

Even though Saint Joseph does not say a word in the Gospels, no one has ever been a better teacher. *In human life, Joseph was Jesus' master in their daily contact, full of refined affection, glad to deny himself in order to take better care of Jesus. Isn't that reason enough for us to consider this just man, this holy patriarch, in whom the faith of the old covenant bears fruit, as a master of interior*

---

[20] St Teresa, *op cit,* 6

life? Interior life is nothing but continual and direct conversation with Christ, so as to become one with him. And Joseph can tell us many things about Jesus.[21] Let us frequently have recourse to his intercession as we approach his feast. *Those souls most sensitive to the impulses of divine love have rightly seen in Joseph a brilliant example of the interior life.*[22] *Saint Joseph, protect us always. We pray that your spirit of peace, of interior silence, of work and prayer, of service to the Holy Church, will bring us life and happiness in union with our Most Blessed Mother. So we shall arrive at an abiding love for Jesus, Our Lord.*[23]

---

[21] St. J. Escrivá, *op cit,* 56
[22] St John Paul II, Apostolic Exhortation, *Redemptoris custos,* 27
[23] John XXIII, AAS, 53, 1961, p 262

19 MARCH

27. SAINT JOSEPH
Solemnity

The season of Lent is interrupted by the Solemnity of Joseph, Husband of Mary. With the exception of Our Lady, there is no greater saint in Heaven than Saint Joseph. This feast originated in the fifteenth century and was then extended to the whole Church in 1621. In 1847 Blessed Pius IX named Saint Joseph Patron of the Universal Church. Saint John XXIII had Saint Joseph's name included in the Roman Canon.

27.1 The promises of the Old Testament were realized in Jesus by means of Saint Joseph.

Behold, a faithful and prudent steward, whom the Lord set over his household.[1]

The household referred to in today's *Entrance Antiphon* is none other than the Holy Family of Nazareth. God entrusted this treasure to Saint Joseph, *his faithful servant,* who dedicated his entire life to their care. The Lord's household also can be understood as the Church, which likewise looks to Saint Joseph as a guardian and patron.

The *First Reading* brings to mind the ancient promises made by God to his chosen people, which were then passed down from generation to generation: the coming of a just and powerful King, the Good Shepherd who will lead his flock to verdant pastures,[2] the Redeemer who will save his people.[3] In this passage from the second book of Samuel

---

[1] *Entrance Antiphon*: Luke 12:42
[2] Ex 34:23
[3] Gen 3:15

God announces to David that the Messiah will arise from his descendants. The Messiah will found an everlasting kingdom. It is through Joseph that Jesus is the son of David. Christ is the fulfilment of the prophecies made from the time of Abraham.[4]

With the Incarnation, the 'promises' and 'figures' of the Old Testament become reality: places, persons, events and rites interrelate according to precise divine commands communicated by Angels and received by creatures who are particularly sensitive to the voice of God. Mary is the Lord's humble servant, prepared from eternity for the task of being the Mother of God. Joseph is the one ... who has the responsibility of looking after the Son of God's 'ordained' entry into the world in accordance with divine dispositions and human laws. All of the so-called 'private' or 'hidden' life of Jesus is entrusted to Joseph's guardianship.[5]

The Gospel of today's Mass places a special emphasis on the fact that Joseph was a member of the House of David: *Jacob was the father of Joseph the husband of Mary, of whom Jesus was born, who is called Christ.*[6] Joseph is the Patriarch of the New Testament.

Here was an ordinary man to whom God granted extraordinary graces. Joseph was to fulfil a most singular mission in the salvific design of God. He experienced indescribable joys along with the trials of doubt and suffering. We recall his perplexity at the mystery of Mary's conception, at the extreme of material poverty in Bethlehem, at the prophecies of Simeon in the Temple, at the hurried flight into Egypt, at the difficulties of having to

---

[4] *Second Reading*: Rom 4:18

[5] St John Paul II, Apostolic Exhortation, *Redemptoris custos,* 15 August 1989, 8

[6] Matt 1:16

live in a foreign land, at the return from Egypt and the threat posed by Archelaus. Joseph proved himself always faithful to the will of God. He showed himself always ready to set aside his own human plans and considerations.

The explanation for this remarkable fidelity is that Jesus and Mary were at the centre of Joseph's life. *Joseph's self-giving is an interweaving of faithful love, loving faith and confident hope. His feast is thus a good opportunity for us to renew our commitment to the Christian calling God has given each of us.*

When you sincerely desire to live by faith, hope and love, the renewal of your commitment is not a matter of picking up again something neglected. When there really is faith, hope and love, renewal means staying in God's hands, despite our personal faults, mistakes and defects. It is a confirmation of our faithfulness. Renewing our commitment means renewing our fidelity to what God wants of us: it means expressing our love in deeds.[7]

We ask the Holy Patriarch to help us to fulfil the will of God in everything. We pray that he will show us how to live out our commitments joyfully and without reservations. Our example will enlighten many others as to the true pathway to Heaven.

27.2 The fidelity of the Holy Patriarch to his vocation.

Well done, good and faithful servant. Come, share your master's joy.[8] Saint Joseph would have heard these words of our *Communion Antiphon* upon his arrival in heaven. One day the Lord will say these blessed words to each one of us if we persevere in our Christian vocation. This will happen despite our many stumbles and falls because we shall have had the humility and the courage to begin again.

---

[7] St. St. J. Escrivá, *Christ is passing by,* 43
[8] *Communion Antiphon*: Matt 25:21

Fidelity to the Lord is what gives meaning to our lives, no matter what our age or personal circumstances. We know that our earthly happiness depends upon our faith. Saint Joseph had his share of difficulties, but he always relied upon the help of God. He refused to deviate from his vocation. *What else was his life if not a total dedication to the service for which he had been called? Husband to Our Lady, legal father to Jesus ... He devoted his life to the attention he paid them, dedicated to fulfilling his vocation – the mission to which he had been called. As a dedicated man is one who does not belong to himself, Joseph ceased to be concerned for himself from the moment when, enlightened by an angel in that first dream, he fully accepted God's designs for him. Receiving Mary as his spouse he began to live for those who had been placed in his care. God had entrusted him with his family, and Joseph did not disappoint him. God sought support in him, and he stood firm in every instance.*[9] God counts on us for many great things. We cannot let him down.

Let us tell the Lord that we want to be unswervingly loyal to what He wants of us just as Joseph was in his life. We should examine ourselves as to how we can be more faithful in our personal conduct, our apostolate and our professional work.

27.3 Our perseverance.

We pray, O Lord, that, just as Saint Joseph served with loving care your Only Begotten Son, born of the Virgin Mary, so we may be worthy to minister with a pure heart at your altar.[10]

We have been preparing for this solemnity by means of the devotion of the Seven Sundays of Saint Joseph. It is a good time for us to reflect on the teaching of Saint

[9] F. Suarez, *Joseph of Nazareth,* pp 215-216
[10] *Prayer over the Offerings*

Thomas concerning divine vocation: *To those whom God calls for his work, God provides the necessary preparation and graces, so that they will be the ideal instruments for that work.*[11] God's fidelity is made manifest in an infinite variety of ways to help us fulfil our commitments. Saint Joseph responded immediately to the countless graces which he received from God.

We ought often to reflect in our prayer on the certainty that the Lord will never let us down. He awaits our mature response, whether it be in youth, in adulthood, in old age, in good times or in bad.

It is possible that we may not *feel* God's presence at times, perhaps for a lengthy period. We may not feel drawn to God because we are full of ourselves. In this kind of situation fidelity to God requires interior recollection. Fidelity requires personal effort to overcome egoism and to begin again a life of prayer.

God wants us to be full of love, alert, brimming over with initiatives. The heart of the Holy Patriarch was always alive with joy, even in the most difficult of trials. We ought to ensure that our journey to God is as new and original as love itself.

Today we ask Saint Joseph to give us a share in his youthful spirit. We ask this of him for the sake of those around us who might find thereby a road to Jesus.

---

[11] St Thomas, *Summa Theologiae,* 3, q 27, a 4, c

25 March

28. THE ANNUNCIATION OF THE LORD

Solemnity

On today's feast the Church celebrates the mystery of the Incarnation and, at the same time, the vocation of Our Lady. It was her faithful response to the angel's message, her *fiat,* that began the work of Redemption.

In the oldest Christian calendars this Solemnity is referred to as a feast of the Lord. Nevertheless, the texts do make special reference to Our Lady. For many centuries this has been considered a Marian feast. The Church has traditionally held that there is a close connection between Eve, the mother of mankind, and Mary, the new Eve, Mother of redeemed humanity.

The setting of this feast day, March 25th, corresponds to Christmas. In addition, there is an ancient tradition that the creation of the world and the commencement and conclusion of the Redemption all happened to coincide at the vernal equinox.

28.1 True God and true man.

But when the fullness of time came, God sent his Son, born of a woman.[1]

As the greatest proof of his love for us, God had his only Son become man to save us from our sins. In this way Jesus merited for us the dignity of becoming children of God. His arrival signalled *the fullness of time.* Saint Paul puts it quite literally that Jesus was *born of a woman.*[2] Jesus did not come to earth as a spirit. He truly became man, like one of us. He received his human nature from Our Lady's immaculate womb. Today's feast, therefore, is

[1] *Divine Office,* cf Gal 4:4-5

[2] cf *The Navarre Bible,* Romans and Galatians, note to Gal 4:4

really in honour of Jesus and Mary. This is why Fr Luis de Granada has pointed out: *It is reasonable to consider, first and foremost, the purity and sanctity of the Woman whom God chose 'ab aeterno' to give form to his humanity.*

When God decided to create the first man, he first took care to create a fitting environment for him, which was the Garden of Eden. It makes sense, then, that when God made ready to send his Son, the Christ, he likewise prepared for him a worthy environment, namely, the body and soul of the Blessed Virgin.[3]

As we consider the significance of this Solemnity, we find Jesus very closely united to Mary. When the Blessed Virgin said Yes, freely, to the plans revealed to her by the Creator, the divine Word assumed a human nature: a rational soul and a body, which was formed in the most pure womb of Mary. The divine nature and the human were united in a single Person: Jesus Christ, true God and, thenceforth, true Man; the only-begotten and eternal Son of the Father and, from that moment on, as Man, the true son of Mary. This is why Our Lady is the Mother of the Incarnate Word, the second Person of the Blessed Trinity who has united our human nature to himself for ever, without any confusion of the two natures. The greatest praise we can give to the Blessed Virgin is to address her loud and clear by the name that expresses her very highest dignity: Mother of God.[4] How many times have we repeated those sweet words: Holy Mary, Mother of God, pray for us sinners ... ! How many times have we meditated upon this, the first Joyful Mystery of the Holy Rosary!

28.2 The ultimate expression of divine love.

And the Word was made flesh, and dwelt among us.[5]

---

[3] Fr. Luis de Granada, *Life of Jesus Christ,* I
[4] St. J. Escrivá, *Friends of God,* 274
[5] John 1:14

Down through the ages, saints and theologians have endeavoured to 'read God's mind' with regard to the Incarnation. It was not necessary that the Son of God should become man, not even for the sake of the Redemption. As Saint Thomas Aquinas has observed: *God could have restored human nature in any number of ways.*[6] The Incarnation is the ultimate expression of God's love for mankind. The best reason for the Incarnation seems to lie in the awesome immensity of this divine love. *For God so loved the world that he gave his only-begotten Son ...*[7] By this lowering of himself, God has made it easier for man to speak with him. The whole history of salvation represents God's reaching out to his beloved creatures. The Catholic Faith reveals to humanity all the goodness, mercy and love that God has for us.

Right from the beginning of time God has been encouraging man to draw close to him. The Incarnation is the culmination of this message. Today's feast celebrates the moment in history when *Emmanuel, God with us,* acquired his human realization. From this moment on, the only-begotten Son would be a man like us. And he would remain human forever. The Incarnation was not a temporary condition. Jesus Christ, the Word made flesh, would be perfect God and perfect man to all eternity. This is the great mystery we may well find overwhelming: God in his infinite love has taken man seriously. Due to his infinite love, God has given man the opportunity to respond to Christ, a full-fledged member of the human race. *Remembering that 'the Word became flesh,' that is, that the Son of God became man, we must become conscious of how great each man has become through this mystery, through the Incarnation of the Son of God! Christ,*

---

[6] St Thomas, *Summa Theologiae,* 3, q 1, a 2
[7] John 3:16

in fact, was conceived in the womb of Mary and became man to reveal the eternal love of the Creator and Father and to make known the dignity of each one of us.[8]

As a result of many religious controversies over the centuries, the Church has sought to define the truths relating to the Incarnation. She has been zealous in this regard because she realizes that to defend the truth about Christ is to defend the truth about the human person. *He Who is 'the image of the invisible God' (Col 1:15), is Himself the perfect man. To the sons of Adam He restores the divine likeness which had been disfigured from the first sin onward. Since human nature as He assumed it was not annulled, by that very fact it has been raised up to a divine dignity in our respect too. For by His incarnation the Son of God has united Himself in some fashion with every man. He worked with human hands, He thought with a human mind, acted by human choice and loved with a human heart. Born of the Virgin Mary, He has truly been made one of us, like us in all things except sin.*[9] *O wonder of your humble care for us! O love, O charity beyond all telling, to ransom a slave you gave away your Son! O truly necessary sin of Adam, destroyed completely by the Death of Christ!*[10] Let us give thanks for this wonderful gift on today's feast. We give thanks to God through his Mother, because *Mary, as God's collaborator in giving a human nature to his eternal Son, was the instrument that linked Jesus with the whole of humanity.*[11]

28.3 The impact of the Incarnation on our life.

The Incarnation should have a pronounced and dramatic impact on our life. This event is the central

---

[8] St John Paul II, *Angelus at the Sanctuary of Jasna Gora,* 5 June 1979
[9] Second Vatican Council, *Gaudium et spes,* 22
[10] *Roman Missal,* Hymn *Exsultet* from the Easter Vigil Mass
[11] St John Paul II, *Address,* 28 January 1987

moment of human history. Without Christ, life has no meaning. *Christ the Redeemer 'fully reveals man to himself'.*[12] It is only through Christ that we will come to comprehend our inner self and everything that matters most to us: the hidden value of pain and of work well-done, the authentic peace and joy which surpass natural feelings and life's uncertainties, the delightful prospect of our supernatural reward in our eternal homeland. *Unceasingly contemplating the whole of Christ's mystery, the Church knows with all the certainty of faith that the Redemption that took place through the cross has definitively restored his dignity to man and given back meaning to this life in the world, a meaning that was lost to a considerable extent because of sin.*[13]

The human testimony of the Son of God teaches us that all earthly realities ought to be loved and offered up to Heaven. Christ has transformed the human condition into a pathway to God. Consequently, the Christian's struggle for perfection takes on a profoundly positive character. This struggle has nothing to do with snuffing out one's humanity so that the divine might shine out instead. Sanctity does not necessitate total separation from worldly affairs. For it is not human nature that opposes God's will, but sin and the effects of original sin which have so severely damaged our souls. Our struggle to become like Christ brings with it a life-long battle against whatsoever degrades our humanity – egoism, envy, sensuality, a critical spirit ... The authentic struggle for sanctity involves every aspect of the proper development of human personality: professional work, human virtues, social virtues, love for everything that is truly human ...

In the same way as the humanity of Christ is not

[12] *idem,* Encyclical, *Redemptor hominis,* 4 March 1979, 11
[13] *ibid,* 10

effaced by his divinity, so it is that through the Incarnation the human condition preserves its integrity and finds its final end. *'Et ego, si exaltatus fuero a terra, omnia traham ad meipsum'. And I, if I be lifted up from the earth, will draw all things to myself.*[14] *Through his incarnation, through his work at Nazareth and his preaching and miracles in Judaea and Galilee, through his death on the cross and through his resurrection, Christ is the centre of the universe, the firstborn and Lord of all creation.*

Our task as Christians is to proclaim this kingship of Christ, announcing it through what we say and do. Our Lord wants men and women of his own in all walks of life. Some he calls away from society, asking them to give up involvement in the world, so that they remind the rest of us by their example that God exists. To others he entrusts the priestly ministry. But he wants the vast majority to stay right where they are, in all earthly occupations in which they work: the factory, the laboratory, the farm, the trades, the streets of the big cities and the trails of the mountains.[15] This is the context of our vocation.

Let us finish our meditation by going to the Mother of Jesus who is also our Mother. *O Mary! Today by your conception you have brought our Saviour to the world ... O Mary, blessed be you among all women for ever ... Today the Godhead has become one with our humanity in such a permanent bond that nothing can break it – not our ingratitude, not even death itself.*[16] Blessed are you!

---

[14] John 12:32
[15] St. J. Escrivá, *Christ is passing by,* 105
[16] St Catherine of Siena, *Elevaciones,* 15

25 March

29. THE VOCATION OF OUR LADY

29.1 Our Lady's example.

When Christ came into the world, He said, 'Lo, I have come to do thy Will, O God'.[1]

The Annunciation and the Incarnation of the Son of God is a most wonderful and extraordinary event. It is the mystery of the enormous love God has for mankind; it is, too, the mystery which has had the greatest bearing on the whole of mankind's history. God becomes man once and for all! Even so, this event took place in Nazareth, a tiny village in a country that was scarcely known to the outside world of its day. There, *God was born in the perfect and entire nature of man. He was whole in what related to human nature. At one and the same time He preserved the totality of the essence that is proper to him, and He assumed the totality of our human essence ... in order to restore that totality.*[2]

Saint Luke tells us very simply about this tremendously important event: *In the sixth month the angel Gabriel was sent from God to a city of Galilee named Nazareth to a virgin betrothed to a man whose name was Joseph, of the house of David; and the virgin's name was Mary.*[3] All down the ages popular piety has represented Mary as being recollected in prayer when she receives the angel's salutation: *Hail, full of grace, the Lord is with you!* Our Mother is disturbed at these words, but her being disturbed

---

[1] Heb 10:5-7
[2] *Divine Office, Second Reading,* St Leo the Great, *Letter 28, to Flavian,* 3
[3] Luke 1:26-37

does not render her inactive. She knows the Scriptures well; she has been instructed in them, as were all good Jews from their earliest years, but above all she has the clarity of mind and the perceptiveness given her by her matchless faith, her deep love and the gifts of the Holy Spirit. This is why she understands the message of God's angel. Her soul is fully open to what God is about to ask of her. The angel hastens to reassure her and reveals to her God's plan for her – her vocation: *You have found favour with God,* he says, *you will conceive in your womb and bear a son, and you shall call his name Jesus. He will be called great, and will be called the Son of the Most High; and the Lord God will give to him the throne of his father David, and he will reign over the house of Jacob forever; and of his kingdom there will be no end.*

The messenger greets Mary as 'full of grace'; he calls her this as if it were her real name. He does not call her by her proper earthly name 'Myriam' (Mary), but by this new name: 'Full of grace'. What does this name mean? Why does the archangel address the Virgin of Nazareth in this way?

In the language of the Bible 'grace' means a special gift, which according to the New Testament has its source precisely in the Trinitarian life of God himself, of God who is love (cf 1 John 4:8).[4] Mary is called 'full of grace' because this name expresses her true being. Whenever God changes a person's name or gives him or her an extra one, He destines him or her to something new, or reveals to that person his or her true mission in the history of salvation. Mary is called 'full of grace', most highly favoured, because of her divine Motherhood.

The angel's announcement revealed to Mary her task in the world, the key to her whole existence. The Annunciation was for her a most perfect light that filled the whole

---

[4] St John Paul II, *Redemptoris Mater,* 25 March 1987, 8

of her life and made her fully aware of her exceptional role in the history of mankind. *Mary is definitively introduced into the mystery of Christ through this event.*[5]

When they say the *Angelus* each day, many Christians throughout the world remind our Mother of this moment, the importance of which, for her and for the whole of mankind, no words can describe. We remind her of it too, when we consider the first joyful mystery of the Rosary. We should try to enter into the scene and to contemplate Our Lady as with loving piety she embraces God's holy Will. *The scene of the Annunciation is a very lovely one. How often have we meditated on this! Mary is recollected in prayer. She is using all her senses and her faculties to speak to God. It is in prayer that she comes to know the divine Will. And with prayer she makes it the life of her life. Do not forget the example of the Virgin Mary.*[6]

29.2 I delight to do thy Will, O my God.[7]

The most Holy Trinity had traced out a plan for Our Lady, a destiny that was unique and quite exceptional: she was to be the Mother of God-made-man. But God asks Mary for her free acceptance. She does not doubt the angel's words, as Zachary had done; however, she points out the incompatibility between her decision to live perpetual virginity (which God himself had placed in her heart), and the conceiving of a son. It is then that the angel announces to her in clear and sublime terms that she is to become a mother without losing her virginity:[8] *The Holy Spirit will come upon you, and the power of the Most High will overshadow you; therefore the Child to be born will be called Holy, the Son of God.*

---

[5] St John Paul II, *loc cit*
[6] St. J. Escrivá, *Furrow,* 481
[7] *Responsorial Psalm,* Ps 39:7
[8] cf M. D. Philippe, *The Mystery of Mary,* Madrid, 1986

Mary listens to these words and ponders them in her heart. There is no resistance in her intellect or in her heart; everything in her is open to the divine Will, without any restriction or limitation. This abandonment of hers to God is what makes Mary's soul *good soil,* capable of receiving the divine seed. *Ecce ancilla Domini* ... behold the handmaid of the Lord, let it be done to me according to your word. Our Lady joyfully agrees to having no will or desire other than that of her Lord and Master, who from that moment on is also her Son – who has been made man in her most pure womb. She surrenders herself joyfully and freely without setting any limits or conditions. *Thus the daughter of Adam, Mary, consenting to the word of God, became the Mother of Jesus. Committing herself wholeheartedly and impeded by no sin to God's saving Will, she devoted herself totally, as a handmaid of the Lord, to the Person and work of her Son, under and with him, serving the mystery of redemption, by the grace of almighty God. Rightly, therefore, the Fathers of the Church see Mary not merely as passively engaged by God, but as freely co-operating in the work of man's salvation through faith and obedience.*[9]

Mary's vocation is the perfect example for any vocation. We understand our own life and the events that encompass it in the light of our own calling. It is in our endeavour to fulfil this divine plan that our way to Heaven and our own human and supernatural fulfilment lie.

Vocation is not the choice we make for ourselves so much as that which God makes of us through the thousand and one events in which we are involved. We need to know how to interpret these circumstances with faith, and with a heart that is at once pure and upright. *You did not choose me, but I chose you.*[10] *Every vocation, every existence, is in*

[9] Second Vatican Council, *Lumen gentium,* 56
[10] John 15:16

itself a grace that encloses within it many others; it is a grace, a gift, that is given to us, that is bestowed on us without our having deserved it, without being evoked by any merit of ours, and with no right to it on our part. It is not necessary that the vocation, the call to fulfil the plan of God, the assigned mission, be great or splendid. It is enough that God has wanted to employ us in his service, that He wants us to aid him, that He trusts in our co-operation. The fact that He wants our co-operation is in itself so extraordinary and magnificent, that an entire life spent in thanksgiving is not enough to repay him for such an honour.[11]

It will please God very much if we thank him today for the many times he has given us light by which to see the path along which he is calling us. We should thank him through his most holy Mother, who corresponded so faithfully to what God asked of her.

29.3 *Ne timeas ...*

Do not be afraid. This injunction is very much at the root of what constitutes a vocation. Man, in fact, is afraid. He is afraid not only of being called to the priesthood but also of being called to live his life with all the obligations that this brings with it, whether in work or in marriage. This fear denotes an immature sense of responsibility. We have to overcome this fear and take on our responsibilities in a way that is mature. We have to accept God's call. We have to listen to that call, to take it upon ourselves and ponder it according to our lights. We have to reply: Yes, yes! *Do not be afraid.* Do not be afraid, for you have found grace. Do not be afraid of life. Do not be afraid of becoming a mother. Do not be afraid of getting married. Do not be afraid of becoming a priest, for you have found grace. This certainty, this awareness of our vocation helps

[11] F. Suarez, *Mary of Nazareth*

us just as it helped Mary. Indeed, *Heaven and earth await your 'Yes', O most pure virgin.* These beautiful and well-known words were Saint Bernard's. He awaits your 'Yes' Mary. He awaits your 'Yes', mother about to have a child. He awaits your 'Yes', O man about to assume some personal, social or family responsibility ...

Yes was Mary's answer. It is the reply of a mother, the reply of a young man. It is a 'yes' for the whole of her or his life.[12] It is a reply by which we joyfully commit ourselves.

Mary's reply *fiat,* is rather more final than a simple 'yes'. It is the complete surrender of her will to what God wanted of her at that moment, and for the whole of her life. This *fiat* will reach its culmination on Calvary, when, standing beside the Cross, she offers herself up with her Son.

The 'yes' that God asks of each one of us, whatever our path in life may be, lasts for the whole of our lives. Sometimes it will be our reply to small occurrences, at other times to larger, more important events. It will be our reply to each call that God makes, and which leads successively to the next. Our 'yes' to Jesus leads us not to think too much about ourselves. It should lead us to keep our hearts alert so that we may be attentive to the voice of God, who tells us who belong to him which is the path He has traced out for us. As we lovingly respond to his call we should see how our freedom and God's Will mingle in perfect harmony.

Let us ask Our Lady today for a great and true desire to perceive our own vocation in greater depth and for light so as to correspond to the successive calls God makes to us. Let us ask her to enable us to give a prompt and firm reply on each occasion. The only thing that can fill our lives and give them their full meaning is our vocation.

---

[12] St John Paul II, *Address,* 25 March 1982

25 April

30. SAINT MARK THE EVANGELIST

Mark, although he had a Roman name, was Jewish by birth and was also known by his Hebrew name John. Although not one of the twelve Apostles, it is more than likely that he knew Jesus personally. Many ecclesiastical writers see a sort of hidden signature of Mark in his Gospel, in the episode of the young man who let go the sheet and fled away at Jesus' arrest in Gethsemane: it may be significant that Mark is the only Evangelist who mentions the incident. This tallies with the fact that he was the son of a woman named Mary, who seems to have been a wealthy widow in whose house the first Jerusalem Christians used to meet. According to an ancient tradition this house was in fact the Cenacle, the place where Our Lord celebrated the Last Supper and instituted the Blessed Eucharist.

Mark was a cousin of Saint Barnabas; he travelled with Saint Paul on his first missionary journey and was with him at the hour of his death. In Rome he was also a disciple of Saint Peter. In his Gospel he expounded faithfully, under the inspiration of the Holy Spirit, the teaching of the Prince of the Apostles. According to an ancient tradition mentioned by Saint Jerome, after the martyrdom of Saints Peter and Paul under the emperor Nero, Saint Mark went to Alexandria, whose Church claims him as its evangelizer and first bishop. In the year 825 his relics were transferred from Alexandria to Venice, where he is now venerated as Patron of that city.

30.1 Saint Mark, Saint Peter's co-worker.

From his early youth Saint Mark belonged to that group of first Christians of Jerusalem who had lived with Our Lady and the Apostles, all of whom he knew well. His mother was one of the first women to provide for Jesus and the Twelve out of her own means. Mark was also a cousin of Barnabas, one of the chief figures of those first days and the man who initiated him in the task of spreading the

Gospel. Mark went with Paul and Barnabas on their first apostolic journey,[1] but on arriving in Cyprus he seemingly felt that he was unable to carry on any further, for at that point he left them and went back to Jerusalem.[2] Paul appears to have been quite disgusted at Mark's inconstancy, to the extent that when, later on, Barnabas and he were planning their second journey, Barnabas wanted to bring Mark with them again but Paul would not hear of it because of the way he had let them down on the previous journey. The argument between Paul and Barnabas waxed so intense that they eventually went their separate ways and undertook separate apostolic missions.

About ten years later we find Mark in Rome, this time helping Peter, who refers to him as *my son Mark,*[3] thereby testifying to a long-standing close relationship. At that time Mark was acting as interpreter for the Prince of the Apostles, and this provided him with a privileged vantage-point which we see reflected in the Gospel he wrote a few years later. Although Saint Mark doesn't provide us with a record of any of the Master's great discourses, he makes up for it by giving us a particularly vivid description of the events of Jesus' life with his disciples. In his accounts we find ourselves once more in those little towns on the shores of the Sea of Galilee; we can sense the hubbub of the crowds that follow Jesus, we can almost converse with the inhabitants of those places and can contemplate Christ's wonderful deeds and the spontaneous reactions of the Twelve. In a word, we find ourselves witnessing the events of the Gospel as if we were actually there in the throng. Through his vivid descriptions the Evangelist manages to imprint on our souls something of the irresistible yet

[1] cf Acts 13:5-13
[2] cf Acts 13:13
[3] 1 Pet 5:13

reassuring fascination that Jesus exercised on people, and which the Apostles themselves experienced in their life with the Master. Saint Mark in effect gives us a faithful account of Saint Peter's most intimate recollections of his Master: with the passage of the years his memories had not grown dim, but became ever more profound and perceptive, more penetrating and more fond. It can be said that Mark's message is the living mirror of Saint Peter's preaching.[4]

Saint Jerome tells us that *Mark, the disciple and interpreter of Peter, wrote down his Gospel at the request of the brethren living in Rome, according to what he had heard Peter preach. And Peter himself, having heard it, approved it with his authority to be read in the Church.*[5] This was without doubt Mark's principal mission in life – to transmit Peter's teachings faithfully. What a lot of good he has done right down the centuries! We really have to thank him today for the love he put into his work and for his fidelity to the inspiration of the Holy Spirit! His feast is also a good opportunity to consider how well and how lovingly we do our daily Gospel reading, which is God's Word directed to us personally. We can also ask ourselves how often we act out the role of the Prodigal Son, or make our own that prayer of blind Bartimaeus: *Domine, ut videam!* Lord, let me see; or the prayer of the leper: *Domine, si vis, potes me mundare!* Lord, if you will, you can make me clean! How often have we felt in the depths of our soul that Christ is looking at us and inviting us to follow him more closely, perhaps asking us to overcome a habit that separates us from him, or, like faithful disciples, to be more charitable with those we find it difficult to get on with?

---

[4] cf *The Navarre Bible,* Introduction, St Mark, p.60
[5] St Jerome, *De script. eccl.*

30.2 To be good instruments of God we always have to be ready to make a new beginning.

Mark spent a number of years in Rome where, as well as assisting Peter, we also find him collaborating with Paul in his ministry.[6] So the man for whom Paul could find no use for on his second missionary journey is now *a comfort*[7] and a faithful companion for him. Later still, around the year 66, the Apostle writes to Timothy: *Get Mark, and bring him with you, for he is a great help to me.*[8] The Cyprus incident, which at the time seemed to loom so large, is now completely forgotten. Rather is it the case now that Paul and Mark are friends and collaborators in the all-important venture of extending Christ's Kingdom. It is indeed a great example of how we should never write people off conclusively, and a wonderful lesson, should we ever need one, on how to reconstruct a friendship that appears to have been ruined forever!

The Church proposes Saint Mark to us today as a model. It can be a great source of hope and consolation to contemplate the life of this holy Evangelist, because in spite of our weaknesses we can trust like him in divine grace and in the assistance of our Mother the Church. Our defeats and our acts of cowardice, be they small or great, have to help us to be more humble, to unite us more closely with Jesus and to draw from him the strength we find lacking in ourselves.

Our imperfections should not cause us to turn away from God or to abandon our apostolic mission, even though at times it may be true that we have failed to respond properly to God's grace, or that we have wavered when we were being relied upon not to. In these and other

[6] cf Philem 24
[7] Col 4:10-11
[8] 2 Tim 4:11

circumstances, if they occur, we should not be taken aback, because, as Saint Francis de Sales says, *there is nothing surprising about the fact that sickness is sick, or that weakness is weak, or that wretchedness is wretched. Nevertheless, detest with all your strength the offence you did to God, and with confidence in his mercy follow courageously the path of virtue you had forsaken.*[9]

Failures and acts of cowardice are important and that is why we turn to Our Lord asking his pardon and help. But precisely because He trusts us and because we can count on receiving grace anew, we ought to begin again immediately and make up our minds to be more faithful in future. With Our Lord's help we learn to draw good from our weaknesses, especially when the enemy, who never rests, tries to dishearten us and get us to give up the struggle. Jesus wants us to be his in spite of any previous history of weakness we might have had.

30.3 The apostolic mandate.

Go into all the world, and proclaim the Gospel to every creature,[10] we read in the Entrance Antiphon of today's Mass. This is the apostolic mandate recorded by Saint Mark. Further on, the Evangelist, moved by the Holy Spirit, testifies to the fact that this command of Christ was already being fulfilled when he was writing his Gospel: the Apostles *went forth and preached everywhere, while the Lord worked with them and confirmed the message by the signs that attended it.*[11] These are the closing words of his Gospel.

Saint Mark was faithful to the apostolic mandate he had so often heard Peter preach: *Go into all the world.* He himself, personally and through his Gospel, was an

---

[9] St Francis de Sales, *Introduction to the Devout Life,* 3, 9
[10] *Entrance Antiphon*: Mark 16:15
[11] Mark 16:20

effective leaven in his own time, as we ought to be too in ours. If in the face of his first reverse he had not reacted humbly and energetically, perhaps we would now not have the treasure of Jesus' words and deeds on which we have so often meditated, and many men and women would never have known, through him, that Jesus is the Saviour of mankind.

Mark's mission, like that of the Apostles, like the mission of evangelizers of all times, and like the example of every Christian who tries to live up to his or her vocation, was certainly not an easy one, as we can see from his martyrdom. He must have had many wonderful experiences as well as his fair share of opposition, weariness and danger in following Our Lord's footsteps.

We can thank God, and also the men and women of the Apostolic age, that the strength and joy of Christ have been handed down to us in our day. But every generation of Christians, and every individual, is called to receive the Gospel message and to pass it on in turn. God's grace is never lacking: *non est abbreviata manus Domini,*[12] the Lord's hand is not shortened. *The Christian knows that God works miracles, that he performed them centuries ago, and that he still works them now.*[13] Each one of us, with God's help, will work miracles in the souls of relatives, friends and acquaintances as long as we remain united to Christ through prayer.

---

[12] Is 59:1

[13] St. J. Escrivá, *Christ is passing by,* 50

27 April

31. OUR LADY OF MONTSERRAT

The veneration of Our Lady of Montserrat, Patroness of Catalonia, is extremely ancient, predating the seventh-century Arab invasion of Spain.

The statue was hidden at the time of the Islamic incursion and discovered in the ninth century, at which point a chapel was built to venerate it. King Wilfrid later founded a Benedictine abbey there.

At first the shrine was mainly regional in its appeal, but the miracles attributed to the Virgin of Montserrat became so numerous that news of them was carried far and wide, particularly by pilgrims travelling to Santiago de Compostela, so that the fame of the shrine spread well beyond the borders of Catalonia. So it is, for example, that in Italy one can find more than one hundred and fifty churches or chapels dedicated to Our Lady of Montserrat. Likewise, to her were dedicated some of the first churches to be founded in Mexico, Chile and Peru, not to mention numerous monasteries, towns, mountains and islands throughout the American continent that were named in her honour.

31.1 Marian shrines are 'divine signs'.

Many peoples shall come and say: 'Come, let us go up to the mountain of the Lord, to the house of the God of Jacob; that He may teach us his ways and that we may walk in his paths.' For out of Zion shall go forth the law, and the word of the Lord from Jerusalem.[1]

Countless pilgrims daily make their way to the innumerable shrines dedicated to Our Lady to discover God's ways or to undertake them anew, to find peace of soul and consolation in affliction. In these places of prayer, the Blessed Virgin makes the soul's encounter with her

[1] Is 2:3

Son easier and his presence more accessible. Every Marian shrine is a *permanent antenna of the Good News of salvation.*[2]

Today we celebrate the feast of Our Lady of Montserrat. For centuries countless Christians have had recourse to her intercession to keep them going when life was hard; there at her shrine they all found what they sought: peace of soul, God's call to a greater self-giving, a cure, or consolation in tribulation. The liturgy of this feast is centred on the mystery of the Visitation, *which is the first undertaking of the Blessed Virgin. Montserrat offers us, therefore, very worthwhile lessons for our journey as pilgrims,*[3] which is what we are. We must not forget that we are heading towards a specific and very well defined goal, namely, heaven. The end of a journey determines to a great extent what mode of transport to use, what baggage to bring, and what to provide along the way. The Blessed Virgin tells us not to carry too many things with us, not to wear clothes that are too heavy or cumbersome, and to walk briskly towards our Father's house. She reminds us that nothing on this earth is permanent, and that everything has to be subordinated to the completion of the journey, of which perhaps we have already covered a considerable portion.

Moreover, on the journey we have to do as Mary did when she went to visit her cousin Elizabeth: *In those days Mary arose and went with haste into the hill country, to a city of Judah.*[4] She went *with haste,* with a quick and joyful tread, just the way we too have to go on our path towards God. And we too must bear in our heart the joy and the spirit of service that Our Lady carried in hers.

---

[2] St John Paul II, *Address to rectors of Marian shrines,* 22 January 1981
[3] St John Paul II, *Address at Montserrat,* 17 November 1982
[4] Luke 1:39

31.2 Our Lady is our hope in all our needs.

Hope is the pilgrim's virtue; without it the wayfarer would simply give up or his pace would slacken and become lethargic. The Blessed Virgin is our hope because she encourages us continually to keep going, helps us overcome discouragement and sustains us with her maternal solicitude in moments of difficulty. Whenever we have recourse to her, be it simply through a short aspiration or a glance at her image, we feel ourselves strengthened. *Even without our realizing it, she always intervenes on our behalf and with a mother's tact, as she did with the young couple in Cana of Galilee. She did so too in an exemplary fashion in the mystery of the Visitation, which is indelibly outlined in the liturgy of Montserrat. And so,* says St John Paul II, *there echoes daily on this mountain the melodious accents of that greeting to Our Lady, Queen and Mother, repository of the hope that nourishes the pilgrim: Hail, our life, our sweetness and our hope.*[5] This is how we too can greet her frequently.

Our Lady was a source of joy, peace and hope to all who knew her during her life on earth. When, after Jesus' death, the world was plunged in utter darkness, on that first Holy Saturday only the light of Mary's hope shone forth undimmed; and so it was to her that the Apostles then turned for protection. Now, from heaven, *in her maternal charity she cares for the brethren of her Son, who still journey on earth surrounded by dangers and difficulties, until they are led into their blessed home.*[6] St Bernard explains very beautifully that the Virgin Mary is the *aqueduct* which receives divine grace from the fountain that springs from the Father's heart and distributes it to us. This stream of heavenly water descends upon mankind, *not*

---

[5] *ibid*

[6] Second Vatican Council, *Lumen gentium,* 62

all at once, but causes grace to fall drop by drop upon our parched hearts,[7] according to our needs and our desire to receive it.

The Blessed Virgin always comforts us, and is present throughout our earthly voyage whenever we need her protection from the stormy winds that blow; *she is a sure haven where no ship can be lost.*[8] We can never carry out routinely the devotional practices whereby we shelter daily under her protection – the Angelus, the Rosary, the three Hail Marys for purity, the scapular ... Whenever we go to seek her intercession in some shrine or place dedicated to her, she always receives us with special mercy and love.

31.3 Hope and divine filiation.

Because life's journey forever moves us onwards, and *we have no lasting city*[9] here below, it is an elementary measure of prudence to ask our Heavenly Mother for *provision of energies for the stages yet to come,*[10] for the distances that remain to be covered. One of the wayfarer's biggest enemies, and the one that most insidiously undermines his strength, is discouragement, the thought that the goal is beyond his reach. What causes discouragement is not just the presence of suffering and setback, but ceasing to aspire to holiness and, after a fall, not getting up again quickly and keeping on going.

The soul that hopes in Christ lives by that hope, and already carries within itself something of the joy of heaven, because hope is the source of joy and is what enables difficulties to be borne patiently.[11] Such a soul prays constantly and confidently at all times; it bears temptation,

---

[7] St Bernard, *Homily on Our Lady's Nativity,* 3-5

[8] cf St John Damascene, *Homily on Our Lady's Dormition*

[9] Heb 13:14

[10] St John Paul II, *Address at Montserrat*

[11] cf Col 1:11-24

pain and tribulation patiently; it works hard and effectively for the Kingdom of God, principally with those with whom it is in most direct contact. Hope leads to abandonment in God and to the conviction of our divine filiation, because the christian soul is aware that God knows and reckons with all the situations it has to undergo – old age, sickness, family or professional problems – and in every situation will provide it with all the help it needs to persevere. It is the Blessed Virgin who channels them and multiplies all those graces in the soul. She offers us her hand whenever we stumble or fall, helps us to be truly sorry for our sins and places in our heart the sentiments that moved the prodigal son's decision to return to his father's house.

Saint Teresa describes how, at the age of twelve, when her mother died, she realized what she had really lost: and *I went in my distress to an image of Our Lady, and with many tears besought her to be a mother to me. Though I did this in my simplicity, I believe it was of some avail to me; for whenever I have commended myself to this sovereign Virgin I have been conscious of her aid; and eventually she brought me back to herself.*[12] With this simplicity and confidence we have to go to Our Lady on her feasts and approach her through our invocations. Today we have recourse to Our Lady of Montserrat, asking her to teach us the way of hope, which is also the way of divine filiation. She, *seated upon her throne, with her Son in her lap, seems to want to enfold all her children with him in one embrace. Our spiritual pilgrimage consists precisely in achieving the certainty of our divine filiation. Our vocation is a fact; through the unfathomable predilection of the Father, she has made us sons in the Son: 'Blessed be the God and Father of our Lord Jesus Christ, who has blessed us in Christ with every spiritual blessing in the heavenly places,*

[12] St Teresa, *Life,* 1, 7

even as He chose us in him before the foundation of the world, that we should be holy and blameless before him. He destined us in love to be his sons through Jesus Christ, according to the purpose of his will, to the praise of his glorious grace which he freely bestowed upon us in the Beloved' (Eph 1:3-6).[13]

[13] St John Paul II, *Address at Montserrat*

29 April

32. SAINT CATHERINE OF SIENA

Born in Siena in 1347, Catherine Benincasa as a young girl joined the Dominican Third Order and was outstanding for her spirit of prayer and penance. Impelled by a great love for God, the Church and the Roman Pontiff, she worked tirelessly for the peace and unity of the Church in the difficult years of the Avignon captivity. She spent much time at the Papal court trying to persuade Pope Gregory XI to return to Rome, because that was the place from which Christ's Vicar on earth ought to rule the Church. 'If I die, let it be known that I die of passion for the Church,' she said a few days before her death, which took place on the 29th of April 1380.

She wrote very many letters, of which about four hundred have survived, along with some prayers and 'elevations', and just one book, the 'Dialogue', which contains her own account of her intimate conversations with Our Lord. She was canonized by Pius II and her veneration spread rapidly throughout the whole of Europe. Saint Teresa of Avila said that, after God, the person she felt most indebted to for her spiritual progress was Saint Catherine of Siena. Pius IX declared her the second patron saint of Italy (along with Saint Francis of Assisi), and in 1970 Saint Paul VI proclaimed her a doctor of the Church.

32.1 Love for the Church and the Pope, the 'sweet Christ on earth'.

Although she did not have the benefit of a very formal education (she learned to read and write as an adult), and was only thirty-three years old when she died, Saint Catherine of Siena led an extraordinarily full and fruitful life, *as if she was in a great hurry to reach the eternal tabernacle of the Blessed Trinity.*[1] She is a wonderful

[1] St John Paul II, *Homily in Siena,* 14 October 1980

example to us of love for the Church and for the Roman Pontiff, whom she described as *the sweet Christ on earth,*[2] and of forthrightness and courage in making herself heard by the men of her time.

At that time, which was a particularly troublesome one in the Church's history, the Popes reigned at Avignon, in the south of France; Rome, as the centre of Christianity, had been allowed to fall into decay. Our Lord made Saint Catherine see that it was necessary for the Popes to return to Rome in order to inaugurate the long-awaited and very urgent reform of Church life. To this end she prayed tirelessly, practised penance and wrote unceasingly to the Pope, to cardinals and to the various princes of Christendom.

Saint Catherine always professed unswerving obedience and love for the Roman Pontiff, of whom she wrote: *Anyone who refuses to obey the Christ on earth, who is in the place of Christ in heaven, does not participate in the fruit of the blood of the Son of God.*[3]

She continuously sent urgent appeals to cardinals, bishops and priests for the reform of the Church and christian living, and didn't shrink from taking them to task seriously, although always with great humility and respect for their dignity, because *they are ministers of the blood of Christ.*[4] It was principally to the Church's pastors that she addressed herself again and again, realizing that the spiritual health of their flock depended to a great extent on their own conversion and exemplary behaviour.

Today we ask Saint Catherine to enable us to rejoice with the joys of our Mother the Church and to suffer with

---

[2] St Catherine of Siena, *Letters,* Siena 1913, III, p.211

[3] *idem, Letter 207,* III, p.270

[4] cf St Paul VI, *Homily proclaiming St Catherine a Doctor of the Church,* 4 October 1970

her in her sorrows. Let us ask ourselves how hard we pray each day for her pastors, and how generously we offer mortifications and hours of work and bear patiently life's difficulties, all of which sacrifices help the Holy Father to carry the tremendous responsibility that God has placed on his shoulders. Let us also pray for her intercession, that 'the sweet Christ on earth' may never be short of trustworthy helpers.

I thought the comment on loyalty you had written to me was very appropriate to all those moments in history which the devil makes it his business to repeat: 'I carry with me every day in my heart, in my mind and on my lips, an aspiration: Rome!'[5] That one word – Rome – can help our daily presence of God, and serve as an expression of our unity with the Roman Pontiff and our prayer for him. Perhaps it will also help us to increase our love for the Church.

32.2 Saint Catherine offered her life for the Church.

Saint Catherine had an admirably feminine temperament,[6] at the same time displaying an unusual drive and energy, a feature somehow distinguishing those women who are capable of undergoing great sacrifices and of taking their place beside the Cross of Christ. She refused to tolerate any faintheartedness in the service of God. She was utterly convinced that when the salvation of souls was at stake being unduly tolerant or *understanding* with mediocrity was totally unacceptable, because it is in effect only a concession to laziness or cowardice. *Enough of all this soft soap!,* she cried out. *All it does is cause the members of Christ's Spouse to stink!*

Always fundamentally optimistic, she would not allow herself to become downhearted if, in spite of having done

---

[5] St. J. Escrivá, *Furrow,* 344
[6] cf St John Paul II, *Homily,* 29 April 1980

all she could, things did not work out as she had hoped. All her life long she had a profoundly serious and gentle manner. Her followers always remembered her radiant expression and her open gaze; spotlessly neat and well-groomed in her person, she was fond of flowers and loved to sing as she moved about. When an important person of the time went at a friend's insistence to interview her, he expected to meet a demure woman with downcast eyes and diffident manner, and was greatly surprised to find himself in the presence of a young lady who greeted him warmly with a welcoming smile, *as if he had been a brother returning from a long journey*.

Eventually the Pope did return to Rome, in 1377, but a year later he died. His successor's election marked the beginning of what is known to history as the Great Western Schism, an upheaval that caused tremendous division and suffering in the Church. Saint Catherine spoke and wrote to cardinals and kings, to princes and bishops, but all in vain. Utterly worn out and in great sorrow, she offered herself to God as a victim for the Church. One day in January 1380, as she was praying at Saint Peter's tomb, she experienced something that other saints too have shared: she felt upon her shoulders the immense weight of the Church. Her agony lasted just a few months. On the 29th of April, around midday, God called her to his glory. On her deathbed she directed to God this moving prayer: *O eternal God, receive the sacrifice of my life on behalf of the Mystical Body of Holy Church. I have nothing else to give, except what you have given me.*[7] A few days earlier she had told her confessor: *I assure you that, if I die, the sole cause of my death is the zeal and love for the Church which burns me up and consumes me.* Let us pray to her today for this incandescent love for our Mother the Church, which is

[7] St Catherine of Siena, *Letter 371,* V, pp.301-302

an inseparable concommitant of being close to Christ.

Our own times too are days of trial and sorrow for Christ's Mystical Body. *We have to ask the Lord with an unceasing clamour (cf Is 58:1) to shorten them, to look mercifully on his Church, and to grant once again his supernatural light to the souls of her shepherds and of all the faithful.*[8] Let us offer the thousand little incidents of everyday life for the welfare of Christ's Mystical Body. God will surely bless us for it, and Our Lady, *Mater Ecclesiae,* will pour out his grace generously upon us.

32.3 Making the truth known. Helping to shape public opinion.

Saint Catherine's example teaches us to speak forthrightly and courageously whenever matters affecting the Church, the Roman Pontiff or the good of souls are at stake. We will often have the serious obligation to defend the truth. In this we can learn a lot from Saint Catherine: she never gave way in the fundamentals, because she placed all her trust in God.

In the first reading of today's Mass, the Apostle Saint John says: *This is the message we have heard from him and proclaim to you, that God is light, and in him is no darkness at all.*[9] This is where the first Christians, and the saints of all times got their strength: what they proclaimed was not some doctrine of their own creation, but rather the message of Christ, handed on from each generation to the next. The power of this Truth transcends the changing fashions and attitudes of mankind's history. We have to learn to speak about the things of God more and more naturally and straightforwardly, but at the same time with all the conviction that Christ has placed in our hearts. The Roman Pontiffs have often denounced the systematic

---

[8] St. J. Escrivá, *In Love with the Church,* 28

[9] 1 John 1:5

attempt by certain sectors of the media to misrepresent the truth by passing over in silence the sufferings of Catholics for the Faith, or their noble endeavours for good. Faced with this situation, each one of us in his or her place in society has to act as a mouthpiece for the truth. Some Popes have described the playing down of the contribution of Catholics to the literary, scientific, religious, or social life of nations as a *conspiracy of silence.*[10] Often the very fact that something is Catholic is enough to ensure that it never gets mentioned by the media.

We all have an important part to play in the apostolate of public opinion. At times our personal sphere of influence may extend no farther than the neighbours or friends we visit or who call on us. Or we may be in a position to clarify some doctrinal issue by writing a letter to the editor of a newspaper, or by making a telephone call to a radio programme where audience reaction on some controversial topic has been invited. Again, we may have the opportunity to reply constructively to the questions of a survey, or to recommend a good book to someone. We have to overcome any temptation to discouragement, thinking perhaps that *we can do very little.* Just as the current of a great river is fed by a network of tiny streams which in their turn have been formed drop by drop, our opportunity to contribute to the river of truth should never be omitted. That was how the first Christians started spreading the Gospel message.

Let us ask Saint Catherine today to let us share something of her love for the Church and for the Roman Pontiff, along with the holy desire to make the doctrine of Jesus Christ known everywhere, imaginatively and lovingly, always trying to see the positive side of things and not missing a single opportunity. Let us petition Our

---

[10] cf Pius XI, *Divini Redemptoris,* 10 March 1937

Blessed Lady in Saint Catherine's own words: *To you I have recourse, O Mary, offering you my supplication for the sweet Spouse of Christ and for his Vicar on earth. May he always have the light to rule Holy Church prudently and with discernment.*[11]

[11] St Catherine of Siena, *Prayer 11*

1 May

33. SAINT JOSEPH THE WORKER

Memorial

The *Memorial* of Saint Joseph the Worker has been celebrated liturgically since 1955. On this day the Church, inspired by Saint Joseph's example and under his patronage, commemorates in a special way the human and supernatural value of work. All work is a collaboration in God's own work of creation, and, through Jesus Christ, in accordance with our love for God and for our fellow men and women, it can become true prayer and apostolate.

33.1 Work is a gift from God.

By the labour of your hands you shall eat.[1] The Church, in presenting Saint Joseph to us today as a model, is not endorsing just one particular form of work, manual labour, but is testifying to the dignity and value of all honest human occupations. In the first reading at Mass[2] we read the Genesis account of man's participation in the work of Creation. Sacred Scripture also tells us that God placed man in the garden of Eden *to till it and keep it.*[3] From the beginning of man's existence, work is for him a command of nature, a feature of his condition as created being, an expression of his dignity, and a means whereby he co-operates in the great overall task of divine Providence. All that original sin did was to change the *form* of this co-operation, as we also read in the Book of Genesis: *Cursed is the ground because of you; in toil you shall eat of it all the days of your life ... In the sweat of your face you shall eat bread.*[4]

---

[1] *Entrance Antiphon*: Ps 127:1-2
[2] Gen 1:26; 2:3
[3] Gen 2:15
[4] Gen 3:17-19

After the fall of our first parents, what had been intended originally as something pleasant and agreeable has since become difficult, and very often exhausting; but there has been no change in the relationship of man's work to his Creator and its role in the redemption of mankind. The conditions attaching to work cause some people to look upon it as a punishment, or, alternatively because of the malice of the human heart estranged from God, as a mere form of merchandise or an 'instrument of oppression', to such an extent that on occasions it is difficult to appreciate its very real grandeur and dignity. Others see work exclusively in terms of a means for making money, or as an expression of selfish personal affirmation, and fail to realize the value of work *in itself* as something divine, whereby man collaborates with God and offers his Creator something in which all his natural and supernatural virtues come into play.

For many centuries manual work was looked down on as no more than a way of earning a living, and was considered to be something basically worthless or degrading. Nowadays materialistic societies tend to classify people according to 'how much they make' and to their ability to obtain a greater level of material well-being at more or less any cost. *It is time for us Christians to shout from the rooftops that work is a gift from God and that it makes no sense to classify men differently, according to their occupation, as if some jobs were nobler or of less significance than others. Work, all work, bears witness to the dignity of man, to his dominion over creation. It is an opportunity to develop one's personality. It is a bond of union with others, the way to support one's family, a means of contributing to the improvement of the society in which we live and to the progress of all humanity.*[5] Saint Joseph was a tradesman who worked for his living, and today's feast proposes him to us as a model

[5] St. J. Escrivá, *Christ is passing by,* 47

and patron.[6] We should have frequent recourse to him to ensure that the work we do never loses its innate dignity or value, for it is not uncommon that, when God is forgotten, *from the factory dead matter goes out improved, whereas the men there are corrupted and degraded.*[7] Our work, with Saint Joseph's help, ought to leave our hands as a prayerful and pleasing offering to God.

33.2 The natural and the supernatural meaning of work.

In the Gospel of today's Mass we see once again how Jesus is identified in Nazareth by his occupation: *Is not this the carpenter, the son of Mary?*[8] When he returned to his native town (sons here as elsewhere often following the same trade as their fathers), the neighbours remarked: *Is not this the carpenter's son? Is not his mother called Mary?*[9] In another place it says that Jesus practised the same profession as Saint Joseph, the man who occupied the place of his father here on earth. Man's work by being taken up by the Son of God, has been sanctified, and can now be something redemptive, through being united to Christ the Redeemer of the world. All the negative qualities that attach themselves to work as a consequence of original sin – weariness, toil, hardship and difficulties – become, in Christ, something of immense value for every individual and for all of mankind. Man is now associated with the work of redemption wrought by Christ, *whose labour with his hands at Nazareth greatly ennobled the dignity of work.*[10]

Any honest occupation can be a task adapted to the perfection of the individual who carries it out, and indeed of the whole of society itself. Through the communion that

---

[6] St John Paul II, *Redemptoris custos,* 15 August 1989, 22
[7] Pius XI, *Quadragesimo anno,* 15 May 1931, 135
[8] Mark 6:3
[9] Matt 13:54-58
[10] Second Vatican Council, *Gaudium et spes,* 67

exists among all the members of Christ's Mystical Body – the Church – man's work, in all its incidental detail, can become a means of helping others. But for this to be so, it is essential for us not to lose sight of the fact that every human enterprise, even the most arduous and difficult of achievement, has to have a *supernatural* as well as a human purpose. *The galley slave is well aware that he rows in order to make the ship move; but for this to give meaning to his life, he needs to appreciate the meaning that suffering and punishment have for a Christian. That is, he has to see his situation as a means of identifying himself with Christ. If, through ignorance or rejection, he doesn't manage to see this, he will end up hating his 'work'.*

A similar effect can be seen when the fruit of one's labours (not the financial reward, but the actual product, the thing that has been 'produced' or 'made') is so alienated from its maker that it scarcely impinges on his consciousness.[11] Many people go to 'work' every morning as if they were going to the galleys, to row a ship to a destination they are neither aware of nor care about; all they look forward to is the weekend and the pay-packet. This sort of work, evidently, can do nothing to ennoble or sanctify man, and only with difficulty can it develop his personality and be of real benefit to society.

Let us meditate today, with Saint Joseph's help, on various aspects of love and esteem for our job. How hard do we try to do things perfectly and punctually? What is our professional standing like? Do we have a methodical approach to things – which does not at all exclude having a sense of urgency about them? Do we always carry out every little detail of our work as carefully and considerately as we can? If our daily enterprise is engaged in as conscientiously as is humanly possible, we can say with the

[11] P. Berglar, *Opus Dei,* Salzburg, 1983

liturgy of today's Mass: *O God, fount of all mercy, look upon our offerings, which we bring before your majesty in commemoration of Saint Joseph, and mercifully grant that the gifts we offer may become the means of protection for those who call on you.*[12]

33.3 Loving our work.

Work well done is work done with love. To have a proper regard for the task we are engaged in is, perhaps, the first step in ennobling it and raising it to the level of the supernatural. We have to put our heart into the things we do, and not just do them mechanically, automatically, 'because we haven't any option'. *My son, do you remember that man who came to see me this morning, the one with the brown jacket? He's not an honest man ... He works as a cartoonist for an illustrated magazine. It gives him enough to live on and keeps him busy. But he always talks disparagingly about his work, and tells me: 'If only I could be a painter! But I have to draw these stupidities in order to eat. Don't pay any attention to them, old chap, don't even look at them! It's just pure commercialism!' In other words, he's only in it for the money. And he has let his spirit get separated from what his hands are doing, because he has very little regard for his work. But let me say this, my son. If my friend finds his task so repulsive, if his drawings can be said to be rubbish, the reason is precisely because he hasn't put his heart into them. When the spirit is present, there is no job that doesn't become noble and holy. This is as true of a cartoonist as it is of a carpenter or a dustman ... There is a way of drawing cartoons, or of working with wood, or of emptying bins ... which shows that love has been placed there, as well as attention to detail and proportion, and a little spark of*

---

[12] *Roman Missal,* 1st May, *Prayer over the Offerings*

something personal – what artists call individual style – and there is no human undertaking or task in which such a personal ingredient cannot flourish. That's the way things have to be done. The other way, that of loathing one's work and despising it, instead of redeeming it and secretly transforming it, is wrong and immoral. The visitor in the brown jacket is, therefore, an immoral person, because he doesn't love his work.[13]

Saint Joseph teaches us to love the occupation in which we spend so much of our life: keeping the home, working in the laboratory, at the plough or the computer, delivering parcels or being a receptionist. The status of a job depends on its capacity to perfect us in a human way and supernaturally as well, on the opportunities it offers to provide for our family and collaborate in good works on behalf of mankind, and on the social contribution we can make in the world through its means.

Saint Joseph had Jesus beside him while he worked. At times he would have asked him to hold a piece of wood while he sawed it, and at others he would have shown him how to use a chisel or a plane. Whenever he got tired he would have been able to look at his son, who was the Son of God, and his work would thereby acquire a new value because he would realize that through it he was collaborating mysteriously in the enterprise of salvation. Let us ask Joseph today to teach us the awareness of the presence of God which he had while he was engrossed in his work. Let us not forget, either, our Mother the Blessed Virgin, to whom we lovingly dedicate the month of May that begins today. Let us not forget to offer daily in her honour a particular hour of work or study, each day better than the previous one, and more perfectly done.

---

[13] E. D'Ors, *Learning and heroism: greatness and service of the intellect,* Pamplona 1973

3 May

34. SAINTS PHILIP AND JAMES
Apostles

34.1 The calling of Philip and James.

Among those Galileans who were fortunate enough to be chosen by Jesus to form part of his intimate circle were Philip the son of Alphaeus and James the Less.

James was born in Cana of Galilee, near Nazareth, and was a relative of Jesus. The Gospel does not mention the exact moment Jesus called him. Sacred Scripture testifies to the important position James held in the Church at Jerusalem.[1]

Saint James was one of the people privileged to receive a private appearance of the Risen Lord, as we read in the first reading of today's Mass.[2]

Philip was a native of Bethsaida, a little town along the shore of Lake Gennesaret, as were also Peter and his brother Andrew,[3] who were very probably close friends of his. One day on the banks of the Jordan, Philip met Jesus as he was making his way towards Galilee in the company of his first disciples. Thc Master said to him: *Follow me.*[4] That was how Jesus invited his disciples to join his little company, just as the rabbis used to do with their own followers. Philip followed him forthwith, and at once began introducing his own friends in turn to the one who had become for him the centre of his life. *Philip found Nathanael, and said to him, 'We have found him of whom*

---

[1] Gal 1:18-19; Acts 12:17; 21:15-18; Gal 2:9
[2] 2 Cor 15:7
[3] John 1:44
[4] John 1:43

Moses in the law and also the prophets wrote, Jesus of Nazareth, the son of Joseph.[5] And faced with Nathanael's doubts, Philip gives him the best of all replies: *Come and see.* Nathanael went along, and remained with Christ forever.

Jesus never disappoints. Apostolate always entails leading our relatives, friends and acquaintances to Our Lord; our task consists in clearing the way for them and removing any obstacles blocking their view. Christ, who has already called us, wishes to enter into the souls of the people who approach him, just as he did with Nathanael, who afterwards became one of the chosen Twelve in spite of his initial unwillingness to believe his friend's claims. His first reaction to Philip's invitation was: *Can anything good come out of Nazareth?* Frequently too it has fallen to us to say to the people we want to bring closer to God: *Come and see!* And anybody who took us at our word and came to Jesus never felt cheated.

Philip and James are today our intercessors before Jesus. We entrust to them particularly our apostolate with our friends and relatives.

34.2 Jesus was always close to his disciples, and is now close to us.

In the Gospel at Mass today[6] we read how, during the Last Supper, Jesus explains to his disciples that he has prepared a place for them in heaven so that they can be with him forever, and they already know how to get there. The conversation continues – the disciples asking questions, and the Master answering. At this point Philip intervenes with a request that seems to all of them to be out of place: *Lord, show us the Father, and we shall be satisfied.* And Jesus, chiding his disciple affectionately,

---

[5] John 1:45

[6] John 14:6-14

replies: *Have I been with you so long, and yet you do not know me, Philip? He who has seen me has seen the Father; how can you say, 'Show us the Father'.* How often, perhaps, has Jesus had to make the same reproach to us as to Philip! *Look how often I have been beside you and you have not noticed!* And Our Lord could list for us one occasion after another, times perhaps when we found ourselves under pressure from circumstances and let ourselves get flustered by losing our sense of divine filiation and closeness to God. We find Our Lord's reply to his Apostle so wonderfully reassuring! In him, we too are represented.

Jesus reveals the Father. Christ's Sacred Humanity is the means whereby we get to know and love God the Father, God the Son and God the Holy Spirit. The normal way we have of reaching the Blessed Trinity is through contemplating Christ. In him we have the supreme revelation of God to mankind. *He himself ... completed and perfected Revelation, and confirmed it with divine guarantees. He did this by the total fact of his presence and self-manifestation – by words and works, signs and miracles, but above all by his death and glorious resurrection from the dead, and finally by sending the Spirit of truth. He revealed that God was with us, to deliver us from the darkness of sin and death, and to raise us up to eternal life.*[7] He fills our life completely. *He is sufficient for you,* says Saint Augustine. *Apart from him, nothing can be said to be at all. Philip knew this well when he said, 'Lord, show us the Father and we shall be satisfied.'*[8] Do we too have this same conviction?

---

[7] Second Vatican Council, *Dei Verbum,* 4
[8] St Augustine, *Sermon 334,* 4

34.3 Spreading the Apostles' message. Apostolate is based on a supernatural foundation.

In the first reading at Mass this morning we read Saint Paul's words to the Christians of Corinth: *For I delivered to you as of first importance what I also received, that Christ died for our sins in accordance with the Scriptures, that he was buried, that he was raised on the third day in accordance with the Scriptures, and that he appeared to Cephas.*[9] Paul received from the Apostles a divine message which he in turn passed on. It was the same message as the one preached by Philip and James, who gave their lives in witness to it. They, like the Apostle of the Gentiles, knew well what the core of their preaching had to be: Jesus Christ, the Way to the Father. This is the Good News that is handed on from generation to generation: *Day unto day takes up the story, and night unto night makes known the message,*[10] we read in the responsorial psalm. We do not have any new message to announce, because the Good News is unchanging: that Christ died for our sins, that he rose again, that he lives beside us, that he loves us as nobody can ever love us, that he has destined us for eternal happiness beside him, when we shall see him face to face.

Our apostolate consists in proclaiming to the four winds in every conceivable way the same doctrine that the Apostles preached: that Christ lives, that only he can satisfy the anxieties of the human mind and heart, that only in Christ can one find happiness, that it is he who reveals the Father. The Apostles, like us, encountered difficulties and obstacles in trying to spread Christ's kingdom. If they had decided to wait for a more suitable occasion, then the message which has so transformed our entire existence would probably never have reached us. When, later on,

---

[9] 1 Cor 15:3-5

[10] *Responsorial Psalm*: Ps 18:3

they found themselves bereft of resources and faced with the resistance of those who heard them, the Apostles, and especially Philip, perhaps recalled the day they were called upon to feed a great multitude while having no food and no possibility of obtaining any.[11] Jesus saw the crowd approaching him and said to Philip: *How are we to buy bread, so that these people may eat?* Philip made a rapid estimate and said to the Master: *Two hundred denarii would not buy enough bread for each of them to get a little.* He did his calculations, and quickly realized that the means at their disposal were quite insufficient to meet the needs of the multitude.

Once again we see how Jesus is moved and filled with pity for the crowd, which is so much in need of understanding and comforting. But he also wants his disciples not to lose sight of the fact that he is always by their side. *I am with you always,*[12] he tells them at the end of his life here on earth. *Have I been with you so long, and yet you do not know me, Philip?* God is the indispensable factor we have to rely upon to get our accounts to balance. In our personal apostolate with friends, relatives, acquaintances and clients, it is true that we have to reckon with the two hundred denarii, the human means, which is never enough; but we cannot forget that Jesus is always present with his power and his mercy. He is beside us now too. The greater our needs and difficulties in the apostolate, the more help Jesus offers us. We cannot shrink from having recourse to him.

Philip was from Bethsaida, like Peter and Andrew. He was first of all a disciple of John the Baptist, and afterwards followed Jesus, who called him to form part of the company of the Twelve. He was the one who

---

[11] 1 cf John 6:4ff
[12] cf Matt 28:20

announced to Nathanael that he had met the Messiah. We know from Saint John that Philip was present when Jesus worked his first miracle at the wedding feast of Cana. From the account of the miraculous multiplication of the loaves we can gather that Philip was in charge of provisions: he is the one who quickly calculates how much is needed – two hundred denarii – to satisfy the hunger of the crowd. He intervenes along with Andrew in the episode of the Greek pilgrims – devout Gentiles – who wanted to meet Jesus. Philip is also the one who in the Cenacle asks Our Lord to show them the Father. Tradition has it that he was the apostle of Phrygia in Asia Minor, where he suffered martyrdom by crucifixion.

James, a blood relative of Jesus, is called the Less, to distinguish him from James the brother of John. He was the first bishop of Jerusalem, and carried out an intense work of evangelization among the Jews of that city. Tradition depicts him to us as a man who was personally very austere, and full of goodness towards others. Peter, John and James the Less were known as the 'pillars' of the primitive Church. James died a martyr's death in Jerusalem around the year 62 A.D. He is the author of one of the *Catholic* Epistles.

13 May

35. OUR LADY OF FATIMA

From the 13th of May to the 13th of October 1917, the Blessed Virgin appeared at Fatima (Portugal) to the three children, Lucia, Francisco and Jacinta. The apparitions were preceded by three apparitions of an angel in the spring of 1916. On each occasion Our Lady asked them to say the Rosary and to offer reparation for the offences made to her Immaculate Heart. On the 13th of October there took place the prodigious event, seen by thousands of people, which had been foretold by Our Lady, so that the world would believe the message of the apparitions: for about ten minutes or so, the sun spun in the sky like a wheel of fire.

The Blessed Virgin asked for the world to be consecrated to her Immaculate Heart. At the request of the Portuguese hierarchy, this consecration was solemnly performed by Pope Pius XII on the 31st of October 1942. It was renewed by St John Paul II in 1982.

35.1 Our Lady's apparitions at Fatima.

On the 13th of May 1917, around midday, Our Lady appeared for the first time to the three young shepherds Lucia, Jacinta and Francisco, while they were pasturing their sheep in a hollow dotted with holm oaks and olive trees, known locally as the *Cova da Iria.*[1] The Blessed Virgin asked the children to return there on the thirteenth of each month for the following six months. The message she revealed to them speaks about penance for sins, about saying the Rosary, and the consecration of the world to her Immaculate Heart. Each time the beautiful Lady appeared to the children she asked them to say the Rosary every day. She also taught them a prayer to say often in which they

---

[1] C. Barthas, *The Virgin of Fatima,* Madrid, 1963

would offer God the events of their lives and especially many small mortifications and sacrifices: *O Jesus, this is for love of you, for the conversion of sinners and in reparation for the offences made to the Immaculate Heart of Mary.*

In August the Blessed Virgin promised to give the children a sign that would be seen by everybody, as a proof of the truth of her message. In each apparition she reminded them to pray for the conversion of sinners by offering sacrifices and saying the Rosary. On the 13th of October there took place what is known as *the miracle of the sun.* Tens of thousands of people who were present in the Cova da Iria that day witnessed the extraordinary event; it was seen even by people many miles away. On that occasion Our Lady told the children that she was the *Virgin of the Rosary.* She also told them: 'Men have to mend their ways and ask for pardon for their sins ... They shouldn't offend Our Lord any more; he is already far too much offended.'

St John Paul II, speaking in 1987, recalled his visit to Fatima in 1982, where he went, he said, *with my Rosary in my hand, with Mary's name on my lips and the song of mercy in my heart,* to give thanks to Our Lady for his having survived the assassination attempt on his life the previous year. *The apparitions at Fatima in 1917, testified to by extraordinary signs, form as it were a point of reference and enlightenment for our century. Mary, our heavenly Mother, came to awaken men's consciences, to illuminate the authentic meaning of life, to call men to conversion from sin and to spiritual fervour, to inflame souls with love for God and with charity towards their neighbour. Mary came to help us, because many, unfortunately, do not wish to accept the invitation of the Son of God to return to their Father's house.*

From her sanctuary at Fatima Mary renews even today her maternal and urgent petition: the conversion to Truth and Grace; the return to the life of the sacraments, especially Penance and the Eucharist; the devotion to her Immaculate Heart, accompanied by a spirit of penance.[2]

Today we can ask ourselves: how well do we respond to the frequent inspirations of the Holy Spirit to purify our souls, especially through the sacrament of Penance? How constant are we at making reparation for our own past sins and for the sins of mankind? How well do we say the Rosary, especially during this month of May? Can we be said to have 'ambitious' expectations as regards the friends and companions we want to lead, like repentant prodigals, humbly back to Christ?

35.2 The Blessed Virgin asks us to do penance for the sins of mankind.

The message of Fatima is, in its basic meaning, a call to conversion and repentance, as in the Gospel ... The Lady of the message seems to have read with special insight the 'signs of the times', the signs of our age. The call to repentance is a motherly one, and at the same time it is strong and decisive.[3] Today in our prayer we hear Our Lady's voice, sweet yet insistent, calling us individually to action.

Throughout the Gospel there resound the words *repent and do penance.*[4] Jesus begins his mission asking for penance: *Repent, for the kingdom of heaven is at hand.*[5] The word 'penance' signifies the conversion of the sinner, and stands for a whole array of internal and external actions directed at making reparation for sins committed.[6]

Mary reminds us that without penance man does not receive the Kingdom of her Son; without penance man is in the kingdom of sin. In Our Lord's own words, without

---

[2] St John Paul II, *Angelus,* 26 July 1987
[3] St John Paul II, *Homily at Fatima,* 13 May 1982
[4] cf Mark 1:15
[5] Matt 4:17
[6] cf L. Bouyer, *Penitence,* in *Dictionary of Theology,* Barcelona, 1983

penance *all likewise perish.*[7] So too in the Apostles' preaching to the infant Church this truth occupied an essential place.[8] All the days of the pilgrim Church on earth are a *spatium verae poenitentiae,* a time of true penance granted by God so that no one may be lost.[9] Penance is necessary because sin exists and we are no strangers to it, because we have to make reparation for all our own faults and weaknesses and for those of our fellow men, and because no human being, without a special and extraordinary privilege, is confirmed in grace. *The ultimate purpose of penance,* St John Paul II taught, *is to get us to love God intensely and to consecrate ourselves to him.*[10] The Curé d'Ars used to say that penance is as necessary for the soul as breathing is for the life of the body.[11]

The first expression of the virtue of penance consists in having a great love for frequent confession of present and past sins. Firstly, we should always have a great desire to receive this Sacrament ourselves; then, to prepare for it very well and contritely; and finally, to do an effective apostolate among our relatives and friends to bring them to this sacrament of joy and mercy. The virtue of penance has to be present, to some degree, in all the everyday actions of life: in *fulfilling exactly the timetable you have fixed for yourself, even though your body resists or your mind tries to avoid it by dreaming up useless fantasies. Penance is getting up on time and also not leaving for later, without any real reason, that particular job that you find harder or most difficult to begin and finish.*

Penance is knowing how to reconcile your duties to God, to others and to yourself, by making demands on

---

[7] Luke 13:3
[8] cf Acts 2:38
[9] cf 2 Pet 3:9
[10] St John Paul II, *Homily at Fatima*
[11] St Jean Vianney, (The Curé d'Ars), *Sermon on Penance*

yourself so that you find enough time for each of your tasks. You are practising penance when you lovingly keep to your schedule of prayer, despite feeling worn out, listless or cold.

Penance means being very charitable at all times towards those around you, starting with the members of your own family. It is to be full of tenderness and kindness towards the suffering, the sick and the infirm. It is to give patient answers to people who are boring and annoying. It means interrupting our work or changing our plans, when circumstances make this necessary, above all when the just and rightful needs of others are involved.

Penance consists in putting up good-humouredly with the thousand and one little pinpricks of each day; in not abandoning your task, although you have momentarily lost the enthusiasm with which you started it; in eating gladly whatever is served, without being fussy.

For parents and in general for those whose work involves supervision or teaching, penance is to correct whenever it is necessary. This should be done bearing in mind the type of fault committed and the situation of the person who needs to be so helped, not letting oneself be swayed by subjective viewpoints, which are often cowardly and sentimental.

A spirit of penance keeps us from becoming too attached to the vast imaginative blueprints we have made for our future projects, where we have already foreseen our master-strokes and brilliant successes. What joy we give to God when we are happy to lay aside our third-rate painting efforts and let him put in the features and colours of his choice![12] What a wonderful masterpiece then appears!

---

[12] St. J. Escrivá, *Friends of God,* 138

35.3 Consecration of the world to the Immaculate Heart of Mary.

One part of the message of Fatima was Our Lady's desire for the world to be consecrated to her Immaculate Heart. And indeed, what safer refuge could there be for this poor world of ours? Where else could it find better protection and shelter? This consecration means *drawing near, through the Mother's intercession, to the very Fountain of life that sprang from Golgotha. This Fountain pours forth unceasingly redemption and grace. In it, reparation is made continually for the sins of the world. It is a ceaseless source of new life and holiness.*[13]

Pope Pius XII, whose episcopal ordination took place precisely on the 13th of May 1917, the date of the first apparition, consecrated the human race, and especially the peoples of Russia, to the Immaculate Heart of Mary.[14] St John Paul II later renewed it, and we in turn can unite ourselves to his petition: *O Mother of individuals and peoples, you who know all their sufferings and their hopes, you who have a mother's awareness of all the struggles between good and evil, between light and darkness, which afflict the modern world, accept the cry which we, as though moved by the Holy Spirit, address directly to your heart. Embrace, with the love of the Mother and Handmaid, this human world of ours, which we entrust and consecrate to you, for we are full of disquiet for the earthly and eternal destiny of individuals and peoples.*

In a special way we entrust and consecrate to you those individuals and nations which particularly need to be entrusted and consecrated. 'We fly to your patronage, O holy Mother of God: despise not our petitions in our necessities.'

---

[13] St John Paul II, *Homily at Fatima*

[14] Pius XII, Radio message *Benedicite Deum,* 31 October 1942

Reject them not!

Accept our humble trust – and our act of entrusting![15]

The Virgin Mary, always attentive to what we ask her for, enables us to find refuge and shelter in her most pure heart.

[15] St John Paul II, *Consecration to Our Lady of Fatima,* 13 May 1982

14 May

36. SAINT MATTHIAS
Apostle

After the Ascension, while the Apostles were awaiting the coming of the Holy Spirit, they chose Matthias in Judas' place to make up the number of the Twelve, since they were to represent the twelve tribes of Israel. Matthias had been a disciple of Our Lord and a witness to his Resurrection. According to tradition he evangelized Ethiopia, where he suffered martyrdom. Through the agency of Saint Helena his relics were later brought to Trier in Germany, where he is venerated as Patron of the city.

36.1 God is the one who chooses.

It was not you who chose me, says the Lord, but I who chose you and appointed you to go and bear fruit, fruit that will last.[1]

After Judas' betrayal his place among the Twelve became vacant. The election of his successor fulfilled something that the Holy Spirit had prophesied and Jesus had expressly instituted: Our Lord wanted there to be *twelve* Apostles,[2] because the new People of God was to be founded upon twelve supports, just as the former one had been based on the twelve tribes of Israel.[3] Saint Peter, exercising his primacy in the assembly of the one hundred and twenty disciples, sets out the conditions laid down by the Master – conditions that had to be met by whichever disciple was chosen to complete the Apostolic College: he had to have known Jesus personally, and would have to bear witness to him. Peter explains this in his discourse to

---

[1] *Entrance Antiphon*: John 15:16
[2] cf Matt 19:28
[3] cf Eph 2:20

the assembly: *One of the men who have accompanied us during all the time that the Lord Jesus went in and out among us, beginning from the baptism of John until the day when he was taken up from us – one of these men must become with us a witness to his resurrection.*[4] The Apostle emphasises that the man selected has to have been an eyewitness of the preaching and the events of Jesus' entire public life, and especially of his Resurrection. Thirty years later we find him saying the same thing in his last written testimony to all Christians: *For we did not follow cleverly-devised myths when we made known to you the power and coming of our Lord Jesus Christ, but were eyewitnesses of his majesty.*[5]

Peter does not make the choice himself: he leaves that to God, just as used to be the case at times in the Old Testament.[6] *The lot is cast into the lap, but the decision is wholly from the Lord,* we read in the Book of Proverbs.[7] *They put forward two, Joseph called Barsabbas, who was surnamed Justus, and Matthias* – a shortened form of Mattathias, which means 'God's gift'. *And they cast lots for them, and the lot fell on Matthias; and he was enrolled with the eleven apostles.* An ancient historian records a tradition that this disciple belonged to the group of the seventy-two who had been sent by Jesus to preach to the cities of Israel.[8]

Before the election, Peter and the whole community pray to God, because the choice is not to be theirs: vocation is always a divine choice. And so they pray: *Lord, who knowest the hearts of all men, show which one of these two thou hast chosen.* The Eleven and the other disciples

---

[4] Acts 1:21-22
[5] 2 Pet 1:16
[6] cf Lev 16:8-9; Num 26:55
[7] Prov 16:33
[8] cf Eusebius, *Ecclesiastical History,* 1, 12

do not dare take upon themselves, by expressing any personal preference or inclination, the responsibility of choosing Judas' successor. When, later on, Saint Paul feels compelled to declare the origin of his mission, he says that he has been appointed *not by men nor through man, but through Jesus Christ and God the Father.*[9] It is God who chooses and sends forth, now just as much as then.

Each of us has a divine vocation to holiness and apostolate; we received it first in Baptism, and it has been subsequently underscored by God's successive interventions in our lives. At certain moments in life this call to follow Jesus becomes particularly intense and clear. *I didn't think God would get hold of me the way he did either. But ... God doesn't ask our permission to 'complicate' our lives. He just gets in: and that's that!*[10] It's then up to each of us to respond. Today we can ask ourselves in our prayer: Am I faithful to what God wants of me? Do I try to do God's will in all my undertakings? Am I prepared to respond all life long to what Our Lord asks of me?

36.2 We are never denied the graces necessary to respond to vocation.

... and the lot fell on Matthias. Matthias' calling reminds us that vocation is always an unmerited gift. God destines us to become ever more identified with his Son and to participate in his divine life; he gives us a mission in life and intends us to enjoy the happiness of heaven with him forever. God has called us to be close to Christ and to extend his kingdom, each one in his or her own surroundings and circumstances.

Apart from this universal call to holiness, Jesus calls many individuals in a special way: some, to give witness by separating themselves from the world; others, to serve

---

[9] Gal 1:1

[10] St. J. Escrivá, *The Forge,* 902

him in a specific way through the priesthood. But in the case of the immense majority Our Lord calls them to remain in the world and vivify it from within, either in marriage, which is *a way of holiness,*[11] or in celibacy, which is the complete offering of one's heart for love of God and souls.

Vocation is not born of good desires or great aspirations. The Apostles, and now Matthias, did not choose Our Lord as Master after the fashion of those Jews who used to look for some rabbi to be their teacher. It was Christ who sought them out – some directly, others, like Matthias, through this election which the Church leaves in God's hands. *You did not choose me,* Jesus reminds them in the Last Supper, and we read in today's Gospel, *but I chose you and appointed you that you should go and bear fruit and that your fruit should abide.*[12] How were these men so fortunate as to receive this great privilege? There is really no point in asking why it was they who were the ones to be chosen. It was simply that Our Lord freely called them and not others: *He called to him those whom he desired.*[13] In this their entire good fortune and the whole purpose of their lives is to be found.

From the moment Jesus singles out a soul and invites it to follow him, there follow afterwards many other calls, which may perhaps seem small, but which mark out that soul's path through life. *All through life, ordinarily little by little, but nevertheless constantly and in a compelling fashion, God tenders us many 'determinations' of his initial calling, which always imply a person-to-person relationship with Christ. From the beginning God asks us to make the decision to follow him, but He wisely hides*

[11] cf *Conversations,* 92
[12] John 15:16
[13] Mark 3:13

from us the subsequent implications of that decision, perhaps because at that moment we are not able to accept them.[14] God gives the soul special insights and graces in those impulses by means of which the Holy Spirit seems to draw it upwards, making it aspire to be better, to serve all mankind and especially those it encounters daily. God's grace is never lacking.

Tradition has it that Matthias died a martyr's death, just like the other Apostles. His life consisted essentially in measuring up to the splendid and at times arduous task which the Holy Spirit made him responsible for that day. In our case too, it is in fidelity to our vocation that we find true happiness and the meaning of life, all of it to be revealed to us by God in his own good time.

36.3 Happiness and the meaning of life for every man and woman consists in following God's call.

Jesus chooses his own: He calls them. This calling is their greatest honour, and gives them the right to a very special union with the Master, to special graces which are heard in the intimacy of prayer. *The vocation of each individual is based, up to a certain point, on his or her own being: it can be said that vocation and person become one and the same thing. This means that in God's creative initiative there is present a particular act of love directed towards those who are called, not only to salvation, but to the ministry of salvation. And therefore, from eternity, from the time we began to exist in the plans of the Creator and He willed us to come into being, He also willed us to be called, predisposing in us all the gifts and conditions for a personal and conscious response to the call of Christ or the Church. God, who loves us, who is Love, is also the one who calls us (cf Rom 9:11).*[15]

---

[14] P. Rodriguez, *Vocation, Work and Contemplation,* Pamplona, 1986
[15] St John Paul II, *Address at Porto Alegre,* 5 July 1980

Saint Paul nearly always starts his letters in some such way as the following: *Paul, a servant of Jesus Christ, called to be an apostle, set apart for the gospel of God ...*[16] He is called and chosen *not by men nor through man, but through Jesus Christ and God the Father.*[17] God calls us as he called Moses,[18] Samuel[19] and Isaiah.[20] It is a vocation that is not based on any merit of the individual: *The Lord called me from the womb.*[21] St Paul puts it even more categorically still: *He saved us and called us with a holy calling, not in virtue of our works but in virtue of his own purpose.*[22]

Jesus called his disciples to share his chalice, that is, his life and his mission. He now extends the same invitation to us: we have to be careful not to drown his voice with the noise of things which, if they are not in him and for him, must be of no interest at all. When we hear Christ's voice inviting us to follow him completely, nothing is of any importance compared to the business of following him. And Christ, for his part, all our life long reveals to us little by little the great richness of the call we first heard on the day He passed close beside us.

After his election Matthias once more fades into the background. Along with the other Apostles he experienced the burning joy of Pentecost. He travelled far and wide, he preached and cured the sick, but his name does not appear again in Sacred Scripture. Like the other Apostles, he left behind him an indelible trail of faith which has endured to our own time. He was a burning light that God could contemplate joyfully from heaven.

---

[16] Rom 1:1; 1 Cor 1:1
[17] Gal 1:1
[18] Ex 3:4; 19:20; 24:16
[19] 1 Sam 3:4
[20] Is 6:1ff
[21] Is 49:1
[22] 2 Tim 1:9

31 May

37. THE VISITATION OF THE BLESSED VIRGIN

Feast

Today's feast, established by Urban VI in 1389, is located between Our Lord's Annunciation and the birth of John the Baptist, in keeping with what we read in the Gospel. It commemorates Our Lady's visit to her cousin Elizabeth, who was already advanced in years, to help her during the period of her confinement and at the same time to share with her the jubilation at the wonders wrought by God in both of them. This feast, with which we close the month dedicated to Mary, proclaims to us her mediation, her spirit of service and her profound humility. It teaches us to carry the spirit of christian happiness with us wherever we go, so that, like Mary, we shall be continually a source of joy for all mankind.

37.1 Serving cheerfully.

Come and hear, all who fear God; I will tell what the Lord did for my soul,[1] we read in the Entrance Antiphon of today's Mass.

Shortly after the Annunciation, Our Lady went to visit her cousin Elizabeth, who lived in the hill country of Judea, about four or five days' journey from Nazareth. *In those days,* says St Luke, *Mary arose and went with haste into the hill country, to a city of Judah.*[2] The Blessed Virgin, having learned from the angel about Elizabeth's pregnancy, moved by charity, hurries to lend a hand with her household chores. Nobody obliges her to go: God, through the angel, hadn't asked her to do so, nor had Elizabeth looked for help either. Mary could have remained at home to get on with

---

[1] *Entrance Antiphon*: Ps 66:16

[2] Luke 1:39-56

preparing for the arrival of her Son, the Messiah; but she joyfully sets out on the journey 'with haste' and goes to offer Elizabeth her homely assistance.[3]

We accompany Mary on her way in our prayer, and we tell her, in the words of today's first reading at Mass: *Sing aloud, O daughter of Zion; shout, O Israel! Rejoice and exult with all your heart, O daughter of Jerusalem! ... The Lord your God is in your midst, a warrior who gives victory; He will rejoice over you with gladness, He will renew you in his love; He will exult over you with loud singing as on a day of festival.*[4]

It is easy to imagine the great joy that filled Our Mother's heart and the great desire she had to share it. *Behold, your kinswoman Elizabeth in her old age has also conceived a son,* the angel told her, and gave Mary to understand that Elizabeth's conception was truly extraordinary and was also connected in some way with the Messiah who was to come.[5] After her long journey, Our Lady entered Zachary's house and greeted her cousin. *And when Elizabeth heard the greeting of Mary, the babe leaped in her womb; and Elizabeth was filled with the Holy Spirit.* That house was transformed by the presence of Jesus and Mary. Her greeting *was efficacious: it filled Elizabeth with the Holy Spirit. With her tongue, through her prophetic utterance, she caused a river of divine gifts to spring up in her cousin as from a fountain ... In effect, wherever she who is 'full of grace' goes, everything is filled to overflowing with joy.*[6] This wonderful effect is worked by Jesus through Mary, who right from the beginning is associated with the Redemption and the joy that Christ brings to the world.

---

[3] cf M. D. Philippe, *The Mystery of Mary*
[4] Zeph 3:14,17-18
[5] cf F. M. Willam, *Life of Mary,* p.85
[6] Pseudo-Gregory the Wonderworker, *Homily II on the Annunciation*

Today's feast of the Visitation reveals to us one aspect of Mary's interior life, namely, her disposition of humble service and selfless love for whoever needs her help.[7] This event, which we contemplate in the Second Joyful Mystery of the Rosary, invites us to give ourselves promptly, happily and unpretentiously to the people around us. Very often the best service we can offer is simply to share with them the happiness that overflows from our hearts. But we can only do this if we stay very close to Our Lord through the faithful fulfilment of the moments of prayer we have throughout the day. *Union with God, supernatural virtue, always brings with it the attractive practice of human virtues: Mary brought joy to her cousin's home, because she 'brought' Christ.*[8] Do we 'bring' Christ with us, and with him joy, wherever we go, be it to work, or when visiting friends or someone who is sick? Does our presence habitually cause people to be cheered up?

37.2 Seeking Jesus through Mary.

At Mary's arrival Elizabeth is filled with the Holy Spirit and proclaims in a loud voice: *Blessed are you among women, and blessed is the fruit of your womb! And why is this granted me, that the mother of my Lord should come to me? For behold, when the voice of your greeting came to my ears, the babe in my womb leaped for joy.*

Elizabeth does not just call her *blessed,* but also explains *why*: it is because of the fruit of her womb, her Son who is blessed for ever. Just think of all the times we too repeat the same words whenever we say the Hail Mary: *Blessed art thou among women, and blessed is the fruit of thy womb!* Do we say them as joyfully as Elizabeth did? They can often act as an aspiration to unite us to our heavenly Mother, while we are working, or walking along

---

[7] St John Paul II, *Homily,* 31 May 1979
[8] St. J. Escrivá, *Furrow,* 566

the street, or whenever we see one of her images.

Mary and Jesus are always together. Jesus' most wonderful deeds are performed, as they are now, in intimate union with his Mother, the Mediatrix of all graces. *This union of the Mother with the Son in the work of salvation,* says the Second Vatican Council, *is made manifest from the time of Christ's virginal conception up to his death.*[9]

Today we learn once more that each encounter with Mary implies a new discovery of Jesus. *If you seek Mary, you will find Jesus. And you will learn a bit more about what is in the heart of a God who humbles himself,*[10] who makes himself accessible in the midst of the routine of ordinary life. God's great gift to mankind, whereby we can get to know and love Christ, had its beginning in Mary's faith, whose perfect fulfilment Elizabeth now openly reveals: *The fullness of grace announced by the angel means the gift of God himself. Mary's faith, proclaimed by Elizabeth at the Visitation, indicates how the Virgin of Nazareth responded to this gift.*[11] The Virgin Mary, who had already pronounced her complete and unconditional *fiat,* presents herself at the threshold of Zachary's house as the Mother of the Son of God. This is Elizabeth's joyful discovery,[12] and ours too; it is one we can never get used to.

37.3 The *Magnificat*.

The characteristic feature of this mystery of the Rosary is the all-pervading atmosphere of gladness that surrounds it: the mystery of the Visitation is a mystery of joy. John the Baptist stirs exultantly in his mother's womb; Elizabeth, rejoicing at the gift of maternity, bursts forth in

---

[9] Second Vatican Council, *Lumen gentium,* 57
[10] St. J. Escrivá, *Christ is passing by,* 144
[11] St John Paul II, *Redemptoris Mater,* 25 March 1987, 12
[12] cf *ibid,* 13

blessings to the Lord; and, in response to Elizabeth's praises, Mary elevates her heart to God in the *Magnificat,* a hymn overflowing with Messianic joy.[13] The house of Zachary and Elizabeth exudes the spirit of the Old Testament at its most sublime, while Mary encloses in her womb the Mystery which inaugurates the New. The *Magnificat* is *the song of the Messianic times in which there mingles the joy of the ancient and the new Israel ... Mary's hymn has spread far and wide and has become the prayer of the whole Church in all ages.*[14]

This is the backdrop against which we perceive the full significance of the secret Mary treasured in her heart. The great mystery revealed to her by the angel finds its purest expression in the *Magnificat*. There is no trace in it of pretence or affectation. *My soul magnifies the Lord, and my spirit rejoices in God my Saviour*: the words, so full of nobility and of intimate union with the Creator, are a perfect mirror of Our Lady's soul.

Together with this canticle of joy and humility, the Blessed Virgin has also left us a prophecy: *Henceforth,* she exclaims, *all generations will call me blessed. From the earliest times the Blessed Virgin is honoured under the title of Mother of God, under whose protection the faithful take refuge together in prayer in all their perils and necessities. Accordingly, following the Council of Ephesus, there was a remarkable growth in the cult of the People of God towards Mary, in veneration and love, in invocation and imitation, according to her own prophetic words: 'All generations will call me blessed; for he who is mighty has done great things for me'.*[15]

During her lifetime our mother Mary was not

---

[13] St John Paul II, *Homily,* 31 May 1979
[14] St Paul VI, *Marialis cultus,* 2 February 1974, 18
[15] Second Vatican Council, *Lumen gentium,* 66

conspicuous for spectacular deeds: the Gospel makes no mention of any miracles she did while she was on earth, and has left us a very scanty record of the words she spoke. Externally her life was like that of any housewife who has to look after her family. Nevertheless, her marvellous prophecy has been fulfilled literally. Who can record all the praises made in Mary's honour, the invocations, the sanctuaries, the offerings, the Marian devotions? For twenty centuries she has been called 'blessed' by people in all walks of life: intellectuals, illiterates, kings, warriors, tradesmen, men and women, infants and elderly. We are fulfilling that prophecy at this very moment, as we say to her in the intimacy of our heart: *Hail Mary, full of grace, the Lord is with thee, blessed art thou among women.*

We have invoked her in a special way during this month of May, *but the month of May cannot end. It has to continue in our life, because our veneration and our love for her, the devotion we have to Our Lady cannot disappear from our hearts, but rather has to grow and express itself in a witness of Christian living, fashioned according to the example of Mary, 'the name of the beautiful flower that I ever invoke morning and evening', as Dante put it (Paradiso, 23, 88).*[16] In discovering Mary, we discover Jesus. *What must the cheerful way Jesus looked at people have been like? His must have been the same look as shone from the eyes of his Mother, who could not contain her joy – 'Magnificat anima mea Dominum!' – and her soul glorified the Lord while she carried him within her and walked with him by her side.*

Oh, Mother! May we, like you, rejoice to be with him and to hold him.[17]

[16] St John Paul II, *Homily,* 25 May 1979
[17] St. J. Escrivá, *Furrow,* 95

THURSDAY AFTER PENTECOST

38. OUR LORD JESUS CHRIST ETERNAL HIGH PRIEST

Memorial

The whole Church participates in the mission of Christ the Priest. Through the sacraments of christian initiation the lay faithful participate in Christ's priesthood and are rendered capable of sanctifying the world through secular affairs. Priests, in a way that is different in essence and not just in degree, also participate in Christ's priesthood and are constituted as mediators between God and man, especially through the Sacrifice of the Mass, which they realize *in persona Christi.* Today is a day when we ought to pray for all priests in a special way.

38.1 Jesus is High Priest forever.

The Lord has sworn an oath he will not change: You are a priest for ever according to the order of Melchizedek.[1]

The Epistle to the Hebrews gives us a precise definition of priesthood when it tells us that *every high priest chosen from among men is appointed to act on behalf of men in relation to God, to offer gifts and sacrifices for sins.*[2] And so the priest, who is a mediator between God and man, is intimately connected with the sacrifice he offers; this is the principal act of worship whereby man adores his Creator.

The Old Testament sacrifices were offerings made to God in recognition of his sovereignty and in thanksgiving for favours received. The act of total or partial destruction

[1] *Entrance Antiphon*: Ps 109:4
[2] Heb 5:1

of the victim on the altar was a symbol and image of the authentic sacrifice which, in the fullness of time, Christ was to offer on Calvary. Jesus, being made High Priest forever, offered himself to God as a most pleasing victim of infinite value. At one and the same time he *showed himself the Priest, the Altar, and the Lamb of sacrifice.*[3] On Calvary, Jesus the High Priest made a most acceptable offering of praise and thanksgiving to God; *it was so perfect that none greater can be thought of.*[4] This sacrifice was also a supreme act of expiation and propitiation for our sins: one drop of Christ's Blood would have been sufficient to redeem all the sins of mankind. Christ's petition on the Cross for his brethren was heard most readily by his Father, and now in heaven *he never ceases to offer himself for us.*[5] *Christ is priest indeed; but He is priest for us, not for himself. It is in the name of the whole human race that He offers prayer and acts of human religious homage to his Eternal Father. He is likewise victim; but victim for us, since He substitutes himself for guilty mankind. Now the Apostle's exhortation, 'Have this mind among yourselves, which was in Christ Jesus,' requires all Christians, so far as human power allows, to reproduce in themselves the sentiments that Christ had when He was offering himself in sacrifice – sentiments of humility, of adoration, praise, and thanksgiving to the divine Majesty. It requires them also to become victims, as it were; cultivating a spirit of self-denial according to the precepts of the Gospel, willingly doing works of penance, detesting and expiating their sins.*[6] This is the resolution we make today.

---

[3] *Roman Missal, Easter Preface V*
[4] cf St Thomas, *Summa Theologiae,* III, q.48, a.3
[5] Heb 7:25
[6] Pius XII, *Mediator Dei,* 20 February 1947, 85

38.2 All Christians have a priestly soul. Dignity of the priesthood.

The whole Church participates in the redemptive mission of Christ the priest, *which is entrusted to all the members of the people of God, who through the sacraments of initiation have been made sharers in the priesthood of Christ, to offer to God a spiritual sacrifice and bear witness to Christ before man.*[7] All the lay faithful participate in Christ's priesthood, although in a manner which is different from that of priests – not only in degree, but essentially. With *a truly priestly soul,* they sanctify the world through the perfect exercise of their secular activities, seeking in everything the glory of God: in the case of the housewife, for example, it will be through her domestic duties; or, with the army officer, by demonstrating his patriotism principally through the cultivation of the military virtues; or with the businessman, by improving his company's situation and promoting social justice. In this way all of them, offering their lives and their work through the Mass, make daily reparation for the sins of the world.

Priests and bishops have been expressly called by God, *not in order that they should be separated from the people or from any man, but that they should be completely consecrated to the task for which God chooses them. They could not be the servants of Christ unless they were witnesses to and dispensers of a life other than that of this earth. On the other hand they would be powerless to serve men if they remained aloof from their life and circumstances.*[8] The priest has been *chosen from among men* to be invested with a dignity that astounds even the angels, and then sent back to men to serve them *in relation to God* with a special and unique salvific mission. The

[7] Bl. A. del Portillo, *On priesthood,* Scepter, Chicago 1974, p.20
[8] Second Vatican Council, *Presbyterorum ordinis,* 3

priest repeatedly takes the place of Christ on earth: he has received Christ's power to forgive sins, he teaches men the way to heaven, and above all he lends his hands and his voice to Christ in the most sublime moment of the Mass: in the Sacrifice of the Altar he consecrates *in persona Christi,* taking Christ's place. There is no dignity comparable to that of the priest. *Only the divine maternity of Mary is superior to this divine ministry.*[9]

The priesthood is a marvellous gift which Christ has given his Church. The priest is *a direct and daily instrument of the saving grace which Christ has won for us. If you grasp this, if you meditate on it in the active silence of prayer, how could you ever think of the priesthood in terms of renunciation? It is a gain, an incalculable gain. Our mother Mary, the holiest of creatures – only God is holier – brought Jesus Christ into the world just once; priests bring him on earth, to our soul and body, every day: Christ comes to be our food, to give us life, to be, even now, a pledge of future life.*[10]

Today is a good day to thank Jesus for this great gift. Thank you, Lord, for the invitations to the priesthood that you constantly issue to men! We, for our part, can make the resolution of treating Christ's priests ever more lovingly and reverently, seeing them as *Christ who is passing by,* and bringing us thc most marvellous gifts we can desire: what they bring us is eternal life.

38.3 The priest, an instrument of unity.

Saint John Chrysostom, very conscious of the dignity and responsibility of the priesthood, at first resisted the idea of being ordained, and justified his behaviour as follows: *If the captain of a great ship, with a big crew full of oarsmen and laden with precious merchandise, ordered*

---

[9] R. Garrigou-Lagrange, *The priest's union with Christ,* Madrid, 1962
[10] St. J. Escrivá, *In Love with the Church,* 39

me to take the tiller and cross the Aegean or the Tyrrhenian Sea, my first reaction would be to resist. And if I were asked why, I would immediately reply: because I don't want the vessel to sink.[11] But, as the saint appreciated well, Christ is always close to the priest, close to the ship. Moreover, it is his Will that priests would continually feel supported by the esteem and the prayer of all the Church's faithful. *They should treat them with filial love as being their fathers and pastors,* says the Second Vatican Council. *They should also share their priests' anxieties and help them as far as possible by prayer and active work so that they may be better able to overcome difficulties and carry out their duties with greater success.*[12] What the faithful require of their priests is that they be always exemplary and base their efficacy on prayer, that they celebrate the Holy Mass lovingly and that they care for God's holy things with the consideration and respect they deserve, that they visit the sick and attach great importance to catechesis, that they always retain the joy which is born of self-surrender and which is so helpful even to those who are separated from God.

One thing we can ask God for today is that his priests be always available and open to everybody, and detached from themselves, *because the priest does not belong to himself, as he does not belong to his relatives and friends, nor even to a particular country: the charity he has to breathe must be universal. His very thoughts, his desires, his sentiments, are not his own: they belong to Christ, who is his life.*[13]

The priest is an instrument of unity. It is the will of

---

[11] St John Chrysostom, *On priesthood,* 3, 7

[12] Second Vatican Council, *Presbyterorum ordinis,* 9

[13] Pius XII, *Posthumous address,* quoted by John XXIII in *Sacerdotii Nostri primordia,* 4 August 1959

God *ut omnes unum sint,* that they may all be one.[14] Our Lord has said that every kingdom divided against itself will be laid waste, and that no city or household can survive if unity is lost. Priests ought to be *eager to maintain the unity of the Spirit*;[15] this exhortation of Saint Paul *is directed especially to those raised to sacred Orders so that the mission of Christ may be continued.*[16] It is principally the priest's responsibility to work for peace and harmony among his brothers, and to ensure that the unity of the faith is proof against differences of outlook in accidental and earthly affairs;[17] with his word and example he has to safeguard the conviction that nothing in this world warrants destroying the marvellous reality of the *cor unum et anima una,* one heart and soul,[18] which animated the first Christians and which must be the same for us. He will manage to fulfil his mission of unity more easily if he is open to all, if he is held in high regard by his brothers and sisters. *Pray for the priests of today, and for those who are to come, that they may really love their fellow men, every day more and without distinction, and that they may know also how to make themselves loved by them.*[19]

St John Paul II, addressing all the priests of the world, exhorted them in these words: *As we celebrate the Eucharist at so many altars throughout the world, let us give thanks to the Eternal Priest for the gift which he has bestowed on us in the Sacrament of the Priesthood. And in this thanksgiving may there be heard the words which the Evangelist puts on Mary's lips on the occasion of her visit to her cousin Elizabeth: 'the Almighty has done great*

---

[14] John 17:21
[15] Eph 4:3
[16] Second Vatican Council, *Unitatis redintegratio,* 7
[17] cf F. Suarez, *On priesthood,* Madrid, 1969
[18] Acts 4:32
[19] St. J. Escrivá, *The Forge,* 964

things for me, and holy is his name' (Luke 1:49). Let us also give thanks to Mary for the indescribable gift of the Priesthood, whereby we are able to serve in the Church every human being. May gratitude also awaken our zeal! ...

Let us unceasingly give thanks for this. Let us give thanks with the whole of our lives. Let us give thanks with all our strength. Let us give thanks together with Mary, the Mother of Priests. 'How can I repay the Lord for his goodness to me? The cup of salvation I will raise; I will call on the Lord's name' (Ps 116:12-13).[20]

---

[20] St John Paul II, *Letter to priests,* 25 March 1988, 8

Sunday After Pentecost

39. THE BLESSED TRINITY
Solemnity

Today the Church celebrates the feast of the Blessed Trinity. This, the ineffable mystery of God's intimate life, is the central truth of our faith and the source of all gifts and graces. The liturgy of the Mass invites us to loving union with each of the Three Divine Persons: Father, Son and Holy Spirit. This feast was established for the Latin Church by Pope John XXII, to be celebrated on the Sunday after the coming of the Holy Spirit, which is the last of the mysteries of our salvation. Today we can say many times, savouring it, the prayer: Glory be to the Father, and to the Son, and to the Holy Spirit.

39.1 Revelation of the mystery of the Trinity.

'Tibi laus, Tibi gloria, Tibi gratiarum actio:' to You be praise, to You be glory, to You be thanksgiving, world without end, O Blessed Trinity![1]

Having completed the commemoration of the mysteries of salvation, from Christ's birth in Bethlehem to the descent of the Holy Spirit at Pentecost, the liturgy now invites us to contemplate the central mystery of our faith: the Blessed Trinity, the ineffable mystery of God's own inner life and the fountain of all gifts and graces.

In his infinitely wise providence God gradually revealed to mankind his inmost being, that is, as he is in himself, and not just as the cause of created things. In the Old Testament he makes known above all his oneness, and his complete transcendence from the world as its creator and lord. We learn that God, unlike the world, is *uncreated*; that he is not limited in space (he is *immense*) or in time (he is *eternal*);

---

[1] *Trisagium Angelicum*

and that his power knows no limits (he is *omnipotent*). *Know therefore this day, and lay it to your heart,* says the liturgy, *that the Lord is God in heaven above and on the earth beneath; there is no other.*[2] Only you, Lord, are God.

The Old Testament proclaims above all the greatness of Yahweh, the one God, Creator and Lord of the universe. But he is also revealed as *the shepherd who seeks his flock,* who looks after his own indulgently and tenderly, who forgives and forgets the frequent infidelities of his chosen people. At the same time we get glimpses of the paternity of God the Father, of the Incarnation of God the Son (whose advent is foretold by the prophets), and of the action of the Holy Spirit, who vivifies all things.

But it is Christ who reveals to us in all its fullness the inner workings of the Trinitarian mystery and calls us to participate in it. *No one knows the Father except the Son and any one to whom the Son chooses to reveal him.*[3] It is he who speaks to us of the co-existence of the Holy Spirit with the Father, and who sends him to the Church to sanctify it until the end of time; and he it is who reveals to us the perfect oneness of life of the Three Divine Persons.[4]

The mystery of the Trinity is the starting point of all revealed truth, the fountain from which proceeds supernatural life, and the goal whither we are headed: we are children of the Father, brothers and co-heirs with the Son, and continually sanctified by the Holy Spirit to make us ever more and more resemble Christ; accordingly, we deepen in the understanding of our divine filiation and become living temples of the Blessed Trinity.

Since it is the central mystery of the Church's faith, the Blessed Trinity is continually invoked in the liturgy.

---

[2] *First Reading, Year B*: Deut 4:39

[3] Matt 11:27

[4] *Gospel, Year C*: John 16:12-15

We were baptized in the name of the Father and of the Son and of the Holy Spirit; and in their name also are our sins forgiven. We begin and end many prayers by invoking the Father, through Jesus Christ, in the unity of the Holy Spirit. Often during the day we say the prayer: *Glory be to the Father, and to the Son, and to the Holy Spirit.*

God is my Father! If you meditate on it, you will never let go of this consoling thought!

Jesus is my dear Friend (another thrilling discovery) who loves me with all the divine madness of his Heart.

The Holy Spirit is my Consoler, who guides my every step along the road.

Consider this often: you are God's – and God is yours.[5]

39.2 The soul's relationship with each of the Three Divine Persons.

The divine life in which we are called to participate is extraordinarily bounteous indeed. The Father eternally engenders the Son, and the Father and the Son together breathe forth the Holy Spirit. This generation of the Son and the spiration of the Holy Spirit is not something that took place at a particular moment in time and gave rise once and for all to the Three Divine Persons. No. These 'processions', as theologians call them, are eternal.

In the case of human generation, a father begets a son but thereafter both father and son continue to exist independently of the act of begetting, even if one of them later dies. The man who is father is not just 'father': both before and after begetting he is 'man'. In God, by contrast, the essence of the Father consists in giving life to the Son: this is what determines him as a Divine Person really distinct from the others. Among human beings, the son who is begotten has a separate existence from his father;

[5] St. J. Escrivá, *The Forge,* 2

but the essence of the Only-begotten Son of God consists precisely in being Son.[6] And it is through him, making ourselves like him by the constant impulse of the Holy Spirit that we obtain and grow in the awareness of our divine filiation. *For all who are led by the Spirit of God are sons of God. For you did not receive the spirit of slavery to fall back into fear, but you have received the spirit of sonship. When we cry, 'Abba! Father!' it is the Spirit himself bearing witness with our spirit that we are children of God, and if children, then heirs, heirs of God and fellow heirs with Christ.*[7]

Among men, paternity and filiation are circumstances that fall short of defining the subject completely; but in God, paternity, filiation and spiration constitute the entire being of the Father, Son and Holy Spirit.[8]

From the moment man is first called to participate in the divine life through the grace of Baptism, he is destined to participate in it ever more and more; along this path he must journey continually. From the Holy Spirit we constantly receive impulses, motions and inspirations to encourage us to travel faster along the way that leads to God, and to revolve in an ever tighter 'orbit' around Our Lord. *Our heart now needs to distinguish and adore each one of the divine Persons. The soul is, as it were, making a discovery in the supernatural life, like a little child opening his eyes to the world about him. The soul spends time lovingly with the Father and the Son and the Holy Spirit, and readily submits to the work of the lifegiving Paraclete, who gives himself to us without the slightest merit on our part, bestowing on us his gifts and the supernatural virtues!*

We have run 'like the deer, longing for flowing

---

[6] cf J. M. Pero-Sanz, *The Athanasian Symbol,* Madrid, 1976
[7] *Second Reading, Year C*: Rom 8:14-17
[8] A Carthusian, *The Trinity and Interior life,* Madrid, 1958

streams' (Ps 41:2), thirsting, our lips parched and dry. We want to drink at this source of living water. All day long, without doing anything strange, we move in this abundant, clear spring of fresh waters that leap up to eternal life (cf John 4:14). Words are not needed, because the tongue cannot express this wonder. The intellect grows calm. One does not reason; one looks! And the soul breaks out once more into song, a new song, because it feels and knows it is under the loving gaze of God, all day long.[9]

39.3 Praying to the Blessed Trinity.

The Blessed Trinity dwells in the christian soul as in a temple. Saint Paul explains that *God's love has been poured into our hearts through the Holy Spirit who has been given to us.*[10] And there, in the inner recesses of the soul, we learn to be intimate with God – Father, Son and Holy Spirit. *You, O Eternal Trinity, are a deep ocean, into which the more I penetrate, the more I discover, and the more I discover, the more I seek you,*[11] we say in the intimacy of prayer.

My God, Blessed Trinity! Draw from my poor being what most contributes to your glory, and do with me what you wish both now and in eternity. May I no longer place between us any voluntary hindrance to your transforming action ... Second by second, with a forever 'actual' intention, I desire to offer you all that I am and all that I have. Make my poor life, in intimate union with the Word Incarnate, an unceasing sacrifice of glory to the Blessed Trinity ...

My God, how I wish to glorify you! O, if only in exchange for my complete immolation, or for any other condition, it were in my power to enkindle the hearts of all your creatures and the whole of creation in the flames of

---

[9] St. J. Escrivá, *Friends of God,* 306-307
[10] *Second Reading, Year C*: Rom 5:5
[11] St Catherine of Siena, *Dialogue,* 167

your love, how I would desire to do so! May at least my poor heart belong to you completely, may I keep nothing for myself nor for creatures, not even a single heartbeat. May I have a burning love for all mankind, but only with you, through you and for you ... I desire above all to love you with the heart of Saint Joseph, with the Immaculate Heart of Mary, and with the adorable Heart of Jesus; and, finally, to submerge myself in that infinite ocean, that abyss of fire that consumes the Father and the Son in the unity of the Holy Spirit, and love you with your own infinite love ...

O Eternal Father, beginning and end of all things! Through the Immaculate Heart of Mary I offer you Jesus, your Word Incarnate, and through him, with him and in him, I want to repeat ceaselessly this cry that rises from the bottom of my soul: Father, glorify continually your Son, that your Son may glorify you, in the unity of the Holy Spirit for ever and ever (John 17:1).

O Jesus, who said: 'No one knows the Son except the Father, and no one knows the Father except the Son and any one to whom the Son chooses to reveal him' (Matt 11:27), 'Show us the Father, and we shall be satisfied!' (John 14:8).

And you, O Spirit of Love! 'Teach us all things' (John 14:26) and 'form Jesus with Mary in us' (Gal 4:19) until we 'become perfectly one' (John 17:23) in 'the bosom of the Father' (John 1:18). Amen.[12]

[12] Sister Elizabeth of the Trinity, *Elevation to the Blessed Trinity* in *Complete Works,* Burgos 1985

Sunday After Pentecost

40. THE INDWELLING OF THE HOLY TRINITY IN THE SOUL

40.1 The Presence of God, One and Three, in the soul in grace.

At the Last Supper when one of his disciples asked him why He would show himself to them alone and not to the whole world, (which was how the Jews of the day were expecting the Messiah to manifest himself), Jesus answered: *If a man love me, he will keep my word, and my Father will love him, and we will come to him and make our home with him.*[1] Our Lord reveals that not only He but the Blessed Trinity itself would be present, *as in a temple,*[2] in the souls of those who love him. This revelation makes up the whole *substance of the New Testament,*[3] the very heart and quintessence of his teaching.

God – the Father, Son and Holy Spirit – dwells in our soul in grace not only with a presence of immensity, as He is to be found in everything, but in a special way through sanctifying grace.[4] This new presence fills the soul that travels along the paths of sanctity with love, and with an indescribable joy. Indeed, it is there, in the central depths of the soul, that we must accustom ourselves to seeking God, in every one of life's situations, whether it be out in the street, at sport or whilst we are relaxing. *O, then,* exclaimed Saint John of the Cross, *most beautiful soul who dost so much desire to know the place where your Beloved*

---

[1] John 14:23
[2] cf 1 Cor 6:19
[3] Tertullian, *Contra Praxeas,* 31
[4] cf St Thomas, *Summa Theologiae,* 1 ,q 43, a 3

is in order to seek him and to be united with him, He tells you now that you yourself are the abode wherein He dwells, and the closet and hiding place where He is hidden. It is a matter of great contentment and joy for you to see that all your good and all your hope are so near that you cannot be without them. 'Behold', says the Spouse, 'the kingdom of God is within you' (Luke 17:21), and his servant the Apostle Saint Paul says: 'We are the temple of the living God' (2 Cor 6:16).[5]

The good fortune of having the presence of the Blessed Trinity in the soul is not meant only for extraordinary individuals, for people endowed with exceptional charisma or qualities, but for the ordinary Christian, who is called to sanctity in the midst of his or her professional activities and who wants to love God with all his being, even though, as Saint Teresa of Avila points out, *there are many souls who remain in the outer courtyard of the castle (of the soul), which is the place occupied by the sentinels; they are not interested in entering it, and they have no idea of what there is in that wonderful place, or of who dwells inside it ...*[6] In this *wonderful place* – in the soul illuminated by grace – God is with us: the Father, the Son and the Holy Spirit.

This presence that theologians call *indwelling* differs only in quality from the blessedness of those who have already attained the state of eternal happiness in Heaven.[7] Although it belongs to the Three divine Persons, it is attributed to the Holy Spirit, for the work of sanctification is proper to Love.

This revelation that God made to men, as though in loving confidence, amazed the first Christians and filled

---

[5] St John of the Cross, *The Spiritual Canticle,* 1, 7
[6] St Teresa, *The Mansions,* 5, 6
[7] cf Leo XIII, *Divinum illud munus,* 9 May 1897

their hearts with peace and supernatural joy. When we are convinced of this supernatural reality – that God, One and Three, dwells within us as individuals – we turn our lives, with all their troubles, and perhaps even because of such troubles, into *a foretaste of Heaven*: it is like entering into God's inmost being and knowing and loving the divine life, of which we become sharers.

O unfathomable ocean of divine life!
Driven on by faith I have approached your shores.
Tell me, what is it in your great depths
That holds me by its charm?
O bottomless ocean of divine life!
I was swept along by your undertow ...
And already I am out of my depth![8]

40.2 Supernatural life leads a Christian to know and to converse intimately with the Blessed Trinity.

The Christian begins his life in the name of the Father and of the Son and of the Holy Spirit; and in this same Name he leaves this world to find in Heaven the fullness of the vision of these divine Persons whom he has tried to get to know here on earth. One God and three divine Persons: this is the profession of our Faith that the Apostles heard from Jesus' lips and handed down. It is the faith that Christians have held from the very first moment, the faith that the Magisterium of the Church has always taught. As they advance along their journey towards God, Christians of all times have felt the need to meditate on this first truth of our Faith, and to try to get to know each one of the Three Persons. Saint Teresa of Avila tells us in her *Life* how, as she was meditating precisely on one of the oldest instructions of faith in the mystery of the Trinity – the Athanasian Creed or *Quicumque,* as it is called – she

[8] Sister Cristina de Arteaga, *Sow!,* Seville, 1982

received special graces to go deeper into this marvellous reality. The saint writes: *Once when I was reciting the 'Quicumque vult', I was shown so clearly how it was possible for there to be one God alone and three Persons that it caused me both amazement and much comfort. It was of the greatest help to me in teaching me to know more of the greatness of God and of his marvels. When I think of the Most Holy Trinity, or hear it spoken of, I seem to understand how there can be such a mystery, and it is a great joy to me.*[9]

The whole of a Christian's supernatural life is directed towards this knowledge of and intimate conversation with the Trinity, who become eventually the *fruit and the end of our whole life.*[10] It is for this end that we have been created and raised to the supernatural order: to know, to talk to and to love God the Father, God the Son and God the Holy Spirit, who dwell in the soul in grace.

In this life the Christian comes to have an *experiential knowledge* of these three Divine Persons, a knowledge that, far from being something extraordinary, is appreciable within the normal paths of sanctity,[11] a sanctity to which are called the mother of a family who scarcely finds enough hours in the day to look after her home and to make ends meet, the workman who starts his work before daybreak, the sick whose illness prevents them from doing anything ... God, in his infinite love for each individual person, ardently desires to make himself known in this intimate and loving way to all those who really follow in the footsteps of his Son.

On this path towards the Blessed Trinity to which all our efforts must tend, we have as our Guide and Teacher

---

[9] St Teresa, *Life,* 39, 25

[10] St Thomas, *Commentary on Book IV of the Sentences,* 1, d 2, q 1

[11] cf R. Garrigou-Lagrange, *The Three Ages of the Interior Life,* 1

the Holy Spirit. Our Lord promised – and his word never fails: *I will pray the Father, and He will give you another Counsellor, to be with you for ever, even the Spirit of truth, whom the world cannot receive, because it neither sees him nor knows him; you know him for He dwells with you, and will be in you. I will not leave you desolate; I will come to you.*[12] In this *'you'* are fortunately included all of us who have been baptized, and particularly those of us who want to follow Jesus closely, in the very place and circumstances where life has placed us. It is sweet to meditate that this mystery, which is inaccessible to human reason alone, is made clear to us by the light of the Faith and the help of the Holy Spirit. *To you it has been given to know the secrets of the kingdom of heaven.*[13] Let us ask God today to guide us along this path which is filled with light.

40.3 Temples of God.

As well as asking the Holy Spirit to give us a great desire to purify our hearts, we have to desire with real sincerity this intimate meeting with the Holy Trinity, without being put off because perhaps we see our weaknesses and the deficiencies of our attitude towards God more clearly. Saint Teresa tells us that as she considered the presence of the Three Divine Persons in her soul she was *amazed at seeing so much majesty in a thing as lowly as my soul*; then Our Lord said to her: *It is not lowly, my daughter, because it is made in my own image.*[14] And the saint was filled with consolation. It can do us a great deal of good to consider these words as being spoken to us, and they will encourage us to continue along this path that ends in God. We must treat every person we come across each day as the possessor of an immortal soul,

---

[12] John 14:16-18
[13] Matt 13:11
[14] St Teresa, *Matters of Conscience,* 41

the image of God, which is or can become *the temple of God.*

Sister Elizabeth of the Trinity, recently beatified, wrote to her sister on receiving news of the birth and baptism of her first niece: *I feel full of respect,* she said in her letter, *for this little temple of the Blessed Trinity ... If I were near her I would kneel down to adore him who dwells within her.*[15]

The Church recommends us to nourish our piety with solid food, and this is why we should meditate on these instructions on the Faith and recite the prayers composed in honour of the Trinity. Such prayers are the Athanasian Creed or *Quicumque* (which in the past Christians used to say every Sunday after the homily, and which today on the third Sunday of each month, many people say and meditate on in honour of the Blessed Trinity), the *Trisagium Angelicum,* said especially on this solemnity, the *Glory be to the Father, and to the Son and to the Holy Spirit ...* When, with the help of grace, we learn to go deep into these practices of devotion, it is as if we heard again the words of Our Lord: *Blessed are your eyes, for they see, and your ears, for they hear. Truly I say to you, many prophets and righteous men have longed to see what you see, and did not see it, and to hear what you hear, and did not hear it.*[16]

We finish this time of prayer repeating in our hearts, with Saint Augustine: *My Lord and my God, my only hope, hear my prayer so that I may not give in to discouragement and cease to seek you. May I desire always to see your face. Give me strength for the search. You who caused me to find you and gave the hope of a more perfect knowledge*

---

[15] Sister Elizabeth of the Trinity, *Letter to her sister Margaret,* Complete Works, 2

[16] Matt 13:16-17

of you, I place before you my steadfastness, that you may preserve it, and my weakness, that you may heal it. I place before you my knowledge, and my ignorance. If you open the door to me, welcome the one who enters. If you have closed the gate, open it to the one who calls. Make me always remember you, understand you and love you. Increase those gifts in me until I am completely changed ...

When we come up into your presence, these many things we talk about now without understanding them will cease, and you alone will remain everything in everyone, and then we will sing as one an eternal hymn of praise and we too will become one with you.[17]

The substance of our supernatural life is the contemplation and praise of the Blessed Trinity, which is the object of our life, for in Heaven, close to our Mother, Mary – Daughter of God the Father, Mother of God the Son, Spouse of God the Holy Spirit: Greater than she none but God![18] – our joy and our happiness will give eternal praise to the Father, through the Son, in the Holy Spirit.

---

[17] St Augustine, *De Trinitate,* 15, 28, 51
[18] cf St. J. Escrivá, *The Way,* 496

CORPUS CHRISTI

41. THE MOST HOLY BODY AND BLOOD OF CHRIST

Solemnity

This Solemnity goes back to the thirteenth century. It was first established in the diocese of Liége, and Pope Urban IV instituted it in 1264 for the whole Church. The meaning of this feast is the consideration of and devotion to the real presence of Christ in the Eucharist. The centre of the feast was to be, as Pope Urban IV described it, a popular devotion reflected in hymns and joy. In the same year Saint Thomas Aquinas, at the Pope's request, composed for this day two Offices which have nourished the piety of many Christians throughout the centuries. In many different places the procession with the Monstrance through specially bedecked streets gives testimony of the Christian people's faith and love for Christ, who once again passes through our cities and towns. The procession began in the same way as the feast itself.

In places where the Solemnity of the Most Holy Body and Blood is not observed as a holyday of obligation, it is kept on the Sunday after the Most Holy Trinity as its proper day.

41.1 Love and Veneration for Jesus in the Blessed Sacrament.

Lauda, Sion, Salvatorem ...
Sing forth, O Zion, sweetly sing
The praises of thy Shepherd-King,
In hymns and canticles divine.[1]

Today we celebrate this great Solemnity in honour of the mystery of the Holy Eucharist. On this day the liturgy itself and popular piety, which have spared no efforts in their search for inventiveness and beauty, come together to

[1] Sequence, *Lauda, Sion, Salvatorem*

sing to the *Love of loves*. For this day Saint Thomas Aquinas composed those very beautiful texts of the Mass and of the Divine Office. Today we must give many thanks to God for having remained amongst us, make atonement to him and express to him our joy at having him so close to us: *Adoro te devote, latens Deitas ... O Godhead hid, devoutly I adore thee,* we will repeat to him many times this day from the very depths of our hearts.

When we visit the Blessed Sacrament we will be able to say slowly to Our Lord, with love: *Plagas, sicut Thomas, non intueor ...*

I do not see your wounds as Thomas saw them,
but I confess that you are my God.
Make me believe thee ever more and more,
In thee my hope, in thee my love to store.

It was faith in the real presence of Christ in the Holy Eucharist that led to devotion to Jesus in the Blessed Sacrament outside of Mass as well. In the first centuries of the Church the Sacred Species were reserved so that Communion could be taken to the sick and to those who were in prison awaiting martyrdom because they had confessed their faith. As time went by, the faith and love of believers caused them to make both public and private devotion to the Holy Eucharist far richer. Their faith led them to treat the Body of Christ with the greatest possible reverence and this also led to greater public devotion. We can find many testimonies in the most ancient documents of the Church to the veneration by the early Christians which later was to make way for the feast we celebrate today.

Our Lord and our God is in the Tabernacle. Christ is in the Tabernacle, and it is there that we must show him our adoration and our love. This veneration for Jesus in the Blessed Sacrament is expressed in many ways – Benediction of the Blessed Sacrament, processions, prayer before Jesus in the Blessed Sacrament, genuflections that are real acts of faith and of adoration ... Amongst these devotions and various forms of worship, *particularly worthy of mention is the solemnity of Corpus Christi* as a public act by which the Church seeks to pay homage to Christ present in the Eucharist ... The Church and the world have great need of eucharistic devotions. Jesus is waiting for us in this sacrament of Love. Let us not be sparing in the time we spend going to meet him in adoration, in contemplation filled with faith, and let us be prepared to make reparation for the many grave faults and offences committed against him in the world. May our adoration never cease.[2] Today especially has to be filled with acts of faith and of love for Jesus in the Blessed Sacrament.

If we take part in the day's procession, accompanying Jesus, we will be like those simple people who joyfully followed the Master during the days of his life on earth, and who with great naturalness told him of all their needs and about the sufferings they endured. We too will experience the happiness and the joy of being with him. If we see him pass through our streets exposed in the Monstrance, we will tell him from the depths of our hearts how much He means to us ... *Adore him reverently and devoutly; renew in his presence the sincere offerings of your love. Don't be afraid to tell him that you love him. Thank him for giving you this daily proof of his tender mercy, and encourage yourself to go to Communion in a spirit of trust. I am awed by this mystery of Love. Here is the Lord seeking to use my heart as a throne, committed never to leave me, provided I don't run away.*[3] Jesus is happier on this throne of my heart than in the most magnificent Monstrance.

---

[2] St John Paul II, Letter, *Dominicae Cenae,* 24 February 1980

[3] St. J. Escrivá, *Christ is passing by,* 161

41.2 Food for eternal life.

As the words of the *Entrance Antiphon* remind us: *He fed them with the finest wheat and satisfied them with honey from the rock.*[4]

For many years God fed manna to the people of Israel as they wandered in the wilderness. This was an image and symbol of the pilgrim Church and of each individual who journeys towards his or her definitive homeland – Heaven. That food given in the desert of Sinai is a figure of the true food, the Holy Eucharist. *This is the sacrament of the human pilgrimage ... Precisely because of this, the annual feast of the Eucharist that the Church celebrates today contains within its liturgy so many references to the pilgrimage of the people of the Covenant in their wanderings through the wilderness.*[5] Moses often reminded the Israelites of this wonderful deed that God had performed for his People: *Do not then forget the Lord your God, who brought you out of the land of Egypt, out of the house of bondage.*[6]

Today is a day of thanksgiving and of joy because God has wanted to remain with us in order to feed us and to strengthen us, so that we may never feel alone. The Holy Eucharist is the *viaticum,* the food for the long journey of our days on Earth towards the goal of true Life. Jesus accompanies us and strengthens us here in this world, where our life is like a shadow compared to the reality that awaits us. Earthly food is a pale image of the food we receive in Holy Communion. The Holy Eucharist opens up our hearts to a completely new reality.[7]

Although we celebrate this feast only once a year, the

---

[4] *Entrance Antiphon*: Ps 80:17
[5] St John Paul II, *Homily,* 4 June 1988
[6] *First Reading,* Year A: cf Deut 8:2-3; 14-16
[7] cf *Gospel of the Mass,* Year C: Luke 9:11-17

Church really proclaims this most happy truth every day: Jesus gives himself to us daily as our food, and He remains in our Tabernacles to be for us the strength and the hope of a new life, a life without end and without limit. It is a mystery which is ever alive and ever new.

Thank you, Lord, for remaining with us. What would have become of us without you? Where would we have gone to restore our strength and to ask for consolation? From the Tabernacle how easy you make the way for us!

41.3 The Corpus Christi Procession.

One day, as Jesus was leaving the city of Jericho to continue his journey towards Jerusalem, He passed by a blind man who was begging for alms at the side of the road. When he heard the sound of the little crowd that was following the Master, he asked what it meant. The people around him answered: *Jesus of Nazareth is passing by.*[8]

If today, in the many cities and towns where this ancient custom of carrying the Blessed Sacrament in procession is still observed, someone was to ask when he hears the noise of the crowd, 'What is it? What is happening?', we could answer him with the same words with which they answered Bartimaeus: *Jesus of Nazareth is passing by.* It is Christ himself who walks through our streets receiving the homage of our faith and of our love. It is Christ himself! And like the heart of Bartimaeus our hearts too should burst into shouts: *Jesus, Son of David, have mercy on me*! And Our Lord, who went about blessing and doing good,[9] will have compassion on our blindness and on all the ills that sometimes lie heavy on our soul. The Church, by means of the feast we are celebrating today with an exuberance of faith and of love, *desires only to dispel the mysterious silence that surrounds*

[8] Luke 18:37
[9] cf Acts 10:38

the Eucharist, and to emit a triumphant cry that bursts out through the walls of sanctuaries and overwhelms the streets of cities so as to infuse the whole human community with joy at the presence of Christ, of him who is the silent and strong companion of pilgrim man along the paths of time and of earth..[10] This is it that fills our hearts with joy. It is logical, especially on this day, that the hymns that accompany the Blessed Sacrament should be hymns of adoration, of love, and of profound joy.

Let us sing to the Love of loves,
Let us sing to the Lord:
Behold our God is here;
O come, let us adore Christ our Redeemer ...
Pange lingua gloriosi ...
Sing, my tongue the Saviour's glory,
Of his Flesh the mystery sing ...

The solemn procession that takes place in so many towns and cities of Christian tradition is of very ancient origin and is the expression with which Christian people give public testimony of their piety towards the Blessed Sacrament.[11] On this day Our Lord takes possession of our streets and town squares. It is piety that leads the faithful to cover the streets with carpets of flowers and green boughs. Magnificent monstrances have been designed for this feast. The closer their decorations are to the consecrated Host the richer and more intricate they are. Today many Christians will accompany our Lord in procession as He comes to meet those who want to see him and *to make himself available to those who are not looking for him. And so once more He comes among his own people. How should we respond to this call of his? ...*

---

[10] St Paul VI, *Homily,* 11 August 1964
[11] cf J. Abad and M. Garrido, *Initiation into the Liturgy of the Church,* Madrid 1988

The Corpus Christi procession makes Christ present in towns and cities throughout the world. But his presence cannot be limited to only one day, like a sound you hear and then forget. It should remind us that we have to discover Our Lord in our ordinary everyday activities. Side by side with this solemn procession there is the simple, silent procession of the ordinary life of each Christian. He is a man among men, who by a great blessing has received the faith and the divine commission to act so that he renews the message of Our Lord on earth ...

Let us ask Our Lord, then, to make us souls devoted to the Blessed Eucharist, so that our relationship with him brings forth joy and serenity and a desire for justice. In this way will we make it easier for others to recognize Christ; we will put Christ at the centre of all human activities. And Jesus' promise will be fulfilled: 'I, when I am lifted up from the earth, will draw all men to myself' (John 12:32).[12]

---

[12] St. J. Escrivá, *Christ is passing by,* 156

Corpus Christi Octave: Day 2

42. A HIDDEN GOD

42.1 Jesus remains hidden so that He may be sought out by our faith and our love.

Adoro te devote, latens Deitas ...
O Godhead hid, devoutly I adore thee,
Who truly art within the forms before me;
To thee my heart I bow with bended knee,
As failing quite in contemplating thee.[1]

These are the opening words of the hymn Saint Thomas wrote for the feast of *Corpus Christi,* and that have helped so many Christians to meditate upon and to express their faith in and their love for the Blessed Eucharist.

O Godhead hid, devoutly I adore thee ... Isaiah had already proclaimed the same: *Truly thou art a God who hidest thyself.*[2] The Creator of the universe has left upon it the imprint of his work. It seems that He wanted to take second place. But a moment came in the history of mankind when it was God's decision to reveal his most intimate being to us. Moreover, in his goodness He wanted to live among us, to pitch his tent among men. So He took flesh in the most chaste womb of Mary. He came on earth and remained hidden for the great majority of people, who were concerned about other things. Some people recognised him – those who had simplicity of heart and who kept vigilant watch for the things of God. Mary, Joseph, the shepherds, the Magi, Anna, Simeon ... This latter, an old man, had been waiting all his life for the coming of the Messiah who had been promised. This is

[1] Hymn, *Adoro te devote*
[2] Is 45:15

why he was able to exclaim before the Child Jesus: *Lord, now lettest thou thy servant depart in peace according to thy word; for mine eyes have seen thy salvation.*[3] If only we could say the same whenever we approach the tabernacle!

Afterwards, in spite of the miracles by which Jesus manifested his divine power during his public life, many people were unable to recognise him. On other occasions it is Our Lord himself who hides and commands those He has healed not to talk about him. In Gethsemane and in his Passion his divinity seemed totally hidden to men's eyes. As He hung on the Cross Our Lady certainly knew that He who was dying was the Saviour, God made man. But in the eyes of many He was dying simply as a malefactor.

Jesus hides again in the Blessed Eucharist under the appearances of bread and wine so that our faith and our love may seek him out. We say to him in our prayer: *Lord, you who make us share in the miracle of the Eucharist, we beg you not to hide away,* may your face be ever clear to our eyes. *Live with us,* because without you our lives have no meaning. *May we see you,* with our eyes purified by the sacrament of Penance. *May we touch you,* like that woman who dared to finger the hem of your garment and who was healed. *May we too touch you*: without ever wanting to get accustomed to the miracle. *May we want to be beside you all the time*: which is the only place where we are completely happy. *May we have you as the King of our lives and of our work*: because we have given everything to you.[4]

42.2 The Holy Eucharist transforms us.

Love demands the presence of the beloved, and the Master who had left to his followers the supreme commandment of love could not evade this characteristic of true

---

[3] Luke 2:29-30

[4] cf St. J. Escrivá, *The Forge,* 542

friendship – the desire of friends to be together. In order to make this living among us whilst waiting for Heaven a reality, He has remained in our tabernacles. Before He left this earth He commanded his followers: *Abide in me, as I in you. No longer do I call you servants, for the servant does not know what his master is doing. You are my friends. Abide in my love.*[5] He made this possible through the Holy Eucharist. The many times Christ has visited us in Holy Communion and the many times we have gone to see him in the tabernacle have enabled us to develop a deep friendship with him. There, hidden from our senses, but so clear to our faith, He has waited for us: at his feet we have reaffirmed our highest ideals and have abandoned all our worries – those things that may have overwhelmed us at times – into his hands ... A friend understands his friend well. We have gone to drink at the fountain and to learn how to practise all the virtues. We have endeavoured to make his strength our own. We have tried to make his vision of the world and of people our own vision. If only one day we could say like Saint Paul: *It is no longer I who lives, but Christ who lives in me*![6]

Saint Thomas affirms that the virtue of this sacrament is to transform a man into Christ through love.[7] We all have the experience that each one of us lives largely in accordance with what he loves. People devoted to study, to sport or to their profession say that such activities are *their life.* In a similar way, if a man seeks only his own self-interest, he lives for himself alone. If we love Christ and unite ourselves to him. we will live more deeply *through him and in him,* depending on the truth and depth of our

---

[5] John 15:4; 9; 15

[6] Gal 2:20

[7] cf St Thomas, *Commentary on Book IV of the Sentences,* D 12, q 2, a 2, ad 1

love. Moreover, grace forms us inwardly and divinizes us. *Do you love the earth?,* asks Saint Augustine, *You will be earth. Do you love God? What can I say? That you will be God? I do not dare to say it, but Holy Scripture tells you this: 'I say, You are gods, sons of the Most High, all of you' (Ps 81:6).*[8]

We go to see Jesus hidden in the tabernacle. All distance is annihilated and even time loses its boundaries before this Presence which is eternal life, the seed of Resurrection and a foretaste of heavenly bliss. It is from here that a Christian's life radiates forth Christ's life; in the midst of his work, in his habitual smile, in the way he accepts setbacks and pain, the Christian reflects Christ. He who remains for us in the tabernacle manifests himself to men and makes himself present in them in the everyday life of a Christian.

Tabernacles of silver and of gold that give shelter to the omnipresence of Jesus, our treasure, our life, our knowledge, I bless you and adore the One who inhabits you with profound reverence ...[9]

For two thousand years the Son of God has lived among men, *He in whom the Father finds his inexpressible delights, from whom the blessed drink an eternity of bliss! The Incarnate Word is there in the Host, just as He was in the times of the Apostles and of the crowds who followed him in Palestine, with the infinite fullness of a capital grace that asks for nothing except to flow out onto all men in order to transform them into himself. We should approach the saving Word with the same faith as those humble people of the Gospel who hurried forward to meet Christ in order to touch the hem of his garment and were healed.*[10] Let us make a resolution to approach him in the same trustful way.

---

[8] St Augustine, *Commentary on St John's Letter to the Parthans,* 2, 14
[9] Sister Cristina de Arteaga, *Sow!,* XCIX
[10] M. M. Philipon, *The Sacraments in Christian Life*

42.3 Christ gives himself to each one of us personally.

To thee my heart I bow with bended knee,
As failing quite in contemplating thee.

We should not be disconcerted by the outward appearances. Not all reality or even all the created realities of this world are perceived by the senses, which are a source of knowledge but at the same time set a limit to our intellect. The Church in her pilgrimage through this world towards the Father possesses in the Holy Eucharist the Second Person of the Holy Trinity, who cannot be perceived by the senses and who has been assumed by the Sacred Humanity of Christ. *The Word became flesh*[11] in order to dwell among us and to make us partakers of his divinity. He came for the whole world and He would have taken flesh for a single individual, for the least and the most unworthy of men. Saint Paul had a joyful foretaste of this reality, *The Son of God,* he said, *loved me and gave himself for me.*[12] Jesus would have come into the world and would have suffered all He did suffer for me alone. Each one of us should think to himself: this is the great reality that fills my life. In the economy of the redemption, the Eucharist was the providential means chosen by God to enable him to remain with us personally, in a unique and unrepeatable way, within each one of us. We sing joyfully from the depths of our hearts: *Pange, lingua, gloriosi Corporis mysterium ...*

O my tongue, its mysteries sing,
Of the glorious Body telling,
And the Blood, all price excelling,
Which the world's eternal King,
In a noble womb once dwelling,

---

[11] John 1:14
[12] Gal 2:20

Shed for the world's ransoming.[13]

Jesus is not hidden. We see him each day, we receive him, we love him, we visit him ... How clear and unmistakable that Presence becomes when we contemplate him with a gaze that is pure and full of faith! Let us think about how we are going to receive Communion, perhaps in just a few minutes' or a few hours' time, and let us ask God the Father – our Father – to increase the faith and the love we have in our hearts. Perhaps that prayer of Saint Thomas can help us. It is a prayer we may sometimes have said when preparing to receive Jesus on other occasions: *Omnipotent and eternal God, I approach the sacrament of your Only-begotten Son, Our Lord Jesus Christ, like a sick man who goes to the doctor who gives him life; like someone unclean I approach the fount of mercy: as one blind I come to the light of eternity; poor and needy I present myself to the sovereign Lord of Heaven and earth. I pray that in the immensity of your generosity you may deign to heal my sickness, purify my stains, enlighten my darkness, enrich my wretchedness, clothe my nakedness. O most sweet Lord, grant that I may receive the Body of your Only-begotten Son born of the Virgin, with such fervour that I may be intimately united to him and counted among the members of his mystical Body.*

---

[13] Hymn, *Pange Lingua*

Corpus Christi Octave: Day 3

43. THE EUCHARIST: SUBSTANTIAL PRESENCE OF CHRIST

43.1 Transubstantiation.

Visus, tactus, gustus in te fallitur ...
Sight, touch and taste in thee are each deceived;
The ear alone most safely is believed.
I believe all the Son of God has spoken:
Than truth's own word there is no truer token.[1]

When our sight, touch and taste make a judgment about the true, real and substantial presence of Christ in the Eucharist, each one of these senses totally fails us. They can grasp the external appearances, the accidents; they can perceive the colour, the smell, the shape and the quantity of the bread or of the wine, but they are unable to infer from them the underlying reality, because they lack the information that is given only by faith, and that comes to us only in the words by which divine revelation has been transmitted to us: *The ear alone most safely is believed.* That is why when we contemplate this ineffable mystery with the eyes of our soul we must do so *with humble reverence, not following human arguments, which ought to be hushed, but in steadfast adherence to divine Revelation,*[2] in order to make it possible for us to grasp this true and mysterious reality.

The Church teaches us that Christ becomes really present in the Blessed Eucharist *through the conversion of the entire substance of bread into his Body and through the*

---

[1] Hymn, *Adoro te devote*
[2] St Paul VI, *Mysterium fidei,* 3 September 1965

conversion of the entire substance of wine into his Blood, leaving unchanged only those properties of bread and wine which are open to our senses. This hidden conversion is appropriately and justly called by the Church 'transubstantiation'.[3] And Holy Mother Church herself warns us that any explanation given with the object of making this ineffable mystery easier to understand *must maintain, without ambiguity, that order of reality which exists independently of the human mind, the bread and wine cease to exist after the consecration. From then on, therefore, the Body and Blood of the Lord Jesus, under the sacramental species of bread and wine, are truly presented before us for our adoration.*[4]

That order of reality which exists independently of the human mind ... After the Consecration, Jesus is present on the altar or in the tabernacle in which the consecrated Hosts are reserved, even though out of blindness I should fail to make the smallest act of faith, or out of hardness of heart I were to make no manifestation of love. It is not 'my fervour' that causes him to be present – He is there.

In the fourth century, when Saint Cyril of Jerusalem wanted to explain this extraordinary truth to some recent converts, he used, by way of example, the miracle that Our Lord performed at the wedding feast at Cana of Galilee, when he changed the water into wine.[5] Saint Cyril asked: if He was able to do such a wonderful thing as change water into wine, *are we to think it is undignified to believe that He changed wine into his Blood? If He worked this wonderful miracle at a wedding feast, should we not think with still greater reason that He would give the offspring of marriage his Body and his Blood as their food? Therefore,*

[3] *idem, Creed of the People of God,* 30 June 1968
[4] *ibid*
[5] cf St Cyril of Jerusalem, *Mystagogical catechesis,* 4a, 2

do not look on the bread and wine as simple common elements ... and, although your senses may suggest the opposite to you, your faith must give you the certainty of what is there in reality.[6] This reality is Christ himself, who, quite helpless, surrenders himself to us. Our senses are completely deceived, but faith gives us the greatest certainty.

43.2 The real presence of Christ in the tabernacle.

At the miracle in Cana, the colour of the water was changed and became the colour of wine; the taste of the water also changed and was turned into the taste of wine – of good wine. The natural properties of water were changed ... Everything about the water the servants took to Jesus was changed. Not only the appearances of the water, the accidents, but the very being of the water, its substance. The water was turned into wine by Our Lord's words. All the people present not only tasted but drank the excellent real wine that only a few moments before had been ordinary water.

In the Holy Eucharist, Jesus does not change through the words of the priest – as He did in Cana – the accidents of bread and wine (their colour, taste, shape, quantity), but only their substance, the very being of bread and wine, which ceases to be bread and wine and is changed in an admirable and supernatural way into the Body and Blood of Christ. The appearances of bread remain, but there is no longer bread there; the appearances of wine remain, but there is no longer wine there. The substance of bread and the substance of wine have changed from what they were before in themselves, from that by which a thing is such and such a thing in the eyes of the Creator. God, who can create and who can annihilate, can also transform one thing

---

[6] *ibid,* 4a, 2 and 5

into another; in the Blessed Eucharist He wanted to effect this miraculous transformation of bread and wine into the Body and Blood of Christ and for the change to be perceived only by means of faith.

In the miracle of the multiplication of the loaves and fishes,[7] the substance and accidents did not undergo any change: there were loaves and fishes to start with, and this same food was eaten by those five thousand men who were fully satisfied. Our Lord had increased the amount of it. In Cana, He changed a certain quantity of water into the same amount of wine, without increasing it at all. In the most Blessed Sacrament, through the action of the priest, Jesus transforms the very substance, whilst the accidents, the outward appearances, remain unchanged. Christ does not come to the Sacrament of the Altar by spatial movement, as when we move from one place to another. He makes himself present through that admirable *conversion* of bread and of wine into his Body and into his Blood.

Quod non capis, quod non vides
animosa firmat fides ...
Sight has failed, nor thought conceives,
But a dauntless faith believes,
Resting on a power divine.[8]

Christ is present in the Holy Eucharist with his Body, his Blood, his Soul and his Divinity. It is the same Jesus as the Jesus who was born in Bethlehem, who had to be carried in the arms of Joseph and Mary on the flight into Egypt. It is the same Jesus as the Jesus who grew up and worked hard in Nazareth, who died and rose again on the third day and who now, glorious, sits at the right hand of God the Father. It is Jesus himself! But it is logical that He cannot be in the same way, even though his presence is the

---

[7] cf John 6:1 *et seq*
[8] Sequence, *Lauda, Sion, Salvatorem*

same presence. *In the order of Christ,* writes St Thomas, *his natural being is not the same as his sacramental being.*[9] But the reality of his presence is no less in the tabernacle than in Heaven: *Christ is present whole and entire, bodily present too, in his physical 'reality' although not in the manner in which bodies are present in a place.*[10] There is little more we can say about this admirable presence.

When we go to visit the Blessed Sacrament we can say, in the literal meaning of the words, 'I am in the presence of Jesus, I am in front of God'. We can say this in just the same way as could have done those people who, filled with faith, encountered him on the roads and streets of Palestine. We too can say, 'Lord, I look at the tabernacle and my sight, touch and taste are all deceived ... but my faith pierces through the veils that cover this little tabernacle and finds you there, truly present, waiting for me to make an act of faith, an act of love or an act of thanksgiving ... just as you patiently hoped those people would do on whom in your public life you poured out your power and your mercy. Lord, I believe, I hope, I love'.

43.3 Trust and respect for Jesus in the Blessed Sacrament.

Sight, touch and taste in Thee are each deceived ... It is truc that in the Blessed Eucharist the senses are unable to perceive the most real presence that exists anywhere. This is because it is a question of the presence of a Body which is both glorified and divine. Therefore it is a divine presence, *a divine mode of existence,* which differs essentially from the modes of being and existing of bodies which are subject to space and time.

The Eucharist never exhausts the ways in which Jesus can be present among us. He announced to us: *Lo, I am*

---

[9] St Thomas, *Summa Theologiae,* 3, q 76, a 6
[10] St Paul VI, *Mysterium fidei,* 46 *cit*

with you always until the close of the age.[11] He is with us in many ways. The Church reminds us that Christ is present in the needy, whether they belong to our family or whether they are strangers to us. He is present whenever we gather together in his name.[12] In a special way He is present in the divine Word ...[13] All these are real ways of being present among us, but in the Holy Eucharist, God is present among us in a way *par excellence,* given that in this sacrament Christ is there in his very person, in a *true, real and substantial* way. *This presence,* Saint Paul VI teaches, *is called 'real' not in an exclusive sense as though the other forms of presence were not 'real', but by reason of its excellence. It is the substantial presence, by which Christ is made present here among us, whole and entire, without doubt, both God and Man.*[14]

Let us consider today how we should behave in his presence, and what kind of trust and respect we should have for him. Let us ask ourselves whether our faith becomes deeper and more penetrating when we are before the tabernacle, or whether the darkness of the senses prevails and they remain as though blind in the presence of this divine reality. How often have we said to Jesus: *I firmly believe, Lord, that you are here, that you see me, that you hear me; I adore you with profound reverence ....*

The miracles of the wedding feast of Cana and the multiplication of the loaves and fishes that we considered earlier can help us try to understand better this wonder of divine love. In both these miracles Jesus asks others for their collaboration. The disciples distributed the food to the crowds and everyone was satisfied. In Cana He said to the

---

[11] Matt 28:20
[12] cf Matt 18:20
[13] cf Second Vatican Council, *Sacrosanctum Concilium,* 7
[14] St Paul VI, *Mysterium fidei,* 39 cit

servants, *Fill the jars with water*; and they *filled them to the brim,* until they could hold no more. If they had been careless and had put in less water, the amount of wine would also have been smaller. Something similar happens in Holy Communion. Even though grace is always without limit and we have not merited the honour we receive, Jesus asks us too for our collaboration; He invites us to correspond, with our own devotion, to the grace we receive. He rewards us in proportion as He finds in our hearts that good disposition He asks us for. The constantly greater desire, the purity of our hearts, the spiritual communions, our sense of the presence of God throughout the day, and particularly when we pass close to a tabernacle ... will enable us to receive more and more grace and love whenever Jesus comes into our hearts.

CORPUS CHRISTI OCTAVE: DAY 4

44. LIKE THE REPENTANT THIEF

44.1 The tabernacles we find along our way.

In Cruce latebat sola Deitas ...
God only on the cross lay hid from view,
But here lies hid at once the manhood too:
And I, in both professing my belief,
Make the same prayer as the repentant thief.

As Jesus hung dying on the Cross, the good thief was able to see in him the Messiah, the Son of God. By an extraordinary grace from God, that man's faith enabled him to overcome the difficulties presented to him by what he could only see and hear – appearances that spoke only of a man who had been condemned to death. Christ's divinity was hidden from the eyes of all onlookers, but that man was at least able to look upon the Saviour's most holy humanity. He was able to contemplate Christ's loving gaze, the forgiveness that He poured out with all his heart upon those who were jeering at him, and his moving silence in response to all insults and offences hurled upon him. Even on the Cross, in the midst of so much suffering, Jesus pours out his love.

We look at the sacred Host and our eyes can see nothing of him: they do not see the loving gaze of Jesus, or his compassion ... But with the strength of faith we proclaim him as our God and our Lord. Often, to express in some way the certainty of our soul and of our love, we have said to him: *I firmly believe, Lord that you are here, that you see me, that you hear me ...* Your gaze is just as loving as the gaze the good thief was able to contemplate, and your compassion is still infinite. I know that you are always attentive to the very least of my petitions, sorrows and joys.

Although in different ways, Jesus is equally present in Heaven and in the consecrated Host. *There are not two Christs, but a single Christ. We possess in the Host the Christ who is present in all the mysteries of the Redemption – the Christ known by Mary Magdalen and the Samaritan woman; the Christ of Mount Tabor and of Gethsemane; the Christ who rose from the dead and is seated at the right hand of the Father ... This wonderful presence of Christ among us should revolutionise our lives ... He is here with us – in each city and in each town.*[1] Even every day as we walk along the streets we may be walking just a few yards away from where He is. Do we wonder how many acts of faith may have been made at that particular hour of the morning or of the afternoon in front of that particular tabernacle, either from outside the church or by people going in for a few moments to the place where He is? Do we consider how many acts of love may have been made? ... How sad it would be if we were to go straight past without acknowledging his presence or greeting him! Jesus is not indifferent to our faith and to our love. *Don't be so blind or so thoughtless as not to enter in thought within each Tabernacle when you glimpse the walls or the spires of the houses of God that you pass. He is waiting for you.*[2] What a lot of good this advice filled with wisdom and piety can do to us!

Jesus was moved when He heard that voice acknowledging him as God in the midst of so many insults. It was the voice of a thief who, even though God was so very hidden, was able to recognise him and express his belief in him out loud, at the same time making him known to his compan-

---

[1] M. M. Philipon, *The Sacraments in Christian Life*
[2] St. J. Escrivá, *The Way,* 269

ion. His encounter with Jesus led him to do apostolate.

Love disperses blindness, bewilderment and lukewarmness. This living love – expressed perhaps with a heartfelt ejaculatory prayer – is something we should try to feel whenever we are about to receive Jesus in Holy Communion and when we pass close to a Tabernacle on our way to work. At such times our souls will be filled with joy. *As you make your way through the familiar streets of the city, have you never had the joy of discovering ... another Tabernacle?*.[3] It is the joy experienced by everyone who has ever looked forward to a particular encounter with someone. If our hearts beat faster when we see a person we love in the distance, are we going to remain unmoved as we pass close to a Tabernacle?

44.2 We should imitate the Good Thief.

I ask the same as the repentant thief ... *Jesus, remember me when you come into your kingdom.*[4]

His faith was so great that with a single ejaculatory prayer the Good Thief merited the purification of his whole life. He called Jesus by his name, just as we too have done so often. And He *always gives more than He is asked for. That man asked Our Lord to remember him when He came into his Kingdom, and Our Lord answered him: 'Truly I say to you, today you will be with me in Paradise'. True life consists in being with Christ, for where Christ is, there is his Kingdom.*[5] The Master's longing to have us with him in his glory is so great that He gives us his Body as a foretaste of eternal life.

We have to imitate this man who acknowledged his faults[6] and thus merited the forgiveness of his sins and his

[3] *idem,* 270
[4] Luke 23:42
[5] St Ambrose, *Treatise on St Luke's Gospel, in loc*
[6] cf Luke 23:41

complete purification. *Many times have I repeated that verse of the Eucharistic hymn: 'Peto quod petivit latro poenitens', and it always fills me with emotion: to ask Jesus to remember me as the penitent thief did!*

He recognised that he himself deserved the awful punishment of this barbaric execution ... And with a word he stole Christ's heart and 'opened up for himself' the gates of heaven.[7] When we are in front Jesus himself, if only we could sincerely hate every deliberate venial sin and cleanse our soul of the dross left by so very many ugly things that obscure the image of Jesus within us – selfishness, laziness, disordered attachment to things! ... *Jesus in the Blessed Sacrament is a fountain open to everyone. He is the fountain at which, whenever we wish, we can wash away from our soul every stain of the sins we commit each day.*[8]

If we receive it with the requisite dispositions, frequent Communion will lead us to try also to go frequently and contritely to Confession. In turn, this greater purity of heart will create in us an ardent desire to receive Jesus in the Blessed Sacrament.[9] When it is received with faith and love the Eucharistic Sacrament itself purifies the soul of its faults, weakens our inclination towards evil, divinizes the soul and prepares it to receive the high ideals that the Holy Spirit inspires in the soul of a Christian.

Let us ask our Lord for a real desire to purify ourselves in this life so that we can shorten our Purgatory and be admitted into the company of Jesus and Mary as soon as possible: *If only, My Jesus, it were true that I had never offended you! But now that the damage has been done, I*

---

[7] St. J. Escrivá, *The Way of the Cross,* XII, 4
[8] St Alphonsus Liguori, *Visits to the Blessed Sacrament,* 20
[9] cf St John Paul II, *Address to 'Adoracion Nocturna',* Madrid, 31 October 1982

beg you to forget the displeasure I have caused you and the bitter death that you underwent for me. Lead me into your kingdom after my death, and as long as my life shall last make your love reign always in my soul.[10] Help me, Lord, to hate any deliberate venial sin; give me a great love for frequent Confession.

44.3 The purification of our faults.

The holy Curé d'Ars in one of his sermons tells the pious legend of Saint Alex, and draws from it some consequences that concern the Blessed Eucharist. It is said of this saint that one day, having heard a particular call from God, he left his house and went to live far away from home as a humble beggar. Many years later he returned to the city of his birth, thin and disfigured by his many penances. Without making himself known, he was given shelter in the palace that belonged to his own parents. He lived under the stairs for sixteen years. When he died and his body was being prepared for burial, his mother recognised her son, and, filled with sorrow, exclaimed: 'Oh my son, how late have I recognised you!'

The saintly parish-priest of d'Ars commented that the soul when it leaves this life will at last see the one whom he possessed each day in the Holy Eucharist, the one to whom he spoke, and to whom he poured out his sorrows when he could not bear them any longer. At the sight of Jesus in glory, the soul that has but little love, that has but scant faith, will be forced to exclaim: 'Jesus, what a pity I have only come to know you so late, having had you all the time so close to me!'

Whenever we are in front of the Tabernacle or look at the Sacred Host on the altar we must see Christ present there. We must see the very same Christ as was in

[10] St Alphonsus Liguori, *Meditations on the Passion,* Meditation XII for Wednesday of Holy Week, 1

Bethlehem and Capharnaum. We must see Christ who rose from the dead on the third day, and is now sitting in glory at the right hand of God the Father.

Tantum ergo Sacramentum,
Veneremur cernui ...

We can listen to the words of the liturgy:

Down in adoration falling,
Lo! the sacred host we hail
Lo! o'er ancient forms departing
Newer rites of grace prevail,
Faith for all defects supplying.
Where the feeble senses fail.[11]

This is the expression of a faith that is firm and full of love.

Jesus revealed to us that the clean of heart will see God.[12] This vision of God begins down here on earth, and reaches its fullness and perfection in Heaven. If our heart is filled with dirt, whatever vision we have becomes obscured. The figure of Christ becomes blurred and our capacity for loving is impoverished. *That Christ you see is not Jesus. It is only the pitiful image that your blurred eyes are able to form ... Purify yourself. Clarify your sight with humility and penance. Then ... the pure light of Love will not be denied you. And you will have perfect vision. The image you see will be really his: 'his'.*[13] We will recognise him, just as the good thief did, no matter what the circumstances.

What joy to have Christ so close to us! What joy to see him, to love him and to serve him! ... He listens to us when in the intimacy of our prayer we say to him: 'Lord, remember me, from heaven and from that nearest

---

[11] Hymn, *Tantum ergo*
[12] cf Matt 5:8
[13] St. J. Escrivá, *The Way,* 212

tabernacle where you are also really present'. So that we can fill the emptiness left by our sins whilst we are still in this life, He moves us to greater penance and to greater love for the sacrament of reconciliation. He moves us to accept the sorrows and shortcomings of life in a spirit of reparation. He helps us to look for those little mortifications that enable us to overcome our own selfishness and to help others – mortifications that enable us to carry out our daily tasks with greater perfection.

If we are faithful to these graces, on the last day of our life here on earth, which is perhaps not so very far off, we will hear Jesus saying to us 'Today you shall be with me in Paradise'. Then we will see him and will love him with a joy that has no end.

As we come to the end of our prayer, we say to Jesus in the Blessed Sacrament:

Ave verum Corpus natum ex Maria Virgine ...
Hail true Body, born of the Virgin Mary ...
Let us taste of you at the moment of our death.

We ask our Guardian Angel to remind us of Christ's closeness to us, so that we may never pass him by without stopping. If we have recourse to her, to Mary who is our mother, she will increase our faith and will teach us to treat her Son with greater delicacy and with far more love.

Corpus Christi Octave: Day 5

45. The Wounds That Thomas Saw

45.1 Faith with deeds.

Plagas, sicut Thomas, non intueor,
Deum tamen meum te confiteor...
Thy wounds, as Thomas saw, I do not see;
Yet thee confess my Lord and God to be.
Make me believe thee ever more and more,
In thee my hope, in thee my love to store.

Thomas was not present when Jesus appeared to his disciples. In spite of the testimony each of them gave to him as they firmly declared: *We have seen the Lord,*[1] this Apostle refused to believe in the Master's Resurrection: *Unless I see in his hands the print of the nails and place my finger in the mark of the nails and place my hand in his side, I will not believe.*[2]

Eight days later Our Lord appeared again to his disciples. This time Thomas was with them. Then Jesus spoke to the Apostle, and, reproaching him in a singularly pleasant manner, He said to him: *Put your finger here and see my hands; and put out your hand, and place it in my side; do not be faithless, but believing.* The disciple responded immediately to the delicate consideration shown him by Our Lord and exclaimed: *My Lord and my God*![3] These words were an act of faith and of self-surrender. Thomas's reply was not simply an exclamation of surprise, it was an affirmation, a profound act of faith in Christ's divinity. *My Lord and my God*! These words can be used

---

[1] John 20:25
[2] *idem*
[3] John 20:26-29

as a splendid ejaculatory prayer; we may often have repeated them at the moment of the Consecration or as we genuflect in front of the Tabernacle. With this act of faith we too want to tell Jesus that we firmly believe in his real presence in the Tabernacle, and that He can do whatever He will with the whole of our life.

We do not see or touch the most holy wounds of Jesus in the way Thomas did, but our faith is as strong as that of the Apostle after he had seen Our Lord, because the Holy Spirit sustains us with his constant help. *And,* Saint Gregory the Great comments, *we are delighted by what follows: 'Blessed are those who have not seen and yet believe'. There is no doubt that we are included in this statement, for with our whole soul we confess him whom we have not seen in the flesh. It refers to us, so long as we live in accordance with faith; because only the one who practises what he believes really believes.*[4]

Whenever we are in front of the Tabernacle we should look at Jesus. Jesus speaks to us in order to strengthen our faith. He wants our faith to be manifest in our thoughts, words and deeds. He wants our faith to show in the way we judge others with an open mind and a spirit of charity, in our conversations with people that always encourage them to be honest and to follow Jesus closely. He wants us always to give good example through our deeds, and to finish off perfectly the work that has been entrusted to us, so that we abhor work that is done carelessly and is only poorly finished. *Let us take another look at the Master. You too may find yourself hearing this gentle reproach to Thomas: 'Let me have your finger; see, here are my hands. Let me have your hand; put it into my side. Cease your doubting, and believe' (John 20:27); and, with the Apostle, a sincere cry of contrition will rise from your soul: 'My*

---

[4] St Gregory the Great, *Homilies on the Gospels,* 26, 9

Lord and my God!'(John 20:28). I acknowledge you once and for all as the Master. From now on, with your help, I shall always treasure your teachings and I shall strive to follow them loyally.[5]

45.2 Faith and the Holy Eucharist.

Jesus assured Thomas that they are more blessed who, without seeing with the eyes of the flesh, have, nonetheless the keen sight given by faith. This is why He announced to them at the Last Supper: *It is to your advantage that I go away.*[6] When He was with his disciples and travelled along the roads of Palestine, Christ's divinity was hidden from them to the extent that they had constantly to practise their faith. To see, to hear and to touch are of little worth if grace is not at work in our souls and if our hearts are not pure and disposed to believe. Not even miracles can cause us to have faith if we lack good dispositions. After Jesus had raised Lazarus from the dead, many of the Jews believed in him, but others went over to the Pharisees with a view to doing away with him.[7] The result of the meeting held by the Sanhedrin immediately after the Jews had given testimony is summed up in a single sentence of Saint John: *So from that day on they took counsel how to put him to death.*[8]

Really, the great good fortune of those who accompanied Our Lord, who saw him, listened to him and spoke to him, is just the same as our own. The deciding factor is faith. This is why Saint Teresa wrote that when she heard people say they wished they had lived when Christ walked on this earth, she would smile to herself, for she knew that we have him as truly with us in the Most

[5] St. J. Escrivá, *Friends of God,* 145
[6] John 16:7
[7] cf John 11:45-46
[8] John 11:53

Blessed Sacrament as people had him then, and wonder what more they could possibly want.[9]

And the holy Curé of Ars points out that our fortune is even greater than that of the people who lived with him during his life on earth, because they sometimes had to walk for hours or for days to find him, whilst we have him so close to us in every tabernacle.[10] Normally we have to make very little effort to find Jesus himself.

In this life we see our Lord through the veils of faith, and one day, if we are faithful, we will see him in glory, in an ineffable vision. *After this life all the veils will disappear so that we can see him face to face.*[11] *Every eye will see him,*[12] Saint John tells us in the Apocalypse, and, again, *his servants shall worship him; they shall see his face.*[13] Meanwhile, in this life, we believe in him and we love him without ever having seen him.[14] But one day we will see him with his glorified body, with those holy wounds that he showed to Thomas. Now we confess him as our Lord and as our God: *My Lord and my God*! we say so often to him. As we pray to him now we can say: *Make me believe thee ever more and more.* Give me a stronger faith. *In thee my hope, in thee my love to store.* May my hope become stronger and ever more cheerful, may I love you with my whole being.

Today, as we once again consider this closeness of Jesus in the Holy Eucharist, we make a resolution to live closely united to the nearest tabernacle. It would be helpful to know which tabernacle is closest to our place of work or to our home. Then we will always be able to relate in our

---

[9] cf St Teresa, *The Way of Perfection,* 34, 6

[10] cf St Jean Vianney, (The Curé d'Ars), *Sermon on Maundy Thursday*

[11] St Augustine, *In Catena Aurea,* VIII

[12] Rev 1:7

[13] Rev 22:4

[14] cf 1 Pet 1:8

hearts to his presence there: as we can when we are engaged in some sport, whilst we are travelling ... *for the company of our good Jesus is too good for us ever to forsake him and his most holy Mother.*[15] Mary is always beside her son.

Go perseveringly to the Tabernacle, either bodily or in your heart, so as to feel safe and calm: but also in order to feel loved ... and to love.[16]

45.3 Our conversation with Jesus who is present in the Tabernacle.

Wherever Jesus went, his faithful friends would anxiously await his arrival. It could not be any other way. Saint Luke tells us that on one occasion Jesus crossed over the lake to Capharnaum, and *they were all waiting for him.*[17] We can imagine the joy experienced by each one of them as they waited for the Master, thinking of the petitions they wanted to present to him, longing to be with him. There in Capharnaum, the Evangelist tells us, He worked two wonderful miracles. He cured a woman who dared just to touch the hem of his garment, and He raised Jairus's daughter from the dead. At the same time everyone felt strengthened by Jesus' words, by a glance or by a question from him about members of his or her family... Perhaps some of them made up their minds that day to follow him more generously. His friends gave all their attention to the Friend.

We who do not see him physically are as close to him as those people who waited for him and went forward to meet him as he reached the shore. We too have constantly to summon up a more vivid sense of his presence in our cities and towns. We have to talk to him – He wants us to –

---

[15] St Teresa, *The Mansions,* 6, 7, 13
[16] St. J. Escrivá, *The Forge,* 116
[17] Luke 8:40

as our God and our Lord, but at the same time as our very special Friend. *Christ, the risen Christ, is our companion and friend. He is a companion whom we can see only in the shadows – but the fact that He is really there fills our whole life and makes us yearn to be with him forever.*[18]

Each day we go to meet him. And He is waiting for us. He lends us a hand, if sometimes – what a pity if it should be the case – we forget to speak to him with confidence, 'without anonymity', with the same sense of reality we have as we talk to the people we meet at work, in the lift or out in the street. Our senses, on which we rely so much in ordinary life, will not help us much to find him. Often we will feel *as though blind in front of the Friend,*[19] and this initial darkness will eventually become a brightness such as our senses could never give us. Saint Teresa says that the humility of the good Jesus was so great that He wanted, as it were, to ask leave of his Father to remain with us.[20] How can we fail to thank him for all the goodness and all the love he has shown us?

As we come to an end of our prayer we say to him, Lord, we would speak to you even if we had to wait in many waiting rooms, even though we had to ask for many appointments. But we do not have to do any such thing! You are so powerful, all powerful – in your mercy too – that, although you are the Lord of lords and the King of all those who rule, you have humbled yourself in order to wait like a poor beggar who clings to our door-post. We do not have to wait – you wait constantly for us.

You await us in Heaven, in Paradise. You await us in the Sacred Host. You wait for us in our prayer. You are so very good, that whilst you are there hidden through Love,

---

[18] St. J. Escrivá, *Christ is passing by,* 116
[19] St Paul VI, *General Audience,* 13 January 1971
[20] cf St Teresa, *The Way of Perfection,* 33, 2

hidden in the sacramental species – this is what I firmly believe, for you are there really, truly and substantially, with your Body and your Blood, with your Soul and your Divinity – the holy Trinity is there too, the Father, the Son and the Holy Spirit. Moreover, through the inhabitation of the Paraclete, God is in the centre of our souls, seeking us out.[21] We must not make him wait. Our Mother Mary constantly encourages us to go on to meet him. What care we should put into making our daily Visit to the Blessed Sacrament!

---

[21] S. Bernal, *Profile of the Life of the Founder of Opus Dei,* 1976

CORPUS CHRISTI OCTAVE: DAY 6

46. FOOD FOR THE WEAK

46.1 The Holy Eucharist: a memorial of the Passion.

O memoriale mortis Domini!
Panis vivus...
O thou memorial of our Lord's own dying!
O living bread, to mortals life supplying!
Make thou my soul henceforth on thee to live;
Ever a taste of heavenly sweetness give.[1]

From the very beginning of the Church, Christians have cherished as a special treasure the words spoken by Our Lord at the Last Supper, those words by which bread and wine were changed for the very first time into his most sacred Body and Blood. Some years after the great night on which the Holy Eucharist was instituted, Saint Paul reminded the first Christians in Corinth of what he had already taught them. He says that he himself received this doctrine from Our Lord – that is to say, it was a zealously guarded tradition that went back to Christ himself. The Apostle says: *I received from the Lord what I also delivered to you This is in the tradition of the Church: first to 'receive' and then to 'transmit': the tradition was that the Lord Jesus on the night He was betrayed took bread, and when He had given thanks, He broke it and said, 'This is my Body, which is for you. Do this in remembrance of me'. In the same way also He took the cup, after supper, saying, 'This is the cup of the new covenant in my blood. As often as you drink it do this in remembrance of me'.*[2] These words are substantially the same as the words pronounced by the priest when he causes Christ to be

---

[1] Hymn, *Adoro te devote*
[2] 1 Cor 11:23-25

present on the altar.

Do this in remembrance of me. The Holy Mass, which is the unbloody renewal of the sacrifice on Calvary, is a banquet in which Christ gives himself as food, and as a remembrance – a memorial – which becomes a reality on each altar whenever the Eucharistic mystery is renewed.[3] The word *remembrance* has a different meaning from that of the subjective remembering of a fact or of a past happening that we make present to our minds by bringing it into our memories. Our Lord does not commission the Apostles and the Church simply to *remember* that event at which they are present, but to *make it present once again.* The word *remembrance* derives its meaning from a Hebrew term which was used to designate what was the essence of the feast of the Passover – that it was a remembrance or memorial of the flight from Egypt and of the pact or covenant that God had made with his chosen People. Through the paschal rite the Israelites did not only recall an event that was already past, but they were conscious of making that event present once more and of reliving it, so that all generations might share in it.[4] At the paschal meal the covenant that God had made with them on Mount Sinai was made present once again. When Jesus says to his disciples *Do this in remembrance of me,* it is not a matter of simply remembering the paschal meal of that particular night, but of enacting the paschal sacrifice of Calvary itself, which is already present in an anticipated way at the Last Supper. Saint Thomas teaches that *Christ instituted this sacrament as the perpetual memorial of his Passion, as the fulfilment of the ancient 'figures' that had preceded it and as the most marvellous of all his works;*

---

[3] cf Second Vatican Council, *Sacrosanctum Concilium,* 47

[4] cf *The Navarre Bible,* Epistles of St Paul to the Corinthians, note to 1 Cor 11, 24; cf L. Bouyer, *Dictionary of Theology,* Memorial

and He left it to his disciples as a special way of consoling them during the sadness caused them by his absence.[5]

The Holy Mass is the memorial of Our Lord's death, a memorial in which there really takes place the paschal banquet, *in which Christ is consumed, the mind is filled with grace and a pledge of future glory is given us.*[6]

As we meditate on the Holy Eucharist let us unite ourselves to the prayer that the liturgy puts before us: *O God you have left us this wonderful sacrament to be the memorial of your Passion. Grant that through honouring the mystery of your Body and Blood, we may always experience your redeeming grace.*

46.2 Living Bread.

He gave them bread from heaven,[7] wrote the Psalmist, as he thought of that wonderful substance, white like dew, that the Israelites found one day lying on the ground in the desert when they were beginning to run out of food. But that bread, Our Lord declared in the synagogue of Capharnaum, was not the true *bread from heaven. Truly, truly, I say to you, it was not Moses who gave you the bread from heaven; my Father gives you the true bread from heaven. For the bread of God is that which comes down from heaven, and gives life to the world. They said to him, 'Lord, give us this bread always'.*[8]

The true reality is in Heaven; here on earth we find many things we consider to be definitive, whereas they are in reality but impermanent copies of those true things that await us. When, for example, Jesus speaks to the Samaritan woman about *living water,* He does not mean 'fresh water' or clear 'running water' as the woman supposes. He wants

---

[5] St Thomas, *Sermon for the Feast of Corpus Christi*
[6] Second Vatican Council, *loc cit*
[7] Ps 77:24; 104:40
[8] John 6:32-34

to point out to us that we shall never know what water really means until we have the direct experience of that reality of grace of which water is only the pale image.[9]

The same happens with *bread,* which for many centuries has been the staple and sometimes almost the only food by which many nations have been sustained. Bread which serves as food and the manna gathered in the desert each day by the Israelites are both signs and images that God makes use of so that we can understand what the Eucharist represents for us – *Living bread* that gives us life during the whole of our earthly existence. The people who listened to Jesus knew that the manna their ancestors had gathered each morning[10] was a symbol of the good things the Messiah was to bring us; this is why on that occasion they asked Jesus to give them a similar sign. But they could not grasp that the manna was a figure of the ineffable gift of the Eucharist; *The bread of God is that which comes down from Heaven, and gives life to the world.*[11] *That manna fell from heaven, this manna is above Heaven itself. That kind was corruptible; this is not only free from all corruption, but it communicates incorruptibility to all who eat it reverently ... That was the shadow, but this is the reality.*[12]

This admirable sacrament is doubtless the most loving action of Jesus. For he gives himself not only to humanity as a whole, but to each person in particular. Communion is always unique and unrepeatable: today's is always different from yesterday's. Just as Jesus adds a new element to this loving action from day to day, so too should we renew our love as we approach the eucharistic banquet anew.

---

[9] cf R. A. Knox, *Pastoral Sermons,* 13: *Real Bread*
[10] cf Ex 16:13 *et seq*
[11] cf John 6:33
[12] St Ambrose, *Treatise on the Mysteries,* 48

Ecce panis angelorum...
Behold the bread of angels, sent
For pilgrims in their banishment,
The bread for God's true children meant,
That may not unto dogs be given,[13]

sings the liturgy. Day after day, year after year, it is our indispensable food. The Prophet Elijah travelled through the desert for forty days with the strength given to him by a single meal that had been offered to him by an angel of the Lord.[14] God will doubtless give the necessary graces to Christians who live in places where it is impossible for them to receive Holy Communion. Normally, however, it is the Holy Eucharist that restores our strength on each day of our journey through this world where we are as pilgrims.

46.3 Sustenance for the journey. Ardently desiring to receive Holy Communion. Avoiding all sense of routine.

O living bread, to mortals life supplying!
Make thou my soul henceforth on thee to live;
Ever a taste of heavenly sweetness give.

Jesus Christ, who gives himself to us in the Holy Eucharist, is utterly indispensable as nourishment for us. Without him we very soon fall into an extreme state of weakness. *Material food first changes into the one who eats it, and then, as a consequence, restores to him his lost strength and increases his vitality. Spiritual food, on the other hand, changes the person who eats it into itself. Thus the effect proper to this sacrament is the conversion of a man into Christ, so that he may no longer live, but Christ lives in him; consequently, it has the double effect of restoring the spiritual strength he had lost by his sins and*

---

[13] Sequence, *Lauda, Sion, Salvatorem*
[14] cf 1 Kings 19:6

defects, and of increasing the strength of his virtues.[15]

He gives us strength for the journey, because each day we tread a new bit of the path that leads us to Heaven. At the end of our lives God must find in us fullness of love. But *marching food is meant for the march, and you must have stretched your muscles if you are to enjoy it; how dull picnic-fare tastes, if you are weatherbound, and compelled to eat in your armchair. 'Your loins must by girt', Our Lord says; we must be 'bonafide' pilgrims if we are to find proper food in the Holy Eucharist.*[16] Our desires to improve each day, to be daily a little closer to Our Lord, are the best means we have of preparing to receive Holy Communion. Our *hunger for God,* our desire for sanctity, urge us on to really get to know Jesus and to long ardently for the moment when we will receive him; then we will count the hours ... and the minutes still to pass, until we have him within our soul. We will turn to our Guardian Angel and ask him to help us to prepare well, and then to thank him properly. We will be sorry that the brief time Jesus in the Sacred Species remains within us after Holy Communion passes so rapidly. During the day we will longingly recall those minutes when we had Jesus so close to us. We will try to identify ourselves with him and will wait impatiently for the next time we will be receiving him. We should never allow routine, laziness or a desire to hurry, to creep into these moments that are the most important ones of our life.

Gratitude is a sign of good manners, and we must thank Jesus for *the wonderful way He has given Himself up for us. The incarnate Word comes within our breast! Inside us, inside our littleness, lies the Creator of heaven and earth! ... The Virgin Mary was conceived without sin to*

---

[15] St Thomas, *Commentary on Book IV of the Sentences,* d 12, q 2, a 11
[16] R. A. Knox, *op cit,* 17: *A Better Country*

prepare her to receive Christ in her womb. If the action of grace is to be in proportion to the difference between the gift and the merits, should we not turn the whole day into a continuous Eucharist? Do not leave the Church almost immediately after receiving the Blessed Sacrament. Surely you have nothing so important on that you cannot give Our Lord ten minutes to say 'thanks'. Let's not be mean. Love is repaid with love.[17] Let us never be in a hurry as we express our gratitude to Jesus after Holy Communion! There can be nothing more important than fully savouring those moments with him.

[17] St. J. Escrivá, *In Love with the Church,* 48

Corpus Christi Octave: Day 7

47. CLEANSE ME, LORD JESUS

47.1 Christ's surrender on the Cross, renewed in the Blessed Eucharist, purifies us of our weakness.

Pie pellicane, Jesu Domine,
Me immundum munda tuo sanguine...
O loving Pelican! O Jesus Lord!
Unclean I am, but cleanse me in thy blood;
Of which a single drop for sinners spilt,
Can purge the entire world from all its guilt.[1]

An ancient legend has it that the pelican brought its dead young ones back to life by wounding its breast and giving them its blood.[2] Christians applied this image to Jesus Christ from the very earliest times. A single drop of the most sacred blood of Jesus, shed on Calvary, would have been sufficient to make reparation for all the crimes, all the acts of hatred, impurity and envy of all men of all the ages – past and present. But Christ went still further: He shed the very last drop of his blood for mankind and for each individual, as though only that particular person existed on earth... *This is the cup of my Blood, the Blood of the new and everlasting covenant. It will be shed for you and for all so that sins may be forgiven.* Jesus Christ said these words at the Last Supper. They are repeated by the priest each day at Holy Mass as he renews the sacrifice of Our Lord, which continues to be offered until the end of the world. The next day on Calvary, when, already dead,

---

[1] Hymn, *Adoro te devote*
[2] cf St Isidore of Seville, *Etymology,* 12, 7, 26

having surrendered his life to his Father, *One of the soldiers pierced his side with a spear, and at once there came out blood and water*[3]– therefore the very last drop of his blood. The Fathers of the Church see the sacraments and the very life of the Church as springing from this pierced side of Christ: *Oh death that gives life to the dead,* exclaims Saint Augustine! *What can be purer than this blood? What wound was ever more health-giving than this?*[4] It is through this wound that we are healed.

Saint Thomas Aquinas commenting on this passage of the Gospel points out that John chooses to say: *aperuit, non vulneravit,* that the soldier with the lance 'opened' the crucified Saviour's side, not that he 'wounded' it, *because in this side of his the gate of eternal life was opened up for us.*[5] All of this happened, Saint Thomas affirms, in one place, to show us that it is through Christ's Passion that we receive purification from our sins and the removal of any stain of sin.

The Jews considered life – the vital principle – to be contained in the blood. Jesus shed his blood for us in giving his life for ours. He showed his love for us when in his blood He washed us from our sins and raised us to a new life.[6] Saint Paul reminds us that for us Jesus was exposed to the public gaze on the Cross: He hung there in the sight of all in order to attract the attention of all who passed by. He still wants to attract our attention. This is why we say to him, today, in the intimacy of our prayer: *O loving Pelican! O Jesus Lord, unclean am I,* I am full of wretchedness, *Cleanse me in thy blood...*

---

[3] John 19:34
[4] St Augustine, *Treatise on St John's Gospel,* 120, 2
[5] St Thomas, *Reading on the Gospel of St John, in loc,* 2458
[6] cf Rev 1:5

47.2 Jesus comes in Person to heal and strengthen us.

Our Lord comes to us in the Blessed Eucharist as the Physician who will cleanse and heal our wounds, the wounds that cause such grievous harm to our souls. When we go to visit him, his loving glance from the tabernacle purifies us. But if we let him, He does much more each day – He comes right into our heart and fills it with his grace. Before himself receiving Holy Communion the priest presents the Sacred Host to us and repeats some words that recall what John the Baptist said quietly to John and to Andrew, pointing Jesus out to them as He passed by: *This is the Lamb of God who takes away the sins of the world.* And the faithful reply with the words of the centurion of Capharnaum, words that are full of faith and love: *Lord, I am not worthy to receive you under my roof* ... On that occasion Jesus limited himself to healing the servant of this Gentile from a distance. He could see the great faith the man had. But in Holy Communion, even though we tell Jesus that we are not worthy, that our soul will never be sufficiently well disposed to receive him, He wants to come to us in Person – with his Body and his Soul – into our hearts, stained as they are with so many major and minor infidelities. Every day He repeats the words He spoke to his disciples as they began the Last Supper: *I have earnestly desired to eat this passover with you ...*[7] How our hearts should fill with love and joy as we meditate on this great desire of Jesus to come into our soul! It is right to reflect seriously on the fact that *the miracle of transubstantiation was performed just for you – just for me. He came and dwelt there just for you ... No secondary agent, no intermediary, shall communicate to us the influence our souls need; He will come to us himself. How He must love us to want to do that! How resolute He must be that*

[7] Luke 22:15

nothing on his side should be wanting, that no loophole of excuse should be given us for refusing what He offers when He brings it himself! And we so blind, we so hesitating, we so neglectful – we so unwilling to give ourselves wholly to him who thus gives himself wholly to us![8]

Our daily failures and wretchedness – from which not one of us is ever free – should not be an obstacle to our receiving Holy Communion. *It is not that we should abstain from receiving Our Lord in Communion because we acknowledge ourselves to be sinners; rather should we hasten to receive him, with ever-growing desire, as a remedy for our soul and a purification for our spirit, but with such humility and such faith that, judging ourselves unworthy of receiving such a great favour, we should go rather to seek healing for our sores.*[9] Only grave sins prevent us from receiving the Blessed Eucharist worthily if we have not been to sacramental Confession, when the priest will have forgiven our sins in Christ's name.

The are many different ways in which the Redemption, the Blood that He shed, is applied to us. It is applied to us in a very special way in the Holy Mass, which is the unbloody renewal of the sacrifice of Calvary. At the moment when we receive Communion from the hands of the priest, our souls become a second Heaven, full of a splendour and glory before which the angels feel amazement and admiration. *When you receive him, tell him: 'Lord, I hope in you. I adore you, I love you; increase my faith. Be the support of my weakness, you who have remained defenceless in the Eucharist so as to be the remedy for the weakness of your creatures'.*[10]

---

[8] R. A. Knox, *Pastoral Sermons,* 23 *Prope est Verbum,* Burns and Oates, London 1960, p. 306
[9] Cassian, *Collationes,* 23, 21
[10] St. J. Escrivá, *The Forge,* 832

47.3 The Sacred Humanity of Christ in the Eucharist.

...Me immundum, munda tuo sanguine...
Unclean I am, but cleanse me in thy blood.

We should ask God to grant us a great desire for cleanness of heart. We should at least do what that leper did one day in Capharnaum – he knelt down before Jesus and begged him to cure him of his illness, which must already have been at a very advanced stage, for the Evangelist says he was *full of leprosy.*[11] Jesus stretched out his hand, touched his sores and said: *I will; be clean. And immediately the leprosy left him.* Our Lord will do the same for us, for He does not merely touch us, but comes to dwell in our soul and to fill us with his grace and his gifts.

At the moment of our receiving Holy Communion we really are in possession of Life. *We have within us the Incarnate Word, whole and entire, with all that He is and all that He does. We have within us Jesus, who is God and man, together with all the graces of his Humanity and all the treasures of his Divinity. We possess, in the words of Saint Paul, 'the unsearchable riches of Christ' (Eph 3:8).*[12] First of all, Jesus is within us as man. Holy Communion pours into us the actual, heavenly and glorified life of his Humanity, of his Heart and of his Soul. In Heaven the angels are filled to overflowing with happiness through the tremendous effusion of this Life.

Some saints have been favoured with a vision of Christ's glorified Body, as it is in Heaven, resplendent with glory, and as it is in our soul at the moment of Holy Communion whilst the Sacred Species remain within us. Saint Angela of Foligno spoke of *a beauty that caused human words to fail,* and for a long time after her vision she was able to recollect *an immense joy, a sublime*

---

[11] cf Luke 5:12 *et seq*

[12] P. M. Bernadot, *From the Eucharist to the Trinity*

illumination, a continuous delight beyond words, a dazzling and delectable light which surpasses all other brightness.[13] It is the same Jesus who visits us each day in this sacrament and works the same wonders.

Our Lord comes into our soul also as God. At such times we are especially united to the divine life of Jesus, to his life as the Only Son of the Father. *He himself says to us 'I live because of the Father' (John 6:58). From eternity, the Father gives his Son the life He has within himself. He gives it to him totally, without reserve or limitation, and with such loving generosity that, whilst remaining distinct from each other, they form a single Godhead with a single Life which possesses the fullness of love, of joy and of peace.*

This is the life we receive.[14] Faced with such an impenetrable mystery, how shall we not want to go to Confession, to the sacrament that will prepare us to receive Jesus better? How shall we refrain from asking him, when our soul is in a state of grace, to purify us from so many stains, from so many of those sorry imperfections of ours? If the leper was healed when Jesus touched him, how can our heart fail to be cleansed also, so long as a lack of faith and of love on our part do not prevent it? Today in the intimacy of our prayer we say to Jesus: *'Lord, if you will' (and you are always willing), 'you can make me clean' (Matt 8:2). You know my weaknesses; I feel these symptoms; I suffer from these failings ... We show him the wound, with simplicity, and if the wound is festering, we show the pus too; Lord, you have cured so many souls; help me to recognise you as the divine physician, when I have you in my heart or when I contemplate your presence in the tabernacle.*[15]

---

[13] *idem*
[14] *idem*
[15] St. J. Escrivá, *Christ is passing by,* 93

CORPUS CHRISTI OCTAVE: DAY 8

48. A PLEDGE OF ETERNAL LIFE

48.1 A foretaste of Heaven.

Iesu, quem velatum nunc aspicio...
Jesus, whom for the present veiled I see,
What I so thirst for, do vouchsafe to me;
That I may see thy countenance unfolding,
And may be blest thy glory in beholding. Amen.[1]

By God's mercy we will one day see Jesus face to face, without anything to obscure our vision, as He is in Heaven. We will see him in his glorified body, see the marks of the nails, his loving glance and his ever-welcoming demeanour. We will recognise him immediately. And He will recognise each one of us personally and will come forward to greet us after waiting so long for this meeting. Now, we see him in a veiled manner, in which He is hidden from our senses. We encounter him in the thousand and one situations of each day. We meet him at our work, in the little acts of service that we do for the people around us. He is to be found in every one of the people who share with us our labours and our joys... But we find him in a very special way in the Blessed Eucharist. It is there that He waits for us, and gives himself to us completely in Holy Communion – a foretaste here and now of heavenly glory. When we adore him in the Blessed Eucharist we are taking part in that liturgy which is celebrated in the *heavenly Jerusalem* towards which we make our way as pilgrims, and where He is seated at the right hand of God the Father. Already here on earth we unite ourselves to the angels who praise him endlessly in Heaven, for this sacrament *unites*

---

[1] Hymn, *Adoro te devote*

time and eternity.[2]

The Blessed Eucharist is here and now a foretaste and a pledge of the love that awaits us; by it, *a pledge of future glory is given to us.*[3] It gives us strength and consolation, it keeps alive the memory of Jesus and is the *viaticum,* the *victuals* we need to sustain us as we walk along the path which at times may seem very steep. *When in the celebration of the Eucharist the Church announces the death of the Lord, she also proclaims his coming again. This announcement is made to the whole world and to her faithful children – that is to say, to herself.*[4] It reminds us that our bodies when they receive this sacrament *are no longer corruptible, but possess the hope of an everlasting resurrection.*[5] Our Lord made this clear revelation at the synagogue in Capharnaum: *He who eats my flesh and drinks my blood has eternal life, and I will raise him up on the last day.*[6]

Jesus, whom we now see hidden – *Iesu quem velatum nunc aspicio...* – did not want to wait until our definitive meeting, which will take place once our days of work here on earth are ended. To unite himself intimately with us He allows us now, in the Most Holy Sacrament of the Altar, a glimpse of what it will be like to possess him in Heaven. In the tabernacle, hidden from our senses, but not from our faith, He waits for whatever times we choose to visit him. *He is there as though behind a wall, and from there He looks at us as though from behind the lattice (Song 2:9). Even though we cannot see him He looks at us from that place where He is truly present, so that we may possess him, even though He conceals himself in order that we may*

---

[2] St Paul VI, *Apostolic Brief to Cardinal Lercaro,* 16 July 1968
[3] Second Vatican Council, *Sacrosanctum Concilium,* 47
[4] M. Schmaus, *Dogmatic Theology,* vol. VI
[5] St Irenaeus, *Against Heresies,* 1, 4, 18
[6] John 6:56

seek him out. Until such time as we reach our celestial home, Jesus wants to surrender himself entirely to us, and to live united to us in this way.[7]

48.2 Our participation in the Life that never ends.

Our Lord often lets us see us by means of the Gospels that many of the things we consider to be real and substantial are no more than images or copies of the things that await us in Heaven. Christ is the only true reality, and Heaven is our authentic and definitive Life – a life of eternal happiness, a happiness with true depths and dimensions, in the shade of which this life is as insubstantial as a dream. When our Lord says to us *He who eats this bread will live for ever,*[8] He is speaking of the Food *par excellence,* and of the everlasting Life which is the fulfilment of all earthly existence.

So as to thank Jesus with all our heart for the gift of himself present in the Blessed Eucharist, we should consider that He already gives himself to us as our real Life, as a foretaste of the Life we will one day have for ever in eternity. As we reflect on this we can think of these words of Ronald Knox: *All the din and clatter of the streets, all the great factories which dominate our landscape are only echoes and shadows if you think of them for a moment in the light of eternity; the reality is in here, is there above the altar, is that part of it which our eyes cannot see and our senses cannot distinguish. The motto on Cardinal Newman's tomb ought to be the funeral motto of every Catholic: 'Ex umbris et imaginibus in veritatem', it says. Out of the shadows and appearances into the truth. When death brings us into another world the experience will not be that of one who falls asleep and dreams, but that of one who wakes from a dream into the*

---

[7] St Alphonsus Liguori, *The Practice of the Love of Christ,* 2
[8] John 6:58

full light of day. Here, we are so surrounded by the things of sense that we take them for the full reality. Only sometimes we have a glimpse which corrects that wrong perspective. And above all when we see the Blessed Sacrament enthroned we should look up towards that white disc which shines in the monstrance as towards a chink through which, just for a moment, the light of the other world shines through.[9] It is He alone who contains all fullness of Being.

When we contemplate the Sacred Host on the altar or in the monstrance, we see there Christ himself, encouraging us and helping us to live on earth with our gaze on Heaven, on himself, whom one day we will see coming in glory, surrounded by the angels and the saints. Here on earth it is Christ himself who welcomes man, his friend so often harshly treated on his pilgrim journey, and strengthens him with the warmth of his understanding and of his love. In the Eucharist the sweet words, *Come to me all you who labour and are heavy laden and I will give you rest,*[10] acquire their full meaning. This personal and profound relief that He offers us, and which is the only true recompense and solace for all our labours along the paths of the world, can be found – at least partially and in anticipation – in the divine Bread that Christ offers us at the Eucharistic table.[11] May we not fail to receive him as He deserves.

48.3 Mary and the Blessed Eucharist.

We always find Our Lady very close to Jesus – in Heaven, and here on earth in the Blessed Eucharist. The *Acts of the Apostles* tells us that after Christ's Ascension into Heaven, Mary was with them, united to them – already

[9] R. A. Knox, *Pastoral Sermons,* 23
[10] Matt 11:28
[11] cf St John Paul II, *Homily,* 9 July 1980

fulfilling her role as Mother of the Church – *in prayer and in the breaking of bread.*[12] She was there, *receiving Communion in the midst of the faithful, with the Body, Blood, Soul and Divinity of her own Son ... In the Christ of the Mass and of her Eucharistic Communions Mary recognised the Christ of all the mysteries of the Redemption. What human gaze would dare to fathom the depths of the intimacy with which the soul of the Mother and the soul of the Son met once again in the Eucharist?*[13] What must Our Lady's Communions have been like whilst she remained on this earth?

Since her Assumption into Heaven Mary again contemplates her glorified Son face to face. She is intimately united to Jesus, and in contemplating him she knows the whole plan of the redemption, central to which can be found the Incarnation and her own divine Maternity. All around him, in Heaven and on earth, the angels and saints ceaselessly adore him. Mary, more than all other beings together, loves and adores her Son, really present as He is in Heaven and in the Eucharist. She teaches us to have within ourselves the same sentiments she had in Nazareth, in Bethlehem, on Calvary, in the Cenacle; she encourages us to talk to him with the same love with which she adores her Son in Heaven and in the Blessed Sacrament of the Altar.[14] As we look on Our Lady's great piety, we too can repeat: *I wish, Lord to receive you with the purity, humility and devotion with which your most holy Mother received you...*

The most holy Virgin, who is always close to her Son, strengthens us and teaches us how to receive him, to visit him and to see him as the centre of our day, as the One to

---

[12] Acts 2:42
[13] M. M. Philipon, *The Sacraments in Christian Life*
[14] cf R. M. Spiazzi, *Mary in the Christian Mystery*

whom we frequently turn our thoughts and to whom we turn in our need. In Heaven, very close to Jesus, we will see Mary, and beside her our Father and Lord Saint Joseph. In some way the glory of Heaven will simply be a continuation of the relationship we have with them whilst we are still on earth.

Medieval authors often compared Mary to the biblical Boat which brings the Bread to us from afar. It really is like that. Mary is the one who brings the Eucharistic Bread to us; she is the Mediatrix; she is the Mother of the divine life that Christ gives to souls. Above all, by the light shed on it for us by the spiritual motherhood of Mary, we are happy to meditate upon the relationship between Mary and the Blessed Eucharist. It is as our Mother that Mary says to us: Come, eat the Bread that I have prepared for you; eat plenty, for it will give you true life.[15]

It is our mother's invitation that makes present to our minds at this particular time – and always – the recently celebrated feast of the Body and Blood of Christ.

[15] *idem*

THE SACRED HEART OF JESUS: I

FRIDAY AFTER THE SECOND SUNDAY AFTER PENTECOST

49. THE SACRED HEART OF JESUS

Solemnity

This devotion already existed in the Middle Ages as a private devotion; it appears as a liturgical feast in 1675 following the apparitions of Our Lord to Saint Margaret Mary Alacoque. In these revelations the saint was given to know with special depth the need to make reparation for her personal sins and for the sins of the whole world, and to respond to Christ's love. Our Lord asked her to extend the practice of frequent Communion, especially on the first Friday of every month, in a spirit of reparation. He asked for *the first Friday after the octave of the Most Holy Sacrament* to be dedicated to a *special feast to glorify his Heart.* The feast was celebrated for the first time on the 21 June 1686. Pius IX extended it to the whole Church. In 1928 Pius XI gave it the splendour it has today.

Beneath the symbol of the human Heart of Jesus we consider above all the infinite Love of Christ for each individual soul. This is why devotion to the Sacred Heart *stems from the principles of Christian doctrine,* as St John Paul II made clear in his abundant teaching about this consoling mystery.

49.1 The origin and significance of this feast.

The designs of his Heart are from age to age, to rescue their souls from death, and to keep them alive in famine,[1] we read at the beginning of today's Mass.

There is a two-fold aspect to the Solemnity we celebrate today: on the one hand there is thanksgiving for

---

[1] *Entrance Antiphon*: Ps 32:11,19

the wonders of God's love for us, and on the other there is reparation, because this love is often poorly responded to or scarcely repaid,[2] even by those of us who have so many reasons for loving and thanking God. The basis of Christian piety has always been consideration of Christ's love for all men; this is why devotion to the Sacred Heart of Jesus *stems from the principles of Christian doctrine.*[3] This devotion received a special impulse from the devotion and piety of many saints to whom Our Lord disclosed the secrets of his most loving Heart, moving them to spread devotion to the Sacred Heart and to foster a spirit of reparation.

On the Friday after the octave of the feast of *Corpus Christi,* Our Lord asked Saint Margaret Mary Alacoque to promote love for frequent communion ... especially on the first Friday of every month, in a spirit of reparation, and promised that He would let her share, each Thursday to Friday night, in his suffering in the Garden of Olives. One year later Our Lord appeared to her. Laying bare his most Sacred Heart He spoke to her in words that have nourished the piety of many souls: *See this Heart that has loved men so much and has spared itself nothing until it has exhausted itself and consumed itself in order to show them its love. I receive in return scarcely anything but ingratitude because of their irreverence and sacrileges, and because of the coldness and disdain they show towards Me in this sacrament of love. But what hurts me still more is that it is hearts who are consecrated to me who treat me thus. This is why I ask you that on the first Friday after the octave of the Most Holy Sacrament a special feast may be dedicated to the honour of my Heart by receiving Communion on that day and making reparation with some*

---

[2] cf A. G. Martimort, *The Church at Prayer*

[3] Pius XII, *Haurietis aquas,* 15 May 1956, 27

act of atonement...

In many parts of the Church there exists the private custom of making reparation on the first Friday of the month with some Eucharistic act, or by saying the Litany of the Sacred Heart. Moreover, *the month of June is dedicated in a special way to the veneration of the divine Heart. Not just on one day – the liturgical feast, which generally falls in June – but every day.*[4]

The Heart of Jesus is the source and expression of his infinite love for each person, whatever his situation may be. The Lord seeks out each one of us. A very beautiful Messianic text taken from the Prophet Ezechiel reads: *I am going to look after my flock myself and keep all of it in view. As a shepherd keeps all his flock in sight when he stands up in the middle of his scattered sheep, so shall I keep my sheep in view. I shall rescue them from wherever they have been scattered during the mist and darkness.*[5] Each one is an individual whom the Father has entrusted to the Son so that he or she shall not perish, even though he may have strayed far away.

Jesus, true God and true man, loves the world with *a human heart,*[6] a heart that serves as a channel for God's infinite love. Nobody has ever loved us more than Jesus does, nobody ever will love us more. *He loved me,* said Saint Paul, *and gave himself for me.*[7] Each one of us can repeat the same words. His Heart is full of the Father's love – full in a way that is at once divine and human.

49.2 Christ's love for each one of us.

Christ's Heart loved as no other heart has ever loved. It experienced sadness and joy, compassion and sorrow.

---

[4] St John Paul II, *Angelus,* 27 June 1982
[5] *First Reading, Year C*: Ez 34:11-16
[6] Second Vatican Council, *Gaudium et spes,* 22
[7] Gal 2:20

The Evangelists frequently tell us of Jesus saying: *I have compassion on the crowd*;[8] *He had compassion on them because they were like sheep without a shepherd.*[9] The successful outcome of his Apostles' first venture into evangelisation made him feel as we do when we receive some good news: *He rejoiced,* says Saint Luke:[10] and He weeps when death takes his friend from him.[11]

Neither did He hide from us his disappointments: *O Jerusalem, Jerusalem, killing the prophets ... How often would I have gathered your children together ...*[12] How often! Jesus sees the whole history of the Old Testament and of mankind: a portion of the Jewish people and of the Gentiles of all times will reject God's love and mercy. We can say that in this passage God is somehow weeping with human eyes for the sorrow He feels in his human heart. And this is the real meaning of devotion to the Sacred Heart – to translate God's nature into human terms for ourselves. It is not a matter of indifference to Jesus – any less than is our daily relationship with him at the present time – that some lepers failed to return to thank him after they had been cured. He is not indifferent to the hospitality and consideration shown towards a guest, as He told Simon the Pharisee. On many occasions He experienced the great joy of seeing someone repent of his sins and become his disciple, of seeing the generosity of those who left everything to follow him. He was affected by the joy of blind men who were able to see, perhaps for the first time in their lives.

Before celebrating the Last Supper He was already thinking that He would remain with us for ever by means

---

[8] Mark 8:2
[9] Mark 6:34
[10] Luke 10:21
[11] cf John 11:35
[12] Matt 23:37

of the Holy Eucharist that He was about to institute; *I have earnestly desired to eat this passover with you,* He said to his friends, *before I suffer.*[13] This emotion must have been even stronger when He *took bread, gave thanks, broke it and gave it to his disciples, saying, 'This is my Body ...*[14] Who shall ever be able to express the feelings in his most loving Heart as He gave his mother to us on Calvary to be our Mother?

When He had already surrendered his life to his Father, *one of the soldiers pierced his side with a spear, and at once there came out blood and water.*[15] This open wound reminds us today of the immense love that Jesus has for us, because He willingly gave the very last drop of his precious Blood for us, as though each of us were alone in the world. Are we not, then, going to approach Christ with confidence? What amount of wretchedness can prevent our loving him, so long as our heart is big enough to ask for forgiveness?

49.3 Reparatory love.

After He had ascended into Heaven in his glorified Body, Christ did not cease to love us. He does not stop calling us now to live always close to his most loving Heart. Even in the glory of Heaven, *in his hands and feet and side He bears the glowing marks of the wounds which represent the triple victory gained by him over the devil, sin and death.*

He likewise has in his heart, placed, as it were, in a most precious shrine, those treasures of merit, the fruits of his triple triumph. These He bestows generously on redeemed mankind.[16]

---

[13] Luke 22:15
[14] cf Luke 22:19-20
[15] John 19:34
[16] Pius XII, *loc cit,* 22

Today, on this Solemnity, we adore the Most Sacred Heart of Jesus *since that Heart of his participates in and is the natural and most expressive symbol of the inexhaustible love with which our divine Redeemer still loves mankind. That heart indeed, although it is no longer liable to the disturbances of this mortal life, still lives and beats. It is now inseparably joined with the Person of the divine Word, and in it and through it with his divine Will.*

Wherefore, since the heart of Christ overflows with divine and human love, and since it is abundantly rich with the treasures of all the graces our Redeemer acquired by his life, his sufferings and his death, it is truly the unfailing fountain of that love which his Spirit pours forth into all the members of his Mystical Body.[17] As we meditate today on the love Christ has for us, we will feel a desire to thank him for such a great gift and for so much unmerited mercy. As we consider how so very many turn their backs on God, let us remember that often we ourselves are not altogether faithful, that we have many personal weaknesses. We should turn then to his most loving Heart, where we shall find peace. We often need to have recourse to his merciful love, and to seek that peace which is one of the fruits given us by the Holy Spirit: *Cor Iesu sacratissimum et misericors, dona nobis pacem. Most sweet and merciful Heart of Jesus, grant us peace.*

As we see Jesus so close to our concerns, to our problems, to our ideals, we say to him: *I give you thanks, my Jesus, for your decision to become perfect Man, with a Heart which loves and is most lovable, which loved unto death and suffered, which was filled with joy and sorrow, which delighted in the things of men and showed us the way to Heaven, which subjected itself heroically to duty and acted with mercy, which watched over the poor and*

---

[17] *idem,* 24

the rich and cared for the sinner and the just alike.

I give you thanks, my Jesus. Give us hearts that will measure up to yours![18]

Close to Jesus we always find his Mother. We turn to her as we come to the end of our prayer, and ask her to make the way that leads us to her Son both firm and safe.

---

[18] St. J. Escrivá, *Furrow,* 813

THE SACRED HEART OF JESUS: II

FRIDAY AFTER THE SECOND SUNDAY AFTER PENTECOST

50. CHRIST'S LOVE FOR US

Solemnity

50.1 A unique and personal love for each individual.

In one of the Readings of today's Mass we hear: *so we know and believe the love God has for us. God is love, and he who abides in love abides in God, and God abides in him.*[1]

God expresses the fullness of his love for man by sending the Person of his Only-begotten Son. We have come to know that God loves us not only because this was the constant teaching of Jesus Christ, but because his presence amongst us is the greatest proof of that love. He himself is the complete revelation of God and of his love for men.[2] Saint Augustine teaches that the fount of all graces is the love God has for us, the love that He has revealed not only with words, but also with deeds. The supreme act of this love occurred when his Only-begotten Son assumed mortal flesh and became man like us, in all things except sin.[3]

Today we should ask for new light so that we may understand in an ever-deeper way God's love for men, for each individual. We must beg the Holy Spirit to enable us, with his grace and our correspondence, to say personally

---

[1] *Second Reading, Year A:* 1 John 4:16

[2] cf John 1:18; Heb 1:1

[3] cf St Augustine, *De Trinitate,* 9, 10

and with ever-greater depth of understanding: 'I have known the love that God has for me.' We will reach that wisdom, the wisdom that really matters, with the help of grace if we frequently meditate on the most Sacred Humanity of Jesus – his life, his deeds, all He suffered in order to redeem us from the slavery in which we found ourselves, and to raise us to friendship with him, a friendship that will last for all eternity. The Heart of Jesus, a heart with human feelings, was the instrument united to the Divinity by which He gave expression to his indescribable love: the Heart of Jesus is the heart of a divine Person, that is, of the Incarnate Word. *By it all the love with which He loved, and even now continues to love us, is represented and, so to speak, placed before our very eyes.*

Therefore devotion to the Sacred Heart is so important that it may be considered, so far as practice is concerned, a perfect profession of the Christian religion.

For this is the religion of Jesus, which rests entirely on a Mediator who is man and God, so that no one can come to the heart of God except through the heart of Christ, as He himself says: 'I am the way, and the truth, and the life. No one comes to the Father but by me' (John 14:6).[4]

There was not a single act of Christ's soul or of his will that was not directed towards our redemption and to obtaining for us all possible help so that we should never separate ourselves from him or so that, should we ever stray from the path, we would come back to him. There was not a single part of his body that did not suffer for love of us. He gladly accepted all types of sorrow, insult and shame for our salvation. Not a single drop of his most precious Blood remained unshed for our sake.

God loves me. This is the most consoling truth of all

[4] Pius XII, *Haurietis aquas,* 15 May 1956

and the one that should bring the most practical repercussions in our lives. Who can ever understand the depths of Christ's goodness manifested in the call that we have received to share his own Life with him, to share his friendship? ... A Life and a friendship that even death cannot rupture; rather, death will make it stronger and safer.

God loves me. And John the Apostle writes: 'Let us love God, then, since God loved us first.' As if this were not enough, Jesus comes to each one of us, in spite of our patent wretchedness, to ask us, as he asked Peter: 'Simon, son of John, do you love me more than these others?'

This is the moment to reply: 'Lord, you know all things, you know that I love you!' adding, with humility, 'Help me to love you more. Increase my love!'[5]

50.2 Atonement and reparation.

During the Mass of this Solemnity we pray that we *who glory in the Heart of your beloved Son and recall the wonders of his love for us, may be made worthy to receive an overflowing measure of grace from that fount of heavenly gifts.*[6]

We should draw from these moments of prayer the immense joy of considering, once again, the deep love that Jesus has at this moment for each one of us. A God with a heart of flesh like ours! Jesus of Nazareth still goes about the streets and squares of our cities doing good[7] just as when He was clothed in mortal flesh among men – helping, healing, consoling, forgiving, and through his sacraments conferring eternal life on us ... These are the infinite treasures of his Heart which He continues to pour out copiously upon us. Saint Paul teaches that *When He*

[5] St. J. Escrivá, *The Forge,* 497
[6] *Roman Missal, Collect*
[7] cf Acts 10:38

ascended on high He led a host of captives, and He gave gifts to men.[8] Every day we receive immeasurable graces – inspirations and all types of material and spiritual help from the loving Heart of Jesus. However, He *does not lord it over us. He begs us to give him a little love, as he silently shows us his wounds.*[9] How often have we refused him this love! How often has He hoped we would show more love, greater fervour as we make that *Visit to the Blessed Sacrament* or receive Holy Communion! ...

We must make a great deal of reparation and atonement to the Most Sacred Heart of Jesus for our past life, for so much wasted time, for so much roughness in the way we deal with him, for so much lack of love. We can say to him in the words written by Saint Bernard, *I beg you to receive the offering of the years remaining to me. Do not despise, O my God, this heart which is contrite and humble because of all the years that I have spent so foolishly.*[10] Give me, Lord, the gift of contrition for still being so clumsy in the way I talk to you and show my love for you. Increase my aversion from any deliberate venial sin. Teach me to offer you in expiation all the physical and moral setbacks of each day – my tiredness at work and my efforts to finish off my daily tasks the way you would like me to.

When we see so many people who seem set on fleeing from grace, we cannot remain indifferent. *Don't be content to ask from Jesus pardon just for your own faults: don't love him with your heart alone ...*

Console him for every offence that has been, is, or will be done him. Love him with all the strength of all the hearts of all those who have most loved him.

Be daring: tell him that you are crazier about him than

---

[8] Eph 4:8

[9] St. J. Escrivá, *Christ is passing by,* 179

[10] St Bernard, *Sermon 20,* 1

Mary Magdalen, than either of his two Teresas, that you love him madly, more than Augustine and Dominic and Francis, more than Ignatius and Xavier.[11]

50.3 A furnace burning with charity.

Those two disciples whom Jesus accompanied along the way to Emmaus finally recognise him in the breaking of bread, after having travelled with him for several hours. *They said to each other, 'Did not our hearts burn within us while he talked to us on the road, while He opened to us the scriptures*?[12] Their hearts, which only shortly before had been discouraged, downcast and sad, are now filled with fervour and joy. This would have been reason enough for them to have realised that it was Christ who was accompanying them. It is the very same effect that Jesus has on those who struggle to be close to his most lovable Heart. It happened then and it continues to happen every day.

In this most *precious ark* of the Heart of Jesus is to be found the perfection of all charity. This most precious gift *of the Heart of Christ and of his Spirit. It gave the apostles and martyrs the fortitude with which they were strengthened to fight even to death itself, which they met with an heroic spirit, to preach the truth of the Gospel and to bear witness to it by the shedding of their blood.*[13] From his Heart we draw the conviction we need with which to make others know Christ. It is in our conversation with Jesus that true apostolic zeal is enkindled, a zeal that can survive any number of apparent failures, or surmount all the obstacles placed in its way by living in an environment that seems totally hostile to Jesus.

A friend gives the best he has to his friend. We have

---

[11] St. J. Escrivá, *The Way,* 402

[12] Luke 24:32

[13] Pius XII, *loc cit*

nothing that can be compared with our having discovered Jesus. So we have to make our relatives, our friends and our colleagues get to know him.

It is in the Heart of Jesus that we must enkindle our apostolic zeal for souls. It is in him that we find a *furnace burning with charity* for souls, as we pray in the *Litany of the Sacred Heart.* St John Paul II once commented: *The furnace burns. As it burns it consumes anything material, whether it be timber or any other easily combustible substance.*

The Heart of Jesus, the human Heart of Jesus, burns with the love with which it is overflowing. This love of his is love for the Eternal Father and love for men – the Father's adopted daughters and sons.

A burning furnace dies down little by little. The Heart of Jesus on the contrary is an unquenchable furnace. In this way it is like the 'burning bush' of the Book of Exodus, in which God revealed himself to Moses. The bush that burned with flame but ... 'was not consumed' (Ex 3:2).

Indeed, the love that burns in the Heart of Jesus is more than anything else the Holy Spirit himself through whom the Son of God unites himself eternally to the Father. The Heart of Jesus, the human Heart of God made man, is set on fire by the 'living flame' of the Love of the Trinity which is never extinguished.

The Heart of Jesus, is this 'furnace burning with charity'. Whilst the furnace burns it gives light to the darkness of the night and warms the bodies of frost-bitten travellers.

Today we want to pray to the Mother of the Eternal Word so that the Heart of Jesus, the 'furnace burning with charity', may never cease to burn within the horizon of the life of each one of us. We pray that He may reveal to us the Love that is never extinguished or diminished, the Love that is eternal. We ask that his love may give light to the darkness of our earthly night and give warmth to the cold hearts of men.

As we thank God for the only love capable of transforming the world and all of human life, we turn in the company of the Virgin Immaculate at the moment of the Annunciation, to the Divine Heart which never ceases to be a 'furnace burning with charity'. Burning – like the bush Moses saw at the foot of Mount Horeb.[14]

[14] St John Paul II, *Angelus,* 23 June 1985

THE IMMACULATE HEART OF MARY

SATURDAY AFTER THE SECOND SUNDAY AFTER PENTECOST

51. THE IMMACULATE HEART OF THE BLESSED VIRGIN MARY

Memorial

After the consecration of the world to the most sweet and motherly Heart of Mary in 1942, many petitions were sent to the Roman Pontiff asking him to extend to the whole Church the devotion to the Immaculate Heart of Mary that already existed in some places. Pius XII agreed in 1945 *certain to find in her most loving Heart ... the safe haven in the midst of the tempest that everywhere assails us.* Through the symbol of her heart we venerate in Mary her most pure and perfect love for God and her motherly love for each one of us. In that heart of hers we can find a refuge in the midst of all the difficulties and temptations of life, and we ask her to prepare for us the safe way – *iter para tutum* – the way by which we will soon reach her Son.

51.1 The Heart of Mary.

My heart will rejoice in your salvation. I will sing to the Lord, who has been bountiful with me,[1] we read in the *Entrance Antiphon* of today's Mass.

Yesterday's feastday helped us to consider the heart as an expression and symbol of a person's inmost being. In the Gospels, the first time the Heart of Mary is mentioned it is to express all the richness of Our Lady's interior life. Saint Luke writes: *Mary kept all these things, pondering*

[1] *Entrance Antiphon,* Mass of the Immaculate Heart of Mary

them in her heart.[2]

The *Preface of the Mass* attributes a number of qualities to the Heart of Mary. It is *wise,* because she understood the meaning of the Scriptures as no other person had ever done, and she kept in it the memory of the words and things relating to the mystery of salvation. It is *immaculate,* that is, immune from any stain of sin. It is *docile* because she submitted so faithfully to God's Will and to every one of his wishes. It is *new,* according to the ancient prophecy of Ezechiel – *a new heart I will give you, and a new spirit*[3]- clothed in the newness of grace merited by Christ. It is *humble* because she imitated the humility of Christ, who said *Learn from me; for I am gentle and lowly in heart.*[4] It is *simple,* free from any duplicity and full of the Spirit of truth. It is *clean* and thus able to see God according to the words of the Beatitude.[5] It is *firm* in her acceptance of the Will of God when Simeon announced to her that a sword of sorrow would pierce her heart,[6] when persecution broke out against her Son[7] or when the moment of his death was at hand. It is *ready,* for whilst Christ slept in the sepulchre she kept watch in the expectation of his resurrection, just like the spouse in the *Canticle of Canticles.*[8]

The Immaculate Heart of Mary is called, above all, the *temple of the Holy Spirit,*[9] by reason of her divine motherhood and because of the continuous and all-embracing inhabitation of the Holy Spirit in her soul. This sublime

[2] Luke 2:19
[3] cf Ezek 36:26
[4] Mark 11:29
[5] cf Matt 5:8
[6] cf Luke 2:35
[7] cf Matt 2:13
[8] cf Cant 5:2
[9] cf Second Vatican Council, *Lumen gentium,* 53

maternity that places Mary above all other created beings, was accomplished in her Immaculate Heart before it was accomplished in her most pure womb. The Fathers affirm that she conceived the Word to whom she gave birth according to the flesh first of all in her heart according to faith.[10] By her Immaculate Heart, full of faith and love, a heart that was humble and totally dedicated to the Will of God, Mary merited to carry the Son of God in her virginal womb.

She always protects us as a mother protects her small child who is everywhere surrounded by dangers and difficulties, and helps us to grow continuously. How can we possibly prevent ourselves turning to her each day? *'Sancta Maria, Stella maris' – Holy Mary, Star of the sea, be our guide!*

Make this resolute request, because there is no storm that can shipwreck the most Sweet Heart of Mary. When you see the squall coming, if you seek safety in the firm Refuge that is Mary, there will be no danger of your being hurled off course or going down.[11] In her Heart we find a safe harbour where it is impossible for us to founder.

51.2 A motherly heart.

Mary treasured all these words, reflecting on them in her heart.[12]

Mary kept in her heart the angel's announcement about her divine Motherhood as she would a treasure. She kept for ever in her heart all the things that happened on that night in Bethlehem, all that the shepherds said in front of the manger, the presence – days or months later – of the Magi with their gifts, the prophecy of old Simeon and the difficulties of her journey into Egypt ... Later, a deep

[10] cf St Augustine, *On Holy Virginity,* 3

[11] St. J. Escrivá, *The Forge,* 1055

[12] *Communion Antiphon*: Luke 2:19

impression was made on her heart by the loss of her Son, at the age of twelve, in Jerusalem and the words He spoke to her and to Joseph, when, in a state of great distress, they found him at last. *And he went down with them and came to Nazareth, and was obedient to them; and his mother kept all these things in her heart.*[13] During all the years she lived here on earth Mary never forgot the events that surrounded the death of her Son on the Cross and the words she heard Jesus say as He hung there: *Woman, behold your son*![14] As He pointed to John, She saw each one of us and all mankind. From that moment on she loved us in her heart with a mother's love, with the same love as that with which she loved Jesus. In us she recognised her Son, just as He himself had said: *As you did it to one of the least of these my brethren, you did it to me.*[15]

But Our Lady had already acted as a mother before the redemption was consummated on Calvary, for she has been our mother from the moment when, with her *fiat,* she gave her cooperation to the salvation of all men. In his account of the wedding at Cana, Saint John reveals to us a truly maternal feature of the Heart of Mary – her attentive concern for others. A mother's heart is always an attentive, vigilant heart. A mother never fails to notice anything that affects her child in any way. In Cana, the motherly Heart of Mary bestows her caring vigilance on some relatives or friends of hers, so that they can remedy a situation that might have been embarrassing but would not have had any really serious consequences. The Evangelist, by divine inspiration, wanted to show us that she is not indifferent to anything human and that nobody is excluded from her fervent tenderness. Our little faults and mistakes, as much

---

[13] Luke 2:51
[14] John 19:26
[15] Matt 25:40

as our bigger faults, are the object of her concern. She is interested in everything that can affect our souls – from our little bouts of forgetfulness and anxiety to the great worries we may sometimes have. *They have no wine,*[16] she says to her Son. Everybody is otherwise occupied, nobody else is aware of it. And even though it seems that the *hour* of the miracles has not yet come, she is able to make it arrive sooner.

Mary knows the Heart of her Son well and she knows how to reach it. Now in Heaven, her attitude has not changed. Through her intercession, our prayers reach the Lord's presence *sooner, more certainly and better.* This is why today we can address to her the ancient prayer of the Church, *Recordare, Virgo Mater Dei, dum steteris in conspectu Domini, ut loquaris pro nobis bona*[17]– O Virgin Mother of God, you who are always in his presence, speak good things about us. Say something to him in our favour. We need it so much!

As we meditate on this invocation to Our Lady, it is perhaps not a matter of proposing to ourselves yet another devotion, but of learning to talk to her with more trust, with the simplicity of small children who run to their mothers every moment; they don't talk to them only when they have great need, but also when they are worried by the little things that happen to them. Their mothers gladly help them to solve even the smallest problems. They – all earthly mothers – have learnt this from our Mother in Heaven.

51.3 *Cor Mariae dulcissimum, iter para tutum.*

As we consider the splendour and holiness of the Immaculate Heart of Mary, we can examine today the

---

[16] cf John 2:3
[17] *St Pius V Missal, Prayer over the offerings* from the Mass of Mary Mediatrix of All Graces; cf Jer 18:20

depths of our own soul: whether we are open and docile to the graces and inspirations of the Holy Spirit, whether we jealously guard our heart from anything that could separate it from God, whether we pull up by the roots our little feelings of resentment, of envy ... which tend to bed themselves down within it. We know that from our heart's richness or its poverty our words and deeds will speak. *The good man out of his good treasure brings forth good things.*[18]

From Our Lady there spring forth torrents of the grace of forgiveness, of mercy, of help in necessity ... This is why we ask her today to give us a heart which is pure, human and understanding towards the defects of the people around us. We ask her to make us kind to everyone, to understand people's sorrows whatever their circumstances, and always to be ready to help anyone who needs our assistance. *'Mater Pulchrae dilectionis, Mother of Fair Love', pray for us. Teach us to love God and our brother men as you have loved them; make our love for others always patient, benign, full of respect for them ... Make our joy always authentic and complete, so that we can communicate it to everyone,*[19] and especially to those to whom God has wanted us to be united with stronger ties.

We recall today how, when needs have been pressing, the Church and her children have turned to the Most Sweet Heart of Mary so as to consecrate to her the world, nations or families.[20] We have always had the intuitive feeling that it is only in her Sweet Heart that we are safe. Today we dedicate to her once again all that we are and all that we have. We place on her motherly lap the days that seem

---

[18] Matt 12:35

[19] St John Paul II, *Homily,* 31 May 1979

[20] cf Pius XII, Address, *Benedicite Deum,* 31 October 1942; St John Paul II, *Homily in Fatima,* 13 May 1982

good and those that seem bad, our illnesses, weakness, work, our tiredness and our rest, together with the noble ideals that God has placed in our souls. We place especially in her hands our journey towards Christ so that she may keep it free from all dangers and guard it with tenderness and fortitude, as a mother does. *Cor Mariae dulcissimum, iter para tutum*: Most Sweet Heart of Mary *prepare for me, for them, a safe way.*[21]

We finish our prayer asking God, with the liturgy of the Mass: *O God, who prepared a fitting dwelling place for the Holy Spirit in the heart of the Blessed Virgin Mary, graciously grant that through her intercession, we may be a worthy temple of your glory.*[22]

---

[21] cf Hymn, *Ave Maris Stella*
[22] *Roman Missal, Collect*

1 JUNE

52. SAINT JUSTIN

Martyr

Memorial

Saint Justin was born in the region of Samaria at the beginning of the second century. Like some other thinkers of his day he opened a school of Philosophy in Rome. After his conversion he carried out an effective apostolate from the school. He defended the Christian Faith with his knowledge in times that were difficult for Christianity. The Apologia addressed to the Emperors Antoninus and Marcus Aurelius have been preserved. He died a martyr in Rome during the persecution of the latter Emperor. Because of the effort he made to defend the Faith with his learning and with his knowledge, and for the exemplary value this has for everyone, Leo XIII extended his liturgical feast to the universal Church.

52.1 Defence of the Faith in times of misunderstanding.

To start with, the Faith took root amongst simple working folk: fullers, carders of wool, soldiers in the ranks, blacksmiths ... The many inscriptions that have been found in the catacombs tell us of a great variety of occupations and trades – innkeepers, barbers, tailors, joiners, weavers ... One of these inscriptions depicts a charioteer mounted on his quadriga with a crown in his right hand and in his left the palm of martyrdom.

Very soon Christianity had reached all social classes. Already in the second century there were Christians who were Senators like Apolonius, chief magistrates like the Consul Liberal, lawyers of the Roman forum like Tertullian and philosophers like Saint Justin whose feast we celebrate today and who was converted to Christianity when he was already well on in years.

Christians do not separate themselves from their

fellow citizens. They dress just like everyone else of their time and country. They claim their civic rights and they carry out their duties. They attend state schools like everyone else and they are not ashamed to profess their faith, even though for a long time the pagan environment in which they lived was very much against the Good News. We see them defending the Faith – their right to live it and to be at the same time Roman citizens like everybody else – with admirable constancy, whether in the course of an ordinary conversation in the market place or in the forum, or in the more formal setting of a defence of the Faith with the weapons of the intellect, which was what Saint Justin and others did in their *Apologies* for Christianity.

All of them, each one is his own place, knew how to give a serene testimony of Jesus Christ, which was the best of all *Apologies* for the Faith. One of these living examples of the Faith has come down to us through a piece of graffiti that is still preserved. On the Palatine, the hill on which stood the emperor's palace and the villas of Roman noblemen, there was a school where page-boys of the Imperial court were trained. Among the pupils there must have been a Christian called Alexamenos, because somebody had made a drawing on the wall representing a man with an ass's head nailed to a roughly-hewn cross, with a human figure alongside it. Beside the drawing can be read the inscription: *Alexamenos adores his god.* The young Christian, with valour and pride in his Faith, had written underneath in reply: *Alexamenos is faithful.*[1]

This *graffito* is typical of the sort of slander that was frequently circulated about Christians. The man in the street heard an abundance of rumours, gossip, nonsense and incredible stories ... Among the more cultured classes expressions like those transmitted to us by Tertullian were

[1] cf A. G. Hamman, *The Daily Life of the First Christians,* Madrid 1986

disdainfully passed from mouth to mouth: *That Caius Sextus is a good man. What a pity he's a Christian*! Another important personage says, *I am indeed surprised that Lucius Ticus, a really intelligent man, too, should have suddenly become a Christian.* And Tertullian comments, *It doesn't occur to them to wonder whether Caius is a good man, and Lucius is intelligent precisely because they are Christians, or whether they have become Christians precisely because one man is good and the other intelligent.*[2]

Saint Justin knows how to talk about the greatness of the Christian Faith and how to compare it with all the different ways of thinking and ideologies fashionable in his day: *For,* he points out, *nobody believes Socrates to the point of giving his life for his teaching. However, not only philosophers and men of learning, but lowly workers and totally uneducated men and women have believed in Christ. Such people have taken no notice of the opinion of the world at large. They have scorned fear and even death itself.*[3] Justin himself was later to die giving witness to his faith. God asks us to be every bit as steadfast as he was, whatever our condition in life, even if we sometimes find ourselves in an environment that is completely opposed to Christ's teaching.

52.2 The greater the adversity, the more opportunity for apostolate.

In times of persecution and major tribulation, Christians continued to attract others to the Faith. The very difficulties they faced were the opportunity for carrying out an even more intense apostolate, which was given greater credence than ever by the good example and fortitude of the Christians. Their words took on a new strength – the strength of the Cross. Martyrdom was a kind of testimony

---

[2] cf Tertullian, *On Idolatry,* 20

[3] St Justin, *Apology,* II, 10

that was filled with supernatural vigour and had great apostolic effectiveness. Sometimes the martyrs' very executioner embraced the Christian faith.[4]

If we are really faithful to Christ it is quite possible that we shall encounter difficulties of different kinds, from open slander and persecution to the realisation that a door which should be open is closed to us. We may be relegated to a less prestigious job; perhaps there will be sarcasm or superficial comments ... *The disciple is not greater than his Master.*[5] A Christian's life and the meaning he gives to existence – whether we like it or not – is bound to clash with a world that has fixed its heart on material things.

Such difficulties afford us particularly appropriate opportunities for doing an effective apostolate: teaching the true nature of the Church, spreading writings that can clarify even the most controversial issues; speaking out clearly about Christ and the Christian life ... The first Christians won through by their determination, and they taught us the way: their unconditional fidelity to Christ overcame the pagan atmosphere that surrounded them. *Although they were immersed in the hostile mass of men, they did not look for isolation as a remedy against contagion and as a guarantee of their survival; they knew they were God's leaven. In the end their silent and effective action gave shape to that very mass. In particular, they knew how to be serenely present in their world, how not to despise its values or to scorn any earthly realities.*[6]

If at times of misunderstanding or calumny we remain firm and constant in the personal apostolate that as Christians we are obliged carry out, fruits will come to the Church in the most distant and remote corners of the world,

---

[4] cf D. Ramos, *The Testimony of the First Christians,* Madrid 1969
[5] Matt 10:24
[6] J. Orlandis, *The Christian in the World*

in places where it seemed impossible that any results could be achieved. The more clearly the Cross can be seen, the more effective will be the apostolate.

52.3 We must live charity always. Charity with those who have no regard for us.

Malicious gossip, calumny and even martyrdom itself were unable to make the Christians retreat and resign themselves to being set apart from other citizens in some kind of ghetto, or feel themselves exiled from their own social milieu. Even during the most difficult times of persecution, the presence of Christians in the world was a driving and active force. Christians defended their right to be consistent with their faith. Intellectuals like Saint Justin defended it by their writings, which showed knowledge and common sense. Mothers of families defended it by their friendly conversations and by the example of their lives ... It is in the midst of this storm of contradiction that Christians lived the new commandment of Jesus with even more determination.[7] *It was love that enabled them to make their way through that corrupt pagan world.*[8] *This practice of charity is, more than anything else, what seals us with a special seal in the eyes of many. 'See how they love one another', they say, for they themselves mutually hate one another. And how those Christians are ready to die for one another, whilst they themselves are ready rather to put each other to death,*[9] are words we find written by Tertullian.

The early Christians did not hold a grudge against those who ill-treated them in any way.[10] Like our first brothers in the faith, we too have always striven to drown

---

[7] cf John 13:34
[8] St. J. Escrivá, *Friends of God,* 172
[9] Tertullian, *Apology,* 39
[10] cf *Didache,* I, 1-2

evil in an abundance of good.[11]

In the catechesis he carried out during his short pontificate, John Paul I recalled the exemplary story of the sixteen Carmelite nuns who were martyred during the French Revolution and beatified by Pius X. It seems that during their trial it was suggested that they should be condemned to death *for fanaticism.* One of them asked the judge: *What does fanaticism mean*? He replied, *your foolishness in belonging to religion.* After the sentence had been pronounced and they were being led to the scaffold they sang sacred hymns. When they reached the place of execution, one by one they knelt before the Prioress to renew their vow of obedience. Afterwards they intoned the *Veni Creator,* their singing becoming weaker as the successive heads of the nuns fell under the guillotine. The Prioress was the last to go up. Her last words were these: *Love will always be victorious. Love can overcome everything.*[12] It has always been so.

The charity of the first Christians was aimed first and foremost at strengthening in the Faith their weakest brethren, those who had only recently been converted, and all those who were most in need. On almost every page the *Acts of the Martyrs*[13] relate specific details of this concern for the fidelity of those who were least strong. We must not fail to do the same in times of adversity, calumny and persecution. We must support, *wrap our cloaks round,* those who, owing to their age or other special circumstances have greater need of being fortified. Our steadfastness and cheerfulness at such times will be of great help to others.

As we finish our meditation we say to Our Lady a

---

[11] cf Rom 12:21

[12] cf John Paul I, *Angelus,* 24 September 1978

[13] cf *Acts of the Martyrs,* Madrid 1962

prayer that the first Christians often said: *Sub tuum praesidium confugimus, Sancta Dei Genitrix* ... We fly to your patronage, O holy Mother of God. Despise not our prayers in our necessities, but deliver us from all dangers, O ever glorious and blessed Virgin.[14]

---

[14] A. G. Hamman, *Prayers of the First Christians,* Madrid, 1956

11 June

53. SAINT BARNABAS

Apostle

Memorial

A native of Cyprus, Barnabas was one of the first believers in Jerusalem. It was he who presented Saint Paul to the Apostles after his conversion and accompanied him on his first apostolic journey. He took part in the Council of Jerusalem and was a figure of great importance in the Church at Antioch, the first Christian nucleus of considerable size outside Jerusalem. He was a relative of Mark, on whom he exercised a decisive influence. He returned to his native land, evangelised it, and died a martyr in or about the year 63. His name is mentioned in Eucharistic Prayer I (the Roman Canon).

53.1 The need for having a big heart in the apostolate.

The word *Barnabas* means *son of consolation,* and was the name given by the Apostles to Joseph, a Levite and native of Cyprus.[1] Saint John Chrysostom comments that this surname must have been inspired by his conciliatory spirit and his sympathetic manner.[2]

After the martyrdom of Stephen and the persecution that followed, some Christians went to Antioch, taking with them their faith in Jesus Christ. When word reached the Apostles in Jerusalem about the wonders the Holy Spirit was working there, they sent Barnabas to Antioch.[3] His zeal for extending the Kingdom led him to look for instruments who would be capable of carrying out the enormous task that faced them. So he went to Tarsus to

---

[1] cf Acts 4:36

[2] cf St John Chrysostom, *Homilies on the Acts of the Apostles,* 21

[3] Acts 11:23

look for Paul, *and when he had found him, he brought him to Antioch. For a whole year they met with the church, and taught a large company of people.*[4] He had already detected in the new convert those qualities that, with the help of grace, would transform him into the Apostle of the Gentiles. It was Barnabas who had presented Paul to the Apostles in Jerusalem a short time before, when many Christians were still suspicious of their former persecutor.[5]

With the Apostle he set off on the first missionary journey whose objective was the Island of Cyprus.[6] They were accompanied also by Mark, Barnabas's cousin, who left them in Pergia, half way through the journey, and returned to Jerusalem. When Saint Paul was planning a second great missionary journey Barnabas wanted to take Mark with them again, but Paul thought it better *not to take with them one who had withdrawn from them in Pamphylia, and had not gone with them to the work.*[7] This aroused such strong dissension between them that they separated from one another ...[8]

Barnabas did not afterwards want to leave out his cousin Mark, who was perhaps very young when his strength had failed him at the time of his initial desertion. He was able to encourage and strengthen him, and make of him a great evangelist and a most effective collaborator of Saint Peter and even of Saint Paul, with whom Barnabas was to remain united.[9] Later on, Paul was to express an opinion of the highest esteem for Mark,[10] *as though he saw in him a reflection of his sympathetic manner and recalled*

---

[4] Acts 11:26
[5] cf Acts 9:26
[6] cf Acts 13:1-4
[7] Acts 15:38
[8] Acts 15:40
[9] cf 1 Cor 9:5-6
[10] cf Col 4:10; Phil 24:2; Tim 4:11

pleasant memories of Barnabas, the friend of his youth.[11]

Saint Barnabas invites us today to have a *big heart* in the apostolate, so that we will not become easily discouraged by the defects and the falling away of those friends or relatives of ours whom we want to take to Christ, and so that we do not leave them out when they weaken or perhaps do not respond to our efforts and prayers on their behalf.

If sometimes they fail – quite obviously – to correspond with our concern for them, this should only lead us to do all we can to treat our friends with still greater affection, with a more ready smile, and to make even greater use than we have done previously of the supernatural means.

53.2 Learning to understand people so as to be able to help them.

Preach as you go, saying 'the kingdom of heaven is at hand. Heal the sick, raise the dead, cleanse lepers, cast out demons' ... This command of Christ's that we read of in the Gospel of today's Mass[12] must resound in the hearts of all Christians. It is an apostolate that each one of us has a positive duty to carry out personally in our own surroundings – whether it be in a town or in a part of a great city, in the place where we work, at the University ... We will come across people who are *dead,* whom we have to take to receive the sacrament of Penance so that they recover their supernatural life; people who are *sick,* who cannot manage by themselves and need help in order to approach Christ; *lepers* who will be cleansed by grace through our friendship with them; people *possessed,* whose cure will require of us extraordinary prayer and penance ...

As well as having constancy – we cannot forget that

---

[11] J. Prado, in *Great Encyclopaedia Rialp*
[12] Matt 10:7-13

souls improve with time[13] – we must be aware of the different situations and circumstances of those who need our help. We are told of Saint Barnabas that he was *a good man* who deserved the surname *son of consolation,* and that he brought peace to many hearts. The *Acts of the Apostles* tell us, the first time they mention him, of his large-heartedness, a breadth of sympathy which can be seen in his generosity and his spirit of detachment: *thus Barnabas ... sold a field which belonged to him, and brought the money and laid it at the Apostles' feet.*[14] In this way he was able to follow Our Lord with greater freedom. A generous and detached soul is in a position to give everybody a welcome and to understand the state that souls are really in. When people feel they are understood it is more likely that they will allow themselves to be helped. In the apostolate, the best means a Christian has of winning people over is precisely this welcoming openness towards others, accepting them and really appreciating them as they are, for *nobody can be known except in terms of the friendship we bear towards him.*[15]

If we are to understand others we need to look at everything that is positive about them, and to see their faults only within the context of their good qualities, whether these good qualities be actual or simply potential. And we have to want to help them. We should take the advice of Saint Teresa of Avila: *let us labour, therefore,* she says, *always to consider the virtues and the good qualities we discern in others, and with our own great sins cover our eyes, so that we may see no more of their failings.*[16] Let us listen to the exhortation of Saint Bernard:

---

[13] St. J. Escrivá, *Friends of God,* 78

[14] Acts 4:37

[15] St Augustine, *Sermon 83*

[16] St Teresa, *Life,* 13, 6

Even, he says, *if you do see something bad, do not immediately pass judgment on your neighbour, but rather find excuses for him within yourself. Excuse his intentions if you cannot excuse his deeds. Think that he must have acted out of ignorance, or have been overcome by surprise or misfortune. If his conduct is so obviously bad that it cannot be overlooked, even then try to think in this way and say to yourself: the temptation must have been very strong.*[17]

We have to learn from Our Lord to live harmoniously with everyone, not to think too much about the way people around us fail to correspond with our efforts, or seem deficient in good manners or generosity. Such shortcomings can often be the result of ignorance, of loneliness or no more than just plain tiredness. The good we set out to do can rise above all such mere trifles, and if we consider them in God's presence they cease to have any real importance. *You spend your time with that companion of yours who is scarcely even civil to you: and it's hard.*

Keep at it, and don't judge him. He'll have his 'reasons', just as you have yours, which you strengthen so as to pray for him more each day.[18] Those 'reasons' of ours originate in and are centred upon the Tabernacle.

53.3 Cheerfulness and a positive spirit in our apostolate with our friends.

Sing praises to the Lord with the lyre,
with the lyre and the sound of melody!
With trumpets and the sound of the horn
make a joyful noise before the King, the Lord![19]

It is possible that some Christians allow themselves to be carried away by a *bitter zeal,* as they see everything around them so seemingly far from God, and see the

---

[17] St Bernard, *Sermon 40 on the Canticle of Canticles*
[18] St. J. Escrivá, *The Forge,* 843
[19] *Responsorial Psalm*: Ps 98:5-6

lifestyle adopted by many people who, they feel, should be giving better example. Such zealous Christians try to do good, but they are all the time lamenting the obvious evil they see around them and reproaching society which, according to them, should take drastic measures to put an end to such evil ... God does not want us to be like that; He gave his life serenely and peacefully on the Cross for all men. It would be a great failure if Christians were to adopt a negative attitude towards the world they have to save. We can see the first generations of those who followed Christ always full of joy, in spite of the frequent tribulations they had to undergo. In the Acts of the Apostles, when Saint Luke tries to describe in a few words the little communities that had sprung up everywhere, he tells us that the Church *was built up; and walking in the fear of the Lord and in the comfort of the Holy Spirit it was multiplied.*[20] This is the peace of Christ which we will never lack if we follow him closely. This is the peace we have to give to everyone.

We have to imitate Our Lord and resolutely reject any attitude tainted with harshness, bitterness or a desire for condemnation. If, as Christians, we are to bring joy to the world, how can we think of presenting the Good News as something unattractive and condemnatory? How can we judge others if we do not have the necessary facts on which to judge and, above all, if nobody has in any case given us such a mission? Our attitude towards everyone should always be one of salvation, of peace, of understanding and of joy ... even towards those who at some time or other may have behaved unjustly towards us. *Understanding is real charity. When you really achieve it, you will have a great heart which is open to all without discrimination. Even with those who have treated you badly you will put into living practice that advice of Jesus: 'Come to me all*

[20] Acts 9:31

you that ... are heavy laden, and I will give you rest.'[21] Each Christian is *Christ who passes by* among his own, who lightens their burdens and shows them the way to salvation.

As we come to an end of our prayer we ask Our Lord, with the liturgy of the Mass, for *the flame of your love by which Saint Barnabas brought the light of the Gospel to the nations.*[22] He will grant it to us if we ask him for it particularly through Our Lady: *Sancta Maria, Regina Apostolorum, ora pro nobis* ...; help us in the task of apostolate that we want to carry out among our relatives, friends and acquaintances.

---

[21] St. J. Escrivá, *op cit,* 867
[22] *Roman Missal, Prayer over the Offerings*

22 June

54. SAINTS JOHN FISHER, BISHOP AND THOMAS MORE, MARTYRS

Memorial

John Fisher was ordained priest in 1491. He held several teaching posts at the University of Cambridge, and at the same time was responsible for the spiritual direction of Lady Margaret, the mother of Henry VII. He later occupied the Chair of Theology which the Queen had endowed at Cambridge. Early in 1504 he was named Vice-Chancellor of Cambridge University and at the end of the year was consecrated Bishop of Rochester, the smallest and poorest diocese in England. Two days later he was appointed to office as a member of the King's Council. From 1527 Bishop Fisher upheld the validity of Catherine of Aragon's marriage with Henry VIII. In April 1534 he was imprisoned in the Tower of London, and while he was there, Pope Paul III named him a Cardinal.

Thomas More studied Arts at Oxford and Law at New Inn. In 1504 he was elected member of Parliament and held several public offices. He earned great prestige because of his knowledge of the law and his integrity. Although his professional life was intensely time-consuming, he always found time for his family, which was his most important concern, and for his literary and historical studies. He published various books and essays. In 1529 he was appointed Lord Chancellor of England, in spite of having made it clear to the King that he could not agree with the dissolution of the King's marriage. Taking a full interest in the problems of his day, he dedicated himself to his work with the desire of implementing the laws of his times with a Christian approach.

Both men were beheaded in 1535 for refusing to recognise the supremacy of Henry VIII over the Church in England.

54.1 A testimony of faith, even to the extent of martyrdom.

In England in 1534 all citizens who had come of age were ordered to take the oath under the *Act of Succession,* which acknowledged the union of Henry VIII with Anne Boleyn as a marriage. The King proclaimed himself supreme Head of the Church in England, and denied any authority to the Pope. John Fisher, Bishop of Rochester, and Thomas More, Chancellor of the Realm, refused to take the oath. They were imprisoned in 1534 and were beheaded the following year.

At a time when many acceded to the royal will it would scarcely have been noticed if these two had taken the oath, and they would have saved their lives, their property and their positions as so many others did.[1] Both of these men, however, were true to their Faith even to the point of martyrdom. They were able to give their lives when the time came because they were of the kind who lived their vocation day by day, giving daily witness to the Faith, sometimes in matters that might have seemed of little or no consequence.

Thomas More is a man very close to ourselves, because he was an ordinary Christian who knew how to combine, in perfect unity of life, his vocation as the father of a family with his profession as a lawyer and later as Lord Chancellor of England. He was at home in the world: he loved all the human realities that formed the framework of his life in the place and position where God wanted him to be. At the same time he lived such detachment from earthly things and had such love for the Cross that we can say he drew all of his strength from it.

Thomas More was in the habit of meditating on a passage of the Passion of Our Lord every Friday. When his children or his wife complained about ordinary difficulties and annoyances, he told them they could not expect to *go to Heaven in featherbeds*; and he reminded them of the

---

[1] cf A. Prevost, *Thomas More and the Crisis of European thought,* Madrid 1972

sufferings Our Lord had undergone, and that the servant is not greater than his master. As well as using the ordinary little pinpricks and routine mishaps of the day as a means of identifying himself with the Cross, More offered up other penances. Some days he wore a hair-shirt, a garment of rough cloth next to his skin. He continued this practice during his imprisonment in the Tower of London in spite of the cold, the damp and all the privations he had to put up with during those long months.[2] It was here, in the Cross, that he found his strength.

We are Christians who follow Christ closely in the midst of the world and bear witness, generally silently, to him. Do we too find strength in being detached from earthly things and through the practice of daily mortification and prayer?

54.2 Fortitude and the life of prayer.

When Thomas More had to resign from his post as Lord Chancellor, he gathered his family together to talk to them about the future that awaited them and how they would manage financially. He summarized his whole career saying *I have been brought up at Oxford, at the Inn of Chancery, at Lincoln's Inn, and also in the King's Court ... from the lowest to the highest. Yet I have now little above one hundred pounds a year. If we are to continue together, all must become contributories; but by my counsel it shall not be best for us to fall to the lowest fare first.* Then he suggested to them a gradual descent, reminding them how it is possible to be content at each level. If they were unable to support themselves at even the lowest level, the one at which he had managed to live while in Oxford, he said with peace and good humour, *then we may yet, with bags and wallets go abegging together, and hoping that for pity some good folk*

[2] cf T. J. McGovern, *Thomas More: The Making of a Saint,* New York 1984

will give us of their charity ... and so still keep company and be merry together.[3] He never allowed anything to disturb the unity and peace of his family, even when he was away or in prison. He lived detached from things when he had them, and with great joy when he did not possess or have access to even the most indispensable necessities of life. He was always able to rise above circumstances. He knew how to celebrate important events even behind prison bars. A contemporary biographer tells us that whilst he was imprisoned in the Tower he would dress more elegantly on important feast days, so far as his meagre wardrobe would permit. He always remained cheerful and good-humoured – even at the moment when he was ascending the scaffold – because he relied firmly on prayer.

The things, good Lord, that I pray for, give me thy grace to labour for. He did not expect God to give him those things that, with just a little effort on his part, he could obtain for himself. He worked hard all his life so as to become a lawyer of great prestige before being appointed Lord Chancellor. He never forgot, however, the need for prayer, even though at times, and particularly in circumstances as dramatic as those leading up to his execution, it was not easy for him. During those days he wrote a long prayer in which, among many of the pious and moving considerations made by a man who knew he was about to die, he exclaimed: *Grant me, my lord, a desire to be with you, not so as to avoid the calamities of this world, nor even to avoid the pains of purgatory nor those of hell, not to gain the joys of Heaven, not out of consideration for my own profit, but simply through true love for Thee.*[4]

Saint Thomas More is always presented to us as a man of prayer; this enabled him to be faithful, whatever the

---

[3] *Roper's Life of More,* quoted by T. J. McGovern, *op cit*
[4] St. Thomas More, *A Man Alone, (Letters from the Tower)*

circumstances, to his commitments as a citizen and as a Christian, thereby living a perfect unity of life. This is how we too have to be. *A Catholic, without prayer? It is the same as a soldier without arms.*[5] How is our relationship with Christ? Do we try to grow each day in intimacy with him? Does our prayer influence the rest of our day?

54.3 Christian coherence and unity of life.

Give me thy grace, good Lord, to set the world at naught ... to have my mind well united to you; to not depend on the changing opinions of others ... so that I may think joyfully of God and tenderly implore his help. So that I may lean on God's strength and make an effort to love him ... So as to thank him ceaselessly for his benefits; so as to redeem the time I have wasted ...[6] The Saint wrote these words in the margin of the *Book of Hours* he had with him in the Tower of London. They were days when he gave himself over completely to contemplating the Passion and in this way to preparing himself for his own death in union with the death Christ suffered on the Cross.

Saint Thomas's last moments on earth were seen not only by God. His love for God had been clear to everyone around him; day by day in his family life; in his simple, pleasant manner; in the way he carried out his profession as a lawyer; in holding the highest post in the land – that of Lord Chancellor. It was through fulfilling the duties of each day, some of which were important, others less important, that he sanctified himself and helped others to find God. Among many other examples of his effective apostolate, he has left us that of the apostolate he did with his son-in-law, who had fallen into the Lutheran heresy. *I have borne a long time with your husband,* Sir Thomas said to his daughter Margaret. *I have reasoned and argued with*

---

[5] St. J. Escrivá, *Furrow,* 453
[6] St. Thomas More, *A Man Alone*

him on these points of religion and given to him my poor fatherly counsel but I perceive none of all this able to call him home; and, therefore, Meg, I will no longer dispute with him but will clean give him over and get me to God to pray for him.[7] More's words and prayers were effective as soon afterwards Roper returned to the fullness of the Faith. He became an exemplary Christian and suffered much through remaining loyal to the Catholic Faith.

Saint Thomas More remains among us as a living example for our conduct as Christians. He is the *fruitful seed of peace and joy, as was his passage on earth at home among his family and friends, in the forum, in the law-courts, in the University Chair, at Court, in the embassies, in Parliament and in Government. He is also the silent patron of England, who shed his blood in defence of the unity of the Church and of the spiritual power of the Vicar of Christ. And as the blood of Christians is a germinating seed, the blood of Thomas More slowly seeps into and soaks the souls of those who approach him drawn by his prestige, his sweetness of character and his strength. More will be the silent apostle of the return to the Faith of a whole nation.*[8]

We ask John Fisher and Thomas More to teach us to imitate them in their Christian coherence so that we may live as God wants us to, in all things, both great and small, whatever the circumstances of our lives. In the words of the liturgy of the feast we make our request: *In the death of your martyrs, O God, we see the noblest of testimonies to the true Faith: grant, we pray, that, strengthened by the prayers of St Thomas More and St John Fisher, we may bear witness in our lives to the Faith that we confess with our mouths.*[9]

---

[7] N. Haspsfield, *Sir Thomas More,* London 1963, p.102 ; A. Vazquez de Prada, *Sir Thomas More,* Madrid 1975

[8] A. Vazquez de Prada, *op cit*

[9] *Opening Prayer*

24 June

55. THE BIRTH OF JOHN THE BAPTIST

Solemnity

This Solemnity was already being celebrated in the fourth century. John, the son of Zachary and of Elizabeth, a cousin of Our Lady, is the forerunner of Jesus Christ, and he puts the whole of his life and all his energies into carrying out this mission. It will be a life full of austerity, of penance and zeal for souls. As he himself says: *He (Christ) must increase, but I must decrease.* This is the process that must take place also in the spiritual life of every faithful Christian.

55.1 The mission of Saint John the Baptist.

A man was sent from God, whose name was John. He came to testify to the light, to prepare a people fit for the Lord.[1]

Saint Augustine points out that *the Church celebrates the birth of John as something sacred, and he is in fact the only saint whose day of birth is celebrated; we celebrate the birth of John and that of Christ.*[2] He is the last of the Prophets of the Old Testament and the first to draw our attention to the Messiah. His birth, whose Solemnity we celebrate today, *brought great rejoicing,*[3] for all those who were to get to know Christ through his preaching; he was the dawn that announces the coming of day. This is why Saint Luke emphasises the time of his appearing, at a very definite moment in history: *In the fifteenth year of the reign of Tiberius Caesar, Pontius Pilate being governor of Judaea, and Herod being tetrarch of Galilee ...*[4] John turns

---

[1] *Entrance Antiphon*: John 1:6-7; Luke 1:17

[2] *Divine Office, Second Reading,* St Augustine, *Sermon* 293,1

[3] *Roman Missal, Preface of the Mass of the day*

[4] cf Luke 3:1 *et seq*

out to be the dividing line between the two Testaments. His preaching is the *Beginning of the gospel of Jesus Christ, the Son of God,*[5] and his martyrdom foretells the Saviour's Passion.[6] In spite of all this, John's was a passing voice; Christ was the eternal Word from the beginning.[7]

None of the four Evangelists has any hesitation in applying to John that beautiful prayer of Isaiah: *Behold, I send my messenger before thy face, who shall prepare thy way; the voice of one crying in the wilderness: Prepare the way of the Lord, make his paths straight.*[8] The Prophet refers first of all to the return of the Jews to Palestine after their captivity in Babylon: he sees Yahweh as the king and redeemer of his people, walking at their head through the Syrian desert after so many years of exile, and leading them with sure step back to their native land. A herald goes before him, as was the ancient custom of the East, to announce his arrival and to see to the repair of roads, the condition of which in those days nobody was really concerned about except in very special circumstances. As well as being fulfilled on their return from exile, this prophecy was to take on a still fuller and more profound meaning when it was to be fulfilled a second time with the coming of the messianic era. Our Lord too was to have his herald in the person of the Precursor, who would go before him, preparing the hearts of those to whom the Redeemer would soon be reaching out.[9] Today, on the Solemnity of his birth, as we contemplate the great figure of John the Baptist, he who fulfilled his mission so faithfully, we can ask ourselves whether we too make straight the ways of the Lord so that He may enter into the souls of those friends

---

[5] cf Mark 1:1
[6] cf Matt 17:12
[7] St Augustine, *op cit,* 3
[8] Mark 1:2
[9] cf L. C. Fillion, *Life of Our Lord Jesus Christ,* Madrid 1966

and relatives of ours who are still far from him, and so that those already close to him may give themselves to him more fully. As Christians we are the forerunners of Christ in today's world. *The Lord uses us as torches, to make that light shine out. Much depends on us; if we respond many people will remain in darkness no longer, but will walk instead along paths that lead to eternal life.*[10]

55.2 Our mission is to prepare men's hearts so that Christ may enter in.

The main feature of John's mission is that of Precursor, the one who goes before to foretell the coming of another: *He came for testimony, to bear witness to the light, that all might believe through him. He was not the light, but came to bear witness to the light.*[11] We find these words almost at the beginning of the Gospel written by the very disciple who met Jesus as a result of the specific preparation and indications he received from John the Baptist. *The next day again John was standing with two of his disciples; and he looked at Jesus as he walked, and said, 'Behold, the Lamb of God'. The two disciples heard him say this, and they followed Jesus.*[12] What wonderful memories and what immense gratitude would have come to him when, almost at the end of his life, Saint John the Apostle recalls in his Gospel the time he spent with John the Baptist, who was the instrument used by the Holy Spirit to bring him to Jesus, his treasure and his life!

The Precursor's preaching was in perfect harmony with his austere and mortified life. He proclaimed ceaselessly: *Repent, for the kingdom of heaven is at hand.*[13] Similar words, accompanied by his exemplary life, made a

---

[10] St. J. Escrivá, *The Forge,* 1
[11] John 1:6
[12] John 1:35-37
[13] Matt 3:2

great impression on the whole district, and he was soon surrounded by a large group of disciples ready to listen to his teachings. A strong religious movement stirred the whole of Palestine. People then, just as today, were thirsting for God, and their expectation of the coming of the Messiah was very strong. Saint Matthew and Saint Mark relate that people came from everywhere: from Jerusalem and from all the towns of Judaea.[14] They came too from Galilee, as it was there that Jesus met his first disciples, who were themselves Galileans.[15] To the men sent from the Sanhedrin John makes himself known in the words of Isaiah: *I am the voice of one crying in the wilderness.*

John gave testimony of the truth through his life and his words. He showed no signs of being overawed by those who were in power. He was never influenced or in any way affected by the praise and adulation of the crowds. He never gave in to the constant pressure of the Pharisees. He gave his life defending God's law against all human convention: *It is not lawful for you to have your brother's wife,*[16] was his reproach to Herod.

John had little power with which to oppose the folly of the Tetrarch. There was a limit to the distance his voice could reach so as to prepare for the Messiah a people well disposed. But God's word gathered strength on his lips. In the *Second Reading* of the Mass[17] the Liturgy applies to John the Baptist the words of the Prophet Isaiah: *He made my mouth like a sharp sword; in the shadow of his hand he hid me*; and whilst Isaiah is thinking *I have laboured in vain, I spent my strength for nothing and vanity,* God says

---

[14] cf Matt 3:5; Mark l:1-5
[15] cf John 1:40-43
[16] Mark 6:18
[17] *Second Reading,* Is 49:1-6

to him: *I will give you as a light to the nations, that my salvation may reach to the ends of the earth.*

God wants us to make him manifest through our conduct and our words precisely there where we have our work, our family, our friendships ... in our business affairs, at the University, in the laboratory ... even though it may seem that the field of our apostolate there is restricted. Our Lord is entrusting us now, in our own days, with the same mission as the one He entrusted to Saint John the Baptist: to prepare the way of the Lord, to be his heralds, to open up people's hearts against his arrival. Consistency between our teaching and our behaviour is the very best proof of our conviction and of the validity of what we proclaim. It is often the one essential condition for talking to people about God.

55.3 *Oportet illum crescere* ... Christ must ever increase in our lives whilst our own estimation of ourselves and of what we are worth should decrease.

The mission of the forerunner is to disappear, to take second place, when the one he announces has arrived. Saint John Chrysostom has said: *I myself think that this is why God allowed John to suffer an early death, so that once he had disappeared all the fervour of the crowd would be directed towards Christ rather than being shared between the two.*[18] A serious mistake on the part of any forerunner would be to allow himself, even for a short time, to be confused with the one who is expected.

Essential virtues for anyone who announces Christ are humility and detachment. Of the twelve Apostles, five, as the Gospels mention expressly, had been disciples of John. And it is very likely that the other seven also had been his disciples; at least they had all known him and could give

[18] St John Chrysostom, *Homilies on St John's Gospel,* 29,1

witness of his preaching.[19] In the apostolate the only person it is important to know is Christ. He is the treasure that we announce, and whom we have to take to others.

John's sanctity, his strong and attractive virtues, his preaching ... had contributed little by little to giving substance to some people's thinking that perhaps John himself was the long-awaited Messiah. Deeply humble, John wants only the glory of his Lord and his God. Thus he protests openly: *I baptise you with water; but he who is mightier than I is coming, the thong of whose sandals I am not worthy to untie; he will baptise you with the Holy Spirit and with fire.*[20] Beside Christ, John considers himself unworthy of offering him even the most humble of services, the sort of tasks generally reserved for slaves of the lowest level, such as carrying his master's baggage and undoing the straps of his sandals. Beside the sacrament of Baptism instituted by Our Lord, his baptism is no more than with water, a symbol of the interior cleanliness that those who awaited the Messiah were to effect in their hearts. Christ's Baptism is the Baptism of the Holy Spirit, who purifies in the same way as fire.[21]

Let us look again at John the Baptist, a man of firm character, as Jesus reminds the crowds who listen to him: *What did you go out into the desert to see? A reed bending in the wind*? Our Lord knew, and the people knew too, that John had a markedly outstanding personality quite out of keeping with weakness of character. God asks something similar of us: no less than to pass unnoticed whilst doing good and carrying out our obligations with human perfection.

When the Jews went to tell the disciples of John that

---

[19] cf Acts 1:22
[20] Luke 3:15-16
[21] cf St Cyril of Alexandria, *Catechesis,* 20, 6

Jesus was gathering to him more disciples than their master was, they went to complain to John the Baptist. He answered them: *I am not the Christ, but I have been sent before him ... He must increase, but I must decrease.*[22] *Oportet illum crescere, me autem minui*; it is good that He should increase and I decrease. This is our life's work: that Christ should come to fill the whole of our existence. *Oportet illum crescere* ... Then our joy will know no bounds. In the measure in which Christ, through knowledge and love, penetrates more and more into our poor lives, so will our joy overflow.

Let us ask God, with the poet: *May I be like a reed-pipe, simple and hollow, where only you make sound. May I be no more than the voice of another crying in the wilderness.* I want to be your voice, Lord, in the midst of the world, in the very environment and place in which you want me to live.

---

[22] cf John 3:27-30

26 June

55-A. SAINT JOSEMARÍA ESCRIVÁ
Optional Memorial

St Josemaría Escrivá was born in Barbastro, Spain, on 9 January 1902. He was ordained to the priesthood in Saragossa on 28 March 1925. On 2 October 1928, by divine inspiration he founded Opus Dei. On 26 June 1975, he died suddenly in Rome, after a final affectionate glance at a picture of our Lady in the room where he worked. At the time of his death, Opus Dei had spread to six continents with over 60,000 members of 80 nationalities, serving the Church with the same spirit of complete union with the Pope and bishops which St Josemaría Escrivá had always lived. St John Paul II canonized the founder of Opus Dei in Rome on 6 October 2002, calling him "the saint of the ordinary". The mortal remains of St Josemaría Escrivá rest in the Prelatic Church of Our Lady of Peace at Viale Bruno Buozzi 75, Rome.

55-A.1 Being led by the Holy Spirit.

All day today, we can keep very much in mind the anniversary of St. Josemaría's *dies natalis* – the day of his 'birth' – the day he went to heaven. It is customary to give gifts on such occasions. Let's specify what in particular we can offer St. Josemaría. If you ask yourself what would St. Josemaría ask of you on his anniversary today? the answer will immediately spring to mind and resound in your heart. From you, as well as from all of us, he would ask for *fidelity*. And what must we do to be more faithful? That we strive to imitate his life on earth.

In one of those movies of a get-together, he began with the words from Isaiah, *dicite iusto quoniam bene.*[1] Now we can say the same to St. Josemaría. Each of us can tell him:

---

[1] Is 3:10

quoniam bene, you have done very well! Throughout his earthly life, St. Josemaría always went forward impelled – even "sifted" – by the Holy Spirit: both in his early years, when he was not yet aware of it, as well as later on, when he was fully aware and corresponded heroically to the Spirit of God's action.

St. Josemaría used to say that from 2 October 1928, the only thing he had to do was let himself be led. It is easily said. But if we consider his life carefully, we recognize that this sole concern of his, "letting himself be led", required countless sacrifices: ridicule, misunderstanding, loneliness, calumny, both before and after founding Opus Dei. Let's make the resolution to allow ourselves to be led by God in this way too.[2]

How did St. Josemaría let himself be led by the Holy Spirit? On the basis of practising, in a heroic way, the theological and cardinal virtues. Hope sustained and encouraged him to move forward almost always against the grain, going against what would have pleased him. He assured us that it was "the only thing he had to do." This is spiritual refinement and an example for us who immediately want to give importance to ourselves, to be "the star of the show," the centre of attention, the axis of conversation.

55-A.2 Yearnings of love

Faith, hope and love. This is how St Josemaría corresponded so heroically to the graces that God abundantly granted him. Faith nourished on the Bread and the Word, the Eucharist and prayer. By means of his Eucharistic soul, St. Josemaría converted his whole day into one prolonged Mass, centred and rooted on the sacramental Mass. He always stayed close to our Lord in the Blessed Sacrament, through frequent spiritual communions, acts of love and

[2] cf Rom 8:14

reparation, and acts of self-giving. His prayer was nurtured by the Eucharist and by contemplation of our Lord's mysteries: by speaking with Jesus and imagining himself as present in the Gospel scenes. And I, do I struggle as St. Josemaría did? Do I strive to make an effort – within the limits of my wretchedness – to be a good child of God?

In 1937, recently escaped from the communist zone during the Spanish civil war, he did a retreat in the bishop's residence in Pamplona. During the previous months in Madrid, pursued simply for being a priest, he would flee from one place to another. He suffered enormous hunger. There was no food and when there was, he hardly ate any so as to unite himself more to Christ, and to make the way smoother for those who were to come after him. Before the war, he used to walk everywhere, miles and miles through the poorest Madrid slums, to do good to those misfortunate people. And although his life soon became sedentary during the war, since he had to remain hidden, he lost so much weight that when his mother went to see him once, at the Honduran consulate, she didn't recognize him there, dressed in overalls, until he exclaimed: *Mum!* He was so thin that she recognized him only by his voice. He kept up his strength on the basis of prayer and the Eucharist, sacrifice and self-giving.

In such a state, physically exhausted, he crossed the Pyrenees on foot to the other zone where he could freely exercise his priestly ministry. And on arriving, the first thing he did was to do a retreat for several days, alone as was his custom. Two things that happened during those days of retreat.

He was alone praying in the chapel of the bishop's residence when the vicar general came in to consecrate some chalices and patens. A point from *The Way* comes from this occasion: *Mad? Yes, I saw you (in the bishop's chapel, you thought you were alone) as you left a kiss on each newly-consecrated chalice and paten, so that He might find it there when for the first time he would "come down" to those eucharistic vessels.*[3]

And, at the end of the retreat, he wrote that he made few and very simple resolutions. He probably reduced them to one, since the others he included as implicit in that one. He resolved to sleep only five hours a night, except Thursday to Friday, when he wouldn't sleep at all. He called that a simple resolution. And he decided this when physically he was destroyed, after suffering so much on those incredible treks.

Faced with this example, we feel ashamed at considering our own lukewarmness, our laziness, our lack of self-giving, our seeking compensations. At the same time, we admire the strong soul of St. Josemaría. He calls a "simple resolution" his decision to remain awake from early Thursday morning until late Friday night, almost forty-eight hours straight, in order to have more time for serving God. With such tenacious struggle, one can understand why at the end of his life – not only at the end, but already for years – St. Josemaría could say with simplicity that God had granted him the grace of staying close to him not only throughout the whole day, but also at night, praying while he slept and realizing he was speaking with God.

It was a reward for his effort. What about us? If we desire to resemble St. Josemaría, won't we have to rectify? Shouldn't we formulate resolutions of greater love for God? We ask this from our Lord, since charity is a theological virtue that He alone can grant. He gave it to St. Josemaría in the highest degree, because it was His will and because he asked Him for it so often, so very often. We too implore Him for it, for each of us: Imbue us with faith, hope and charity!

---

[3] *The Way*, 438

55-A.3 Sacrifice for the sake of love

St. Josemaría used to say that each of us is *ipse Christus*:[4] *It is impossible to separate in Christ his reality as God-Man from his role as Redeemer. The Word became Flesh to save men, to make them one with Him: that is the reason for his coming into the world. We ourselves are other Christs, called to co-redeem. Neither can we divide up our life as children of God, separating it from our apostolic zeal.*[5] We can't light one candle to God and another to the devil. We have to truly give ourselves, since it is not possible to be Christ only from time to time, and at other moments behave like allies of the enemy, or be indifferent. which is the same. *We have to devote ourselves only to the glory of God and the good of souls.*[6]

St. Josemaría's love for God, and for all souls for God's sake, was patent. Without any human respect, in front of thousands of people, he would say that when some called him crazy, it was true: *they were not mistaken, I am out of my mind, crazy for the love of God.* A love that demands *not merely to fulfil, but to love, which always means surpassing oneself gladly in duty and sacrifice.*

We know that the life of St. Josemaría was a constant going against the grain. Nevertheless, he never stopped exceeding himself gladly in service. Therefore, if we have to go against the grain, we should do so joyfully, with supernatural refinement, since God deserves everything: *Love is sacrifice; and sacrifice for Love's sake is joy.*[7] From here stemmed his cheerfulness as a son of God, a contagious cheerfulness that he spread to everyone he met. In the midst of the sharpest suffering he was able to smile,

---

[4] cf Gal 2:20
[5] *Letter*, 6 May 1945, 40
[6] *Letter*, 8 August 1956, 8
[7] *The Forge*, 504

and this smile was often one of the hardest mortifications. But he smiled, because *love is sacrifice; and sacrifice for Love's sake is joy*.

We can finish by drawing close to the Blessed Virgin, through a remembrance that make manifest St. Josemaría's humility, so that we may be good instruments in the hands of God and the Blessed Virgin, our Mother. And thus we will truly be of service.

Not long before going to heaven, on 27 March 1975, the eve of his golden anniversary as a priest, St. Josemaría did his meditation aloud.. He saw himself as *a stammering child.*[8] It was an idea he had very much in mind during the final part of his life. A few days later, on 5 April, he said of himself: *A sinner who loves Jesus Christ, who has not finished learning the lessons given by God, a great fool .... Tell it to all who ask you, and they will ask you about it.* Such was the humility of St. Josemaría. He was convinced he was a great fool who had not finished learning the Lord's lessons, when he was filled with God, imbued with the Holy Spirit, dedicated to souls... This is why he travelled, with his eyes wide open, so as to learn; and he learned even from the questions people asked. He was convinced he was a great fool, who had failed to learn God's lessons.

May all of us be fools as great as St. Josemaría. May we be as dedicated as he was. May we learn from God, if possible, as much as he learned: to love, and for the sake of love, to exceed ourselves in carrying out God's will with the help of the Father, the Son and the Holy Spirit; with the help of holy Mary and St. Joseph.

---

[8] Notes taken during a meditation, 27 March 1975

29 June

56. SAINT PETER

Apostle
Solemnity

Solemnity of the beginnings of Christianity. The Apostles Peter and Paul are considered by the faithful, and rightly, as the first pillars, not only of the Holy Roman See, but also of the universal Church of the living God, spread to the utmost bounds of the earth (Saint Paul VI). Founders of the Church of Rome, the Mother and teacher of the other Christian communities, it was they who gave impulse to its growth by the supreme testimony of their martyrdom suffered in Rome with fortitude: Peter, whom Our Lord Jesus Christ chose as the foundation of his Church and Bishop of this illustrious city, and Paul, the Doctor of the Gentiles, teacher and friend of the first community founded here (Paul VI).

56.1 The Vocation of Peter.

Like most of Christ's first followers, Simon Peter came from Bethsaida, a town in Galilee on the shores of the Sea of Tiberias. Like the rest of his family he was a fisherman. He met Jesus through his brother Andrew. Shortly before that meeting which probably took place in the evening, Andrew and John had spent the whole day in the company of Jesus. And Andrew could not keep the immense treasure he had found to himself. Filled with joy he ran to tell his brother about the great benefit he had received.[1]

Peter came up to the Master. *Intuitus eum Iesus ... Jesus looked at him ...* The Master looked straight at the man who had just arrived and his gaze penetrated the very depths of his heart. How we would have liked to contemplate that gaze of Christ's, a look which was

[1] St John Chrysostom, *Catena Aurea,* vol VII

manifestly able to change a person's whole life! Jesus looked at Peter in a masterly and affectionate way. Beyond this fisherman from Galilee Jesus could see his whole Church stretching out through the centuries to the end of time. Our Lord shows that He has always known him: *You are Simon, the son of John,* He says! And he also knows his future: *You will be called Cephas, which means Rock.* These words determine the vocation and the destiny of Peter; they prophesy what is to be his whole task in the world.

From the beginning, *the position of Peter in the Church is that of a rock on which its edifice is built.*[2] All in the Church, as well as our own fidelity to grace, have love, obedience and union with the Roman Pontiff as their corner-stone and firm foundation. *In Peter the strength of all is strengthened,*[3] teaches Saint Leo the Great. If we look at Peter and the Church on her earthly pilgrimage we can apply to them the words of Jesus himself: *and the rain fell, and the floods came, and the winds blew and beat upon that house, but it did not fall, because it had been founded on rock,*[4] the rock, that with all its flaws and rough imperfections, Our Lord chose that day – an ordinary fisherman from Galilee, as He did those who would later succeed him.

The meeting between Peter and Jesus must have deeply impressed those who witnessed it, and who would have been familiar with the scenes of the Old Testament. God himself had changed the name (Abram) of the first Patriarch: *Your name shall be Abraham, for I have made you the father of a multitude of nations.*[5] He also changed

---

[2] St Paul VI, *Address,* 24 November 1965
[3] St Leo the Great, *On the Feast of St Peter, Apostle,* Homily 83, 3
[4] Matt 7:25
[5] cf Gen 17:5

the name of Jacob to Israel – that is, *for you have striven with God and men and have prevailed.*[6] Now the solemnity of the occasion, if not the significance, of the change of Simon's name does not escape the onlookers in spite of the simplicity and matter-of-fact nature of the encounter. 'I have other plans for you,' Jesus has just said to him ...

To change someone's name was to take possession of its owner, a person, and at the same time show him God's Will as it would henceforth affect him in the world. *Cephas* was not a recognisable proper name, but it was one chosen by Our Lord to denote Peter's new function, a function that would be fully revealed to him later on, when he would become the Vicar of Christ.[7] In our prayer today we can examine the sincerity of our love – shown with deeds – towards the one who takes Christ's place on earth. Do we pray for him every day? Do we make his teachings known? Do we second his intentions? Do we promptly spring to his defence when he is attacked or scorned? What joy we give to God when He sees that we love, with deeds, his Vicar here on earth!

56.2 The first of Christ's disciples.

This first meeting with the Master was not the definitive calling. But from that moment on, Peter felt himself captivated by the steady gaze and by the entire Person of Jesus. He did not give up his job as a fisherman, but listened to the Master's teachings, accompanying him on several occasions and witnessing many of his miracles. It is quite probable that he was present at the first miracle of Jesus in Cana of Galilee, where he would have met Mary, the Mother of Jesus. We know that he afterwards went down with Our Lord to Capharnaum. One day, on the shore of the lake after an exceptional and indeed miraculous

---

[6] cf Gen 32:18-19
[7] cf Matt 16:16-18

catch of fish, Jesus did extend to Peter a definitive invitation to follow him.[8] Peter obeyed immediately, his heart having already been gradually prepared by grace. Leaving everything, *relictis omnibus,* he followed Christ as a disciple – one who is prepared to share the lot of his Master in all things.

One day in Caesarea Philippi, while they are out walking, Jesus asks his disciples: *Who do you say that I am? Simon Peter replies 'You are the Christ, the Son of the living God'.*[9] Immediately afterwards Christ solemnly promises him the primacy of the whole Church.[10] How Peter must have remembered those words addressed to him a couple of years earlier on the day his brother Andrew took him to Christ: *You will be called Cephas! ...*

Peter did not change as quickly as his name had changed. He did not display from one day to next the firmness that his new name denoted. As well as a faith firm as a rock, we see in Peter an impulsive character that sometimes wavers. There is even one occasion when Jesus has to reprove the man, who is going to be the very foundation of his Church, for being a hindrance to him.[11] God reckons upon the passage of sufficient time to bring about the formation of each one of the friends He has chosen to be instruments. Meanwhile, He simply counts on their good will. If we have the same good will as Peter, and if we are docile to grace, we too will be turned into instruments fit to serve the Master and to carry out the mission He has entrusted to us. If we start over and over again, if we turn to Jesus, if we open our hearts in spiritual direction, everything – even those events that seem to go

---

[8] cf Luke 5:11
[9] Matt 16:15-16
[10] cf Matt 16:18-19
[11] cf Matt 16:23

against us, even our mistakes and our lack of determination – will help us to come closer to Jesus, who, like a sculptor with a block of marble, never tires of smoothing out our roughnesses. And then, like Peter, we will hear at moments of difficulty those same words: *O man of little faith, why did you doubt*?[12] And we will see Jesus not far away at all holding out his hand to us.

56.3 His fidelity to the point of martyrdom.

The Master showed special signs of his regard for Peter. However, when eventually Jesus needed him most, during those particularly terrible and dramatic moments when He was abandoned and alone, Peter denied him. After the Resurrection, when Simon Peter and the other disciples had returned to their old work of fishing, Jesus went specifically to see Peter and showed himself to him by bringing about a second miraculous catch of fish. This brought back to Simon's soul the memory of that other previous catch, when the Master had invited him quite openly to follow him and promised him that he would be *a fisher of men.*

Jesus waits for him now on the shore. He makes use of material things – sticks, fire, fish – which underline the reality of his presence and reinforce the customary familial atmosphere that always obtained in his relationship with his disciples. *When they had finished breakfast, Jesus said to Simon Peter, 'Simon, son of John, do you love me more than these?'*[13]

Then Our Lord said to Simon: *Truly, truly, I say to you, when you were young, you girded yourself and walked where you would; but when you are old, you will stretch out your hands, and another will gird you and carry you*

---

[12] Matt 14:31
[13] John 21:15 *et seq*

where you do not wish to go.[14] When Saint John comes to write his Gospel this prophecy has already been fulfilled; this is why the Evangelist adds: *This he said to show by what death he was to glorify God.* Then Jesus reminded Peter of those unforgettable words that one day, years before, on the shore of that same lake, had changed Simon's life for ever – *Follow me.*

A pious Roman tradition tells us that, during the bloody persecution of Nero, Peter, having yielded to the fervent pleas of the Christian community, was setting off to seek a safer place from which to continue his governance of the Church. Just outside the gates of the city he met Jesus carrying his Cross. When Peter asked him: *Where are you going, Lord*? (*Quo vadis, Domine?*) The Master replied: *'To Rome, to let myself be crucified again'*. Peter understood the implication perfectly. He returned to the city where the cross awaited him. This legend seems to be the final resonance of the protest Saint Peter made against the cross the first time Jesus announced the imminence of his Passion.[15] Peter met his death a short time afterwards. An early historian recounts that he asked to be crucified head downward, as he considered himself unworthy to die like his Master, holding his head up. His martyrdom is recorded by Saint Clement, successor to Peter in the government of the Roman Church.[16] Since at least the third century, the Church commemorates on this day, the 29th June, the martyrdom of Peter and Paul,[17] their joint *dies natalis,* the day on which they at last and finally saw their Lord and Master face to face.

In spite of his weaknesses Peter was faithful to Christ

---

[14] John 21:18-19
[15] cf O. Hopman, *The Apostles,* Madrid 1982
[16] cf St Paul VI, Apostolic Exhortation, *Petrum et Paulum,* 22 February 1967
[17] St John Paul II, *Angelus,* 29 June 1987

to the point of giving his life for him. As we conclude our meditation we ask him for this same fidelity, in spite of the setbacks we suffer and all the obstacles we shall find placed in our way because we are Christians. We ask him to make us firm in the faith, *fortes in fide,*[18] just as Saint Peter asked the first Christians of his day to be. *What else could we ask of Peter for our own good; what else could we offer in his honour other than our believing exactly what he believed, which is the origin of our spiritual health, and the promise he demands of us to be strong in the Faith*?[19]

This is the strength we ask too of Mary our Mother, so that we may hold fast to our faith without any ambiguity and with a serene firmness, whatever the environment in which we have to live.

---

[18] 1 Pet 5:9
[19] St Paul VI, Apostolic Exhortation, *Petrum et Paulum, cit supra*

29 JUNE

57. SAINT PAUL

Apostle

Solemnity

57.1 Our Lord chooses his disciples.

What shall I do, Lord?[1] Saint Paul asked at the moment of his conversion. Jesus answered him: *Rise and go into Damascus, and there you will be told all that is appointed for you to do.* The persecutor, once he had been transformed by grace, was to receive Christian instruction and Baptism from a man – Ananias – in accordance with the ordinary ways of Providence. Once Paul realises that Christ is all that really matters in his life, we see him give himself immediately with all his strength to making the Good News known to others, without any concern for the danger, tribulations, sufferings and apparent failures that may assail him. He knows that he is the instrument chosen to take the Gospel to many people, as we hear in the *Second Reading* of today's Mass: *But ... He who had set me apart before I was born, and had called me through his grace, was pleased to reveal his Son to me, in order that I might preach him among the Gentiles.*[2]

Saint Augustine says that prior to his encounter with Christ, Paul's passionate zeal was like an impenetrable jungle, but that although it was a great obstacle it nevertheless showed the fertility of the soil. Then God sowed in that soil the seed of the Gospel and the fruits it bore were multitudinous.[3] What happened to Paul can happen to everyone, however serious his or her faults may have been. It is the mysterious action of grace that does not change

---

[1] Acts 22:10

[2] Gal 1:15-16

[3] cf St Augustine, *Contra Fausto,* 22, 70

nature, but heals it, purifies it, elevates it and perfects it.

Saint Paul is convinced that God counted on him from the very moment of his conception; *before I was born,* he repeats on several occasions. In Holy Scripture we find how God chooses even before their birth those He is to send;[4] in this way He shows us that the initiative comes from himself and precedes any personal merit. The Apostle carefully draws attention to this point. He explains to the first Christians in Ephesus this pre-selection by God: *even,* he tells them, *as He chose us in him before the foundation of the world*;[5] to Timothy he says even more specifically: *He called us with a holy calling, not in virtue of our works but in virtue of his own purpose.*[6]

A vocation is a divine gift that God has prepared from all eternity. This is why, when God made known his vocation to him in Damascus, Paul did not ask for advice 'from flesh and blood'. *He did not consult any man,* because he was certain that God himself had called him. He did not heed the counsel of *the prudence of the flesh,* but was totally generous with God. His self-giving was immediate, complete and unconditional. When the Apostles heard Christ's invitation to them, they too had left their nets *immediately,*[7] and, *relictis omnibus,* leaving all things,[8] they had followed the Master. Saul, the ex-persecutor of the Christians, now follows Our Lord with similarly decisive promptitude.

Each of us, in his or her own different way, has received a specific call to serve God. And throughout our lives we receive new invitations to follow him in our own circumstances, and we have to be generous with Our Lord in each new encounter with him. We have to know how to

---

[4] cf Jer 1:5; Is 49:1-5 etc

[5] Eph 1:4

[6] 2 Tim 1:9

[7] Matt 4:20-22; Mark 1:18

[8] Luke 5:11

ask Jesus in the intimacy of our prayer, like Saint Paul: *What shall I do, Lord*? What do you want me to leave for your sake? What do you want me to improve in? At this moment of my life, what can I do to serve you?

57.2 God's call and the apostolic vocation.

God called Saint Paul by means of very extraordinary signs, but the effect they had on him was the same as that which is brought about by the specific call God makes to many individuals to follow him in the midst of their secular activities. God calls all Christians to sanctity and to apostolate. It is a vocation which is demanding, and in many cases heroic, because God does not want lukewarm followers, second-rate disciples. But Christ calls some to dedicate themselves in a special way to spreading his Kingdom amongst all men, while at the same time they continue with their own ordinary duties in the world. As each one of us responds to the specific vocation to which he or she has been called, we have to grasp the apostolic meaning of our lives if we want to be disciples of the Master. This will lead us not to waste any opportunity of bringing others closer to Christ, in a growing friendship with him which at the same time gives them joy and peace and leads them to experience fulfilment in their lives.

The apostolate was for Paul, and is for every Christian who really lives his vocation, an important part of his life – or, rather, an integral part of his life. Work becomes apostolate, and a desire to make Christ known. So too with sickness and with our leisure, with pain and with rest ... at the same time, this apostolic zeal is a food that we cannot do without if we are to get to know Christ. Knowing Our Lord intimately leads necessarily to communicating this discovery of him to others. This communication is the *sure*[9]

---

[9] St. J. Escrivá, *The Way,* 810

sign that you have really 'given yourself' to God. When following Christ is a reality in our lives, there comes the *need to spread out, to do, to give, to speak, to transmit to others one's own treasure, one's own fire ... The apostolate becomes the progressive expansion of a soul, in the exuberance of a personality identified with Christ and animated by his Spirit; we feel the need for urgency, the need to work, to try everything possible to spread God's Kingdom, for the salvation of others, of all men.*[10] *Woe to me if I do not preach the Gospel*![11] exclaims the Apostle.

When we take the Good News to others we are fulfilling the command that Christ gave us: *Go into all the world and preach the gospel to the whole creation.*[12] Then, too, our interior life is enriched, like the plant that receives the water it needs at the right time. Saint Paul gives us an example today and helps us to examine ourselves as to the degree of our determination to bring others a little closer to God. Identified with Christ – the supreme discovery of his life – with him who *came not to be served but to serve, and to give his life as a ransom for many,*[13] the Apostle becomes the servant of all to win as many as he can. He says to the disciples in Corinth: *To the Jews I became a Jew, in order to win Jews; ...To the weak I became weak, that I might win the weak. I have become all things to all men, that I might by all means save some.*[14]

Today we ask him to procure for us a big heart like his, so that we can overlook any small humiliations or the apparent failures that any apostolate brings with it. And we tell Jesus that we are ready to live in fellowship with all, and to offer to all the possibility of getting to know Christ,

---

[10] St Paul VI, *Homily,* 14 October 1968
[11] cf 1 Cor 9:16
[12] Mark 16:15
[13] Matt 20:28
[14] cf 1 Cor 9:19-22

without being too concerned about the sacrifices and the trouble this may cause us.

57.3 The apostolate. A joyful task that demands sacrifice.

Saint Paul exhorts Timothy, and all of us, to speak about God *opportune et importune,*[15] whether the occasion is right or not. In season, he says, and out of season. That is to say, also when circumstances are unfavourable. *For the time is coming when people will not endure sound teaching, but having itching ears, they will accumulate for themselves teachers to suit their own likings, and will turn away from listening to the truth and wander into myths.*[16] It seems as though the Apostle were actually present in our own day. *But you,* he says to Timothy – and in him to every Christian – *always be steady, endure suffering, do the work of an evangelist, fulfil your ministry.*[17] Priests will do this mainly through preaching the word of God, through their personal example, their charity, the advice they give in the sacrament of Penance. Lay people – the great majority of the People of God – generally spread his word through friendship, with their kindly advice, with the conversation they have in private with this or that friend who seems to be getting further and further away from God, or who never has been close to him ... We do it all in the place where we study or work; during our summer holidays ... Parents with their children ... seizing the best moment, or creating the right opportunity.

John Paul II encouraged young people – and every Christian who is a bearer of Christ remains always young at heart – to an apostolate that is intense, direct and cheerful: *Be deeply friends of Jesus and take to your family, your school, the district where you live, the example of a*

---

[15] 2 Tim 4:2
[16] 2 Tim 4:3-4
[17] 2 Tim 4:5

Christian life which is pure and cheerful. Be always young Christians, true witnesses to Christ's teaching. Moreover, be bearers of Christ in this disturbed society, which needs him today more than ever. Announce to everyone by your lives that Christ alone is the true salvation of mankind.[18]

We have to ask Saint Paul today to teach us to turn into *the right situation* whatever situation presents itself to us. Even *those who travel abroad for international activities, on business or on holiday, should keep in mind that no matter where they may be they are the travelling messengers of Christ, and should bear themselves truly as such.*[19] We have to behave with the openness that can only be conveyed by a soul who has made Christ the axis around which everything in his life turns and is organised. Even children – what good instruments of the Holy Spirit they can be – have their own apostolic activity, as the Second Vatican Council tells us, for in their own measure, they can be true living witnesses of Christ among their companions.[20]

The Apostle's untiring apostolic work is quite amazing, staggering, wonderful. Everybody who loves Christ as Paul did will feel the same need to make him known, for, as Saint Thomas Aquinas says, what men much admire they later divulge, since from the abundance of the heart the mouth speaks.[21]

Let us ask Our Lady, Queen of Apostles, *Regina Apostolorum,* to let us come to understand better that the apostolate is a joyous undertaking, even though it may demand sacrifice. Let us ask her for an awareness of the great responsibility we have towards all our fellow men, especially towards the people we meet every day.

---

[18] St John Paul II, *Homily,* 3 December 1978
[19] Second Vatican Council, *Apostolicam actuositatem,* 14
[20] *idem,* 12
[21] cf St Thomas, *Catena Aurea,* vol IV

30 June

58. THE FIRST MARTYRS OF THE CHURCH OF ROME

Optional Memorial

After Jerusalem and Antioch, Rome was the most important early Christian nucleus. Many Christians came from the Jewish colony existing in Rome; the majority came over from paganism.

Today we commemorate the Christians who underwent the first persecution against the Church under the emperor Nero, after the destruction of Rome by fire in the year 64.

58.1 Their exemplary behaviour in the middle of the world.

The Christian Faith very soon reached Rome, which was at that time the centre of the civilized world. Perhaps the first Christians in the capital of the Empire were converted Jews who had come across the Faith in Jerusalem itself or in some of the cities in Asia Minor that had been evangelised by Saint Paul. The Faith was passed on from friend to friend, between workmates and relatives ... The arrival of Saint Peter in about the year 43 brought about a perceptible strengthening of the little Christian community there. From Rome the new religion spread to many parts of the Empire. The internal peace enjoyed by the Imperial world at that time, the improvement in communications that facilitated travel and the rapid transmission of ideas and news, all favoured the spreading of Christianity. The Roman roads that, beginning in the *Urbs,* the great city itself, reached the most remote corners of the Empire, and the commercial fleets that regularly crossed the waters of the Mediterranean all helped to spread the new Christian religion throughout the length and breadth of the Roman world,[1] virtually *orbis terrarum.*

It is difficult to describe the process of conversion, the sequence of experience that affected each person who embraced Christianity in first-century Rome, just as it is now, for each conversion is always a miracle of grace and of personal correspondence with God's gift of it. There is no doubt that a decisive influence was the good example given by the Christians – the *bonus odor Christi*[2]- which had its repercussions in the way they worked, in their joy, their charity and their understanding for everyone, in the austerity of their lives and in their human likeableness ... They were men and women who tried to live their Faith fully in the midst of their ordinary activities. They were now to be found in all levels of society: *Daniel was young, and Joseph a slave. Aquila wrought at a craft. The woman who sold purple dye-stuffs supervised a busy workshop. Another was a prison governor and another a centurion like Cornelius. Yet another was in ill health, like Timothy. Another was a runaway from slavery, like Onesimus. Nothing proved a hindrance to any of these, but all were joyously welcomed and accepted, both men and women, both young and old, both slaves and freemen, both soldiers and civilian citizens alike.*[3]

The *Acts of the Apostles* has left us a delightful account of the hospitality shown by the Christians in Rome. They tell of the welcome given to Paul when he was brought as a prisoner to the Capital. *The brethren there,* Saint Lukc informs us, *when they heard of us, came as far as the Forum of Appius and the Three Taverns to meet us.*

---

[1] cf J. Orlandis, *A Short History of the Church,* Dublin 1978

[2] 2 Cor 2:15

[3] St John Chrysostom, *Homilies on St Matthew's Gospel,* 43, 7

On seeing them Paul thanked God and took courage.[4] Paul felt strengthened by these demonstrations of fraternal charity.

The first Christians did not give up their professional or social activities. (Some people were to do so, with a specific call from God, rather more than two centuries later). With their lives and their words, they considered themselves very much part of this world, of which they were convinced they were destined to be *salt and light.* An early writer summed it up as follows: *Christians are to the world what the soul is to the body.*[5]

We can examine ourselves today to see whether, like those first Christians, we too give good example to the extent that we do in fact move others to come closer to Christ. Do we edify others by our sobriety, by the way we spend money, by our unquenchable cheerfulness, by doing our work well, by keeping our word, by the way we live justice at work with our subordinates and our peers, by carrying out works of mercy and by never having a bad word to say about anybody at all?

58.2 Our attitude in the face of opposition.

The first Christians often came up against serious obstacles and misunderstandings, which in not a few cases led to their death for defending their faith in the Master. Today we celebrate the testimony of the first Roman martyrs, whose execution was the result of the burning of Rome in the year 64.[6] This catastrophe provided the excuse for the first great persecution. To Saint Peter and Saint Paul, whose feast we celebrated yesterday, *were added a great number of chosen ones, who having undergone many sufferings and torments out of envy, were the best model*

---

[4] Acts 28:15
[5] *Epistle to Diognetus,* 6:1
[6] cf Tacitus, *Annals,* 15:44

amongst us,[7] as we read in a vivid account to be found among the earliest Christian writings.

The obstacles and misunderstandings encountered by those who had been converted did not inevitably lead them to martyrdom, but they often experienced in their lives what the words of the Holy Spirit warn us of in Scripture: *Indeed all who desire to live a godly life in Christ Jesus will be persecuted.*[8] Sometimes the pagans' antagonism to the followers of Christ arose because they could not bear the rich fruitfulness and splendour of devotion in the Christian life. At other times it arose because those who had received the Faith had the duty of abstaining from the traditional religious ceremonial which was closely bound up with public life, and was even considered a test of loyalty, an open and formal proof of civic faithfulness to Rome and to the emperor. Consequently, the pagans who embraced Christianity laid themselves open to misunderstandings and slanderous attacks *for not conforming, for not being like the others.*

It is unlikely that God will ask us to shed our blood in order to confess the Christian Faith, although if God were to allow such a trial, we would ask him for the grace to enable us to give our lives in testimony of our love for him. We will, however, in one way or another, meet all kinds of adversity, for *being with Jesus means we shall most certainly come upon his Cross. When we abandon ourselves into God's hands, He frequently permits us to taste sorrow, loneliness, opposition, slander, defamation, ridicule, coming both from within and from outside his Church. This is because He wants to mould and form us into his own image and likeness. He even tolerates our being called lunatics and allows us, if we will, to be taken*

---

[7] St Clement of Rome, *Letter to the Corinthians,* 5
[8] 2 Tim 3:12

for fools ... This is the way Jesus fashions the souls of those he loves, while at the same time never failing to give them inner calm and joy.[9]

Slander, perhaps seeing doors to promotion closed against us at work, friends or workmates who turn their backs on us, sarcastic remarks or derogatory words ... If God allows them, we have to make use of such contradictions in order to live charity in a more heroic way, precisely with those very people who do not have any respect for us, perhaps out of inculpable ignorance. Our attitude can always include a just defence when necessary, especially when we have to avoid the possibility of scandal or of injury being caused to third persons. Such situations will be a great help in enabling us to cleanse ourselves of our own sins and faults, to make reparation for those of others and, finally, to grow in virtue and in love of God. God sometimes wants to purify us like gold in the crucible. Fire cleans gold from the dross, freeing it from impurities and greatly enhancing its value. God does the same with the good servant who hopes and who remains constant in the midst of tribulation.[10]

If contradictions lie in our way and troubles beset us because we follow Jesus closely, we have then to be especially cheerful and give thanks to God, who makes us worthy to suffer something for him as the Apostles did. *Then they left the presence of the council, rejoicing that they were counted worthy to suffer dishonour for the Name.*[11] The Apostles would doubtless have remembered the words of the Master, just as we meditate on them today during this feast of the holy Roman martyrs of the first generation: *Blessed are you when men revile you and*

---

[9] St. J. Escrivá, *Friends of God,* 301
[10] St Jerome Emilianio, *Homily to his brothers in religion,* 21 June 1535
[11] Acts 5:41

persecute you and utter all kinds of evil against you falsely on my account. Rejoice and be glad, for your reward is great in heaven; for so men persecuted the prophets who were before you.[12]

58.3 Apostolate in all circumstances.

In spite of ill-considered slander, infamy itself and outbreaks of persecution, our first brothers in the Faith did not fail to carry out an effective apostolate. They did not fail to tell people about Christ, the treasure they themselves had had the good fortune to find. Moreover, their calm and joyful bearing in the face of adversity, and even of death, was the very reason why many came to know the Master.

The death of the martyrs was the seed of Christians.[13] The Roman community itself after so many men, women and children had given their lives in the course of that terrible persecution went forward invigorated and strengthened. Years later Tertullian wrote: *We are of but yesterday, and already we have filled the world and all your things: cities, islands, towns, villages, hamlets, the army, the palace, the senate, the forum. We have left you only the temples ...*[14]

In our own sphere, in our present circumstances, if we perhaps encounter some slight difficulty to our remaining firm in the faith, we should understand that from this particular spot of bother will come great good for all. It is at such times that we have most reason and most need to speak, with serenity, about the wonder of the Faith, about the immense gift of the sacraments, about the beauty of the fruits of living holy purity well. We should understand that we have elected to be on the *winning side* in the combat of this life, and also in that other glorious life that awaits us

---

[12] Matt 5:11-12
[13] cf Tertullian, *Apology,* 50
[14] *idem,* 37

shortly. Nothing compares with being close to Christ. Even if we had no possessions at all and had to suffer the most painful illnesses or the most vile slander, so long as we possess Jesus we possess *everything.* The effect of this realisation should be noticeable even in our outward behaviour and in our awareness that we are at every moment, even in such circumstances, the *salt of the earth* and the *light of the world,* as the Master has told us.

Referring to the philosophers of his day, Saint Justin rightly said, that *all the good spoken by them belongs to us as Christians, because, after God, we adore and love the Word, who proceeds from the unbegotten and ineffable God himself. Indeed, for love of us He became man so as to share in our sufferings and heal us.*[15]

With the liturgy of the Mass, we ask today: *O God, who consecrated the abundant first fruits of the Roman Church by the blood of the Martyrs, grant we pray, that with firm courage we may together draw strength from so great a struggle*[16] in this world of ours that we have to bring to you.

---

[15] St Justin, *Apology,* II, 13
[16] *Roman Missal, Collect*

Index to Quotations from the Fathers, Popes and the Saints

Note: References are to **Volume**/Chapter.Section

Acts of Thanksgiving
St Augustine, **5**/39.2
St Bede, **5**/78.1
St Bernard, **5**/10.1, **5**/39.3
St Francis de Sales, **4**/84.1
St John Chrysostom, **2**/71.1
St Thomas Aquinas, **5**/78.2

Advent
St Bernard, **1**/1.3

Almsgiving
St Leo the Great, **5**/67.2
St Thomas Aquinas, **3**/17.3

Angels
Origen, **2**/9.3
St Bernard, **7**/30.3
St John Chrysostom, **2**/7.1
St John of the Cross, **2**/7.2
St Peter of Alcantara, **3**/51.2
St John Paul II, **2**/7.1, **2**/30.3, 7/27

Apostolate
Benedict XV, **2**/85.1
Bl. Alvaro, **2**/29.1,
John Paul I, **3**/3.2
Letter to Diognetus, **2**/70.2
St Ambrose, **4**/87.1
St Augustine, **1**/8.3, **2**/59.1, **4**/92.3, **5**/52.1, **5**/87.3
St Cyril of Alexandria, **5**/62.1
St Gregory the Great, **3**/88.2, **4**/69.1
St Ignatius of Antioch, **5**/37.3
St J. H. Newman, **3**/3.2
St John Chrysostom, **1**/4.3, **2**/85.1, **2**/94.1, **3**/88.2, **3**/89.3, **4**/87.1, **7**/42.2
St John Paul II, **1**/45.3, **2**/11.3, **3**/13.3, **4**/37.3, **4**/69.1, **4**/87.3, **5**/10.2, **5**/20.1, **5**/57.1, **5**/68.3, **6**/57.3, **7**/2.3
St Paul VI, **6**/57.2, **7**/25.3
St Teresa, **5**/68.3
St Thomas Aquinas, **1**/9.2, **3**/5.2, **7**/4.3
St Thomas of Villanueva, **4**/40.3
Tertullian, **2**/70.1, **4**/40.2

Ascetical struggle
Cassian, **2**/67.2
St Ambrose, **2**/22.3
St Augustine, **3**/3.1, **3**/18.2, **4**/25.1, **4**/80.2
St Bernard, **5**/50.2, **6**/12.2
St Cyprian, **5**/34.2
St Francis de Sales, **1**/12.3, **4**/25.1
St Gregory the Great, **2**/4.2, **4**/25.2
St Ignatius of Antioch, **4**/96.1
St John Chrysostom, **1**/12.2, **2**/22.3, **4**/14.1, **4**/59.1, **5**/34.2, **5**/50.2, **5**/61.2
St John Climacus, **2**/67.2
St John Paul II, **4**/14.3, **6**/20.1
St Peter Damian, **3**/92.2
St Peter of Alcantara, **1**/13.2

St Teresa, **1**/1.3, **2**/12.2
St Vincent of Lerins, **1**/6.3
Aspirations
St Teresa, **2**/35.3
Atonement
St Bernard, **6**/50.2

Baptism
Origen, **2**/70.3
St Augustine, **1**/51.1
St Cyril of Alexandria, **1**/50.1
St John Chrysostom, **2**/5.1
St John Paul II, **5**/43.2, **5**/59.2, **6**/3.2
St Leo the Great, **1**/51.1
St Thomas Aquinas, **6**/3.3
Blessed Trinity
St Augustine, **6**/40.3
St John of the Cross, **6**/40.1
St Teresa, **6**/40.2, **6**/40.3

Catechism
St John Paul II, **3**/13.2, **4**/86.2
Character
Cassian, **1**/11.1
Charity
St Alphonsus Liguori, **2**/22.2
St Augustine, **3**/52.2, **5**/23.1, **5**/52.1
St Bernard, **4**/85.3
St Cyprian, **2**/94.2, **5**/94.3
St Francis de Sales, **3**/100.1
St Jerome, **5**/23.1
St John Chrysostom, **4**/21.2
St Teresa, **3**/100.1
St Thomas Aquinas, **2**/44.2, **4**/1.2, **5**/15.3
Tertullian, **6**/4.3, **6**/52.3
Chastity
St Jean Vianney, **1**/23.3
St John Chrysostom, **1**/23.3, **4**/62.2, **4**/62.3
St John Paul II, **1**/23.1, **4**/62.2, **4**/83.2, **4**/83.3, **5**/90.3, **6**/22.1
St Leo the Great, **1**/16.3
Christ
Origen, **5**/31.2
Pius XI, **5**/91.1
Pius XII, **5**/52.2, **6**/49.3, **6**/50.1
St Ambrose, **5**/91.3
St Augustine, **1**/2.2, **1**/32.2, **5**/3.2, **5**/31.1, **5**/56.2
St Bernard, **5**/56.1
St Hippolytus, **5**/47.1
St John Chrysostom, **5**/6.1
St John of the Cross, **5**/96.2
St John Paul II, **5**/2.3, **5**/31.1, **5**/64.1, **6**/49.1, **6**/50.3
St Leo, **7**/12.2
St Paul VI, **5**/18.3
St Teresa, **5**/61.3, **7**/35.2
St Thomas Aquinas, **1**/40.1, **7**/12.1
Church
Bl. Alvaro, **6**/18.3
Gregory XVI, **4**/73.3
Pius XI, **3**/10.2, **6**/8.2
Pius XII, **4**/37.3, **6**/8.2
St Ambrose, **4**/73.3, **5**/5.2
St Augustine, **5**/5.2
St Cyprian, **3**/10.2, **4**/13.3
St Cyril of Jerusalem, **3**/10.2
St Gregory the Great, **3**/10.2
St John Chrysostom, **5**/31.2
St John Paul II, **4**/37.2, **5**/28.1, **5**/41.2, **7**/40.3
St John XXIII, **3**/10.2
St Leo the Great, **4**/73.2

St Paul VI, **4**/18.3, **5**/47.2, **6**/8.1
Civic Duties
St Ambrose, **4**/58.1
St Justin, **2**/33.2, **2**/70.2, **4**/58.2
St John Paul II, **5**/21.3
Tertullian, **4**/58.2
Communion of saints
St Ambrose, **5**/68.1
St John Paul II, **1**/10.3, **5**/68.1
St Teresa, **2**/66.1
St Thomas Aquinas, **5**/71.3, **6**/8.3
Compassion
St Augustine, **1**/4.3
St John Paul II, **1**/3.2, **1**/10.1, **1**/10.2, **5**/15.1, **5**/31.3
St Paul VI, **5**/15.1
St Thomas Aquinas, **4**/64.2
Confession
Bl. Alvaro, **3**/7.2, **5**/27.2
St Ambrose, **2**/34.2
St Augustine, **3**/7.3, **4**/60.2
St Bede, **3**/4.1
St Gregory the Great, **2**/39.2
St Jean Vianney, **2**/55.2
St John Chrysostom, **2**/21.1, **2**/34.3
St John Paul II, **1**/4.2, **2**/1.1, **2**/18.3, **2**/34.1, **2**/34.3, **4**/46.3, **5**/5.3
St Paul VI, **5**/27.2
St Thomas Aquinas, **2**/8.3, **2**/21.1
Conscience
St John Paul II, **2**/13.1
Contrition
St Augustine, **2**/41.2
St John Chrysostom, **4**/60.1
St Teresa, **5**/16.2
Conversation
St Augustine, **5**/15.3
St Gregory of Nyssa, **3**/19.2
St John Chrysostom, **5**/9.3
St John Paul II, **5**/6.2
Conversion
St Augustine, **7**/20
St John Paul II, **1**/10.1
Cowardice
St Basil, **2**/69.3
St John Chrysostom, **3**/89.3
Cross
St Athanasius, **3**/56.3
St Augustine, **4**/82.1
St Gregory the Great, **2**/12.1
St Irenaeus, **5**/28.3
St John Damascene, **7**/23.1
St John Paul II, **4**/82.1, **5**/22.2
St Thomas Aquinas, **5**/19.3

Death
Bl. Alvaro, **5**/97.3
Leo X, **5**/80.3
St Bede, **4**/2.2
St Ignatius Loyola, **5**/80.3
St Jerome, **4**/2.3
St John Paul II, **4**/2.1
Dedication
St Augustine, **5**/9.2, **5**/12.1
St Jerome, **3**/86.2
St John Paul II, **3**/104.2
Detachment
St Augustine, **5**/21.3
St Francis de Sales, **5**/24.2
St John of the Cross, **2**/16.1
St John Paul II, **5**/21.3, **5**/38.3
St Teresa, **2**/16.3
St Thomas Aquinas, **7**/50.3
Devil
Cassian, **2**/6.2

St Irenaeus, **2**/6.1
St J. H. Newman, **2**/6.2, **4**/19.1
St Jean Vianney, **2**/6.2
St John of the Cross, **2**/6.3
St John Paul II, **2**/6.1, **2**/6.3, **5**/42.1
Tertullian, **5**/42.2

Difficulties
Bl. Alvaro, **4**/54.2
John Paul I, **5**/44.3
Pius XII, **2**/60.2, **5**/53.2
St Alphonsus Liguori, **5**/69.2
St Athanasius, **4**/3.1
St Augustine, **1**/32.1, **2**/24.3, **2**/64.3, **3**/98.3, **4**/8.1, **4**/25.1, **5**/16.2
St Bernard, **4**/96.1, **7**/43.2
St Cyprian, **1**/36.3
St Francis de Sales, **4**/25.1, **6**/30.2
St Gregory Nazianzen, **1**/13.1
St Gregory the Great, **3**/98.2, **4**/96.3, **5**/9.2, **5**/85.1
St J. H. Newman, **4**/5.3, **4**/96.3
St Jean Vianney, **5**/61.1
St John Chrysostom, **1**/32.1, **1**/43.3, **2**/5.1, **2**/64.1, **2**/64.2, **2**/92.3, **4**/50.3
St John of the Cross, **4**/25.1
St John Paul II, **2**/29.3
St Paul VI, **2**/2.1
St Teresa, **1**/32.3, **4**/25.3
St Theophilus of Antioch, **5**/53.2
St Thomas Aquinas, **2**/60.1

Divine filiation
St Athanasius, **5**/59.1
St Cyprian, **5**/33.1
St Cyril of Jerusalem, **6**/3.2
St Hippolytus, **6**/3.2
St John Chrysostom, **4**/24.3, **7**/5.2
St John Paul II, **1**/17.1, **4**/32, **5**/59.1, **5**/59.2
St Teresa, **5**/60.3
St Thomas Aquinas, **1**/24.3, **1**/36.2, **1**/36.3, **4**/32.1, **4**/98.1, **5**/33.1, **5**/59.1, **5**/59.2, **5**/64.2, **5**/75.3
Tertullian, **5**/33.2

Docility
St John Paul II, **7**/5.1

Doctrine
St J. H. Newman, **3**/18.2
St Pius X, **7**/5.1

Duties
John Paul I, **5**/51.2
St Gregory the Great, **2**/13.3

Early Christians
St Clement, **6**/58.2
St John Chrysostom, **5**/79.1, **6**/58.1
St John Paul II, **5**/2.1, **5**/8.2
St Justin, **2**/70.2

Ecumenism
St John Paul II, **6**/4.3
St Paul VI, **6**/5.2

Eucharist
Bl. Alvaro, **3**/46.2
Cassian, **6**/47.2
St Alphonsus Liguori, **1**/2.1, **6**/44.2, **6**/47.1
St Ambrose, **5**/40.2, **5**/40.3, **6**/46.2
St Augustine, **2**/56.2, **4**/47, **6**/42.2, **6**/45.2, **6**/47.1
St Cyril of Jerusalem, **4**/47.2, **4**/56.2, **6**/43.1
St Fulgentius, **2**/65.3

St Gregory the Great, **4**/70.3
St Ignatius of Antioch, **2**/65.3
St Irenaeus, **4**/65.2
St Jean Vianney, **2**/65.3, **4**/65.3
St John Chrysostom, **1**/2.1, **4**/70.1
St John of the Cross, **5**/7.3
St John Paul II, **2**/51.2, **4**/46.3, **4**/47.1, **4**/65.3, **4**/70.2, **4**/70.3, **6**/41.1, **6**/41.2
St Paul VI, **1**/2.2, **1**/2.3, **2**/44.1, **2**/49.2, **2**/65.1, **2**/65.2, **3**/4.3, **4**/43.2, **4**/56.2, **5**/89.3, **6**/5.1, **6**/41.3, **6**/43.1, **6**/45.3
St Pius X, **1**/2.3
St Teresa, **6**/45.2
St Thomas Aquinas, **2**/65.3, **3**/4.1, **3**/103.2, **4**/43.3, **6**/43.2, **6**/46.1 **6**/46.3, **6**/47.1

Evangelisation
St John Paul II, **2**/32.1, **2**/32.3, **4**/87.3, **5**/12.2, **6**/12.3, **6**/18.2
St Paul VI, **5**/20.2, **5**/20.3, **6**/9.2, **6**/13.2

Examination of conscience
Bl. Alvaro, **4**/93.1
St Augustine, **1**/19.2
St John Chrysostom, **4**/57.2
St John Climacus, **4**/93.2
St John of the Cross, **4**/93.1
St Teresa, **4**/93.3

Example
St Ambrose, **5**/13.2
St Gregory the Great, **2**/32.2
St Ignatius of Antioch, **5**/1.2
St John Chrysostom, **4**/40.2, **4**/72.1, **4**/72.2, **5**/62.2
St John Paul II, **4**/4.3, **4**/73.1
St Teresa, **5**/62.2

Faith
Bl. Alvaro, **6**/18.3
Pius XII, **3**/55.2, **5**/53.2
St Ambrose, **1**/6.1, **4**/13.1, **5**/64.2
St Augustine, **2**/54.3, **4**/54.1, **4**/55.3, **5**/4.2, **5**/48.3, **5**/51.3
St Gregory Nazianzen, **5**/26.1
St Gregory the Great, **2**/54.2, **2**/54.3, **6**/45.1
St Jean Vianney, **3**/44.2
St John Chrysostom, **2**/63.1, **3**/55.1, **3**/89.1, **4**/55.3
St John Paul II, **1**/44.3, **2**/67.1, **6**/6.2, **6**/13.2, **7**/1.3, **7**/12.2
St Justin, **6**/52.1
St Paul VI, **6**/6.2
St Vincent of Lerins, **6**/6.1
St Teresa, **4**/55.1

Family life
St Augustine, **7**/19.1
St John Chrysostom, **2**/70.3
St John Paul II, **1**/31.2, **2**/14.3, **3**/95.1, **4**/91.1, **4**/91.3, **5**/29.3, **7**/6.2, **7**/19, **7**/28.2, **7**/54.3
St Thomas Aquinas, **5**/29.3

Fear
St Augustine, **3**/99.1
St J. H. Newman, **3**/99.1
St John Chrysostom, **6**/12.3
St John Paul II, **2**/93.3, **5**/82.2
St Teresa, **2**/93.1, **2**/93.3

Forgiveness
St Ambrose, **3**/5.1
St Augustine, **1**/37.2
St John Chrysostom, **3**/54.2,

4/61.3, **5**/41.3
St John of the Cross, **5**/1.1
St John Paul II, **5**/1.3
St Therese of Lisieux, **5**/3.1
St Thomas Aquinas, **4**/60.2

Fraternity
St Augustine, **3**/52.2
St Cyprian, **5**/41.3
St Francis de Sales, **5**/78.3
St Gregory the Great, **5**/78.2
St John Chrysostom, **5**/79.1, **5**/88.3
St John Paul II, **5**/78.3,
St Leo the Great, **4**/10.2
St Paul VI, **5**/20.3
Tertullian, **4**/79.2

Freedom
St John Paul II, **4**/74.2, **4**/74.3

Friendship
St Ambrose, **4**/41.2, **4**/41.3, **4**/89.3
St Bernard, **4**/89.1
St Paul VI, **2**/80.2
St Teresa, **1**/36.1
St Thomas Aquinas, **2**/80.2, **3**/5.2

Generosity
Pastor of Hermas, **5**/92.2
St Ambrose, **4**/94.1
St Augustine, **5**/67.2, **5**/74.3, **5**/92.1
St Gregory the Great, **1**/26.2
St Ignatius of Antioch, **4**/97.1
St John Chrysostom, **5**/74.1
St John Paul II, **1**/18.3, **5**/8.3
St Teresa, **1**/26.3, **5**/74.3
St Thomas Aquinas, **5**/74.2

Good Shepherd
St Ambrose, **2**/4.3
St Augustine, **1**/7.2
St Thomas of Villanueva, **1**/7.2

Grace
St Augustine, **5**/77.2, **6**/12.2
St Bede, **4**/99.2
St Irenaeus, **1**/51.1
St John Chrysostom, **4**/97.2
St Teresa, **6**/12.2
St Thomas Aquinas, **2**/17.3, **4**/2.2, **5**/30.1

Heaven
St Augustine, **2**/82.3
St Cyprian, **3**/97.1
St Cyril of Jerusalem, **2**/82.1
St John Chrysostom, **2**/12.2
St John Paul II, **3**/58.2
St Leo the Great, **2**/86.2

Hell
St Teresa, **3**/58.2, **5**/73.2
St Thomas Aquinas, **5**/90.1, **5**/97.2, **5**/97.3

Holy Spirit
Leo XIII, **2**/83.1
St Augustine, **2**/95.3
St Cyril of Jerusalem, **2**/95.3, **2**/96.2
St Francis de Sales, **2**/96.2
St John Paul II, **5**/45.1
St Paul VI, **2**/87.1
St Thomas Aquinas, **2**/90.3, **3**/5.3, **5**/45.1

Hope
John Paul I, **5**/93.3
St Ambrose, **5**/66.3
St Augustine, **1**/4.1, **2**/74.1
St Bernard, **2**/74.3
St John Paul II, **4**/57.1

Human dignity
St John Paul II, **7**/28.3

Humility
John Paul I, **5**/47.3
Leo XIII, **1**/27.1
St Ambrose, **5**/77.1
St Augustine, **1**/2.2, **1**/27.2, **1**/47.3, **5**/21.1, **5**/39.2, **5**/57.2, **5**/60.2
St Bede, **3**/4.1
St Bernard, **3**/45.2
St Cyril of Alexandria, **1**/50.1
St Francis de Sales, **1**/27.2, **4**/84.1, **4**/84.3
St Gregory the Great, **1**/8.2
St Jean Vianney, **1**/27.2
St John Chrysostom, **4**/84.1
St John Paul II, **1**/27.1, **5**/74.2
St Thomas Aquinas, **1**/27.2

Ignorance
St John XXIII, **2**/32.1
St John Chrysostom, **3**/18.2
Incarnation
St Augustine, **3**/3.1
Instruments of God
Cassian, **2**/20.2
John Paul I, **5**/2.1, **5**/65.2
Leo XIII, **5**/77.1
St Augustine, **5**/51.3, **5**/54.2
St Gregory the Great, **3**/98.2
St John Chrysostom, **2**/14.1, **3**/88.2, **4**/55.3
St Pius X, **5**/77.3
St Thomas Aquinas, **2**/70.1, **5**/12.3
St John Paul II, **5**/43.2
Theophylact, **5**/54.2
Interior Life
Bl. Alvaro, **4**/30.1
St John Paul II, **6**/4.3

Joy
St Basil, **4**/67.3
St Bede, **2**/12.2
St John Chrysostom, **4**/26.1
St John Paul II, **1**/30.2, **2**/77.1, **3**/15.3
St Leo the Great, **1**/30.3
St Paul VI, **2**/26.2, **2**/48.3, **5**/27.1
St Thomas Aquinas, **2**/48.3, **2**/94.1, **3**/15.3, **7**/47.2
St Thomas More, **1**/39.2
Judgement
St J. H. Newman, **5**/73.1
Justice
St Cyril of Jerusalem, **5**/83.2
St John Chrysostom, **4**/85.2
St John Paul II, **1**/35.3, **2**/75.1, **3**/19.1, **4**/12.2, **4**/16.3, **4**/77.3
St John XXIII, **4**/77.1
St Paul VI, **4**/12.3
St Thomas Aquinas, **2**/75.1, **4**/77.2, **5**/17.3, **5**/27.2, **5**/55.2

Leisure
St Augustine, **4**/29.1, **4**/29.2
St Gregory Nazianzen, **4**/29.1
St Paul VI, **5**/17.1
St Teresa, **4**/29.2
Lent
St John Paul II, **2**/1.1, **2**/8.2
Little things
St Augustine, **1**/16.2
St Bernard, **5**/39.2
St John Chrysostom, **2**/22.3
St Francis de Sales, **4**/57.2
Love
St Augustine, **3**/52.2
St Gregory of Nyssa, **2**/93.2

St John Chrysostom, **4**/71.2
St John of the Cross, **2**/14.3, **4**/1.2
St John Paul II, **4**/1.2, **5**/8.2, **5**/64.2, **5**/64.3, **5**/88.1
St Teresa, **2**/14.3, **5**/55.2
St Thomas Aquinas, **4**/97.2

Love of God
Clement of Alexandria, **5**/3.1
John Paul I, **2**/24.3, **5**/53.3, **5**/65.1
St Alphonsus Liguori, **4**/66.1
St Ambrose, **5**/28.2
St Augustine, **2**/49.2, **4**/1.3, **4**/92.3, **5**/65.2
St Bernard, **3**/99.1
St Catherine of Siena, **3**/50.2
St Francis de Sales, **5**/77.2
St John Chrysostom, **2**/24.1, **5**/39.2
St John of the Cross, **2**/69.2, **3**/104.2, **4**/95.2
St John Paul II, **3**/104.3, **4**/95.1, **5**/5.1, **5**/5.3, **5**/38.2, **5**/66.2, **5**/75.3
St Teresa, **2**/4.1, **2**/69.1, **2**/69.2, **5**/14.1, **5**/57.3, **5**/92.3, **5**/95.3
St Thomas Aquinas, **4**/66.2, **5**/65.2

Lukewarmness
St Augustine, **5**/3.3
St Gregory the Great, **1**/12.2, **5**/55.1
St John Chrysostom, **4**/19.3, **4**/54.3
St John of the Cross, **4**/19.2, **5**/76.2
St Pius X, **3**/102.3
St Teresa, **4**/19.2
St Thomas Aquinas, **5**/30.1

Marxism
St Paul VI, **2**/33.3

Marriage
John Paul I, **5**/29.2
St Francis de Sales, **4**/62.1
St John Chrysostom, **4**/62.2
St John Paul II, **4**/62.2, **5**/29.1

Mass
Pius XII, **5**/52.2, **5**/92.2
St Augustine, **2**/36.3
St Ephraim, **4**/26.2
St Gregory the Great, **2**/66.2
St Jean Vianney, **2**/30.2, **4**/7.1, **4**/7.3
St John Chrysostom, **4**/26.2
St John Paul II, **2**/30.2, **2**/30.3
St Paul VI, **2**/30.2

Materialism
Bl. Alvaro, **4**/82.2
John Paul I, **5**/46.3
St Augustine, **5**/58.2
St Gregory the Great, **5**/58.2
St John Paul II, **4**/82.2, **5**/25.1, **7**/2.1
St John XXIII, **2**/58.2
St Paul VI, **5**/49.1

Mercy
Clement of Alexandria, **5**/3.1
St Augustine, **5**/15.2, **5**/93.2
St Bernard, **5**/56.2
St Francis de Sales, **5**/93.2
St John Paul II, **4**/85.1, **5**/1.3, **5**/3.2, **5**/5.1, **5**/5.2, **5**/81.2
St Therese of Lisieux, **5**/3.3
St Thomas Aquinas, **3**/42.1, **5**/5.1, **5**/17.3, **5**/41.2, **5**/70.2, **5**/81.2

Morning Offering
St Bernard, **2**/79.1
Cassian, **2**/79.2

Mortification
St Augustine, **4**/8.1
St Francis de Sales, **2**/1.1
St Jean Vianney, **5**/26.1
St John Chrysostom, **2**/15.2, **4**/8.2
St John of the Cross, **2**/2.1, **2**/19.2
St Leo the Great, **2**/19.1
St Paul VI, **2**/15.2, **2**/19.1
St Peter of Alcantara, **3**/101.2
St Teresa, **2**/19.2

Obedience
Cassian, **2**/20.2
St Augustine, **1**/49.1
St Gregory the Great, **1**/5.2, **1**/49.2, **5**/19.3
St John Chrysostom, **1**/5.3, **1**/45.1
St Teresa, **1**/49.3, **5**/19.1, **5**/19.3
St Thomas Aquinas, **4**/88.2, **5**/19.2
St John Paul II, **4**/94.3, **7**/12.2

Optimism
St Teresa, **4**/49.1
St Thomas Aquinas, **4**/49.2

Our Lady
Benedict XV, **3**/105.1, **7**/13.2
Bl. Alvaro, **3**/28.2
Leo XIII, **2**/25.3, **3**/45.3, **5**/18.1, **7**/26.3, **7**/34.1
Origen, **3**/105.3
Pius IX, **1**/25.1, **7**/17.2
Pius XII, **2**/95.1, **7**/3.1, **7**/14.2, **7**/17.2
St Alphonsus Liguori, **1**/21.3, **3**/9.1, **4**/99.2, **5**/81.3, **7**/9.2, **7**/9.3, **7**/41.3, **7**/49.3
St Amadeus of Lausanne, **7**/14.1
St Ambrose, **1**/50.3
St Andrew of Crete, **7**/22.1
St Augustine, **1**/23.1, **1**/47.3
St Bernard, **1**/18.3, **1**/38.3, **1**/40.3, **2**/9.3, **2**/74.3, **2**/79.1, **3**/42.2, **3**/98.3, **5**/48.2, **5**/92.3, **6**/1.1, **6**/1.2, **6**/15.2, **6**/16.1, **6**/31.2, **7**/11.3, **7**/15.3, **7**/43.3
St Bonaventure, **7**/22.1
St Catherine of Siena, **6**/28.3
St Cyril of Alexandria, **1**/38.1, **7**/11.2
St Ephraim, **7**/17.1
St Francis de Sales, **5**/63.2
St Germanus of Constantinop le, **5**/18.2
St Ildephonsus of Toledo, **7**/15.2
St J. H. Newman, **7**/43.2
St Jean Vianney, **2**/30.2, **5**/63.1
St John Damascene, **2**/46.3, **7**/6.1, **7**/14.2
St John Paul II, **1**/22.3, **1**/31.3, **1**/38.2, **2**/47.3, **2**/56.3, **2**/84.3, **2**/95.1, **3**/9.2, **3**/38.3, **3**/42.1, **4**/90.2, **4**/90.3, **4**/94.3, **4**/99.1, **4**/99.3, **5**/14.2, **5**/18.1, **5**/36.1, **6**/10.1, **6**/10.3, **6**/28.2, **6**/31.1, **6**/51.3, **7**/3.2, **7**/3.3, **7**/6.3, **7**/9.1, **7**/11.1, **7**/15.2, **7**/24.3
St Paul VI, **1**/38.3, **2**/48.3, **2**/84.1, **2**/84.3, **2**/95.1, **2**/95.3, **3**/40.3, **3**/105.3, **7**/3.2
St Peter Damian, **4**/90.1, **7**/22.3
St Teresa, **6**/31.3, **7**/3.2
St Thomas Aquinas, **1**/41.1, **4**/90.1, **4**/99.3, **5**/18.1, **7**/43.2
St Vincent Ferrer, **7**/3.2

Passion
St Alphonsus Liguori, **2**/37.1
St Augustine, **2**/39.2, **2**/45.1
St John Chrysostom, **2**/37.1
St John Paul II, **5**/22.2
St Leo the Great, **2**/37.1
St Thomas Aquinas, **2**/37.1
Patience
St Augustine, **5**/94.1
St Francis de Sales, **5**/94.2
St Gregory Nazianzen, **5**/54.3
St John Chrysostom, **2**/28.1, **2**/28.3
St John of the Cross, **5**/5.1
St Thomas Aquinas, **5**/94.2
Peace
St Augustine, **2**/77.2, **2**/94.1, **3**/98.3
St Gregory Nazianzen, **2**/56.2
St Irenaeus, **2**/56.2
St John Chrysostom, **1**/3.2
St John of the Cross, **4**/25.1
St John Paul II, **1**/3.1, **1**/3.3
St Paul VI, **2**/33.1, **4**/12.3
Penance
St Ambrose, **3**/90.3
St Cyril of Jerusalem, **5**/75.2
St Gregory the Great, **3**/90.1
St John Chrysostom, **3**/90.2
St John Paul II, **3**/85.2, **5**/1.3, **5**/41.1
St Paul VI, **2**/3.1
Perseverance
Cassian, **2**/39.1
St Augustine, **5**/4.3, **5**/81.1, **5**/86.3
St Gregory the Great, **7**/4.1
St John Chrysostom, **4**/80.2
St John Paul II, **5**/57.1, **5**/86.2
St Teresa, **2**/92.2, **5**/57.3
St Thomas Aquinas, **2**/92.2
Poverty
St Augustine, **5**/24.3, **7**/31.2
St Gregory the Great, **2**/16.2, **2**/16.3
St John Chrysostom, **4**/48.2
St Leo the Great, **2**/1.2
Prayer
St Alphonsus Liguori, **2**/12.3, **2**/81.3, **5**/48.1, **5**/57.2, **7**/9.1
St Augustine, **2**/9.3, **4**/39.2, **4**/64.1, **4**/64.2, **5**/48.1, **5**/48.3, **5**/56.2, **5**/81.1, **5**/95.2
St Bernard, **5**/48.1
St Cyprian, **3**/94.1
St Gregory the Great, **3**/40.3
St Jean Vianney, **2**/9.1, **3**/40.1, **7**/35.1
St John Chrysostom, **2**/68.2, **4**/64.3
St John of the Cross, **3**/51.1
St John Paul II, **1**/29.2, **3**/93.1, **4**/39.1, 39.3, **4**/91.1, **4**/91.3, **4**/95.2, **5**/33.1, **5**/57.1, **7**/32.1
St Paul VI, **5**/14.3
St Peter of Alcantara, **3**/51.2, **5**/57.3
St Teresa, **1**/29.2, **1**/29.3, **2**/9.3, **2**/15.1, **2**/27.1, **2**/27.3, **3**/51.2, **3**/94.1, **4**/95.2, **5**/14.1, **5**/34.1, **5**/57.1, **5**/57.3, **6**/18.2, **7**/35.1
St Thomas Aquinas, **3**/40.2, **4**/64.2, **4**/80.3
Presence of God
St Alphonsus Liguori, **5**/61.1
St Augustine, **2**/76.1, **2**/76.2, **4**/30.1
St Basil, **5**/72.2
St Gregory the Great, **2**/76.2
St John of the Cross, **2**/76.2

St John Paul II, **2**/61.2, **5**/83.1
Pride
Cassian, **2**/14.1, **5**/63.3
St Ambrose, **5**/54.1
St John Chrysostom, **2**/25.2, **2**/63.1, **2**/63.3, **5**/33.3
St Gregory the Great, **2**/63.2
St Thomas Aquinas, **5**/55.1
Priesthood
Bl. Alvaro, **1**/51.3, 5/11.2
St Ambrose, **7**/10.3
St Catherine of Siena, **4**/20.3
St Ephraim, **5**/71.1
St J. H. Newman, **6**/9,3
St John Paul II, **1**/7.2, **4**/20.1, **5**/57.1, **6**/9.3, **7**/10.1, **7**/10.2
Providence, divine
Cassian, **5**/33.2
St Augustine, **5**/60.2
St Bernard, **3**/96.3
St Jerome, **3**/97.2
St John Paul II, **3**/96.1
St Thomas Aquinas, **3**/96.2
Prudence
St Augustine, **4**/17.1
St John Paul II, **4**/17.1, **4**/17.2
St Teresa, **5**/93.2
Purgatory
St Catherine of Genoa, **7**/39.1
St John Paul II, **7**/39.1
St Teresa, **7**/39.1
Purity
St Ambrose, **5**/90.1
St John Paul II, **3**/8.1, **5**/75.3

Reading of the Gospel
St Augustine, **2**/73.1, **2**/73.3, **4**/86.3, **5**/96.3
St Cyprian, **5**/96.3
St Jerome, **7**/8.3
St John Chrysostom, **5**/96.1
St John Paul II, **4**/86.2
Responsibility
St Augustine, **5**/9.3
St Gregory the Great, **2**/63.2, **5**/68.2
St Ignatius of Antioch, **5**/79.2
St Thomas Aquinas, **5**/51.2
Roman Pontiff
St Ambrose, **6**/7.2
St Augustine, **6**/19.1, **6**/19.3
St Catherine of Siena, **6**/7.2
St Cyprian, **6**/19.1
St John Paul II, **6**/7.3
St Leo the Great, **6**/7.2, **6**/19.2
Rosary
Pius XI, **5**/36.2, **7**/32.3
Pius XII, **2**/81.1
St John Paul II, **2**/81.2, **5**/36.2, **5**/36.3
St John XXIII, **2**/81.1, **7**/33.1
St Paul VI, **2**/81.1, **2**/81.2, **5**/18.3, **5**/36.2

Sacraments
St Augustine, **2**/46.1
St John Chrysostom, **4**/36.1
St Pius X, **4**/46.3
Saints, devotion to
St Catherine of Siena, **6**/32.1
St Jerome, **3**/72.2
St John Paul II, **3**/72.2, **6**/2
St John the Baptist
St Augustine, **1**/8.1
St John Chrysostom, **6**/55.3
St Joseph
Leo XIII, **4**/15.2, **6**/20.1, **6**/26.3
St Ambrose, **1**/22.1
St Augustine, **1**/22.2

St Bernard, **4**/15.3
St Bernardine of Siena, **1**/40.3, **6**/20.3, **6**/25.3
St Francis de Sales, **6**/25.2
St John Chrysostom, **6**/24.1
St John Paul II, **5**/64.3, **5**/84.3, **6**/20.2, **6**/26.3, **6**/27.3
St John XXIII, **6**/26.3
St Teresa, **1**/45.2, **4**/15.2, **6**/26.1, **6**/26.3

St Thomas More
St Thomas More, **6**/54.3

Sanctity
Cassian, **5**/32.3
St John Paul II, **3**/7.3, **4**/4.3, **5**/58.3, **6**/21.3, **7**/38.1

Search for God
St Augustine, **5**/16.3, **5**/37.2, **7**/4.2
St Bernard, **5**/50.3
St Ignatius of Antioch, **5**/32.3
St John of the Cross, **2**/10.2
St John Paul II, **5**/66.1

Self-giving
St Augustine, **5**/3.3
St Gregory the Great, **5**/92.1
St John Paul II, **1**/26.1, **5**/90.3

Service
St Augustine, **5**/3.3
St John Chrysostom, **2**/24.1
St John Paul II, **2**/15.3, **5**/47.3

Simplicity
St Jerome, **1**/24.3
St John Chrysostom, **1**/24.3

Sin
Origen, **5**/93.1
St Augustine, **2**/17.3, **2**/21.3, **5**/31.1, **5**/45.2, **5**/93.1
St Bede, **5**/31.1
St Francis de Sales, **2**/17.3
St Gregory the Great, **5**/9.1
St Jean Vianney, **2**/17.1, **3**/44.2
St John Chrysostom, **4**/85.2
St John of the Cross, **4**/2.2, **5**/45.3
St John Paul II, **2**/17.1, **2**/17.3, **2**/18.2, **2**/29.2, **3**/56.3, **4**/2.2, **4**/34.1, **4**/34.2, **5**/3.2, **5**/41.1, **5**/45.1, **5**/45.2, **5**/70.1, **5**/71.2
St Paul VI, **1**/51.1

Sincerity
St Augustine, **7**/18.2, **7**/18.3
St Francis de Sales, **2**/23.3
St John Chrysostom, **2**/23.1
St Thomas Aquinas, **5**/44.2

Society
Bl. Alvaro, **4**/12.2
Pius XI, **3**/37.1
St John Chrysostom, **3**/52.1
St Paul VI, **1**/35.1

Spiritual childhood
Cassian, **5**/34.1
St Alphonsus Liguori, **5**/57.2
St Ambrose, **4**/63.3

Spiritual direction
St John Climacus, **1**/7.3
St John of the Cross, **4**/76.1, **5**/85.2
St Teresa, **5**/85.2
St Thomas Aquinas, **5**/19.3
St Vincent Ferrer, **4**/92.3

Spiritual reading
St Augustine, **3**/18.2
St Basil, **3**/43.2, **3**/43.3
St Jerome, **7**/36.3
St John Chrysostom, **7**/8.2
St John Eudes, **7**/8.3
St Peter of Alcantara, **7**/8.3

Suffering
St Augustine, **5**/69.2

St Bede, **7**/20.2
St Francis de Sales, **2**/31.2
St John Chrysostom, **2**/64.3, **5**/31.1
St John Paul II, **2**/31.3, **5**/15.1, **5**/15.2, **5**/22.2, **5**/69.1, **6**/17.3, **6**/22.1
St Teresa, **5**/69.3
St Thomas More, **2**/38.3

Supernatural outlook
Pius XII, **3**/55.2
St Augustine, **5**/34.1, **5**/80.1
St Bede, **4**/69.2
St Gregory the Great, **4**/80.2
St John Chrysostom, **4**/82.1
St John Paul II, **5**/58.3, **5**/97.1
St John XXIII, **5**/89.3
St Paul VI, **5**/83.3
St Teresa, **5**/76.3
St Theophilus, **3**/55.2

Temperance
St John Paul II, **4**/35
St Peter Alcantara, **4**/35.1

Temptations
St Athanasius, **4**/3.1
St Basil, **5**/9.2
St Thomas Aquinas, **5**/42.2, **6**/3.3

Time
St Augustine, **4**/65.3
St Paul VI, **5**/17.1

Trust in God
Tertullian, **5**/42.2
St Augustine, **2**/4.3, **5**/67.2, **5**/93.1
St Cyprian, **5**/35.2
St Francis de Sales, **5**/43.3
St Teresa, **5**/60.3, **5**/65.1
St Thomas Aquinas, **5**/33.2
St Thomas More, **5**/61.3

Truth
St Augustine, **4**/18.3
St John Chrysostom, **4**/28.2
St Thomas Aquinas, **5**/44.2

Understanding
St Augustine, **2**/21.2
St Gregory the Great, **2**/72.2
St Jerome, **2**/72.1, **4**/27.3
St John Paul II, **7**/18.2
St Teresa, **2**/87.2

Unity
Aristides, **2**/56.3
Cassian, **3**/72.2
Pius XI, **5**/87.3, **5**/91.2
St Augustine, **2**/56.3, **2**/78.3, **4**/92.1
St Cyprian, **4**/13.3
St Irenaeus, **2**/56.1, **2**/56.2
St John Chrysostom, **2**/56.1, **3**/50.7
St John Paul II, **2**/56.1, **2**/56.2, **3**/57.1, **5**/32.2, **5**/68.2, **6**/18.1
St Paul VI, **2**/56.2, **6**/5.2
St Thomas Aquinas, **2**/56.2

Virtues
Bl. Alvaro, **2**/22.2, **4**/33.1
Pius XI, **4**/33.1
St Augustine, **3**/19.3, **3**/100.1
St Francis de Sales, **3**/6.2
St Gregory the Great, **4**/25.2
St Jerome, **3**/86.3
St John Chrysostom, **3**/52.1
St Teresa, **3**/54.3, **3**/100.1
St Thomas Aquinas, **3**/6.2

Visit to the Blessed

Sacrament
Pius XII, **2**/51.2
St Alphonsus Liguori, **2**/51.3, **4**/56.3
St John Chrysostom, **2**/51.3
St Paul VI, **4**/56.3
St Teresa, **2**/51.3
Vocation
Bl. Alvaro, **2**/32.1,
John Paul I, **1**/45.1
Pius XI, **4**/22.2
St Bernard, **4**/22.1
St Bernardine of Siena, **6**/20.3
St Gregory the Great, **3**/88.2
St John Chrysostom, **7**/25.1
St John Paul II, **4**/22.3, **5**/38.2, **5**/43.1, **5**/90.2, **7**/29.2, **7**/45.1
St Thomas Aquinas, **6**/20.2, **7**/45.2
Will of God
St John Paul II, **5**/43.1
St Augustine, **5**/35.1
St Teresa, **2**/57.2, **5**/35.3
Worldly Respect
St Bede, **5**/44.2
St Jean Vianney, **2**/62.1
St Thomas Aquinas, **5**/30.1
Work
Bl. Alvaro, **4**/30.3
Didache, **4**/78.1
St John Chrysostom, **1**/43.1, **3**/41.2
St John Paul II, **1**/46.2, **3**/11.2, **5**/13.2, **5**/32.2, **5**/84.3
St John XXIII, **3**/11.2

Subject Index

Abandonment
and responsibility, **3**/96.2, **7**/46.2
confidence in God's Will, **3**/61.1, **3**/96.1, **5**/35, **5**/53.1, **5**/58.1
healthy concern for *today*, **3**/61.3
omnia in bonum, **3**/96.3, **5**/58.3, **5**/60.2
unnecessary worries, **3**/61.2, **5**/17.3, **5**/82.3
Advent
expectation of second coming, **1**/20.1
joy of, **1**/2.1
meaning of, **1**/1.3
period of hope, **1**/21.1
period of joy, **1**/15.1
preparation for Christmas, **1**/1.1
Affability, **3**/6.1, **3**/6.2, **3**/6.3
Angels, **7**/27, **7**/28, **7**/29, **7**/30
Anger, can be just and virtuous, **1**/11.3
Anointing of the Sick, **2**/31.3, **3**/31
Apostolate
a duty, **2**/53.1, **2**/85.1, **3**/21.3, **3**/69.1, **4**/40.3, **5**/10.2, **5**/25.1, **5**/51.3, **5**/87.3, **6**/30.3, **7**/2.3
ad fidem, **1**/44.3, **4**/21.1
and difficulties, **1**/9.2, **1**/41.3, **2**/32.3, **2**/53.2, **2**/62.2, **3**/89.2, **5**/52.1, **6**/52.3, **6**/57.3, **6**/58.2
and doctrine, **4**/18.1, **5**/46.3
and example, **2**/32.2, **4**/44.3, **5**/13.1, **5**/51.2, **5**/76.3, **6**/58.1
and faith, **3**/5.1, **7**/34.3
and God's help, **1**/9.2, **2**/59.2, **5**/26.1, **5**/52, **6**/34.3
and humility, **1**/8.2, **5**/57.2
and joy, **1**/15.3, **3**/68.3, **3**/69.1, **5**/25.3, **5**/27.2, **5**/55.1, **5**/55.3, **7**/4.3
and meekness, **1**/11.3
and optimism, **2**/53.3, **3**/21.2
and patience, **2**/52.2, **2**/52.3, **3**/21.2, **5**/94.3
and prayer, **3**/3.1, **3**/88.2, **5**/57.1, **7**/46.3
and prudence, **3**/5.2
and proselytism, **2**/62.2, **5**/10.2, **7**/46.2
and worldly respect, **2**/62.3, **3**/89.3, **4**/44, **5**/30.1, **5**/44.2, **5**/62, **5**/72.3
basis of, **1**/9.1, **3**/3.3, **3**/35.2, **3**/68.1, **5**/10.2
being instruments, **3**/21.1, **3**/36.3, **5**/51.3, **5**/52
constancy in, **1**/12.2, **2**/85.2, **4**/69.2, **5**/20.2, **5**/50.2, **5**/68.3, **5**/94.3, **6**/2.3, **7**/55.3
fruits of, **2**/85.2, **3**/21.3, **5**/52.2, **5**/68.3, **5**/91.3

how to do it, **2**/52.3, **2**/59.3,
needs formation, **2**/54.3
of friendship, **1**/8.3, **1**/9.2, **2**/53.3, **5**/25.2, 7/42.2
of public opinion, **4**/45.2, **4**/45.3, **5**/44, **6**/32.2, 7/2.2
part of the Christian vocation, **1**/8.1, **2**/53.1, **2**/86.3, **3**/69.2, **5**/72.2
role of women, **2**/85.3, **5**/8, 7/36.1
universal meaning of, **1**/44.3, **5**/37.3, **5**/43.1, **6**/58.3, 7/25.3
upright intention, **2**/62.3
virtues required, **3**/36.1, **3**/36.2, **3**/36.3, **4**/33.3, **5**/20.1, **6**/11.2
witnesses to Christ, **1**/6.2, **1**/8.3, **3**/35.2, **4**/66.3, **5**/66.3, **5**/87.3, **6**/53, 7/2

Ascetical Struggle
beginning again, **1**/12.2, **1**/12.3, **1**/24.3, **2**/28.2, **4**/14.3, **5**/9.3, **5**/50.2, **5**/60.2, **5**/70.2, **6**/30.2, 7/20.2
constancy, **2**/28.1, **4**/14.1, **5**/42.3, **5**/48.1, **5**/70.2, **5**/94
develop a spirit of, **1**/13.3, **1**/19.1, **1**/43.3, **5**/34.2, **5**/43.2
expect defeats, **1**/12.3, **4**/14.2, **5**/93.3
fortitude in the face of weaknesses, **1**/12.1, **1**/45.3, **4**/11.2, **5**/42.2, **5**/61.2, **5**/70.2, **5**/93
until the last moments, **1**/12.1, **5**/97.3

Aspirations, **1**/29.3, **1**/40.2, **1**/40.3, **2**/35.3
remembering to say, **2**/35.2

Atonement, **6**/35.3, 49.3, **6**/50.2

Baptism
effects of, **1**/51.2, **5**/43, **5**/59, **5**/71.2
gratitude for having received it, **1**/51.1
incorporation into the Church, **1**/51.3, **4**/13.2
institution of, **1**/51.1
of children, **1**/51.3

Beatitudes, **3**/25.1, **3**/25.2

Blessed Trinity, **2**/76.1, **6**/3.1, **6**/39, **6**/40

Calumny, **3**/19.1, **3**/19.2, **3**/19.3

Celibacy
see Chastity, Virginity

Charity
and forgiveness, **2**/21.1, **2**/21.2, **2**/21.3, **5**/1.1
and judgements, **2**/72.1, **5**/41.3
effectiveness of, **2**/72.3, **4**/10.1, **5**/20.3, **5**/68.2, **5**/94.3
its essence, **3**/27.1, **3**/27.2, **5**/23.1, **5**/31.3, **5**/52.1, **5**/79.3, **6**/50.3
ordered, **1**/25.3, **3**/81.2, **4**/21.3
sins of omission, **4**/21.2
understanding, **2**/72.1, **2**/72.2, **3**/52.1, **3**/52.2, **3**/81.3, **5**/11.2, **5**/6.1, **5**/15.3, **5**/67.3, **5**/93.2

Chastity
and little things, **1**/16.2, **5**/90.3
clean of heart shall see God, **1**/16.3, **3**/8.1, **3**/48.1, **5**/16.1, **5**/53.2, **5**/75.3, **5**/90
fruits of purity, **1**/23.2, **5**/63.3,

5/75.3, **5**/90
guard of the heart, **1**/16.2, **5**/90.3
purity of heart, **1**/16.1, **1**/19.3, **1**/23.1, **4**/62.3, **5**/90
ways of living purity well, **1**/23.3, **3**/8.2, **3**/8.3, **5**/90.3

Christians
early, **2**/70.1, **5**/52.3, **5**/62.3, **5**/68.3, **5**/71.1, **5**/74.2, **5**/79.1, **5**/84.1, **5**/86.2
exemplary, **2**/29.1, **2**/70.2, **3**/74, **3**/102

Christmas
a call to interior purification, **1**/16.1
humility and simplicity in knowing Christ, **1**/30.2
joy at, **1**/30.3
receiving Christ, **1**/30.1
the *Chair of Bethlehem,* **1**/30.2

Church
characteristics of, **3**/10.1, **3**/57.3, **4**/37.1, **5**/5.2, **6**/8
indefectibility, **2**/60.1, **4**/37.2, **4**/37.3
its institution, **3**/47.1, **6**/4.1
love for, **2**/59.2, **3**/10.3, **4**/13.1, **4**/13.3, **7**/16.3
mission of, **4**/16.1, **4**/16.2, **5**/1.3, **5**/28.1, **5**/31.2, **5**/41.1, **5**/47.2, **5**/48.2, **5**/75.3, **5**/87.1
prayer for, **3**/47.2, **6**/4.2, **7**/27.3

Civic Duties, **4**/58.1, **5**/21, **5**/51.2, **5**/67, **5**/74

Commandments of God
first, **3**/76.1, **3**/76.2, **3**/76.3, **5**/55.2, **5**/65.1
fourth, **3**/38.1, **3**/38.2, **3**/38.3
ninth, **3**/86.1, **3**/86.2, **3**/86.3
second, **5**/34

Communion
confession, a preparation for, **1**/2.3, **5**/7.3
dispositions for, **1**/2.1, **1**/2.2, **5**/7.3
effects of, **2**/65.3, **3**/29.3, **4**/46.2, **4**/47.3, **4**/56, **4**/65.3, **5**/40.3, **6**/46.3
preparation for, **1**/2.3, **4**/46.3, **5**/7.2, **5**/7.3, **5**/95.2
spiritual communions, **3**/29.1, **3**/29.2
Viaticum, **4**/56.1
see Eucharist

Communion of the Saints
and optimism, **4**/49.3
and penance, **2**/10.2
entry into, **1**/51.2, **2**/66.2
gaining merit for others, **1**/10.3, **2**/66.1, **5**/**5**/33.3, **5**/68
indulgences, **2**/66.3, **5**/71.3

Compassion, **4**/10.2, **4**/27.3, **5**/7.1, **5**/15.1, **5**/31, **5**/33.1, **5**/58.1, **5**/62.1, **5**/88.1

Concupiscence, **1**/1.2, **5**/58.2

Confession
a good for the whole church, **1**/10.3
and contrition, **1**/37.2, **1**/47.3, **2**/41.2, **2**/41.3, **3**/90.2, **4**/9.2, **5**/5.3
and peace, **1**/3.1, **5**/27.2
and the Good Shepherd, **1**/7.2
apostolate of, **1**/9.1, **2**/34.2, **5**/5.3
frequent, **1**/10.2, **1**/16.2, **3**/7.3, **4**/9.3, **5**/5.3, **5**/27.2
fruits of, **2**/4.2, **2**/8.3, **2**/18.3,

5/1.3, **5**/27.2
institution of, **4**/60.1, **5**/3.2, **5**/93.2
need for and importance of, **1**/10.1, **5**/7.3, **5**/53.2
penance, **2**/34.3, **5**/5.3
personal, auricular and complete, **1**/10.1
preparation for, **1**/9.3, **2**/8.2, **2**/8.3, **3**/7.2, **4**/9.3
preparation for Communion, **1**/1.2, **5**/7.3
respect, gratitude and veneration for, **1**/9.3, **4**/60.2, **5**/39.2
the power of forgiving, **1**/9.3, **2**/8.2, **2**/34.1, **4**/60.3, **5**/.1, **5**/41.2

Confidence in God
and divine filiation, **1**/36.2, **2**/60.3, **4**/5.2, **4**/5.3, **5**/9.3, **5**/33.2, **5**/81, **7**/7.1
its never too late, **1**/36.2, **4**/55.3, **5**/60, **5**/93

Consumerism, **1**/6.2, **5**/25.1, **5**/46.3, **5**/49.1, **5**/55.2, **5**/58.2, **7**/31.3

Contrition, **4**/9.2, **5**/5.3, **5**/9.1, **5**/16.2, **5**/28.2, **5**/60.2

Conversion, **1**/18.3, **2**/1.1, **5**/9.3, **5**/15.3, **5**/54.3, **5**/70.2, **7**/20.1

Culture, **7**/2.1

Death, **3**/63.1, **3**/63.2, **3**/63.3, **5**/71, **5**/75, **5**/80, **5**/97.1, **5**/97.3, **6**/25.1

Dedication, **4**/3.1, **4**/3.3, **5**/9.2, **5**/12.1, **5**/86, **7**/41.2

Detachment
examples, **2**/16.2, **3**/28.3, **3**/64.2, **5**/24.2, **5**/24.3
its need, **1**/28.1, **2**/16.1, **3**/17.1, **4**/19.2, **4**/48.3, **5**/24.1
our practice, **2**/16.3, **3**/17.2, **3**/17.3, **3**/65.2, **4**/6.2, **5**/21.3, **5**/38.3, **5**/49.2

Devil, **2**/6.1, **2**/6.2, **2**/6.3, **5**/42.1, **5**/42.2

Difficulties
and faith, **4**/50.2, **5**/61.1, **5**/85.1, **7**/21.3
current forms of, **1**/32.2, **5**/42.1
Christian reaction to, **1**/32.2, **1**/36.1, **1**/41.3, **4**/25.2, **5**/56.1, **5**/59.2, **5**/60.2, **5**/61.2, **5**/69.2, **5**/82.3, **5**/93, **7**/12.3, **7**/16.2
develop hope, **1**/32.3, **4**/5.3, **4**/25.3, **5**/85.1, **7**/5.2
suffered for Christ, **1**/32.1, **1**/32.3, **4**/25.1, **4**/96.2, **5**/31.3, **7**/12.1, **7**/23.2

Dignity, human, **3**/11.1, **3**/11.2, **3**/11.3, **5**/3.2, **5**/75, **5**/76, **7**/22.2, **7**/28.2

Dispositions, interior
humility, **2**/20.1, **2**/20.2
need for, **1**/18.1, **5**/16.1, **5**/53.2

Divine filiation
and fraternity, **1**/39.2, **4**/98.3, **5**/33.1, **5**/79.3
and petition, **4**/39.2, **4**/39.3, **5**/60.3
consequences of, **1**/39.2, **3**/2.2, **4**/24.2, **4**/24.3, **4**/63.2, **4**/98.2, **5**/33.2, **5**/46.3, **5**/59.3, **5**/60.2, **5**/72, **5**/75.3
everything is for the good, **1**/36.3, **3**/96.3, **5**/22.1, **5**/58.3, **5**/65.1

foundation for peace and joy, **1**/3.3, **1**/39.3, **5**/27.2, **5**/33.1, **5**/59.2
God is our Father, **1**/24.3, **1**/36.3, **3**/2.1, **3**/56, **4**/24.1, **4**/39.1, **4**/58, **4**/98.1, **5**/3.2, **5**/33.2, **5**/59, **5**/60.1, **5**/64
gratitude for, **1**/39.1
truly sons, **1**/39.1, **3**/62.2, **5**/33.1, **5**/47.1, **5**/59.1

Docility
a virtue, **1**/24.3, **1**/43.2, **7**/5.1
and spiritual guidance, **2**/20.3, **5**/45.3

Doctrine
and piety, **6**/14
giving it, **4**/28.2, **4**/28.3, **5**/46.3, **7**/16.1
need for, **7**/13.1

Ecumenism, **6**/4, **6**/5, **6**/6, **6**/7, **6**/8

Education, **7**/6.3

Eucharist
Adoro te devote, **2**/65.1, **3**/4.1, **3**/4.3, **3**/4.2, **4**/43.3, **4**/97.2, **5**/61.1, **5**/95.2, **5**/95.3
and adoration, **1**/44.1, **5**/40.3, **5**/61, **5**/89.3
and faith, **6**/45
institution of, **2**/44.2, **4**/26.1, **4**/26.2
pledge of Heaven, **4**/65.1, **4**/65.2, **5**/40.3, **6**/48
real presence, **4**/43, **5**/7.3, **5**/16.3, **6**/41, **6**/42, **6**/43, **6**/44, **6**/46
true food, **4**/46, **4**/47, **4**/65.1, **5**/40.2, **5**/61
see Communion

Examination of Conscience
a means against evil inclinations, **1**/19.2, **5**/41.3
a meeting with God, **1**/14.2
and hope, **4**/57.2
and self-knowledge, **1**/14.1, **5**/54.2, **5**/73.3
contrition and resolutions, **1**/14.3
fruits of, **1**/14.1, **5**/73.3
how to do it, **1**/14.3
particular, **2**/67.1, **2**/67.2, **2**/67.3, **4**/19.3, **5**/23.3

Example, **3**/34, **3**/74.1, **4**/4.3, **4**/10.1, **4**/40.2, **4**/58.2, **5**/1.2, **5**/13.2, **55**/6.3, **5**/62.2, **5**/68.3, **5**/76.3

Faith
and apostolate, **1**/9.2
and charity, **6**/52.3
and Christ, **1**/43.3, **2**/20.1, **3**/16.1, **3**/67.1, **4**/50.1, **4**/50.2, **4**/55.2, **4**/55.3, **5**/38.3, **5**/56.2, **5**/64.2, **6**/54, **7**/1.1, **7**/37.2
and optimism, **4**/49.2
docility in spiritual guidance, **1**/43.2, **1**/43.3, **5**/45.3
firmness in, **1**/43.1, **3**/73.2, **4**/54.1, **5**/4.3, **5**/30.2, **5**/48, **5**/85.1, **6**/52.1, **7**/1.3
giving it to others, **1**/14.3, **6**/6.3, **6**/13.3, **6**/52.2
need for it, **1**/6.1, **5**/30.3
of Our Lady, **1**/6.3, **3**/43.3, **3**/55.3, **4**/54.3, **5**/51.3, **5**/64.2
operative, **2**/54.2, **2**/60.3, **2**/62.1, **3**/12.3, **3**/67.1, **4**/54.3, **5**/48.3, **5**/60.2

ways to conserve and increase it, **1**/6.1, **1**/6.2, **1**/18.2, **3**/55.1, **4**/31.1, **4**/54.2, **5**/4.2, **6**/6.1, **6**/13

Faithfulness
a virtue, **3**/104.1, **3**/104.2, **5**/86, **7**/14.3
in little things, **2**/50.2, **3**/104.3, **5**/91.3

Family
domestic church, **1**/31.3, **3**/95.1, **5**/29.3, **5**/55.3, **7**/19.1
mission of parents, **1**/31.2, **3**/95.2, **7**/6.2, **7**/19.1, **7**/28.2, **7**/54.2
of Jesus, **4**/32, **7**/54.1
prayer in the, **3**/95.3, **7**/6.3, **7**/19.2, **7**/19.3

Family, Holy
example for all families, **1**/31.3, **7**/6.1, **7**/54.1
love in the, **1**/22.2, **1**/27.3, **5**/64.3
meeting with Simeon, **1**/41.1
Redemption rooted here, **1**/31.1
simplicity and naturalness, **1**/42.2

Fear, **1**/36.1, **2**/93, **3**/99, **5**/82.2

Feasts, **2**/61.1, **2**/61.2, **2**/61.3, **3**/71.1
and Sundays, **3**/71.2, **3**/71.3

Formation, doctrinal
and interior life, **3**/13.3, **3**/18.3
in the truths of the faith, **3**/13.1, **3**/18.1
need to receive and to give it, **3**/13.2, **3**/18.2

Fortitude
gift of, **2**/92.1
in daily life, **1**/45.3, **3**/32.2, **3**/32.3, **3**/97.3, **5**/94.2
in difficult moments, **2**/64.2, **7**/21.1
virtue of, **3**/32.1, **3**/97.3, **4**/44.2, **5**/94.1

Fraternal correction, **1**/7.2, **3**/24.1, **3**/24.2, **3**/24.3

Freedom, **1**/35.1

Friendship
and apostolate, **2**/80.3, **4**/41.3
qualities of a true friendship, **2**/80.2, **5**/6.2, **5**/78.2
true friendship, **2**/80.1, **6**/11.1
with God, **4**/41, **4**/55, **5**/4.2, **5**/61.3, **5**/88.1, **7**/7.2, **7**/7.3

Generosity
prize for it, **1**/26.3
towards God, **3**/46.1, **4**/67.1, **4**/98.1, **5**/38.3, **5**/55.2, **5**/67.2, **5**/72.3, **5**/74, **5**/92
with others, **1**/26.2, **5**/8.3, **5**/66.2, **5**/67

God's Love for men
gratuitous, **3**/62.1, **5**/3.2, **5**/65.2
infinite and eternal, **2**/24.1, **2**/24.2, **3**/62.1, **4**/66.1, **5**/1, **5**/74.3
personal and individual, **3**/62.3, **5**/3.1, **5**/38.2, **5**/66.2, **5**/70.2, **5**/88
returning his love, **2**/57.1, **3**/62.2, **3**/62.3, **4**/66.2, **5**/9.3, **5**/37.2, **5**/39.3, **5**/65.2, **5**/87.3
unconditional reply expected, **2**/24.3, **5**/51.1

Goods of the Earth
supernatural end, **4**/68.1, **5**/21,

5/24, **5**/38.2, **5**/38.3, **5**/49, **5**/55.2
Good Shepherd
and spiritual guidance, **1**/7.3, **1**/43.2
in the Church, **1**/7.2, **2**/68.1
Jesus Christ is, **1**/1, **2**/68.1, **5**/66.3, **5**/70
role of every Christian, **1**/7.2
virtues of, **1**/7.2, **5**/63.3
Gospel
reading of, **1**/48.2, **2**/73.1, **5**/96, **7**/36.3
teaching is current, **1**/48.3, **5**/96.2
Grace
corresponding to it, **2**/40.2, **4**/19.3, **5**/9.3, **5**/51.1, **6**/2.1, **7**/41.2
its effects and fruits, **3**/23.2, **3**/23.3, **3**/84.1, **3**/91.1, **5**/77, **7**/40.3
its nature, **3**/23.2, **3**/84.2, **3**/91.2, **5**/30.1
Guardian Angels
help us, **2**/7.2, **3**/77.2, **3**/77.1, **5**/42.3, **5**/73.3, **5**/77.3, **5**/84.3
love and devotion for, **2**/7.1, **2**/7.3, **3**/77.2, **3**/77.3

Heaven, **2**/82.1, **2**/82.2, **2**/82.3, **5**/21.1, **5**/73.2, **5**/83.3, **5**/90, **5**/97
hope of, **2**/12.2, **2**/82.1, **3**/58.3, **4**/48.2, **5**/37.1, **5**/80.1, **5**/97.1, **7**/12.2, **7**/14.2, **7**/15.3, **7**/52.1
and the Eucharist, **4**/65
Holy days of Obligation, **4**/29.3
Holy Spirit
and Mary, **2**/95.2, **2**/95.3, **7**/44.1
and supernatural virtues, **2**/83.1
devotion to, **2**/76.3
fruits, **2**/94, **5**/23.2, **5**/45, **5**/52.1
gifts,
counsel, **2**/90
fear, **2**/93
fortitude, **2**/92
knowledge, **2**/88
piety, **2**/91
understanding, **2**/87
wisdom, **2**/89
Hope
and discouragement, **1**/21.1, **2**/4.3, **2**/74.2, **3**/79.2, **5**/23.1, **7**/1.2
and heaven, **2**/12.2, **5**/37.1, **5**/80.1, **5**/97.1, **7**/15.3
and Our Lady, **1**/21.1, **2**/74.3, **5**/36.3, **5**/73.3, **6**/31.2, **7**/14.2
confidence in Christ, **1**/23.3, **1**/21.3, **2**/74.1, **5**/49.3, **5**/53.3, **5**/66.3, **5**/83.3, **6**/12
in apostolate, **2**/4.3
its object, **1**/21.2, **3**/79.1, **4**/57.1, **5**/93.3
Humility
and prayer, **1**/29.3, **4**/51.1, **5**/4.1, **5**/57.2
and pride, **2**/25.1, **2**/25.2, **3**/45.2, **3**/50.1, **4**/51.2
and simplicity, **1**/42.1, **1**/47.3, **5**/63.2
founded on charity, **1**/27.2, **2**/25.3, **5**/63.3, **5**/74.2
fruits of, **1**/27.2, **3**/50.1, **5**/21.1, **5**/47.3, **5**/77.1,

5/93.3, **6**/55.3
is truth, **1**/27.1, **5**/39.2, **5**/63.2
needed for the apostolate, **1**/8.2, **5**/77.3
ways to achieve it, **1**/27.3, **2**/14.3, **2**/25.3, **3**/45.3, **3**/50.3, **4**/51.3, **5**/9.2

Illness, **2**/31.1, **2**/31.2, **5**/69.3, **5**/94.2

Jesus Christ
and Our Lady, **1**/17.2, **5**/18.3, **7**/49.1
and the Cross, **1**/20.1, **2**/30.1, **4**/36.1, **4**/53.1, **5**/2.3, **5**/19.3, **5**/22, **5**/28.3, **5**/69, **5**/70.1, **7**/12.2
divinity, **4**/52.1, **6**/28.1
growth of, **1**/50.1
hidden life, **1**/46.1, **1**/46.2, **1**/50.1, **4**/45.1, **5**/84.2
high priest, **6**/38
humanity, **1**/17.3, **1**/50.1, **4**/52.2, **5**/16.2, **5**/28.3, **5**/31.2, **5**/78.1, **5**/84.3, **5**/88, **6**/28, **6**/47.3, **6**/49, **7**/7.2, **7**/35.2
humility, **1**/30.2, **5**/47.2, **5**/52.2, **5**/63.1
Kingship, **2**/42.3, **5**/34.2, **5**/34.3, **5**/83.2, **5**/87, **5**/91
merits of, **4**/4.2
Name of, **1**/40.1, **1**/40.2, **5**/34.1
Only-Begotten Son, **1**/17.1, **5**/59.1
our knowledge of, **1**/17.3, **1**/48.2, **5**/53.3, **5**/96
our Model, **1**/17.3, **1**/49.3, **4**/52.3, **5**/2.2, **5**/15.2, **5**/31.2, **5**/47.1, **5**/66.2, **5**/78.1, **7**/38.3
our support, **1**/36.1, **3**/73.1, **5**/56.1, **5**/61.1, **5**/69.3, **5**/70.1
our Teacher, **1**/48.1, **5**/2.1
search for, **2**/12.3, **2**/49.3, **5**/16.3, **5**/32.2, **5**/37.2, **5**/38.3, **5**/56.2, **5**/66.1, **5**/83.1, **5**/85.1

Joseph, Saint
and work, **6**/33
devotion to, **4**/15.2, **6**/20, **6**/21, **6**/22, **6**/23, **6**/24, **6**/25, **6**/26, **6**/27
exemplar of virtues, **1**/45.2, **4**/15.3, **5**/63.3, **6**/21
his dealings with Jesus and Mary, **1**/22.2, **1**/22.3, **1**/31.1, **4**/15.2, **5**/64.3, **5**/84.3, **6**/22
his intercession, **1**/45.2
his mission, **1**/22.1, **4**/15.1
his obedience and fortitude, **1**/6.3, **1**/45.1
honour and veneration, **1**/22.3
invoking his name, **1**/40.3
ite ad, **4**/15.3
patron of the Church, **4**/15.2, **4**/15.3

Joy
and apostolate, **3**/15.3, **5**/25.3, **5**/55, **5**/76.3, **5**/78.3
and divine filiation, **1**/15.2, **3**/15.1, **5**/27.2, **5**/33.1, **5**/59.2
and generosity, **2**/26.3, **4**/67, **5**/27.2, **5**/38.3, **5**/55.2, **5**/67.2, **5**/74.3
and sadness, **2**/48.2, **3**/15.2, **4**/67.3, **5**/55.1, **7**/47.3
and suffering **2**/26.1, **2**/26.2, **3**/15.2, **4**/96.1, **7**/23.3
being close to Jesus, **1**/15.1,

3/15.1, **3**/25.3, **4**/96.1, **7**/4.2, **7**/47.1
in the family, **3**/15.3
its foundation, **1**/15.2, **3**/15.1, **5**/**5**/27
spreading it, **2**/48.3, **5**/55.3

Judgement
particular, **1**/20.3, **5**/73.2
preparation for, **1**/20.3, **5**/73
universal, **1**/20.2, **5**/73.3, **5**/83

Justice
and charity, **1**/35.3
and mercy, **1**/35.3, **5**/17.3
and the individual, **2**/33.1, **2**/33.2
consequences of, **1**/35.2, **2**/75.1
its aim, **2**/75.3

Laity
role of, **7**/10.2

Leisure
and tiredness, **3**/33.1, **3**/33.3
learning to sanctify it, **3**/33.2, **4**/29, **5**/17.1

Little things
and ascetical struggle, **1**/12.1, **1**/19.2, **1**/50.2, **3**/78.1, **3**/78.2, **3**/78.3, **4**/38, **4**/57.3, **5**/39.2, **5**/50.2, **7**/20.3

Love
seeing God in ordinary things, **1**/33.3, **5**/32.2, **5**/50.2

Love of God
above all things, **4**/1, **5**/35.3, **5**/38.1, **5**/49.1, **5**/55.2, **5**/74.2, **7**/37.3
and the danger of lukewarmness, **1**/13.1, **5**/30.1, **5**/50.3
far-sighted, **1**/33.3
in daily incidents, **2**/24.3, **4**/58
leading to abandonment, **2**/57.3, **5**/55.2, **5**/60.3, **5**/77.2
with deeds, **2**/57.2, **4**/66.2, **5**/51.2, **5**/65.2, **5**/72.3, **5**/73.1, **5**/82.2, **5**/84, **7**/4.1

Loyalty, **3**/87.1, **3**/87.2, **3**/87.3, **5**/21.1, **5**/44.2, **5**/79.3, **5**/86

Lukewarmness
causes of, **1**/13.2, **1**/15.1, **5**/28.2, **5**/50.3
consequences of, **1**/13.1, **1**/47.2, **3**/83.1, **5**/3.3, **5**/16.2, **5**/30.1, **5**/55.1, **5**/76.2
remedy for, **1**/13.3, **1**/47.3, **3**/83.2

Magisterium
God speaks through it, **1**/48.3

Magnanimity, **3**/54.1, **3**/54.2, **3**/54.3, **5**/1.2, **5**/46.2, **5**/64.2

Marriage, **3**/59.1, **3**/59.2, **3**/59.3, **5**/29, **5**/90
dignity of, **4**/62.1, **5**/64.2, **5**/90
see Family life

Mass
attendance at, **4**/36.2, **4**/36.3
centre of interior life, **4**/26.3, **5**/52.3
its value, **2**/30.2, **2**/30.3, **3**/49.1, **4**/7.1, **5**/52.2
fruits of, **3**/103, **4**/7.2, **4**/7.3
our offering, **1**/44.2, **3**/49.3, **4**/61.2, **5**/92.2

Materialism, **7**/2.1

Maturity, **1**/50.3, **1**/51.3

Meekness
and peace, **1**/11.1
dealings with others, **1**/11.1, **5**/1.1

fruits of, **1**/11.3
is foundation, **1**/11.2
Jesus, model of, **1**/11.1, **5**/1, **5**/41.3
need for it, **1**/11.3
Mercy
and justice, **1**/35.3, **3**/82.2, **5**/17.3
fruits of, **3**/82.3
works of, **1**/4.3, **4**/16.3, **4**/27.3, **5**/15
Mercy, divine
an example, **1**/4.1, **3**/82.1, **5**/5.1, **5**/66.3
turn to it, **1**/4.1, **5**/3, **5**/17.3, **5**/39.1, **5**/45.2, **5**/81, **5**/93
with men, **1**/4.2, **4**/27.1, **4**/27.2, **5**/1.3, **5**/3, **5**/41.2, **5**/56.2, **5**/70.2, **5**/81.1
Merit
of good works, **4**/97
Morning Offering, 2/79
Mortification
and purity, **1**/16.3
and the Cross, **2**/2.1, **2**/2.2, **2**/15.2, **2**/43.2, **4**/53.3, **5**/75.3
fasting, **2**/3.1
interior, **1**/19.2, **1**/19.3, **1**/44.2, **2**/3.2, **2**/55.1, **5**/26.1
of imagination, **2**/55.2, **2**/55.3
small sacrifices, **2**/2.3, **2**/3.3, **4**/8, **5**/26, **5**/28.3

Obedience
and docility, **1**/24.3
and faith, **1**/12.3, **1**/45.1
and freedom, **1**/49.3, **5**/19.2
and God's Will, **1**/5.2
and humility, **1**/5.2
because of love, **1**/49.3, **5**/11.2, **5**/19.1
fruits of, **1**/49.2
model of, **1**/49.1, **5**/11.3, **5**/19.3
Optimism, 4/49, **5**/61.3, **5**/78.3
Our Lady
and confession, **7**/51.1
and faithfulness, **7**/14.3
and God's Will, **1**/25.3, **4**/99.1, **6**/29.2, **7**/45.3
and joy, **7**/47
and St John, **1**/33.2
and the Mass, **3**/105, **6**/48.3
and the Old Testament, **7**/5.1
and the Trinity, **6**/1.2
birth of, **7**/22.1
co-redemptrix, **1**/41.2, **3**/105.2, **5**/18, **7**/24.2
devotion, **1**/33.2, **1**/40.3, **1**/38.3, **2**/84.2, **7**/3.1, **7**/9.1, **7**/11, **734.1**, **7**/53.3
full of grace, **4**/99.2, **4**/99.3
generosity, **1**/26.1, **7**/41.1
her gifts, **7**/44.2, **7**/44.3
her help, **1**/38.2, **3**/9.1, **5**/36.1, **5**/48.2, **5**/81.3, **6**/16, **7**/3.2, **7**/34.2, **7**/49.3, **7**/52.3
her vocation, **1**/25.1, **5**/14.1, **6**/29, **7**/6.1, **7**/41.3, **7**/45.3
Immaculate Heart of, **6**/35.3, **6**/51
humility, **1**/27.1, **5**/14.2, **5**/63, **6**/27.3
invoke her name, **1**/40.3, **3**/9.1, **3**/42, **5**/81.3, **5**/92.3, **7**/5.3
mediatrix, **7**/9.2, **7**/9.3, **7**/11.3
Mother of God, **1**/17.2, **1**/38.1, **5**/18.3, **5**/81.3, **6**/1, **7**/11.2, **7**/26.3

our guide, **7**/43.2
our Mother, **1**/38.2, **2**/84.1, **5**/36.3, **5**/63.2, **6**/1.3, **7**/3.3, **7**/11.2, **7**/14.1, **7**/15, **7**/49.2
Queen, **7**/17
pilgrimages, **2**/84.3, **6**/31.1, **6**/35
rosary, **2**/38.3, **2**/79.3, **2**/81.1, **2**/81.2, **2**/81.3, **5**/18.3, **5**/27.3, **5**/36.2, **5**/36.3, **7**/13.2, **7**/13.3, **7**/32.3, **7**/33.1, **7**/48.3
service, **1**/26.1
to Jesus through Mary, **6**/37.2, **7**/52.1

Parables of the Gospel
banquet, **5**/37
good Samaritan, **4**/21, **5**/31
grain of wheat, **5**/34.2
leaven in dough, **4**/40
lost sheep, **4**/59. **5**/70.2
mustard seed, **5**/34.2
pearl of great value, **4**/42
Pharisee and tax-collector, **5**/57.2
prodigal son, **5**/3, **5**/41.1
shrewd steward, **5**/12
sowing seed, **4**/19, **5**/9
talents, **5**/51, **5**/82, **5**/87
two sons sent out, **5**/19
unjust judge, **5**/48, **5**/81.1
vineyard, **5**/10.2, **5**/28.1, **5**/54
virgins, **5**/73
wheat and cockle, **4**/28
working in vineyard, **4**/69, **5**/10, **5**/94.3
Patience, 2/28.2, **2**/28.3, **5**/11.1, **5**/9.3, **5**/54, **5**/94
see Meekness
Peace
and Christ, **1**/3.1, **2**/77.1
causes, lack of, **1**/3.1, **4**/12.2, **5**/14.3
foundation of, **1**/3.3, **1**/35.3, **5**/59.3
fruits of, **1**/3.2
gift of God, **1**/3.1, **2**/77.2, **4**/12.1
source of, **1**/3.2, **4**/12.3
Penance
and Fridays, **3**/85.2
characteristics of, **3**/85.3, **5**/1.3, **5**/5.3, **5**/26.2, **5**/41, **5**/75.2
Persecution
see Difficulties
Perseverance, 2/39.1, **2**/40.3, **5**/4.3, **5**/43.3, **5**/57, **5**/81, **5**/86, **7**/4.1
Piety, 2/91
Way of the Cross, **2**/3.2
see Our Lady, rosary
Pope, 2/68.2, **2**/68.3, **5**/64.1, **6**/7, **6**/19.3, **6**/32.2, **7**/16.3
Poverty
and sobriety, **1**/28.3
evangelical poverty, **1**/28.2
Jesus' example, **1**/28.1
ways of practising it, **1**/28.3, **4**/68.2, **5**/24, **7**/31.1, **7**/31.2, **7**/50.3
Prayer
and humility, **1**/29.3
and St Joseph, **1**/29.3, **3**/93.3, **5**/64.3, **5**/84.3
and thanksgiving, **7**/32
dealings with Jesus, **1**/29.2, **3**/51.1, **5**/56.2, **7**/35.2, **7**/48.1
fruits of, **4**/95.1, **5**/33.3,

5/57.3, **5**/71.1
how to pray, **1**/29.3, **2**/27.2, **2**/27.3, **2**/55.3, **3**/40.1, **3**/55.3, **3**/93.2, **4**/64.2, **5**/4.2, **5**/33, **5**/40.1, **5**/48, **5**/96, **7**/48.2
mental prayer, **7**/34.3
need for it, **1**/29.2, **2**/38.2, **3**/93.1, **5**/9.2, **5**/14, **5**/48.3, **5**/81, **7**/9.1, **7**/35.1
of petition, **2**/9.1, **2**/9.2, **2**/9.3, **3**/9.3, **3**/40.3, **4**/5.1, **4**/39.2, **4**/39.3, **4**/64.1, **4**/64.3, **7**/32.3
vocal prayers, **3**/94.1, **3**/94.2, **3**/94.3, **4**/95.3, **5**/94, **5**/34.1, **5**/95

Presence of God, **2**/12.3, **2**/76.2, **5**/57.3, **5**/61.1, **5**/72.2, **5**/83.1

Priesthood, **2**/44.2
identity and mission, **4**/20.1, **4**/20.2. **5**/48.2, **5**/57.1, **5**/71.1, **6**/9, **6**/38, **7**/10.1
love for, **7**/10.3
prayer for, **4**/20.3, **7**/10.2

Prudence
essence of, **4**/17.1, **5**/93.2
false, **4**/17.3
seeking advice, **4**/17.2

Purgatory, **7**/39.1

Purification
interior mortification, **1**/19.3, **5**/26

Purity
see Chastity

Recollection, interior
union with God, **4**/19.1, **5**/14
Our Lady's example, **1**/29.1, **5**/14

Rectitude of intention, **2**/63, **5**/11.1, **5**/57.1, **5**/67, **5**/72, **5**/74.3

Redemption, **2**/29.2, **2**/36.1, **2**/36.2, **2**/36.3, **5**/52.1, **5**/56.3, **5**/69.1, **5**/75, **5**/80.2

Resurrection
of the body, **3**/75.2, **3**/75.3, **5**/75, **5**/90.1, **5**/97.2

Sacraments, **4**/13.2, **4**/36.1

Saints
as intercessors, **3**/72.1, **7**/50.1
cult to, **3**/72.2
veneration of relics, **3**/72.3

Sanctity
consequences of, **1**/35.2, **4**/4.1, **5**/68.1, **5**/87.1
developing talents, **4**/68.2, **4**/68.3, **5**/12.2, **5**/51.2, **5**/82, **5**/84
in ordinary life, **1**/46.1, **2**/11.2, **2**/57.1, **2**/69, **3**/16.2, **3**/16.3, **3**/92.2, **4**/6.3, **4**/40.1, **4**/45.3, **5**/10.3, **5**/32, **5**/57.3, **5**/72, **6**/9.2, **7**/38.1, **7**/55.2
principal enemies of, **1**/1.2, **5**/50.2
universal call to, **3**/92.1, **5**/10.2, **5**/37.3, **5**/43.1, **6**/9.1, **7**/38.2

Serenity, **3**/98

Service, spirit of
2/14.1, **2**/14.3, **3**/66.3, **5**/3.3, **5**/67, **5**/87.2, **6**/37.1

Simplicity
and humility, **1**/42.1
and spiritual childhood, **1**/24.3, **1**/42.2
fruits of, **1**/42.3

in dealings with God, **1**/42.2, **5**/57.2, **7**/18.3
opposite of, **1**/42.3
rectitude of intention, **1**/42.2, **4**/17.1

Sin
consequences of, **2**/10.1, **2**/17.1, **2**/18.1, **2**/41.1, **3**/80.2, **4**/2, **4**/34.2, **5**/28.2, **5**/31.1, **5**/41.1, **5**/45, **5**/69.1, **5**/71.2, **5**/85.1
forgiveness of, **3**/44.2, **5**/41.2, **5**/70.3
reality of, **1**/47.2, **3**/26.2, **4**/23.1, **4**/34.1, **5**/3.2, **5**/45.3, **5**/93.1
sorrow for, **4**/23.2, **4**/23.3, **5**/9.1, **5**/28.2
see Confession

Sin, venial
deliberate, **2**/17.3, **3**/26.3, **4**/34.3
does damage, **1**/10.2

Sincerity, **2**/23, **3**/60, **4**/18.2, **5**/44, **7**/18.2

Society
and human solidarity, **3**/37.2, **4**/58.3, **5**/46.1, **5**/68
obligations to, **3**/37.3, **3**/53.3, **4**/58.1, **5**/39.3, **5**/44.3, **5**/46.1, **5**/51.2
service to, **3**/53, **4**/58.3, **5**/67, **5**/74

Spiritual childhood
and divine filiation, **1**/24.2, **4**/63.2, **5**/34, **5**/59, **5**/64
and humility, **1**/27.2, **3**/100.1, **4**/63.3, **5**/57.2
consequences of, **1**/42.2, **5**/33.2, **5**/46.3, **5**/59.3, **5**/60.2, **5**/72, **5**/75.3
nature, **1**/24.1, **5**/64
need for, **1**/7.3
virtues associated with it, **1**/24.3, **3**/60.2, **3**/100.2

Spiritual guidance
and joy, **1**/15.3
need for, **1**/7.3, **1**/43.2, **4**/31.3, **5**/19.3, **5**/43.1, **5**/85

Spiritual reading, **7**/8
advice for, **7**/8.3

Suffering
and consolation, **1**/34.3
and divine filiation, **1**/24.2, **5**/59.2, **5**/60.2
cross of each day, **1**/34.2, **4**/53.1, **7**/23.2, **7**/23.3
fruits of, **2**/26.2, **2**/64.1, **4**/53.2, **7**/5.1
helping others through, **1**/34.3, **5**/15, **5**/22.3, **5**/31.3, **5**/60.3
in the world, **1**/34.1, **5**/22.2, **5**/69.1
Our Lady's example, **1**/41.1, **1**/41.3, **5**/69.3, **6**/17, **7**/24.3
redeeming and purifying value, **1**/34.2, **5**/69, **5**/94

Supernatural life
and apostolate, **2**/78.3
and ascetical struggle, **1**/1.3, **3**/9.2, **3**/22, **5**/60.2
and human maturity, **1**/50.3
practice of virtues, **1**/50.1, **5**/84, **5**/87.3

Supernatural outlook
and God's calling, **1**/18.2, **5**/87
examining situations with, **1**/18.2, **5**/12.3, **5**/17.1, **5**/32.2, **5**/53.1, **5**/58.3, **5**/82.3, **5**/84

Temperance, **3**/101, **4**/35
Temptations
4/3.3, **4**/11.1, **4**/11.3, **5**/9.2, **5**/42, **5**/69.2, **5**/90.3
Thanksgiving, acts of
1/37.2, **1**/51.1, **2**/71.1, **2**/71.3, **5**/101.1, **5**/39, **5**/60.2, **5**/78, **5**/95
after Communion, **2**/71.3, **3**/29.3, **5**/95.2, **5**/95.3
human virtue of gratitude, **2**/71.2, **4**/61.1, **4**/61.3, **5**/39, **5**/60.2, **5**/78.2
Time, good use of
acts of contrition, **1**/37.2
acts of thanksgiving, **1**/37.2, **5**/95
Christian value, **1**/37.3, **5**/8.2, **5**/17.1
our life is short, **1**/37.1, **4**/48.2, **4**/48.3, **5**/54.2, **5**/82.3, **5**/84.1
Trust, **4**/5.2
Truth, **2**/23.2, **2**/23.3
love for, **4**/18.1, **4**/31.2, **5**/44
speaking, **4**/18.3, **5**/44
Unity, **2**/56, **5**/32.2, **5**/68.1, **5**/87.3, **5**/91.2, **6**/4.3, **6**/5, **6**/7
Unity of life, **2**/29, **3**/74.2, **4**/16.3, **5**/122.2, **5**/13.3, **5**/32, **5**/46.2, **5**/72, **5**/79, **5**/84, **5**/87, **6**/54.3

Vigilance
against evil inclinations, **1**/19.2, **5**/42.3, **5**/76.2
Come Lord Jesus, **1**/19.1, **5**/83.1
in waiting for Christ, **1**/19.1, **5**/49.2, **5**/73.2, **5**/80, **5**/97.3
the means, **1**/19.2, **5**/43.3
Virginity
apostolic celibacy, matrimony and, **1**/23.1, **4**/62.2, **5**/63.3, **5**/64.2, **5**/90
free choice, **1**/23.1
of Our Lady, **1**/23.1, **5**/64.2
Virtues, **1**/50.3, **2**/22.1, **2**/22.3, **3**/6.3, **4**/3.3, **5**/78, **5**/79.3
Visit to the Blessed Sacrament, **2**/51.2, **2**/51.3, **4**/43.3, **4**/56.3, **5**/61.1, **5**/88.1
Vocation
and apostolate, **7**/25.3, **7**/29.3
and freedom, **4**/22.1, **5**/37.1
and joy, **7**/25.2
and parents, **4**/22.3
grace for, **6**/36.2, **7**/45.2
of each person, **1**/8.1, **1**/33.1, **1**/51.3, **5**/37.3, **6**/36.3
of Our Lady, **1**/25.1, **7**/41.3
of St Andrew, **7**/42.1
of St Bartholomew, **7**/18.1
of St John, **1**/33.1, **5**/23.1
of St John the Baptist, **1**/8.1, **5**/13.1, **6**/55
of St Matthew, **7**/25.1
prayer to St Joseph, **6**/25.3
responding to it, **1**/25.2, **3**/14.3, **4**/22.2, **4**/22.3, **4**/42.3, **5**/38.2, **5**/43, **5**/51.1, **7**/42.3
signs of, **1**/18.2, **1**/18.3
special calling, **1**/25.2, **3**/14.1, **4**/22.1, **4**/42.2, **5**/43.1, **5**/90.2, **6**/34.1, **6**/36.1, **6**/56.1, **6**/57, **7**/37.1

Will of God
above earthly plans, **1**/47.3, **5**/10.1

and peace of soul, **1**/5.3
and sanctity, **1**/5.1, **5**/35
embracing it, **1**/5.1, **1**/5.3, **1**/18.3, **2**/15.1, **3**/20.3, **3**/70.3, **5**/35, **5**/94.2, **7**/45.3
its manifestation, **1**/5.1, **3**/20.2

Work
and prayer, **4**/30.3, **5**/84.3
in God's presence, **4**/30, **5**/84.2, **7**/22.3
its dignity, **1**/46.3, **5**/84, **6**/33.1
of Jesus, **1**/46.1, **1**/46.2, **3**/1.1, **3**/30.2, **3**/41.1, **5**/84.1, **5**/88.2
sanctification of, **1**/46.2, **1**/46.3, **3**/1, **3**/30, **3**/39, **3**/41, **5**/13.2, **5**/17.2, **5**/32.2, **5**/51.2, **5**/84, **6**/33, **7**/36.1

Works of mercy
see Mercy

World
justice in the, **1**/35.1, **5**/60.3
re-evangelisation of, **2**/58.2, **2**/58.3 , **5**/12.2, **5**/20, **5**/25, **5**/87, **6**/18

Worship, divine, **3**/46.2, **3**/46.3, **5**/65.3, **5**/89, **5**/92.2

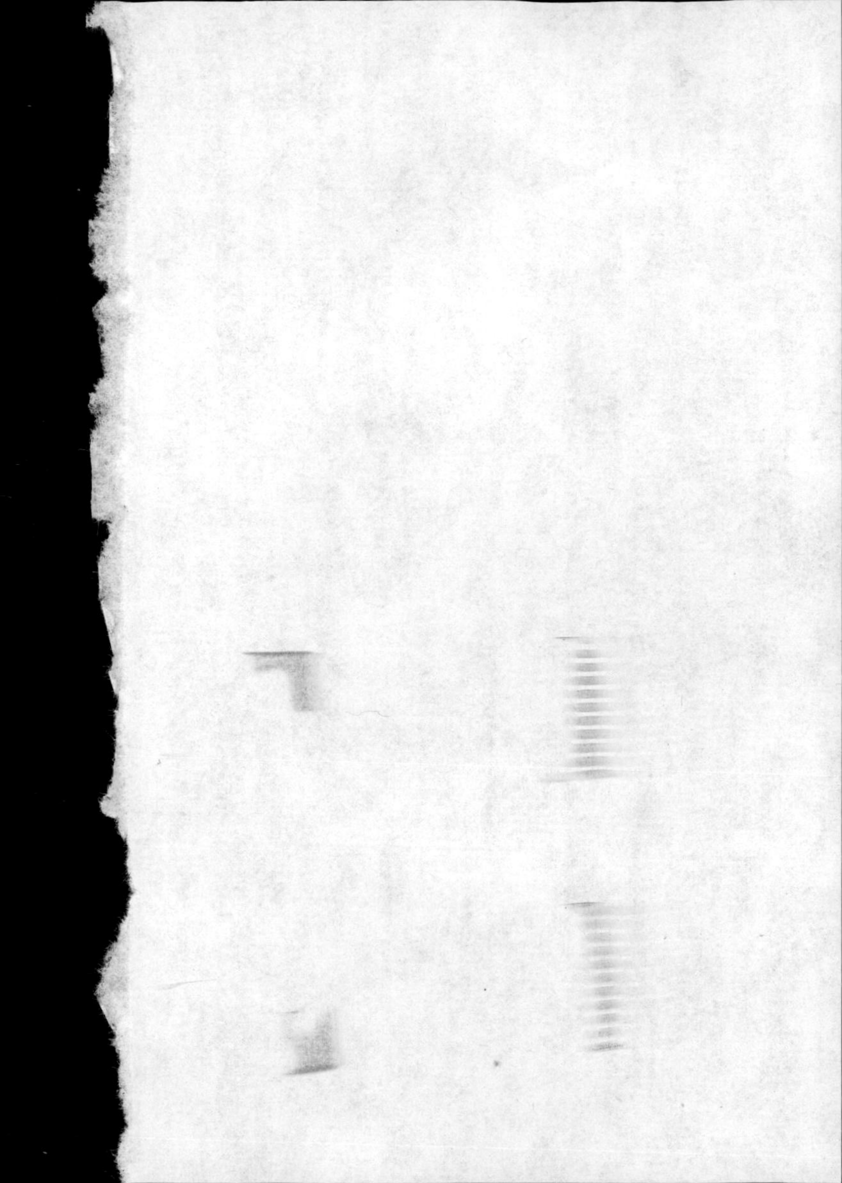